The Ultimate
Home Buyer's Handbook

THE *Ultimate*
HOME BUYER'S
HANDBOOK
What no one tells you
when buying a home...

ERNEST A. SIMPSON

MILL CITY PRESS

Mill City Press, Inc.
2301 Lucien Way #415
Maitland, FL 32751
407.339.4217
www.millcitypress.net

Printed in the United States of America

ISBN-13: 978-1-54565-662-4

Contents

Acknowledgements and Preface

In my effort to complete the (The Ultimate) guide for homebuyer's over the last three years (between doing inspections and trying to have a life outside of work), I've talked to a number of professionals who are directly involved in real estate sales and construction. A few of those who assisted me are noted below.

For help on the sales process and the role of buyer's agents, I thank Nancy Yorgy of Keller Williams (Beverly, Massachusetts) and Melissa Addis and Ronn Huth of Buyer's Choice Realty (Wenham, Massachusetts). These are experienced agents who do buyer agency only. Dianne Pinkham of RE/Max Realty (North Andover, Massachusetts) provided helpful information on 'agency' and assisted in the initial editing.

Attorney Dave Carney of Beliveau Law Group (Salem, New Hampshire) provided input on legal issues and Richard (Ric) Beaudoin of Cross Country Mortgage (Salem, New Hampshire) provided great information on the ins and outs of financing. Kristen Leone of Property North Appraisals Inc. (Haverhill, Massachusetts), a realtor and appraiser detailed the intricacies of the appraisal process. For computer help I have to thank the amazing Jeff Osgood of Osgood Unlimited, Inc. (Haverhill, Massachusetts).

Lastly, thanks to my wife (Martha) for putting up with me (which is not always easy).

To all who may be reading this I'll reiterate a point I've made elsewhere: the Handbook covers a lot of general advice on what to look for when buying a home – and perhaps more important, specific advice on how to evaluate numerous home systems and concerns that are not covered in other books. The chapters on mold, environmental problems affecting homes, septic systems, well systems, and the many system concerns that are not covered by the home inspection are critical reading (in my opinion).

Please feel free to contact me if you have questions. I accept criticisms and corrections and will try to include these in future versions.

Good luck,
Ernest A. Simpson
October 9, 2018

Introduction and Overview . . .

The Ultimate Home Buyer's Handbook is different from other books on buying a home. Many of the other books are very good, but no one has written one that tells you how to look out for your own interests throughout the home-buying process – from making the decision whether to buy, where to buy, what types of areas and homes to avoid, how and when to negotiate most effectively, and how to evaluate the many concerns and problems that can make your home buying experience – if not a nightmare – a less than optimal experience. This is what the Home Buyer's Handbook attempts to do. I also try to provide guidance on working with a real estate agent and how to avoid the traps that people fall into when dealing with sellers, real estate agents, attorneys, and, yes, home inspectors. The chapters on mold, environmental hazards in homes, septic systems, water quality, and wells, in my opinion, are especially important – and this information is not presented in other books on buying a home. (Actually, most of the material in the Handbook IS NOT covered in other books on buying a home).

If you are in the process of buying a home, you should realize that this will most likely be the largest purchase you will ever make. You want to get it right, and you want to avoid as many of costly surprises as you can.

What this book will not do is tell you how to inspect a home. When I wrote a few chapters of this book back in the 1990s, I sent off several chapters to publishers to see if they were interested in publishing it. Unfortunately, the feedback I got was that they had enough books on how to inspect a home and couldn't use another book on this topic, so this got put aside for many years. However, this book never was – and is not – a book on how to inspect a home. You cannot learn how to inspect a home by reading a book; I've been inspecting homes since 1982 and I am still surprised by how much knowledge one requires, given the changes in construction standards and materials and the number of things one needs to recognize. This does not include the ever-expanding ways homeowners and builders have found to screw up their homes for future buyers.

Importantly, the nature of current construction, the demographics of the country, and what people now want for a home, when compared to the situation 20 years ago, is also vastly different. So, instead of telling you how to do a home inspection, the Handbook covers the important concerns that the home inspection *does not deal with but that are critical to your home buying satisfaction.*

For instance, Chapter 1 covers the *Initial Decisions* you need to make when deciding to buy a home (which may be a single-family home, a condominium, or other types of property). You don't want to start off on the home buying journey without knowing the costs of homeownership – and the pluses and minuses of buying versus renting. In the past, this decision was a no-brainer; it may be less so now. While owning your own home makes sense for most people, there are times when renting may be a better option. You need to figure this out, however, before you start looking at homes to buy.

This chapter is not designed to dissuade you from buying a home, since, very simply, the benefits of home ownership in our country are substantial (a truism, I know). But you don't want to ever lose a home to foreclosure and you don't want to have to move in a year or two because you brought the wrong house – or the right house at the wrong time. The book covers how to determine what you can afford to spend and are willing to spend on your mortgage and home ownership costs (discussed in more detail in chapter 10 on the 'ins and outs of financing').

Chapter 2 covers the *First Steps* when buying a home: finding a good buyer's agent, determining what you can afford, devising a 'must have and want list,' and a 'Do not want list.' It's important to know why a buyer's agent is important when buying a home. Lastly, I'll cover getting pre-qualified, as you can't do much until you do this.

Chapter 3*, Regions and Localities that Carry Risks,* covers a number of regions and types of areas that either present significant risks to life, health, and property – or are becoming less desirable places to live, given current trends. This chapter has nothing to do with evaluating the physical condition of the individual property. Instead, it deals with concerns that are specific to certain regions and certain localities that you may want to keep in mind.

(Note: you don't have to read through every chapter of the Homebuyer's Handbook to find something that will be valuable in your home buying efforts. Feel free to read the chapters that are most relevant to your concerns. If you have a private well, I would read Chapter 16, as this has a lot of critical information on evaluating well systems. If the property you are looking at has a septic system, read Chapter 17. For concerns with mold and indoor air quality concerns, read Chapters 14 and 15).

Chapter 4 provides advice on *Evaluating Communities and Neighborhoods.* It's basic stuff – but important.

Chapter 5, *Looking at Homes,* is a practical guide to looking at homes so you can get an idea of what matters and what doesn't (in my opinion, of course).

Chapter 6, *Homes to Rule Out at the Outset: Preliminary Investigations,* covers the types of pre-inspection investigations you should do to avoid the homes that will break your heart and probably your budget. Do these investigations before the home inspection and appraisal and save yourself some money (not to mention heartache)!

Chapter 7 *Making an Offer; Tips and Strategies* covers the strategies and tactics to use to get your offer accepted over others – including getting the best price that may be feasible. I've included some of the negotiating strategies that a good buyer's agent will use to get their offers accepted.

Chapter 8 briefly reviews *Legal Issues* you need to be aware of. Your attorney (assuming you have one) will cover many of these. I'll also review a few of the more unusual concerns that are not typical issues – but you need to know about, including a brief section on buying a foreclosure. As properties commonly come with title problems, easements, and other legal impediments, I've provided an overview of how these can affect you. While you need to be mindful of these concerns, you will rely on an attorney for guidance.

Chapter 9 covers *Avoiding Financing Pitfalls.* This is not the sexiest topic – but I've tried to clarify a few of the choices and options you may have so the process will go more smoothly. I'll also go over important issues about homeowner's insurance that you need to be aware of.

Chapter 10, *Getting the Most from your Home Inspection,* covers finding a qualified home inspector. You also need to know how to get the most out of the home inspection process AND understand what the inspection won't tell you. I'll also cover the other possible investigations you may want to do and when they are warranted. Following up on the inspection findings is critical, so we'll go through this as well.

Chapter 11, *Overcoming the Limitations of the Home Inspection*, tells you about the shortcomings of the home inspection process – and how to work around these limitations.

Chapter 12 covers *Post-Inspection Negotiations.* This chapter is important since negotiations often occur not only when getting your offer accepted but *after* the home inspection has been done. Negotiations may also occur due to other investigations you will/should be doing. I'll note guidelines on what is typically 'doable' in negotiations and what isn't, as well as strategies you can utilize.

Chapter 13, *What Slips through the Cracks,* deals with the many systems, components, and concerns that may be present on the property you are buying – but <u>are</u> <u>not</u> part of the home inspection. This may be because they can't be evaluated by a limited, visual inspection, because they require a specialized knowledge or procedures, or because they are just not present on most residential properties. I'll also note how to deal with many of the seasonal limitations that you and your inspector may face. Note: this chapter covers a lot of important stuff as you may assume home inspectors cover these concerns – but really, you may be on your own.

Chapter 14 covers *Environmental Hazards* and how these may affect your purchase decision. There's lots of stuff here.

Chapter 15, *Avoiding mold and Indoor Air Quality Problems,* deserves its own chapter, given how much of a hot button issue this has become. Read this!

Chapter 16, *Evaluating Water Quality and Private Wells,* covers what you should know about water quality and private wells. I'll note what you should test for when you have a private well system.

Chapter 17 covers *How to Evaluate Private Waste Disposal (Septic Systems).* This is an important chapter if you are buying a home that is <u>not</u> on municipal sewers. Replacing a failed septic system can involve huge amounts of money, so you want to avoid this at all costs.

Chapter 18, *A Brief Review of New Construction Concerns,* is a brief overview of things you need to be aware of if you are buying a newly-constructed home. This could be its own book. As I am a building consultant and home inspector and not a builder, I'll concentrate on new construction concerns related to the inspection – plus other evaluations you may need to do. I'll just touch on legal issues, but these are very important when buying a 'new' home.

Chapter 19 provides a brief overview of concerns specific to *Condominiums, Condexes, Over-55 Developments.*

Chapter 20, *Special Types: Vacation Properties, Investment Properties, and Mobile Homes* notes the special considerations with these types of properties.

As a final thought: take this all in, but don't get overwhelmed.

Good luck,
E.A. Simpson

P.S. Please feel free to contact me (esimpson@evergreenhomeinspection.com) for any items you feel are erroneous or need clarification – or if you'd like to see something included in a future edition.

CHAPTER 1
Initial Decisions

What you will learn in this chapter . . .

- *When to rent, when to wait . . .*
- *The reasons to buy a home . . .*
- *Pitfalls to avoid when deciding to buy . . .*
- *The risks of buying a fixer-upper . . .*
- *Making the purchase decision . . .*

When to rent, when to wait, when to buy . . .

Before you start your home buying search, you may want to step back and look at the overall picture and a few of the pitfalls you can encounter when buying – and owning – a home. This may be coming a bit late, if you are already actively looking at homes or perhaps have even made an offer on a property (That's o.k.. There are still a lot of things you can learn in the later chapters). It is important, however, to understand the potential costs of homeownership, as well as a few of the larger concerns and challenges, before plunging ahead.

So, before getting into the reasons about when to put off buying a home and the list of potential problems you may encounter, I'll list a few of the reasons why buying a home is (or has been) a good idea. Hey, this is the obvious stuff, but it still needs to be said. I'm not just setting you up for the downsides.

Reasons to buy a home:

Historically speaking (and this is what all other books on home buying will point out), owning your own home is desirable. It makes sense financially, emotionally, and physically. Home ownership benefits you, your community, and the nation (not to mention your local Home Depot). Almost everyone, at some point in their lives, would like to own their own home.

As you probably realize, real estate is a national obsession. Just look at the HGTV channel TV. Prior to 2007, owning a home was one of the best ways to invest your earnings for long-term financial stability, mainly by building equity (but also as a speculation). The long-term performance of the real estate market, from the early 1950s into the mid-2000s, overall* was on a fairly steady upward trend. The tax system in the U.S. is geared to support real estate by allowing the home-owner to write off mortgage interest payments and property taxes. For those who were lucky and astute enough to purchase homes at the right price and were able to hold on or continually trade up, real estate has probably been their largest source of wealth.

*'Overall' doesn't account for the fact that real estate in the 'oil patch' states suffered a serious downturn in the 1980s and New England real estate had a 'mini-crash' from 1988 to 1992.

I'm saying the obvious, but I'll say it anyhow: Owning your own home allows you to make the property something you can be happy and proud to live in and gives you control over your living situation. Having a yard, even a small one, is something most people want, whether for gardening, for entertaining, for kids to play in, for their pets – or just for the need to get outside in nice weather. For young people planning on starting a family, having a home of one's own is seen as almost a necessity. Owning a home is also valuable, as it necessitates fiscal discipline. (I have a brother-in-law who never held onto money until he and his wife bought a house. After that, they wouldn't part with a dime.) Owning a home is enforced saving.

Renting means you are building your landlord's equity, not your own. Renting means you can't control whom you have for neighbors, you can't plant a garden out back, you can't have too much stuff, you can't play your music too loud or have a large party, and you very often don't have a lot of privacy. In short, you may suffer financially and you certainly suffer a loss of control over what you can do with your life if you don't own your own home. Renting is also very con-stricting. Rules, regulations, and a lack of control over your neighbors are often disheartening. Signing a lease, as is typically required, will tie you the property for longer than you may want.

That said . . .

There are times to buy and times not to buy – and there are <u>reasons</u> to buy and reasons not to buy. You need to think about these things before you decide to purchase real estate. What you don't want to do is rush in and buy at the top of the market. You don't want most of your income going toward your mortgage payment and other household expenses so you will be 'house poor.' You don't want to buy something that you will have to sell in a couple of years because it no longer meets your needs or is something you are not happy with.

A piece of advice I've heard that applies to real estate as well as life in general is:

Avoid making the big mistake . . .

Not to digress, but for life in general, this could include:

- working hard to get into a good college, only to get expelled one month short of high school graduation due to getting caught with drugs.
- taking out 100K in student loans with no realistic career plan on paying it back.
- taking just a little hit of some addictive drug that someone hands you at a party (usually while you're young).
- drinking and driving, especially when this results in a DUI and an accident with injuries. I would now include 'texting' and driving as well.
- believing the Food and Drug Administration has your interests at heart . . . (this could be another book . . .)
- not wearing a seat belt when you are young and thinking you are invincible . . .
- assuming that the future will always look like the past . . . .

Thinking things through . . .

Making the big mistake on a home purchase usually would include simply not thinking through your own situation and your future needs, being too cautious in your decision, or taking risks you shouldn't be taking. Let's look at a few of the things that you need to think about . . .

First, how stable is your family income? Is your job/income relatively secure? Police officers, firefighters, and teachers with at least some years 'in' may not have worries about their industry shutting down. The same is true for many professions and occupations: there seems to be no shortage of need for nurses, medical staff in general, pharmacists, many categories of state and municipal employees, accountants, etc. If you own or work in an established family-owned business, you probably have a stability of income or prospects for doing well in the future. If you have a degree of income certainty, you can be a bit more aggressive in what you can afford for a mortgage and you can perhaps stretch a bit on what properties you can look at. If you already have enough money set aside to pay a substantial portion of the cost of the home, this obviously also makes a difference. The same is true if you have a guaranteed pension or source of income. Lots of people are fortunate to have family money or at least a 'backstop' of help should things go wrong. In this case, you can go for the larger home and, in some cases, the larger mortgage without putting yourself at risk. Without a backstop, <u>you are at risk</u>.

But you need to think about your spouse's income also. Maybe your income appears to be secure, but your spouse's or 'significant other's isn't. The loss of one income could make a huge difference in your ability to afford a large mortgage. This is one of the problems that was researched by Elizabeth Warren (now a senator for Massachusetts) in the early 2000s. One of the warnings that came up in these studies, at a time when the economy was going well, was about how young couples could afford to pay the then astronomical real estate prices and high mortgages if one party lost their job. While getting financially overextended didn't cause the real estate crisis, it did make things worse for many families when the economy tanked in 2007–2008.

But losing a job is not the only thing that can occur. If you are a young couple planning to have kids, can you or your spouse suffer the loss of income (in terms of being able to pay your mortgage) when the baby comes? Will your job – or your spouse's/significant other's job – still be there? Will you pay so much for childcare that it will hardly be worth having both parties working? You need to think these concerns through ahead of your home buying search. It may be that you will look for a home that is something that you'd be happy living in but isn't the dream home you'd eventually like to own. Maybe you need to wait a bit. You most definitely don't want to be in a situation where you can't make the payments because you've become overextended.

. . . it is not the responsibility or role of your real estate agent, attorney, or mortgage professional to evaluate market risk or your ability to withstand a declining job, stock, or property market. You still need to make sure you think things through AND have the right people on your side. This means a good buyer's broker, financing professional, attorney, and home inspector – all of whom will help you look out for your interests. The decision to buy a home, however, is yours: no one is going to tell you to wait.

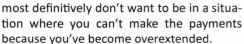

Another pitfall is simply getting caught up in the type of insanity that prevailed just prior to 2007, when anyone and everyone who could get a mortgage – and even an exorbitant mortgage – was able to qualify. This is not quite the situation now (late 2018), but it is getting crazy in different ways. The same lesson, however, needs to be understood: it is not the responsibility or role of your real estate agent, attorney, or mortgage professional to evaluate market risk or your ability to withstand a declining job, stock, or property market. You still need to make sure you think things through AND have the right people on your side. This means a good buyer's broker, financing professional, attorney, and home inspector – all of whom will help you look out for your interests. The decision to buy a home, however, is yours: no one is going to tell you to wait.

The problem with market risk is that no one can foresee the future. I would love to be able to predict when and if interest rates will rise substantially (small

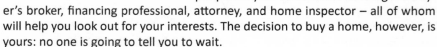

increases may not make much difference, in my opinion). Higher rates will impact real estate prices. So will the state of the economy. Give me a crystal ball on this, and I'll quit being a home inspector and become a financial trader (I won't, but it's a thought). Nor can anyone tell you when the economy may 'roll over' (although, in 2018, this seems a lot closer than far away).

What you should consider when looking at your timeframe for ownership . . .

First, unless you are going to be in the home for at least three years – and some authorities say five years – you may be better off renting. There are a lot of transaction costs when buying a home and selling a home. Not only will you have the initial mortgage financing costs and the costs for at least some improvements or repairs on the home, but you will also be paying a real estate agent 4 or 5 percent of the sales price when you sell. That said, renting is not a desirable option when you have a family or if you are already a homeowner and have all the stuff that needs to go into another home. The timeframe may not apply if you are 'flipping' the home or, at the other extreme, are purchasing something you plan on owning for a long time.

At the time of this writing, we are still experiencing a rising economy, and interest rates, while rising, are still relatively low. If and when the economy falters, real estate will take another tumble. How far down, I don't know. Real estate does well when the economy does well. It may do okay in the initial stages of an inflationary scenario (until fuel costs rise substantially), but not in a deflationary depression (think the 1930s).

I also think there are important long-term risks – financial, location, and environmental – that you need to stay aware of while making your home buying decision. I'll cover these in the later chapters.

Okay, enough with the doomsday stuff. The risk I want you to avoid is losing your home because you can't afford the payments (or the taxes). So, it is important to understand ALL the costs that go with home ownership – as there are many. I've listed a few below.

Costs of Home Ownership . . .

#1 Mortgage payments. This is your payment to the bank or financing company for the home. As I think everyone knows, this includes the interest on the loan as well as the loan principal. I won't get into details on what type of mortgage can work best. Fixed-term rate mortgages are usually preferable, but there are situations where a variable rate mortgage is the better option, especially when you may be moving or refinancing in the next few years. You can determine what you can – and may be willing – to spend and the type of mortgage (FHA versus conventional) when you sit down with a loan officer.

*The tax 'Reform' act of 2017 will not allow homeowners to write off the costs of real estate tax bills over $10,000 on their federal income tax, making the more expensive properties in towns with higher property taxes less 'affordable.'

Your mortgage payment will probably be the largest expense you will have. The nice thing, however, is that you can write off your interest payments (up to a certain amount) on your federal tax returns.

#2. Real estate taxes. Depending on where you live, these taxes can range from the tolerable to the outrageous. The suburbs in much of the northeast and northcentral states, excluding cities with a broad tax base or rural areas with limited services, tend to have high real estate taxes*. These taxes and the spending they fund are not under your – or sometimes anyone's – control. No one wants to cut spending on schools, police, and fire protection – and when people do, there really is no good or legal way to do this as everything is contractually obligated. My worry is that, should the economy suffer a severe downturn, it will be the young teachers, police officers, and other workers who will be laid off, and all the programs that make the community life most livable will disappear. The highly paid older workers with lucrative retirements and benefits will not be impacted. Complicating the picture is the fact that no legal mechanism exists to reform or change the system where the negotiated pensions may be excessive.

There are no 'bad guys' in this scenario. The point is that the taxes that are affordable now may not be so in the future as the retired population gets larger and the costs of paying the pensions for retirees rises. Also, while the economy may go down the tubes and your income –and your community's income – may decline, this will not be reflected in lower property taxes.

#3. Homeowner's insurance. The cost of homeowner's insurance has been going up and up, and with the revised standards for 'flood insurance,' many homeowners are paying more for this than for simple property insurance. For homes on the coast or other waterways, these costs have gone up dramatically. I recently had a client who conveyed that a home they were interested in had a $12,000 annual flood insurance bill. The home was near the water – but it wasn't a spectacular home. (They didn't pursue that home). See the later sections of the Handbook on flood insurance.

#4.Utility and fuel bills (and where these are trending). Utility expenses tend to 'yo-yo,' as fuel costs have gone up and down. Natural gas, in particular, has been fairly inexpensive in recent years. Fuel and utility costs may be a small part of your overall budget or a substantial part – more so if you heat with oil, propane, or direct resistance electricity than if you heat with natural gas. More than the fuel source, however, the size of the home, how well it is insulated, your lifestyle (how high do you keep the heat?), and the efficiency of the heating and cooling systems will determine your energy costs. Fuel and utility bills can get quite high, depending on these factors. The risk is that these can go a LOT higher – and probably will, in time. The good thing is that a lot of these costs may be at least somewhat controllable.

#5. Repair, replacement, and maintenance costs for heating and cooling systems. Maintenance costs need to be factored into your budget; parts break down and unexpected servicing is often required. As a general estimate, the newer high-efficiency furnaces may only last 15 to 25 years. A lot of 40-year old boilers are out there that are still working fine, so you never know. Air conditioning and heat pump systems may last 15 to 30 years in northern areas and 10 years in southern climates.

#6. Appliance repairs and upgrades. Appliances don't last forever. Most will need replacement within six to ten years, with notable exceptions (certain types of electric and gas ranges, most exhaust fans). Anything mechanical, I should note, will have a finite life.

#7. Lawn and yard maintenance . . . This may not be a large expense for those with small yards or for homeowners who do most of the work themselves. Then it's a matter of how much time can you spare. Some people love working on their yards; for others, it's a chore. This can be where condominium living can be attractive – assuming that the condo takes care of the lawn and the fees are not excessive. Large yards mean a ride-on mower or paying someone to do your lawn. A large lawn mower and other yard equipment may require a garage or shed (don't plan to store these under your deck!). Can you afford to pay a landscaping company for taking care of your yard? You must budget for this expense.

#8. Snow plowing and removal. In the northern states, this may be a necessity unless you have a snowplow or snow blower – or a strong back and heart. Snow removal from roofs can be a necessity in winters with extremely heavy snow covers (as occurred in New England in 2015). Due to heavy snows and severe ice dam problems, some homeowners spent thousands in snow removal costs. Most of the expenses from damage, I should note, would normally have been covered by homeowner's insurance.

#9. Other costs:

- Plumbing repairs: water heaters don't last forever; gas-fired stand-alone units seem to have an average life of 10 to12 years; electric a bit more. Pipes corrode out. Leaks will occur. Sewer lines will back up, etc.

- Septic system pumping; sewer ejection systems, and grinder pumps will have a finite life . . .
- Well systems require maintenance and well pumps will eventually need replacement.
- Pools require maintenance and proper start-up and shut down seasonally. Chemicals need to be added to keep the water clear. Covers are needed for the winter and solar covers are desirable for the summer months.
- For condominiums, you will have monthly condominium fees. These can range from minimal to very large. The larger fees may be tolerable if they include heating and cooling costs, parking and snow plowing, amenities such as pools, workout rooms, etc. Special assessments may be applied for major capital improvements or repairs, but, as I will discuss in Chapter 18, you should be able to research pending assessments before you buy.

Unanticipated repairs and replacements . . .

While the home inspection can be useful in estimating the typical remaining life of the larger mechanical systems and the typical life-span for major systems and components, no absolutes exist. As a home inspector, I see 50-year-old heating systems (usually boilers) still working fine and 15-year-old systems that are failing. Unfortunately, putting an exact time frame and the cost of system replacements is difficult (if not impossible). That said, buying a home with 'older' systems means you will be replacing at least some of these 'sooner than later.' Also, the fact that the home inspection does not cover a lot of major systems and concerns (covered in Chapters 12 through 16) that can be a source of significant expense means you may need to look at these items also.

*As contrary advice: if you can expect to be in the home for years, feel free to make improvements you may get a lot of enjoyment out of – even though you may not get your money back when reselling. Pools, basketball courts, hot tubs, etc., come to mind.

Renovation costs . . .

If you are like most home buyers, you will want to change something. This work can range from the very minimal (painting walls and ceilings, new flooring) to complete 'gut jobs.' The overall condition of the home and the amount of needed work is very often obvious and is – or should be – reflected in the market value or selling price. The money you spend on renovations (viz., new kitchen, new bathroom, new siding, etc.), if done carefully, will usually increase the value of the home (although usually not as much as you spend to do the improvements). Renovations are also optional and/or deferrable. Renovations that are done with 'sweat equity' will generally increase the value of the property, assuming they are done in a workmanlike manner, are really needed, and are done with budget restraint. Renovations should always be done with resale in mind. What you like, a future buyer of your home may not*.

Warning on fixer-uppers . . .

READ THIS! Buying what is termed a 'fixer-upper' is always a temptation for first-time buyers. These can work great IF you get the right house at the right price – which, to be honest, I don't see people get very often these days. Usually, by the time you include the costs to fix all of the problems and make the home right, you could have bought a home with all the work done already – without undergoing the years of hardship and sacrifice. Also, as I'll cover in later chapters, there is a vast difference between an older home that is solid but just needs updating and a home that was poorly built, minimally-improved, or where everything that was done was done badly and needs to be ripped out.

Too often, I see first time buyers looking to buy the cheapest homes in the market when it is obvious that, after incurring the costs (and time) to renovate the property, they would have been better off spending more money and buying something that didn't need so much work.

Too often, I see first time buyers looking to buy the cheapest homes in the market when it is obvious that, after incurring the costs (and time) to renovate the property, they would have been better off spending a bit more money and buying something that didn't need so much work. <u>Read this twice</u>!!

You also need to honestly assess your willingness to take on a fixer-upper or home in severe distress. These homes can be great for the right person, but you can become overwhelmed by the amount of work, money, and resources needed to make a fixer-upper into something you are happy with. If you are busy with your career, family, or other pursuits, you need to carefully assess how much time you are willing to put into the home. <u>Also assess your skill set</u>. If you can do a lot of repairs and renovations yourself or at less than market rates, buying a distressed property can work. Also, if you are willing to learn, you should not necessarily be dissuaded from a property that needs a lot of work. Skills can be acquired. Just be realistic. Again, know the difference between a sound home that is perhaps very dated and a money pit that you'll never make right. Getting a good home inspection (and reading the rest of the Handbook) is critical.

To summarize my point regarding 'fixer uppers', remember that

> *the true price of the home is not what you spend to purchase it, it's the cost to purchase it AND the costs you will incur for repairs, system*

replacements, maintenance, and renovations. (I credit Bob Mulloy of Allsafe Home Inspection for this insight)

The purchase decision . . .

Your decision whether to purchase a home and what to purchase depends on what stage you are at in life – and what stage you will enter within some reasonable time frame. As this is common sense and is something you probably know, I do not need to go into detail here, but a few of the things you need to think about are:

-   if you are just starting out, will you be having kids and how soon? Can you stay in your condo – or buy a condo – with a baby coming, or would the conditions be unsuitable for infants or toddlers? Most condos are fine for young children. Others, not so much.
-   If you are older and are considering downsizing and moving to a warmer climate, will you miss your kids and grandkids too much? If downsizing, will you have room for family functions? I've had older clients who downsized too soon and regretted giving up the larger home for a condo or over-55 development. They ended up buying another single-family home.
-   Is the home easily livable as you get older? A new trend is for 'universal' design, with wider interior doorways and a full bathroom on the first floor. Some homes are easier to 'age in' than others – and many homes can be altered easily to accommodate older occupants – while others can't (think old Victorian or Colonial era properties).
-   If you have a small family, is it going to get larger? An obvious question, but I've had clients who were buying a two-bedroom home when they had one child already and another on the way. You normally have a few years grace period before you have to move, but still . . .
-   Will you have elderly parents or in-laws who may need a place to live in a few years? Lots of people are now buying homes with finished in-law suites or homes they can convert into additional living space. See Chapters 4 and5 on researching whether the town you may be looking in will allow in-law apartments.
-   Don't assume you can simply add on to a home that becomes too small for your needs. Maybe you can, but you had better get an idea of what this will cost. *

The upshot is: *always think ahead.*

When can renting make sense?

Without the ability to have a down payment or enough monthly income, renting may be your only option. If your credit score is low, then you may be better off trying to repair it before you go looking for a mortgage. (I'll review a few ways to establish credit in chapter 8. You may look to get into a down payment assistance program if you have a decent income but no savings.

Renting can make a lot of sense for many people who may even be able to afford a home. As noted, two important factors are your time frame and your personal situation. Renting can be the most viable option when:

> *I recently had a young buyer who assumed he could put on a separate wing with a master bedroom and bath-room for $20,000. The cost for what he was planning more realistically would have been $80,000 – if not more. He was not happy to hear this.

- You may have to move out of the area within the next three years, or when you simply don't know if you will want to stay in that town or region for an extended length of time.
- Your job security is uncertain or you have a high risk of your income declining
- You are new to an area and don't know which community or neighbor-hood you may want to live in on a permanent basis.
- You don't have enough money saved, or a high enough income, to purchase a home without putting yourself at significant financial risk.
- Your credit score is low, as noted. You may be able to get a mortgage – but you will pay a higher rate than if you have a higher credit score.
- You are downsizing and need time to think things out before deciding where and how you want to live.
- When the rental situation is a bargain and includes a tolerable location and conditions. Occasionally, young couples will rent from relatives until they have enough saved for a down payment. (My wife and I did this when starting out).
- You live 'day to day' financially and cannot afford to have any unantici-pated expense.

There are a lot of costs entailed in buying a home, so you don't want to have to sell after just a year or two. If you think you may be moving to another region or area, or if you expect your situation will substantially change (for the better or worse) in the next couple of years, then renting may make sense even if you can afford to buy. On the other hand, if you are getting a 'desirable' and/or easily saleable property at a great price that gives you a built-in exit strategy, then the advice 'rent with the intention of buying' is worth heeding. Save money and improve your credit score, so if and when the right property comes along, you will be prepared.

CHAPTER 2
First Steps

. . .Working with a real estate agent . . . getting prequalified . . .

What we will cover in this chapter . . .

- *Why finding a good buyer's agent is essential . . .*
- *Pitfalls of going it alone . . .*
- *Determining what you can afford, getting pre-qualified' . . .*
- *Using the Internet resources to look at homes . . .*
- *Creating a want/do not want list . . .*
- *Understanding the sequence of how things proceed . . .*
- *Where to get information on properties you may want to look at . . .*
- *What a listing agent has to tell you – and what they don't . . .*

If you have already started looking at homes on the internet, you need do a couple of things. First, find a good buyer's agent you like, trust, and who you feel will work hard for you. Second, you need to develop a relationship with a qualified mortgage lender, as you need to determine what you can afford to buy based on your income, living expenses, and your financial situation. You need to know how large a mortgage you qualify for and what price range of homes you should be looking at. You are wasting everyone's time if you don't know this. Third, you want to make up your 'want' list, 'must have' list, and, just as important, your 'Do not want' list. A list is provided in the website HomebuyersHBook.com. You can copy and use this when looking at homes. Fourth, if you haven't done this yet, go online and check out the homes in the communities you may want to live in. Fifth, understand the sequence of how things proceed, so you will be prepared to make an offer, get the home inspected, know what other evaluations you need to do, and follow up on concerns revealed by the inspection. (How to do this will be covered in later Chapters). Lastly, I've provided information on utilizing web resources when looking at homes.

Working with a Buyer's Agent . . .

In my opinion, the first thing you should do when buying a home is find a real estate agent who will act as your *buyer's agent*. Having a buyer's agent is important, as they are contractually obligated to work for you and can guide you through the whole buying process. You must understand: real estate agents do not work for you unless they are a *buyer's agent* that you have formally engaged to work on your behalf. Other types of agencies exist. A listing agent – whom you may deal with if you simply go to an open house or respond directly to an advertised home – works for the seller. They are trying to get the best possible price and terms for the seller and they have a fiduciary relationship (loosely defined as a 'relationship of trust') with that seller. They cannot, legally or ethically, lie or make any fraudulent representations. But they are not working for you either, and they are not obligated to tell you everything you may need to know – or help you get the best deal.

(Note: in many states, an attorney can act as a real estate agent just by the fact of being an attorney. This can work IF the attorney is an experienced agent; I'd be cautious otherwise. Most attorneys stay away from acting as buyer's agents unless they do this regularly).

In some areas of the country, you may work with a 'sub agent' (who used to be called a 'selling agent'). The sub agent works *for* the seller but *with* the buyer but not *for* the buyer. (Confusing, I know). In other words, a subagent could help you to find a home you may want to purchase, but their allegiance is still to the seller. This means they cannot do anything that would be against the seller's interests (such as offering a lower price, negotiating aggressively, or using knowledge about the seller's situation that would give you an edge in the transaction). Does this sound like something that could work against you? The confusion and ethical dilemmas with the whole 'subagent' type of agency led to the rise of *buyer's agency*, where, unless otherwise specified, a real estate agent will act either as a listing agent (working for the seller) or *for* you, as a buyer's agent.

Only 'buyer's agents' work for you and are legally required to represent your interests throughout the real estate purchase. They can tell you to 'walk away' from a property that doesn't fit your needs or needs serious work, offer a lower price, renegotiate if the inspection reveals problems, find a qualified home inspector and financing professional, and direct you to an attorney who knows what (s)he is doing. *Without this help, you are on your own.* In terms of finding a buyer's agent, you may know someone already or have been referred to someone and that's fine. Just make sure that you both like and trust them to work for you. I won't go into what you may need to do when interviewing an agent. Just make sure you are compatible and that the agent won't rush you to buy something/anything just to make a sale. Although rarely the case in recent years (at least with the agents my clients work with), back in the 80s and 90s, I saw buyer's agents who just wanted to make the sale happen, whether it was really in their client's interest or not.

In real estate offices in the states where I work (Massachusetts and New Hampshire), the selling agents are now largely gone and agents who represent buyers are now all *buyer's agents*, meaning they are not a subagent of the home seller, as they were in the past. That is not to say, however, that you will get equal representation from every office or every agent out there. Some of the 'old timers', I think, are still in the old subagent mold.

If I had a choice, I would choose an agency that does buyer representation only – or, if working with a traditional agency that takes listings also, with an agent who works mainly with buyers. Importantly, what you want is an agent

who puts your interests over the deal going through . . .

In other words, you want an agent who will tell you to walk away from over-priced homes, from homes with intractable problems – or even when they feel the home isn't right for your needs or budget. A good buyer's agent should also have the knowledge and ability to negotiate for you – and the wherewithal to tell you not to negotiate when further efforts will cause you to lose the property to another buyer. In general, if the agent is not comfortable with negotiations or has no skills in this area, they probably aren't selling real estate.

One option that is occasionally found is something called 'dual agency.' This is a situation where the agent will represent the buyer and seller with both sides' permission. This is a less desirable situation, as the agent must be absolutely honest and straightforward with every issue relating to the transaction, and you, as a buyer, would have to explicitly understand how you may need to proceed when the issues are not clear-cut. I've seen this work when you have very ethical, skilled agents – but, in general, it is something to avoid.

Pitfalls . . .

A pitfall to avoid is to find yourself dealing directly with a listing agent without first engaging your own buyer's agent. Listing agents love it when a buyer comes directly to them. If they can act as the agent for both the listing and selling side, they get to keep the entire commission instead of splitting it with the buyer's agent. You can't blame a listing agent for seeking to get the full commission; it's perfectly legal and really a smart business practice. Real estate agents, like everyone else, are in the business of making money. *It's just not in your interest.*

Here are a couple of examples of how you can lose in this scenario. A listing agent, with the owner's permission, may offer to take $10,000 off the selling price if you buy directly from them. You think you are coming out ahead. Maybe you are – but what if the home was overpriced by $30,000 to begin with? A good buyer's agent can tell you that the home you like, listed for $480,000, is only worth $450,000 and not the $470,000 'bargain price' you are getting it for. You just lost $20,000 by not having someone to advise you on market values. A listing agent will not – and legally, cannot – tell you that the home is overpriced or may not be the home that is right for you. Also, while your home inspector may give you a lot of good information, it is not their function to help you with negotiations. We don't know the price of the home, the local market, whether there are back-up offers, and the many factors that go into the buying decision. Importantly, home inspectors <u>cannot legally</u> tell you to walk away from a property or what to negotiate. In many states, a home inspector can lose his or her license if (s)he does this. (That said, any good home inspector will warn you off when serious problems are found). If you are unsure if you want to proceed with a sale or want advice on whether and what to negotiate, you will need a buyer's agent.

The way people end up dealing directly with the listing agent is that they see a listing online and directly call the agent. Or, they see an 'open house' and they go in and meet the listing agent and begin the process of making an offer if they are interested in the property. At this point, bringing in a buyer agent may not be practical and, while I am not an attorney, may not be legal. What you should do is find a buyer's agent you want to work with and engage them <u>before</u> you start actively looking. In this case, if you see a property on your own, such as at an open house, you would simply inform the listing agent that you already have representation.

I should note something else that can occur – and this is a reason I am glad I am a home inspector and not a real estate agent. This is a situation where there is a bidding war on a property. In this case, it can happen that the offer from the buyer's agent somehow doesn't find its way to the seller in a timely manner and the buyer who is working directly with the listing agent gets the home. There are legalities involved (as well as ethics), but it does occur and can be difficult to prove. Listing agents are supposed to provide all offers to a seller. I have also heard of buyers going directly to the listing agent before they have a buyer's agent in bidding war situations, as they feel this provides them with the best chance of 'winning' the home from other buyers. Maybe it can – but there are still significant downsides to doing this. As a home inspector, I can't get involved in these choices, but you really need guidance when a bidding war erupts.

So what would I consider bad agent practices?

First, not taking the time to understand your particular needs and wants. I think most agents are fine on this, as it would be fairly obvious if they weren't – and you would go elsewhere. A corollary to this would an agent who is simply too busy to put out the effort to be helpful. Getting a super successful agent whose name is on every billboard may be a great idea for homeowners who are listing their home. It's not so good for buyers, as you'll just get one of their assistants to work with you. They may not have the expertise, ability, or commitment to work with a buyer.

Another agent practice to be careful of is when they refer you to a home inspector who does not do thorough, critical inspections. Instead they refer you to someone who does 'quick' inspections that do not endanger the deal from going through or keep them at the inspection too long. (See Getting the most from your Home Inspection in Chapter 10 for more on finding a qualified inspector). This was a problem back in the 1980s when I started out. Ever since buyer agency came into practice, this has not been as much of an issue in my area – but I'd be naïve to say it doesn't happen – usually with new or inexperienced agents. Buyer's agents are legally obligated to work for you – and this normally includes finding a qualified, experienced inspector. A public official I know related a conversation he recently had with the owner of a large real estate agency. The agency owner told him that they screen out home inspectors who are too thorough or take longer than two hours to do the inspection, so this stuff still happens.

A problem I hear of – but don't personally see in my area – is when buyer's agents don't believe it is their function to attend the inspection. This is the norm in many states. If they are not present, however, how are they going to understand the problems that may be revealed by the home inspection and how are they going to address these with the seller (or seller's agent)? Yes, the inspection report is useful, but it really can't provide the context and additional information that a verbal discussion at the inspection can provide. In many cases, the report can make a problem sound either more serious or less serious than it warrants. Systems that don't appear to be working properly may just need to be serviced or have limited repairs. When evidence of suspected problems is found, requesting clarification on what occurred and what was done to correct the problem may be all that is needed.

To really understand the home and the conditions found, both you AND the buyer's broker need to attend the inspection and be active participants. Another practice I hear of is that agents in some areas don't believe that they should influence the inspector or their client in terms of what they should regard as 'acceptable' or 'not acceptable.' In this case, you should review your concerns with your buyer's agent regarding what the inspection revealed. I have no objection (and in fact, sometimes prefer) showing the listing agent serious problems, as now the 'issues are out on the table.' (Very often, they won't want to know what is found as they will have to disclose these conditions to another buyer should you not proceed with the sale). The buyer's agent should also be forwarded a copy of the report so that, where appropriate, they can negotiate problematic issues with the listing agent (or seller, where no agent is involved). (See Chapter 10).

A good buyer's agent should have the willingness and ability to steer you through any post-inspection negotiations. This is important. I saw numerous cases (mostly in the 80s and 90s) where buyers did not get help with resolving or renegotiating issues that came up – issues that in no way should have caused them to 'walk away' from the property. When the agents didn't negotiate for allowances or for repairs, the buyer would be either stuck with the cost of repairs or would walk away from a perfectly good house due to problems that were easily correctable.

Also, be aware of agents still in the mindset of the old sub-agent seller mentality. Even when the market was 'dead' a few years back, I heard real estate agents argue that the inspection was being done for 'information purposes only.' This may be true in a seller's market, where properties may have multiple offers and renegotiations may not be possible. (Note: at the time this was written [mid-2018], most of the country was in a seller's market, so many inspections are, in fact, done for information purposes only.) But to say that the home inspection is always being done for 'information only' purposes, even when serious problems or issues that need repairs are revealed, doesn't serve your interest. Why do the inspection if you are never going to going to ask for allowances (when warranted) or that suspect conditions be resolved? It does not benefit the seller either if you walk away from the deal, as they must start over with another buyer.

If the agent is not willing to renegotiate or tell you to 'walk' when this is warranted, then you need to find another agent – or at least realize you are on your own in these matters.

There are important exceptions, however, to this advice. First is with 'as is' properties, often bank owned, or properties where the listed or negotiated price is well below the market value of the home. It is also the case, as noted, for properties that have multiple offers and where bidding wars are occurring. In these cases, the buyer can use the inspection to either 'walk' on the home or accept it 'as is.' *You may not be able to do any negotiations in these situations*.

When sellers SAY that there will be no renegotiation after the home inspection, this is not 'written in stone.' I did an inspection last year on a property where the buyer agreed to 'no renegotiation.' When the inspection revealed a serious problem with the structure that would probably cause most buyers to 'walk,' the seller lowered the price by $10,000 due to the efforts of the buyer's agent. The seller probably realized that other buyers would not go forward due to this problem.

As a final note about dealing with real estate agents, it is important that you treat them with respect. Not often – but occasionally – I see buyers who treat agents with disrespect. There is no reason for this and this reflects most on those who can't show respect for all the parties involved. A listing agent is required to represent the seller's interest. As such, they have to treat the buyer fairly and answer your questions truthfully – but they are not there to represent your interest. Flowery language describing the merits of the property is the norm and should be taken with the appropriate regard. (In any case, you would want them to do the same when you have them listing your house for sale.)

The majority of real estate agents in today's world are ethical and professional and look out for their clients' interests. You'll hear stories about 'bad agents' or 'bad practices' – but you'll hear these most from other agents who don't condone these practices (just listen in when the buyer's and seller's agents are talking at the kitchen table while at the inspection). Bad (read: unethical) practices obviously can occur. We'd be naive to think otherwise with so much money at stake in every deal. But this is the exception and not the rule. That said, never confuse the real estate agent's interests with your own. While I believe that most buyer's brokers put their clients' interests first, real estate brokers have an immense interest in the deal going through. For the listing agent, this could mean not providing you with information that would affect your purchase decision but that they are not required to provide (for instance, is that beautiful meadow next to your intended home in the process of being developed or being sold to a Confined Animal Feeding Operation?). You need to do your own research, as noted in the next few chapters – AND you need to take steps to protect your own interests.

Using the web to look at homes . . .

Today, many home buyers – especially the younger, tech-savvy buyers – use the web to look at homes for sale. They'll then contact their agent to arrange showings of the properties they are most interested in. This can work great – but I still have reservations. First, the temptation will be to contact the listing agent, so you can arrange to see the property as soon as possible. You can do this, but as noted, you are better off engaging a buyer's agent who you will work with. You'll pay the same in broker commissions (well, almost), so you might as well have your own representation. Second, you can push the savings from technology too far. I've read articles that forecast the end of using real estate agents in the sale of homes. Eliminating the buyer's agents would not be to your advantage, as you would not be aware of what is going on in that local market and what may be changing. You would also not get information particular to the home that you should know (like: does the owner have to sell quickly, are their multiple offers, is the home underpriced or over-priced, etc.).

My advice is: don't sign in to the websites to look at homes– at least not at the outset. I have no experience dealing with these companies, other than that a lot of my them and I've generally had good feedback. A few of the most popular sites are provided below.

Redfin.com
Zillow.com
ZipRealty.com
Trulia.com
Realestate.com
Forsalebyowner.com
Realtor.com
Walkscore.com
Estately.com
HUD.gov

Just looking at realtor.com, by the way, I was able to get a listing of all of the homes in each town plus a listing and the price on all of the homes sold in these towns over the last six months. These sites can be a great screening tool in your house hunting search.

Looking up information about a property . . .

A lot of information will be on the **listing sheet**. Look at how many days the property was on the market. Look at price reductions. And, of course, look at the number of bedrooms, the size of the home, and whatever features will be make this home attractive to you.

Registry of Deeds. The registry of deeds in most counties can provide a history of ownership. In many states, this information can be obtained online. You may find something interesting in the ownership record.

Building Inspection Office. You can check on whether building permits were issued for work done. See Chapter 7 for more on this. You'll want to go to the building department in the town the home is located in. Some information may be online – but you may get more information by going in. Also check on any variances that may affect the use of the property.

What does an agent have to tell you – and what they don't . . . other questions to ask.

By the way, there is a whole list of things that a seller – and seller's agent – do not have to tell you, unless you ask. But if you ask, they are <u>obligated</u> to provide honest information. A few of the questions you can ask are:

- Did a serious crime occur on the property? Was someone killed or did someone nefarious live at this home?

- Is the home haunted? (Some buyers, I've been told, actually want to buy a home that is haunted . . . Interesting).
- Are there problems with the neighbors? (This can be important!) Does their dog bark endlessly?
- Did someone in the home die of AIDS or some other disease? (Less of a stigma now than in the past).
- Was the property used for some criminal purposes? Is the land around the property slated for development? (<u>This is an important one!</u>)Have there been other inspections on the property? What did they reveal?Why are the homeowners selling?
- Did the home suffer damage in recent storms or other weather event? Again, the seller and listing agent must answer this (to the best of their knowledge) if asked – but they don't have to volunteer information.
- Did the home suffer damage in recent storms or other weather event? Again, the seller and listing agent must answer this (to the best of their knowledge) if asked – but they don't have to volunteer information.
- Does the current homeowner have flood insurance? *If they have no mortgage, they may not be paying for flood insurance – but you will have to if you have a mortgage.* Your insurance company may even require this.

I'm sure there are other questions you can ask – but these are a few I'm familiar with.

Understanding the sequence of how things proceed . . .

As a very brief summary of how things unfold when you are buying a home, I've noted the following sequence.

#1 Make the decision to buy and understand the type of the market you are buying into.

#2 Find a buyer's agent before you start looking at homes seriously. While you can check out what's for sale before you have an agent – see the caution about going to 'open houses' or calling the listing agent before engaging a buyer's agent.

#3 Talk to a good loan officer/financing professional. You'll need to do this before you look at homes. Get pre-qualified from a lender. Even better, get 'pre-approved,' where the bank or lending company is actually ready to lend you the money. You can very often get the names of qualified lending officers from your agent. This is critical. You don't want to try to figure this stuff out on your own.

#4 WAIT – this should go first: read the early chapters of the Handbook. Think things through and devise a 'Want/Do Not Want' list, as noted above.

#5. Ideally, look at a lot of homes – but be ready to move quickly if you need to. Use the strategies noted in Chapter 8 to get your offer accepted.

#6. Make your offer, based on what you think you can get the home for. This may be the listing price – or a higher or lower price, depending on the market conditions. Your agent (or attorney) will have an inspection contingency clause inserted into your offer. Try to get this for 10 days; 7 days is a minimum. Sometimes 5 days is all you will get. Financing and other contingencies may need to be inserted into the offer. Counteroffers could occur. We'll assume your offer gets accepted (meaning you have reached agreement on the critical terms with the seller).

[Note: in most states, you will be signing a Purchase and Sales Agreement when your offer is accepted. This will give you a specified number of days to have the home inspected. In other states, such as Massachusetts, it's a bit different. You will make an Offer to Purchase that gives you a specified amount of time to have the home inspected. At the end of the inspection period, you will then sign the actual Purchase and Sales Agreement. In each case, you should have time to do the inspection and other investigations after your offer is accepted.]

#7. If you plan on adding onto or expanding the home, check with the local building inspector and possibly the conservation commission. You want to make sure you can do what you want to do with the property before you get too far into the process. See more on this in Chapter 6.

#8. Do your home inspection and the other relevant investigations noted in the later chapters. Don't forgo the inspection as a negotiating strategy! Radon testing is also typically done at the time of the inspection. Possible renegotiations may occur based on the inspection – or allowances are made by the seller due to verbal requests that fall short of a renegotiation effort. See the chapter on post-inspection negotiations for what may be possible in a 'seller's market.'

#9 As soon as you have reached an agreement with the seller, your attorney – or the attorney provided by the lender – will do a Title search and will order the Appraisal. They will also review the Purchase and Sales document. A final approval of the loan will occur if the home 'appraises out' (meets the appraised value to justify what the bank is giving you for your mortgage). Essentially, the bank wants to make sure the property has enough value so they can sell the property and recoup what they have loaned should you default on the loan. If the property doesn't appraise, either the seller would need to reduce the price – or you would need to come up with a larger down payment.

#10 You will need to have Homeowner's Insurance in place before you can close. Note: if you are a cash buyer, no one will require that you have a Homeowner's policy before you buy the property – but you had better do this. If you put this off now, you may continue to put this off.

#11. Do a final 'walk through' inspection with your agent the morning of the day you will 'close' (take legal possession of the property). Notify your attorney if things are amiss (debris or abandoned goods left that will cost you to remove; failed systems; things taken, such as attached light fixtures, that should not have been removed, etc.). Most of the time, there will not be significant issues; sometimes there will be.

#12. Assuming everything is okay at the walk-through inspection, go to the closing (also termed the 'settlement'), where you will be signing the paperwork involved in the legal transfer of the property. Expect a couple of hours signing forms. Expect many hours, if you choose to read everything you will be signing. I advise looking at the plot plan, if nothing else, to make sure you are getting what you think you are getting. (See Chapter 8, on Legal matters).

#13. Done. Go home, have a glass of wine, and start packing.

©Ernest A. Simpson, 2018.

CHAPTER 3
Regions and Localities that Carry Risks . . .

What we'll cover in this chapter . . .

- Coastal living . . . the good, the bad, and the ugly . . . (sorry, I couldn't help it)
- Assessing flood risks . . .
- Knowing the risks of earthquakes in specific regions . . .
- How to assess fire and extreme heat risks . . .
- Impacts of living in areas with industrial agriculture . . .
- Risks of living in areas where fracking for natural gas is occurring . . .
- States that are financial 'time bombs' . . .

Now, before getting into the nitty-gritty of looking at homes – which I'll do in Chapter 4, 5, and 6, I'm going to backtrack a bit. Before you start looking at homes, it will be desirable to look at some of the risks specific to certain regions. While you may be familiar with these, maybe you are not. The fact is: there are short or long-term risks of living in certain types of areas and even specific localities. In some cases, you may want to ask whether it will it be prudent to live the next 'X' (fill in) number of years with the hazards I've noted below. At the least, thinking about these issues ahead of time could make a difference in how you live and what you do to minimize your risks – if not where you live.

Regions, localities at risk . . .

#1. Living near the coast and low-lying areas – with the effects of global warming . . .

This is an obvious one – but it is still important to discuss. I'm not going to debate this issue of global warming (and the euphemism: climate change). As far as science goes, it's a settled matter. The earth has been warming for some time, but nothing can account for the current degree of warming by explanations other than the increase in greenhouse gases (principally carbon dioxide and methane). For those still in doubt: I can't help you. It's important to question everything, but there's also time to accept what scientific evidence has concluded. The climate change deniers still questioning why this is occurring generally have an economic interest in questioning this, such as ties to or financial support from oil, gas, and coal interests – or just the fact that people who believe in science believe in facts, and facts are not in fashion at the moment. A lot of very ignorant – but very rich – billionaires oppose anything that reeks of scientific inquiry – or something that will take a dime out of their future profits. And finally, while the so-called scientific objections you still find floating around can sound very convincing, they rely on statistical 'tricks' to make something seem true that isn't. They never submit their theories or explanations for rising temperatures for scientific review. Enough said . . .

The problem is that buyers, while accepting that climate change is real, are ignoring this issue and are buying homes in areas that are projected to be impacted by rising sea levels. In my area, I see a lot of retirees moving to be near the coast – especially coastal cities. The need for flood insurance – and the costs and negative baggage this carries – seems to be discounted by a lot of home buyers.

I think the explanation for why buyers are ignoring the sea level rise projections lies in the belief that while this is occurring, the impacts before mid-century (2050) may be somewhat relatively modest (at least compared to what happens after that). The really severe impacts in terms of sea level rise may not be felt in the next twenty years or so (other than the occasional mass destruction of entire communities from storms such as Sandy, Katrina, Irma, etc.). The year 2050 seems like a long ways away. It is and it isn't. Coastal areas are already seeing the impacts of what are, to date, fairly minimal rises. The streets in parts of Miami, for instance, are prone to routine flooding during extreme high tides. The storm drains that used to allow water to flow out now have ocean water flowing in. Along portions of the east coast, homes on coastal islands are being picked up and moved inland due to the erosion of the land facing the water. Many coastal islands are disappearing and are no longer habitable. Lastly, a new study predicts that, with limited human intervention, 31 to 67 percent of Southern California beaches could completely erode back to coastal infrastructure or sea cliffs by the year 2100 with sea-level rises of 3.3 feet (1 meter) to 6.5 feet (2 meters).

Just how bad will it get? This is where things get tricky. According to a 2015 study out of Princeton and Germany's Potsdam University, our total emissions of greenhouse gases are enough to lock in roughly five feet of sea level rise by the end of this century. According to other projections I've seen, this could be conservative – and substantial rises could occur much sooner. Some of the projections are scary, showing a ten foot – or greater – sea level rise. The increase in extreme storms and weather events is another consequence of global warming, with low-lying coastal communities obviously most at risk for flooding and damage. This has already come about with hurricanes Harvey, Irma, and Maria. Hurricane Sandy obliterated whole sections of coastal New York not thought to be at risk. And its not just coastal areas that are at risk. The rising sea levels will impact cities – and even development well inland due to storm surges and the fact that higher sea levels will cause rivers to back up and rise as well.

A complicating factor is that the higher water temperatures lead to greater evaporation from the seas. This leads to more intense storms and more intense rainfalls. Can we say 'Houston'?

But even if the really serious sea levels rises are a ways off, you still need to question whether you want to be subjecting yourself to the increased costs of flood insurance – and the negatives that living in a projected flood zone may have when the currently healthy real estate turns into a bear market (it may have, by the time you read this). In the current tight market, buyers have had to take on the added costs of flood insurance – as well as the risks of living where flooding may occur. In a bear market, these homes will be marked down relative to homes where flood insurance is not required. The costs of flood insurance vary, with an average cost of roughly $1200 a year in Massachusetts in 2016. On expensive homes and homes particularly at risk, the insurance premiums will obviously be much higher. I just had a client who walked away from a home for sale near the coast due to the $12,000 <u>annual</u> flood insurance assessment.

Another problem is that long before the sea levels rise to the point where homes are flooded, it is likely that the property values of homes in the highest risk areas will crash. Areas such as south Florida are particularly at risk. Sea levels in South Florida are roughly four inches higher now than they were in 1992. The National Oceanic and Atmospheric Administration predicts sea levels will rise <u>as much as three feet</u> in Miami by 2060. By the end of the century, according to projections by Zillow, some 934,000 existing Florida properties, <u>worth more than $400 billion</u>, are at risk of being submerged. Some of the doomsayers (doesn't mean they aren't right, however) say that one third of Florida will be a saltwater swamp at some point.

The impact is already being felt in South Florida. Tidal flooding now predictably drenches inland streets even when the sun is out, and thanks to the region's porous limestone bedrock, saltwater is creeping into the drinking water supply. The area's drainage canals rely on gravity; as oceans rise, the water utilities have had to install giant pumps to push water out to the ocean.

Existing homeowners in these areas face what is called the 'prisoner's dilemma'; that is, should they sell now, before the rush for the exits starts? By doing so, however, they will cause the problem they are trying to avoid (the crash in real estate values). The problem may become more apparent when banks refuse to provide mortgages to homes in at-risk areas. So far, however, the sun has not set on coastal Florida real estate. Some commentators have described the real estate market in South Florida as 'pessimists selling to optimists.' This may characterize lots of areas with low-lying coastal real estate. It also likely that some of the low-lying areas of Houston that were subject to flooding are no longer viable places to live. (Note: roughly 90 percent of the housing stock In Houston did not suffer flood damage, so one can't argue that the city itself is at risk – not yet, anyhow).

Many coastal homes are now being raised up or are built on elevated piers. That's great, but it is expensive to do. Costs are reputed be roughly $70,000 – but these can run a lot higher. Also, most homes weren't built to be put on piers. Homes with their living space ten feet about the street don't exactly provide a nice urban streetscape. Another problem: flood insurance is limited to $250,000. Your homeowner's insurance does not cover losses from land movement, such as beach or riverfront erosion or loss of value due to flooding concerns.

But even if your future home is not prone to flooding – for instance, if your home sits on an elevated spot or is raised up on piers – many of the roadways and public transportation networks are low-lying and will be subject to occasional or chronic flooding. A Boston Globe article noted that, with a three-foot rise in sea levels, roughly 48.5 miles of roadways on the Cape (Cod) would be submerged, with another 160 miles disconnected from the network. You may find neighborhoods or whole communities that are isolated by floodwaters in the future. Conceivably, whole communities may be wiped out. (Please don't think I'm being alarmist. The projections noted above are conservative).

I will note that I have seen homes that are in flood zones where the risks are minimal. In one section of the city I live in, flood insurance is required due to a severe river flooding that occurred in 1936. After that event, flood control dams were built upstream and there have been no subsequent floods. Some of the FEMA flood control maps, in my opinion, may extend the risks to areas not likely to experience flooding (or, at least, not soon). Also, just being near the coast or a river is not a problem if the land is elevated well above the waterways. A lot of coastal development will probably do fine.

I recommend that, if the home you are looking at has any chance of requiring flood insurance, you should ask the listing agent for a copy of the elevation certificate and whether the existing flood policy can be transferred to the new owner at the same rate. (Note: Elevation certificates are now required in my area for homes in coastal locations). Be careful: a real estate broker could note that the current owners do not pay flood insurance. That could be true if the current owner doesn't carry a mortgage. It won't be true for you, the new owner.

What can you do to protect your investment? First, do your research. Study the FEMA flood maps (msc.fema.gov) to see whether the home you may be buying is in a low or high-risk zone. You can also utilize resources such as Climate Central's Risk Zone map at ss2.climatecentral.org. Regional authorities may also have flood zone maps. In Boston, there is the Sasaki Associates Interactive Sea Change map at seachange.sasaki.com/map. Also, note that flood maps change, so you need to look at the most current maps. The redrawing of the flood maps in recent years greatly expanded the areas where flood insurance is required. I recommend that you research the flood insurance costs before you get too far into the process of buying a home.

Also, the risks of serious flooding are usually known – but not always. I don't think most of the population of the New York metropolitan area ever thought they could see something like 'super-storm' Sandy. Homes that had sat alongside small streams in Vermont for the last 200 years were wiped out due to flooding from the remnants of Hurricane Irene in 2012.

For homes that have flooded or appear 'at risk,' you may want to research whether it is feasible to have the home raised so the living areas and utilities will not be subject to damage if flooding does occur.

In other words, this is a giant case of buyer beware.

As a final note: would I personally live near the coast or in areas designated as a flood zone? Surprisingly, I would – assuming that: #1: the property is at a low-risk area, elevated above the areas projected to be at risk of flooding, #2: I am compensated for my risk by getting a good deal on the property, and #3: I have no plans to leave the property to my son, much less my grandchildren. (I am at an age where I shouldn't have to worry about flooding 30 years down the road).

#2. Susceptibility to catastrophic earthquake damage on the Northwest coast . . .

When we think of earthquakes, we usually think of California due to its known history of severe earthquakes. But other regions of the country have suffered devastating earthquakes as well – just not as frequently. The New Madrid earthquake, centered in Missouri in the early 1800s, and the Alaskan quake from the 1960s come to mind. No one ever really thought much about the upper Pacific coast, even though that region is along the 'rim of fire' which extends up the west coast to Alaska and across the Pacific to Japan. Unfortunately, the lack of severe earthquakes in the northwest will not last forever – and when it occurs, the rupture of the fault under what is called the Cascadia subduction zone is likely to be devastating. The consequences of an earthquake along this fault line may be enough to affect where you will buy in this region. If nothing else, it should give you plenty of incentives to prepare your home (and your life) should this event occur.

A bit of background . . .

Everyone has heard of the San Andreas fault that runs up through California. This fault has resulted in the periodic earthquakes – ranging from light to severe – along the fault line. But no one ever thought of the Pacific Northwest as being at risk of a major quake simply because, from the time of Lewis and Clarke's expedition in 1804 when this area was first explored, none have ever occurred.

What is known is that the upper Pacific coast, from Northern California up to Vancouver, is over the intersection of the North American continental plate and what is termed the Juan de Fuca plate, roughly 90,000 square miles in size, which extends out into the Pacific Ocean. The Juan de Fuca plate is gradually pushing under the North American plate and is the source of the volcanoes along the Cascadian mountain range.

Given the knowledge of plate tectonics and the lack of a recorded history of earthquakes where the Juan de Fuca plate rides under the North American plate, geologists back in the 1980s began to look at for evidence for past quakes. What they found indicated a massive earthquake in the (somewhat) distant past. The evidence provided by a grove of dead cedar trees in a coastal location provided one of the first clues. Interestingly, geologists found that this die-off did not occur gradually, as would occur from rising sea levels inundating the roots with salt water. Instead, the die-off occurred simultaneously, as if trees in the low-lying area were suddenly submerged in salt water. By correlating this evidence with a history of tsunamis (tidal waves) in Japan (Japan has kept meticulous records of the dates of tsunamis going back centuries), they were able to pinpoint the date of the last earthquake as January 26 in the year 1700. The tidal wave that occurred in Japan at that time was termed a mystery tsunami, as there was no earthquake that preceded the event. Instead, the wave had to occur from an earthquake that occurred *across* the Pacific.

Further research indicated that the Cascadian fault experiences an earthquake roughly every 240 years, with a lot of variation in this time frame. Statistically, we are well overdue for a quake to occur.

The scary thing about the possibility of an earthquake in the Cascadian fault line is the likely magnitude of the quake. Whereas California routinely experiences earthquakes registering anywhere from 4.0 up to 8.2 on the Richter scale, a full break of the Cascadian fault may produce an earthquake at a 9.2. And since the Richter is logarithmic scale; a 9.00 earthquake is ten times worse than an 8.0 quake. The second problem is the complete unpreparedness of the area for a quake of this magnitude.

What you need realize is that, if the 'big one' hits in this region:

- there is no early warning system
- virtually none of the buildings were built to withstand a severe earthquake. Many homes, unless properly reinforced, will simply slide off their foundation. (Oregon had no seismic code for new buildings until 1994).
- The damage caused by shaking during the earthquake, however bad, will be outweighed by the likely tsunami (tidal wave) that follows. (Remember the 2011 Fukuyama quake in Japan?).
- The electrical grid will go down, probably for months
- An evacuation of low-lying areas – and especially the beaches – will be impossible.
- Homes and buildings built on filled land, as found in areas of Seattle, simply won't exist anymore. This type of soil simply 'liquefies' and loses its bearing capacity during a severe earthquake.
- FEMA calculates that, across the region, something on the order of a million buildings – more than three thousand of them schools – will collapse or be compromised in the earthquake. So will half of all highway bridges, fifteen of the seventeen bridges spanning Portland's two rivers, and two-thirds of railways and airports; also, one-third of all fire stations, half of all police stations, and two-thirds of all hospitals.

(The whole story, from an article in the New Yorker magazine (July 20, 2015) is quite fascinating. I've included a link below and on the Home Buyer's Handbook website (HomeBuyersHBook.com) to the full article. (http://www.newyorker.com/magazine/2015/07/20/the-really-big-one. (Note: if you are reading this as a book, and not an on-line version, I have provided the hyperlinks at HomebuyersHBook.com so you can look up these articles).

Obviously, I am not telling you to avoid living in the northwest. Although I haven't been there it appears to be one of the more interesting and beautiful places in the country. But if you are going to buy a home there, I would do some research on where you may NOT want to be if the 'big one' hits. (One can't say statistically that an earthquake is 'overdue,' but unless geologic history reverses itself, it will happen, perhaps sooner than later). A brief list of properties to avoid would include: homes built on, above, or below steep hillsides; homes built in low-lying areas that would be submerged by a tsunami; homes built over filled land (commonly found in the Seattle area).

If you will be buying a home in any earthquake-prone area you will want to research the risk factors for the site. For homes along the Pacific rim in areas with a history of severe earthquakes, evaluate whether the home you are looking will still be standing after a severe quake. Has the structure been reinforced to limit the possible damage. If not, can it be reinforced? In general, older homes and buildings are more 'at risk' – especially those built with unreinforced masonry. For homes and buildings built on 'filled land' – forget it.

For a good article on preparing for this type of event, read the follow-up article from the New Yorker at the following link. https://www.newyorker.com/tech/elements/how-to-stay-safe-when-the-big-one-comes. Again, you can follow this link at the website: HomebuyersHBook.com)

Other earthquake risks

I'm not saying anyone can – or should – avoid living in areas where earthquakes occur. You can't do this unless you rule out much of the west coast. Even areas not thought to be subject to earthquakes, such as Oklahoma, now have quakes. This is believed to be due to the injection deep back into the ground of fracking waste from oil and gas drilling. Even New England reportedly suffered a moderate quake back in the 1700s. You can't live in many areas of California without having a risk of damage from a major earthquake. But who knows when and where this will occur? Most (but not all) buildings will survive all but the most severe quakes, and they should not cause a wholesale destruction of the communities. Life goes on (for most) and lastly, in many regions, only limited areas are affected by any given incident.

That said, you may want to just be careful about what and where you buy in an area that has a history of severe earthquakes – or is overdue for a major quake. Look for something that will survive and assess the potential for having a structural retrofit so that the damage may be minimized. While the California building codes are more stringent about limiting earthquake damage from non-severe quakes, unfortunately, most of the older unreinforced brick masonry will still fail during an earthquake. Do you think all of the underground gas lines could be a problem too? In areas where fracking-induced quakes are occurring, get supplemental coverage for earthquake damage from your insurance company (assuming they offer this). As covered in the chapter on Financing, the homeowner's insurance policies in most states DO NOT cover earthquake damage, but you may be able to get it as a 'rider.'

#3. Risk of tornadoes and wind damage

Again, tornadoes are extremely prevalent in the south and Midwest (does it seem like there are more and more these days?). Nevertheless, the actual risk that any one town or neighborhood will be hit in any ten or twenty year period is extremely low. That said, if you live in these regions, there is always a risk of tornadoes – and given the severity of the winds during a severe tornado, there are few conventionally built homes that can survive.

But, while no construction can survive a EF4 or EF5 tornado, with winds typically above 160 mph, newer homes that are built with enhanced measures to resist tornadoes and high wind conditions may survive a less severe tornado (which, fortunately, most are). Unfortunately, a lot of shoddy construction has been made in the Midwest and southern states. I've seen pictures of homes blown apart by non-severe tornadoes, where the damage could have been minimized if the construction had been at least somewhat wind-resistant.

If you are building or buying a new home in a tornado- or hurricane-prone area of the country, there are techniques and methods that can be implemented that would make the home resistant to damage from high winds. Again, given the limitations of this book, you will need to research this. If you are buying a home that was designed to resist wind and storm damage, I think this would be a plus, but you would need to have a qualified structural engineer review the plans AND the implementation of the structural reinforcements.

If you are buying (or living) in a conventionally-framed home, there are measures you can take that will help you survive a tornado or other high-wind conditions. One measure would be to have – or build – a safe room that is structurally reinforced to withstand tornado damage. For some properties – and especially mobile homes – having a below-ground room designed to withstand a tornado would be advisable. Mobile homes should be strapped down in regions where tornados frequently occur. See Chapter 20 for more discussion of this.

#4. Homes in areas at extreme fire risk

While vast sections of the western states are most at risk of severe fire, as severe droughts and high wind conditions have resulted in fires that no one anticipated (note the Gatlinburg fires in October 2016 or the fires that devastated western Canada a couple of years ago). The 2015 Canadian fires, incidentally, reportedly burned an area equal to the size of Massachusetts.

California and most of the western states have always had a semi-desert climate for much of the year. The effect of global warming is causing these areas to become even drier and hotter, extending the fire season far beyond what it was in the past. (Note: I don't think the forested areas of the eastern half of the country are necessarily immune to catastrophic fires either, should a prolonged drought and the right conditions occur).

For many people, building a home in the rural inland forested areas of the West has held an enormous appeal – and it's understandable: it's a beautiful land-scape. The problem is that many of these homes were built at a time when large fires were not as much a risk as they are now. Homes have been built out in the middle of the forest or grasslands, surrounded by trees and vegetation that dry out for much of the year. This poses a high risk of losing the home unless aggressive measures are done to make the site and home more fireproof (think metal roofs, removal of vegetation, and other measures). Very often, the homes near or in the towns can be saved, but those in outlying areas can't be.

For those buying (or living) in California, I think the fire risk is known. The wild-fires that occurred in October 2017 in northern California and December 2017 in southern California were among the most severe on record. Over 10,000 struc-tures were destroyed or damaged. The fire risk is exacerbated by the effect of global warming, which has extended the fire season in the west by two months. Another problem is that the California population increasingly is living in high-risk fire corridors, with residential neighborhoods spilling into rural or remote territory. According to a 2017 risk analysis by Verisk, 15% – or over two million – of California's homes are concentrated in high or extremely high wildfire risk zones. Another 12% are located in moderate risk areas. This means that more than a quarter of the state's homes are at moderate to extremely high risk of being ravaged in an annual wildfire. What is also troubling is that homeowners who lost their homes in the 2017 fires are rebuilding in the same locations. They are supposed to implement measures to prevent fire damage in the future, but whether these efforts are sufficient has been questioned.

Throughout the West, much of the development over the last forty years has occurred in forested areas, mainly at the forest edges. Fire suppression scientists call this the 'wildland urban interface' (WUI). These areas offered cheaper land, open space, wildlife, and distance from neighbors, not to mention distance from building inspectors and those not of a like mind. Between 1990 and 2010, some 2 million new homes were built in the WUI, right in the path of the fires.

As a home buyer, you need to think about whether you want to live where the fire risk is extremely high and you stand a good chance of losing everything you've got – including your life.

Wherever you buy, you will need to assess the fire risk of both the area and the site. Where the risk is 'significant' and you still want to live in the areas designated as a WUI, research on how you can make the property more fire-resistant. Colorado has programs that will help homeowners in fire-prone areas redesign the landscaping and take other measures to minimize the risk of a fire taking their homes. Where this has been done, there have been some preliminary results that indicate this will increase your home's survivability in a severe fire. I should note that counties in Montana tried to implement a similar program but were shot down by newly elected firebrand conservatives who saw this as an infringement on their private property rights. Check out the state you are buying in to see if similar programs are available, as the preliminary studies indicate that fewer properties that have been fireproofed have lost homes to fire. If nothing else, know your evacuation routes and what you will need to take if you need to leave quickly.

#5. Areas subject to water shortage risks . . . extreme heat . . .

Much of the southwest and southern California are basically deserts. Will some of these areas become uninhabitable? I don't think that is likely in the near future, but perhaps, with the global warming and continued droughts, you can't rule it out – especially if the water supplies from the Colorado River are cut off at some point. A more severe rationing of water is likely to occur. You can probably expect to see fewer lawns and irrigated golf courses in Arizona, California, and the rest of the southwest (Note: this has already occurred in many areas.) A lot of the water that is diverted from the Colorado River ends up being used in agriculture. At some point, this will not happen.

In terms of heat, this can be a problem anywhere when prolonged heat waves occur. Severe heat waves increase heat-related deaths. Cities and urban areas form 'heat islands' that have higher temperatures due to the prevalence of asphalt and the lack of vegetation. While most of the country will experience increased risks of extreme temperature periods, the southwest faces a double whammy as the temperatures are extreme much of the year – and not just occasionally. Temperatures in Phoenix commonly reach 115 F degrees during the summer. You can't live there without air conditioning (but I have to admit, that's true for most of the country today). While many people prefer the heat to the cold and snow, there are limits. If you are moving to the southwest, you may want to rent for a year or two to make sure you can adjust to the temperatures. I think the 'desert' areas of the southwest may be a great place to live – for eight months of the year. Eventually, many areas will not be habitable for most people. Just my opinion . . .

#6. States and cities at risk of going broke due to pension obligations and bad decisions . . .

To put it bluntly, the municipal and state pension systems in this country are a mess. For a lot of reasons we don't need to get into here, numerous cities and states have pension obligations that far exceed their ability to pay. Basically, it comes down to the fact that many states found it way too easy to promise more future benefits when times were good so they could use the money for other purposes. Also, many states and cities grossly overestimated the investment returns that the pension funds would accrue. When the tech bust occurred in 2000, and with the real estate and financial markets bust in 2008, the funds' assumed high rate of return (usually around seven to eight percent) proved to be fiction. Also, the fact that people are living longer quickly overrode all the assumptions on how much the pension funds should have set aside. And lastly, the municipal and state workers in many states have guaranteed pensions that far exceed anything that anyone in the private section will ever get.

So how could this affect you as a homeowner? Unfortunately, for the state's taxpayers, the pensions are typically guaranteed by law. They can't be lowered except by a bankruptcy filing. That would be a last resort – and this would not be allowed by the courts, except in the most extreme circumstances. Detroit comes to mind, and now Puerto Rico.

If the pension benefits can't be lowered, then the money has to come from somewhere – and that usually means higher real estate and other taxes or greatly reduced services. For the states that planned responsibly (for instance, Oregon, Wisconsin, North and South Dakota, and Idaho), enough money was set aside to largely cover the expected pensions (at least at this time). In other states, including Illinois (a fiscal basket case), New Jersey, Kentucky, and Connecticut, the pension shortfalls are extreme. This is likely to result in much higher real estate and sales taxes – and these could be much higher in places like Chicago and areas of California. The prospect of much higher taxes and the fiscal impasse in Illinois is already causing an outflow of people who are trying to escape before the #%^& hits the fan. High taxes may be desirable when they result in great schools and increased public amenities. On the other hand, they negatively affect real estate values when they are way out of line relative to the benefits of living in that community.

I should note that the alternative to higher taxes is the gutting of all services in the public sphere that make the community worth living in. The creditors and the younger workers will be screwed. When the union members in city of Harvey, Illinois sued to ensure they would get their retirements, the courts ruled they were entitled to the payments they were promised. The city did not have the money, so they had to lay off one quarter of the police force and half of the firefighters.

If you are retiring or just moving you should research the fiscal health of the town and state. This data can be hard to come by, but the Government Accounting Standards Board (GASB) requires that government entities report their pension funding status. Florida and California maintain websites that will give you this information. Don't get blindsided.

#7 Living in states where industrial agriculture is dominant . . .

Despite our idealistic picture of farms and rural areas, the effects of industrial agriculture have made many areas of the country less-than-desirable places to live. While it is hard to generalize on this, areas of the Midwest and southern states, where intensive farming is occurring, come to mind.

The problems are several fold:

First, in a number of states, particularly Iowa and North Carolina, concentrated animal feeding operations (CAFOs) are present where literally thousands – or tens of thousands – of pigs, chickens, and cows are housed in huge containment buildings (I hesitate to call these 'barns'). These operations have enormous waste pit lagoons of manure that generate extremely noxious smells and wastes. In some areas, these wastes are shot high into the air, where the residue falls down onto the downwind residential areas (usually poor and without recourse). The manure pits are something akin to hell. These have the unfortunate habit of failing or leaking, thereby flooding rivers with toxic wastes. (You can't fish in these waters.) The effect of excessive and poorly applied fertilizers, meanwhile, has made dead zones in downstream rivers.

Living near or downwind of these operations literally stinks. Have you smelled ammonia? The ammonia also combines with the sulfates from coal-fired power plants to form types of small particle pollution that is an air pollution problem.

Moreover, due to the political power of the industrial farm operations, the measures that could prevent or mitigate the dumping or spillage of manure into streams and the watersheds are not implemented. Downstream cities have to spend huge monies on water pollution controls for the drinking water, as they can't control the CAFO operations. The politicians in power, as is often the case, have sold out the people for the corporate money.

A second problem with living in areas with large agricultural operations is the higher level of exposure to pesticides and herbicides. Large farms – or, should I say, the 'agricultural operations' – in much of the country use a simply unbelievable amount of pesticides and herbicides (such as atrazine, chlorpyrifos, and Roundup) on their crops. Roundup was found to be a likely carcinogenic substance by European researchers and has been banned in many countries (but, of course, it is still widely used here). See the Chapter on water quality for a discussion of these herbicides.) The amount of pesticides, herbicides, and other chemicals used in present-day agriculture in this country makes these areas much less healthy to live in. Those living in the major California agricultural valleys, for instance, show much higher rates of asthma and other conditions.

The third problem with living in agricultural areas is the economic effect of industrial agriculture. A landscape that used to have independent farmers and vibrant agricultural communities now has been hollowed out in many areas. Family farms and businesses that used to provide good incomes are gone: everything gets contracted out by the large agricultural corporations, as there is no market except to grow for the large conglomerates – which pay only minimal prices. The subsequent effect is that the once thriving local economies have died, the downtowns are largely ghost towns. Unless changes occur, you don't want to buy in one of these areas. There simply is not much 'community' left.

#8 Areas subject to fracking, fossil fuel operations, and environmental degradation . . .

Not only are many rural communities impacted by Confined Animal Feeding Operations (CAFOs) and industrial agriculture, but many areas of the rural heartland are now subject to industrial operations for fuel extraction utilizing hydraulic fracturing (fracking). These processes inject huge amounts of water, chemicals, and propants (sand and other materials used to keep the seams open) under high pressures to fracture gas or oil-laden bedrock deep in the earth to release natural gas or oil. Prior to the development of fracking technology, extracting this gas was not possible or economically viable.

The problem is that these operations, despite efforts to paint a bright picture of fracking, use huge amounts of toxic chemicals that end up polluting the waterways and groundwater. The reinjection of the wastewater/sludge deep into the earth is another problem, as this is believed to be causing the earthquakes recently besetting Oklahoma. Most of the toxic waste, full of heavy metals and volatile organic compounds, reportedly ends up dumped on the ground, where it then pollutes the groundwater and streams.

Leakage of methane, possibly through cracked or poorly sealed casings, has resulted in this gas mixing in with well water. The film *Gasland* showed homeowners setting fire to the water that came out of their taps. This is reportedly not an uncommon problem in areas of Pennsylvania where fracking is done. I would be cautious about buying a home in localities where fracking is occurring – or even where I could not control whether one of these operations will set up shop next to my property. States most at risk include rural sections of Pennsylvania, Ohio, Texas, North Dakota – in other words, large portions of the Midwest and plains.

And lastly, no sane person would move to areas voluntarily where mountaintop removal is done, but you have to question why the residents of the states of West Virginia, Virginia, and Kentucky would allow this to occur. Mountaintop removal is the process whereby mountains are leveled to extract the coal inside. If you can bear seeing it, Google 'mountaintop removal' and look at the pictures of what this entails. This process not only destroys the mountains and fills the valleys with toxic waste, but it destroys the lives of the people who used to call these areas 'home.' ('For what?' you have to ask. Millions of years of a landscape destroyed to supply cheap electricity for air conditioning?) All for the benefit of the wealthy coal operators and a relatively small number of coal miners. And yes, I feel for the coal miners – but they should be asking themselves how much of their region are they willing to turn into a permanent wasteland for their own short-term benefit.

A final question:

#9 How safe – and sustainable – is an area if, as the saying goes, the SHTF?

This is something no one wants to think about a whole lot. But I look at the jammed highways and the tightly packed cities and suburbs and ask myself: what happens if gasoline or heating oil becomes extremely expensive or not available? What happens if the food trucks can't roll in? What do people do? Are there some areas that are more likely to remain sane and good places to live? There are no easy answers here. You would think rural areas would be preferable, but isolated properties may be more at risk from those who are desperate. Crime rates are rising rapidly in rural areas at this time. Cities would be at high risk in many ways, but many cities have educated and higher income inhabitants. Resources may also get funneled to cities if things go bad, as this is where they would be most needed. Cities could be the worst and among the better places to be, when and if things go downhill. Small towns could work, assuming they are not overrun with refugees from the coasts or the cities. I suspect that a lot of tightly packed rim suburbs simply won't be the place to be.

I'm not sure what to recommend here: whether urban, suburban, or rural areas would be the best place to live should things fall apart. All could be o.k. – or terrible – depending on the neighbors, the region, and a whole bunch of factors. Maybe it would be safest to live on a cul-de-sac or self-contained community with a lot of hard-working, non-violent neighbors who think like you do. This will be hard to find – but it is worth thinking about. Neighbors and community are important.

CHAPTER 4

Evaluating Communities and Neighborhoods

What we'll cover in this chapter:

- What you should look for in a community? . . . the obvious stuff . . .
- What you should look for? . . . the non-obvious stuff . . .
- What matters to you?
- Pitfalls from living in some types of communities . . .

Unlike the last chapter, this is a more conventional (but I hope more informative) guide to looking at where to live. It is also a chapter that, for many buyers, may be less critical if you are familiar with the area you will be purchasing in. With the availability of internet searches and a good real estate agent, you may have this information before you begin your home search.

If relocating from another region, some of the pitfalls listed below could be very important. It's a good idea to look at community and neighborhood issues in a fresh light, as sometimes things you think matter may not – and the things you think don't matter really may.

Critical things to look for in a community

The following are the things most real estate advisors and professionals say you should look for in a community. I will go over these briefly – and then note when I think the conventional advice can sometimes be ignored.

#1 The conventional wisdom says to buy in the nicest community you can afford to buy in. While this is obviously good advice, the fact is, 'nice' means different things to different people.

#2 Do you commute to work? If so, you will want to think about access to commuter rail or highways. The availability of commuter rail lines or easy highway access – or just proximity to your workplace – may determine where you buy.

Look at what you might deal with if the area you are looking at is not close to your workplace. Long commutes are a drag and sooner or later this gets to most people. This is especially true if you have children or are planning to. If commuting by car, most real estate advisors recommend doing a couple of practice commutes so you have an idea of how long it will typically take. For most people, the less time you spend in the car, the happier you will be – although dealing with traffic is a lot more aggravating than simply dealing with the distance you travel. Consider both carefully.

#3 You are buying the neighborhood. Walk the area around the home you are looking at. Walk the land or streets in back, where possible. It's important to do a several block search and not just look at the particular street where the home is located. Are the homes similar to the one you are looking to buy? (The advice to buy the least expensive home on the street generally holds, but only if you aren't paying a huge premium for the location).

#4 Assess the trends affecting the town. Is it on the upswing or downswing? In my region, the 'rim suburbs' near Boston – or those on commuter rail lines – are seeing the most interest (and highest prices for what you get). Both young and older buyers don't want a long commute and want semi-urban living, with access to restaurants, parks, walking trails, and other amenities. In general, when the economy overall is improving, the real estate market will also be improving – just more so in some areas than others.

When we think of communities on a downswing, we most often think of those with industries that have shut down or are at risk of shutting down. This happened in New England when manufacturing went south, in the southern states when the jobs went to Mexico, and in the south and Midwest when jobs when to China. Small towns in agricultural areas are also being hollowed out for the reasons noted in the last chapter.

Some of the afflicted areas could be on their way back, where the communities are stabilizing. You may be able to get nice homes that you could never afford elsewhere. I can't generalize on this. Conversely, the less upscale rim suburbs that are considered desirable places to live are becoming overcrowded. These properties may not hold their value – or at least they won't where the prices have risen too high or if the economy falters. Be careful in areas with explosive growth, as these will need new infrastructure and schools – which means higher taxes.

#5 The reputation of the schools may be important if you have kids or are planning to. The more expensive towns often have more programs and resources for kids, including better special education programs. If you don't have kids or they are done with school, this will not be an issue. This may also not matter if you are home schooling or sending the kids to private school.

The school academic ratings are readily available online at state websites. Most real estate agents have the town profiles on school issues. This may or may not matter to you. See contrary advice below.

#6 Many young buyers – and many retirees – want to live in areas with good restaurants, hiking paths, and a high degree of walkability. Automotive transportation is increasingly avoided by the Millennial generation. Homes near parks, walking paths, the ocean, or nice lakes are increasingly desired and sought after. The traditional desire to buy what is called a McMansion in suburbia is losing its attractiveness. McMansions may not become undesirable in the coming years, but they won't be as popular as in-town houses and smaller homes. There simply aren't enough younger buyers in the post-baby boom generation to purchase them – and many of the current 20- to 35-year-old potential buyers are burdened with huge student loans. They couldn't buy the large suburban home even if they wanted to – at least not at today's prices. Old farmhouses out in the 'sticks' are the ideal for a few – but not for most young buyers (these were a 'boomer' generation thing).

Contrary Advice . . .

#1 If you want or need more house, land, etc., there are still communities that are perfectly nice and offer more reasonable prices than the 'more prestigious' communities. I've occasionally inspected expensive 'starter' homes in expensive suburbs around Boston that I couldn't afford – but wouldn't even live in, in any case, without spending lots of money to make the home reasonably livable. Buying a starter home in a nice but not spectacular town, with the plan to move up later as your family and income (hopefully) expands, can make sense. Also, shooting for the most 'upscale' community is fine – but not if it will increase your risk of foreclosure should you lose your job.

While McMansions may not be selling for what they were a few years back, some are now a relative bargain. (That does not mean 'cheap' – just a relative bargain).

#2 If you are 'getting on' (that means getting older, for those in denial) and downsizing, you may not only want a smaller home, but you might want a community geared toward 'active retirement.' This can be an over-55 development, a nice condominium, or just a community that has a lot of opportunities and support for elderly residents. Over-55 developments and assisted living communities can be a great way to avoid the isolation of living alone.

Lastly, homes with in-law apartments – or at least separate space for additional family members – can be an attractive option. If you have a parent who is selling their home and can help with the down payment on the 'new' home with an in-law set up (or the potential for one), this can work for both parties. I see this happening a lot. If you are the younger party in this scenario, you may get free child care and a larger down payment; if the older party, you may see a lot more of your grandkids.

#3 *Trends.* Try took a bit down the road for trends that are likely to develop and how they will affect the community. How will higher fuel costs affect you – and your town? What about a severe economic downturn? Will you want to live in that town (or that neighborhood) in that scenario? See Chapter 3.

#4 *Property taxes.* Are they affordable? These seem to be going up and up, and there is really no mechanism to control them. As more and more municipal employees retire and the medical costs rise, property taxes will continue to rise accordingly. You would think that that, in towns and states with high property taxes, this would have a negative effect on the property values – but it doesn't appear to have had much of an effect – yet. This is more of an issue in the northeast and other higher tax states. The high taxes are a plus when they provide you with better schools and services. They are not so much a plus if they are so high you can't afford to live there. *Affordability trumps all.*

#5 *Schools.* If you do not have children (or plan on having them), do you need to be in the highest rated school district? The school districts with the highest test scores come with the biggest ticket price!

If your kids are grown or you will not be having kids soon, you may not want to pay a premium to live in a town where the costs of the homes are high and the real estate taxes even higher, largely to support the school system. I see lots of 'boomers' selling their homes and moving to less expensive towns once their kids are out of school. As noted, the quality of the schools may also not matter if you will be home schooling or sending your kids to private schools.

Also, listing agents will sell a town (and buyers look for a town) based on the reputed quality of the schools. Those communities with the highest average SAT scores and statistics on student performance are considered to have the best schools. This may be the case, but it is also a self-reinforcing situation, where high achieving, highly educated parents with, of course, high achieving kids who will do well academically anywhere, choose to live. So, are the schools always better? Perhaps – but not as much as the housing prices in these towns would lead you to believe.

#6 Understand the plusses and minuses of *Homeowners' Associations (HOAs)* and the restrictions they impose. When you buy a condominium or a single-family home in a subdivision, there may be an HOA that governs what you can and can't do with your property. In general, the larger and more upscale the development, the more likely you are to have an HOA. The oversight that an HOA provides will protect the property values by not allowing undesirable activities or property modifications that do not meet community standards. You want your neighbors to keep their lawns mowed, you do not want them to paint their houses purple, you may not want mechanical equipment in the yard or auto repairs in the driveway. Restrictions are a necessity.

But, there is always a 'but.' Some people chafe at the restrictions imposed by the HOA. Occasionally you will get an overzealous mini-dictator running the show and they can make life miserable for everyone. I've had clients move from an over-55 community as they simply found it too restrictive for their tastes. These clients just couldn't adapt to limitations put on their landscaping, gardening, and other pursuits. You decide – but make sure you can pursue your favorite hobbies and interests in your new home or you won't be happy there.

#7 *Be aware of parking and traffic issues . . .*

For many buyers, living on busy street will simply not matter, especially if there are no kids or the kids are grown. Very often, however, the nicest homes are on the main streets near the town center. It's hard to avoid busy roads. What you want to avoid is buying a home where you think you are getting a quiet street – and it becomes a throughway during commuting hours. (Go to the property during commuting hours of the day to assess this).

Parking issues. Homes in congested neighborhoods often must utilize on-street parking. This may not be a reason to reject a home with on-street parking only, but this can be a real hassle – especially during snowy winters. Check for alternative parking arrangements. The lack of on-street parking is often reflected in the price of the home. For condominiums, it is nice when you have underground garages where you can simply walk to your unit. Having any garage is desirable. Again, this may be very important to some buyers and of no concern to others.

#8 *Avoid visual Pollution.* You really can't always avoid all of the below, but they are all 'negatives' and could affect market values. They may be something that you would find intolerable – or that would at least affect your enjoyment of living at that site. You may find you can live with them too.

- public utility substations that you look out on.
- <u>close</u> proximity to major utility lines (see more in Chapter 15 on Environmental Hazards).
- <u>close</u> proximity of radio and TV broadcasting towers. Besides the risk of exposure to electromagnetic radio waves, you may get poor radio reception on channels closest on the dial to the broadcast signal from the nearby tower.
- <u>gas stations.</u>
- <u>auto dealerships.</u>
- <u>salvage yards.</u>
- <u>overnight layover site for trains</u> (diesel locomotives are kept running all night long at these spots). Both noise and air quality may suffer. Visual pollution is also possible, but these spots are usually not adjacent to residential areas.
- <u>Bus stations or even bus stops.</u>
- <u>Homes next to ball fields or major stadiums.</u> (This may not be a strong negative – and can even be a plus for some people. I think living next to most usable parks would be a plus). Just realize: there are times when the traffic and crowds (and discarded trash) may be a pain to deal with.

#9 *Close proximity to major power transmission lines.* I'm going to cover exposure to electromagnetic fields (EMFs) in chapter 15. Whether homes sited near major transmission lines pose a hazard due to increased electromagnetic fields has been intensively studied and debated. I'm not convinced that this is a problem for most properties – but it could be for some. In many states, you can have the utility company serving the home assess this further. The problem is, however, that even when the electromagnetic fields are found to be at no more than background levels, the <u>close</u> presence of a high-power transmission line constitutes a negative that could affect the future resale of the property. *You need to buy with resale in mind.*

#10 *Wooded sites due to Lyme disease concerns.* Consider Lyme disease concerns. You just can't go out in the woods anymore without recognizing the potential for getting Lyme or other tick-borne diseases. Lyme disease is one of several serious diseases carried by ticks (mainly deer ticks). This is a serious concern in the Northeast, but Lyme disease is expanding throughout much of the eastern half of the country. Getting Lyme disease is bad enough (and it is normally treatable – if caught in time), but if the symptoms of the disease are not recognized, it can cause untold harm to children and adults. I worry about children the most, as they can have serious life-long complications from an untreated condition. Living in tighter suburban or semi-urban neighborhoods, where deer are not present, would lessen the risk.

#11 *Cell towers?* No one wants to live close to cell towers, but they are every-where. Towers at a good distance from the home or not in the line of sight may not lead to increased exposure to electromagnetic fields (but we'll get into this further in Chapter 15).

#12 *Avoid living next to a highway or busy road* if you can't control your exposure to the exhaust fumes. New studies indicate that those living next to busy roads who keep their windows open or spend significant amounts of time outside may have elevated exposure to the microscopic metals and chemicals that are spewed from vehicle exhaust pipes. A recent study cited in the Boston Globe noted the growing body of evidence of the dangers of living near highways or other high traffic areas. The evidence suggests that those living within 1500 feet of a highway have a greater risk of developing cardiovascular disease. Reportedly, the effect of fine particles emitted by power plants and vehicles have been studied and have been shown to result in higher rates of asthma for those exposed. The EPA regulates 'fine particle' exposure. Ultrafine particles, by contrast, have not been studied and no regulations currently exist.

The contrary advice: if you live in a condominium, high-rise building, or even a single-family home where you will utilize air conditioning, and do not keep the windows open – and do not spend a lot of time outside in proximity to the highway, this concern may not matter. Being upwind and not downwind of the roadway can also make a difference, as upwind houses may experience vastly lower levels of exposure to airborne pollutants.

#13 *Avoid homes impacted by bad smells and sounds.* An example is homes near – or simply downwind of – municipal sewage treatment plants. Almost every town has these. You may not know they are present when you look at a home – until the wind changes direction at your family barbeque. Surprising, however, modern sewage treatment technology can be very effective at minimizing odors – and if you live upwind of the plants, they may affect you minimally, if at all. Even restaurants in tightly congested neighborhoods can sometimes produce a lot of odors. Some many make you want to go out to eat all the time – or not eat at all.

If the home you are looking at borders or is near a working farm – especially a farm with livestock – make sure that you can tolerate manure smells. Many people would not find this to be a big negative; others would. The farms were usually there first.

Noise pollution could be an issue with facilities where loud outside mechanical work is done. Body shops, etc. could fit the bill. Not everything is bad about a mixed-use neighborhood, but having a salvage shop two doors down would not be a 'plus.'

#14 Homes near major oil and gas pipelines . . .

Pipelines are everywhere and anywhere – but we really can't do without them. They are, by far, the most economical and even environmentally safe way of transporting fuels from the areas where production is occurring to refineries and to the consuming areas. That doesn't mean they are safe – or that you want to live near one. Spills do occur. As the pipes and infrastructure age, you can expect more problems. Pipelines carrying oil or natural gas liquids would be more of a concern than natural gas lines in terms of the pollution effects.

Major gas lines, however, have their own issue: they occasionally explode. Case in point: the San Bruno, California explosion in 2010 that killed eight people. This was an older, high capacity gas line with what was found to be, by today's standards, improper welds. Not everyone in the neighborhood that blew up even knew there was a major gas line under the street. In terms of buying a home, do you want to live right over a major gas line? Nearby may be unavoidable – but what are the criteria for 'nearby'? A few hundred feet? A lot would depend on the type of fuel and the capacity and age of the line. In my area, the location of major gas transmission lines is well marked. Living next to smaller gas lines is unavoidable; they supply the gas that heats most of our homes. I've had some clients – although not many – who do not want a gas line coming into their home. Choose accordingly.

#15 Be careful with zoning restrictions . . . .

"See chapter 13 for more on this".

#16 Future development . . .

Future development is important and <u>you will need to research this</u>. My first home bordered 25 acres of rolling meadow. This, of course, was sold and developed, reducing my incentive to stay at that property. Similarly, I inspected a home a few years back that was beautiful and problem-free but then was surprised to find out that my client walked out on the deal. It turned out that the woods surrounding the home would soon be a massive subdivision. No one told him until he was well along in the buying process. <u>Due diligence is critical</u>!

> *Unless protected by the state or completely undevelopable land (such as a marsh), ASSUME THAT VACANT LAND NEAR OR AROUND THE HOME WILL BE DEVELOPED.*

Even properties given to charitable organizations and intended by the beneficiary to be left as open space are sometimes sold off for development if they 'need' the money. Investigate this further where you border a property that reputedly has preservation easements.

And now for the 'nitty gritty' of looking at homes . . .

CHAPTER 5
Looking at Homes . . .

What we'll cover in this chapter . . .

- Understand how things play out in a seller's market versus a neutral or buyer's market . . .
- How to measure the pros and cons of a property. . .
- The nitty-gritty of looking at homes: what's good (or desirable) and what could be a negative . . .
- Creating a wish list with 'must have' versus 'would like'. . .

This chapter will, I hope, provide you with a guide to looking at properties so you can both weed out the bad stuff and find a home that meets most of your needs. You'll also want to look at Chapter 7, as this will cover some of the types of situations you need to be careful with.

First Steps

As noted previously, your first step will be to find a buyer's agent to represent you through the transaction.

Second, you will have gotten pre-qualified (or pre-approved) by a financing professional so you know how much you can afford in a mortgage and therefore what price range you should be looking at.

Third, you will want take stock of your local real estate market. Note that the local market can differ from the regional market. Also realize that the market can differ for properties in different price ranges. The market will also vary between towns and the types of homes. Very simply: if you are in a buyer's market, the inventory is higher than the buyer demand, whereas in a seller's market, you have limited inventory with lots of competing buyers. Buying in a 'buyer's market' is to your advantage, as it allows more time to look and less urgency get your offer accepted. If you think the market is declining, you could even decide to sit things out – but this is harder to do than you think.

During a seller's market, everything is selling quickly and multiple offers are common. You may not have a lot of time to make an offer if you find the 'right home' – one that gives you most of what you want in the price range you can afford. The need to move quickly can be a problem if you are in such a rush that you don't have the home inspected or do the other investigations that are recommended.

The time of year also makes a difference. Late fall and winter tend to be slower times. Homeowners tend to hunker down for the Holidays and winter, making this a good time to buy as there are not as many competing buyers as in the spring or summer. The spring market is when real estate activity increases. In the spring market, things can get crazy in a hurry.

Most people have a pretty good idea of what towns or areas they want to buy in. You probably know what type of community you would like to live in and what you can afford. If you are not set, look at communities that fall within your price range and commuting time, as noted in Chapter 4.

Creating a 'Must Have list,' a 'Want list,' and 'Do Not Want' list . . .

One of those things that is useful when starting out is to have a 'Want/Must Have' list and – just as important – a 'Do Not Want' list of features you will be looking for – or wanting to avoid. After determining what you can afford and what type of neighborhood and community you will be looking in, having a 'Want' list will help you narrow down your search. A 'Do Not Want' list will help you narrow your search further. That said, this is an imperfect process, as very often you will fall in love with a property that doesn't match either your *Want* or *Do Not Want* lists and what you thought would be a deal breaker really isn't.

I've included a *WANT/DO NOT WANT LIST* in the website HomeBuyersHBook. com. It will be easier to copy out and print this list from the web site.

Special requirements . . .

Special requirements can be critical to your search – and may not matter for others. I'll note several important concerns first, before reviewing what you may want to specifically look for when touring homes.

Concerns with kids . . .

Is the home child safe and child friendly? Homes in a cul-de-sac or in a settled neighborhood may be better for kids on bikes, walking, etc. This is the traditional appeal of suburbs: they provide more space for kids to roam. Fenced-in yards are popular if you have young kids (but honestly, you won't keep them fenced in for long). Fenced yards matter more for dogs.

Be careful with busy streets. Investigate the traffic by visiting at different times during the day. A roadway with fast-moving traffic – even if intermittent – could be a concern.

Open floor plans are desirable, as you can watch the kids from the kitchen. Kids or no kids, people like open floor plans today. (Note: this can be overdone – see later comments).

The proximity of parks and playgrounds. If you have these close by and can walk to them, this is a real plus.

Neighborhoods that are child centered and not isolated . . . If you have young kids, you may want to look at a neighborhood with other young families. Don't dismiss this need. I had clients who sold the home they loved in order to move to a neighborhood with more young families – just so their child would have someone to play with.

Pools – or lack of. Pools are viewed as desirable by many buyers – and are a total turn off to others. For young children, pool safety is a definite concern. For older kids, this may be less of an issue.

> A home with a pool should have safe, lockable gates and other barriers. Pool safety is critical for children and pets. I had a neighbor who got rid of his pool when his kids were born. For above-ground pools, you can always reinstall the pool later. Pools require a lot of maintenance and will increase your home-owner's insurance. Conversely, people love their pools – both for the kids/ grandkids and for social gatherings in the summer. Many in-ground pools get filled in when the kids leave and the pool maintenance becomes a burden. (In other words, there is no one 'right' choice).

Watercourses, such as ponds, etc. can be a wonderful attribute – but they are also a concern for young kids. As an example: I inspected a lovely old upscale antique on a large lot. What looked like a slightly swampy area just to the back of the house turned out to be a 12-foot deep pool of water that reportedly was always present. As there was no way to fence this area off, this was a concern to the buyers as they had young children. Koi ponds could be an issue.

Sex offenders. One thing you will want to do is check the local sex offender registry. Do this ahead of the inspection, if you can. I had clients a few years back who walked away from a home that didn't have a lot of inspection issues – but after the inspection, they found the (semi-urban) neighborhood was loaded with Level 3 sex offenders.

Concerns for older buyers . . .

Is the home suitable for aging in place? Younger buyers may not be concerned, but older buyers or those with physical limits may avoid homes with stairs. As people get older, they often want single-level living and low maintenance homes – both on the interior and exterior. This may be something to look for.

As a piece of contrary advice: I have sometimes counseled existing homeowners that, if they really love their home, they may simply consider modifying it rather than selling it. Most homes can be adapted for easier maintenance and greater safety: doorways can be enlarged; walk-in showers installed with grab bars; stairs can be negotiated with stair lifts. You may simply want to hire people to do the needed yard work. The risk is that you'll sell too early. I have had middle-aged clients buying single-family homes after downsizing from their larger home to a condo and finding they had no place for the grandchildren to stay. Some just couldn't get used to condominium living. But if you are definitely moving and getting on in years, look for age-friendly construction and age-friendly neighborhoods.

Elderly or Disability-friendly? Is the home designed to be usable for the disabled – or can it be made to be? A home designed for someone in a wheelchair would typically have a ramp access, wider door frames, bathrooms with a shower stall flush with the floor, lower kitchen cabinets and countertops, etc. In general, a modern ranch style home or a home where one can live on one level will be the best candidate for aging in place modifications. Also note that the home may need to be ADA compliant to get subsidized funding to support disabled occupants.

If you either can't or don't want to deal with *icy sidewalks or driveway maintenance*, think about moving to a condominium where this work will be done by the association's maintenance staff. Look for condos with parking under the building. Having parking where you don't have to go outside to get in your car makes a lot of sense for the elderly – and everyone, really. Icy conditions are a real hazard. Lots of people get seriously hurt every winter from slips and falls. You may not be big on 'going south' for the winter, but it is something to consider for this reason.

Always read the condo docs to verify what maintenance is included in the condo association fee. Don't assume that the driveways will be maintained just because the sidewalks are. Condo developments with just two or three units in a building may not do as much as larger condo complexes. Most condo associations, however, have the responsibility of keeping sidewalks and driveways safe for use.

Other issues that can be important . . .

Is commercial use allowed? While home offices are normally allowed, you really need to be careful if you are planning to have any type of business that is run out of the home. This means anything with employees, signs, a regular picking up of products, or customers or clients coming to the property. Depending on the zoning and the nature of the neighborhood and community, some things may be tolerated (hairdressers in semi-rural neighborhoods are common), but you really need to be careful with this. Do not assume that you can do anything unless the property is zoned for commercial use (or no zoning restrictions are present). As an example: If the property will be used for a daycare, then you will need to assess the requirements your state (or municipality) and insurance company may have regarding these. These would include: no lead paint; windows sized properly for egress; hard-wired smoke and carbon monoxide systems; fully compliant, safe stairwells; no safety hazards of any kind; zoning restrictions, etc.

Possible to have an in-law unit or space? Having an in-law apartment is increasingly sought after. Some homes already have these. Other homes may be amenable. If an in-law apartment is present OR if you are planning to install one, make sure you check with the town to ensure #1 that they are allowed and #2 that any existing in-law unit was fully permitted (meaning allowed under the zoning or provided with a variance to allow the in-law unit).

Pet-friendly. Many homebuyers will only buy a home with an enclosed yard for their dog. Others will look for a home near dog-walking paths. Hey, maybe this isn't why you may purchase one home over another – but then again, if you are a dog lover, maybe it is.

Space for special hobbies. This can be where having a dry, usable basement or heated outbuilding is highly desirable – and may be critical.

Office space for working at home. Again, this could be critical to your search.

Sufficient garage space, ideally capable of being heated if you like to work on cars. Having any garage, in general, is desirable for the winter months. It's better if it is an attached garage.

Land for gardening. This can be very important for some people. (I know a couple who sold their lovely existing home and purchased a new property with more land just so they could have a large garden).

Solar friendly? This is seldom a reason to choose or reject a home (with exceptions), but it is important to some buyers. There are a bunch of factors to consider here. See Chapter 14.

The 'nitty-gritty' of looking at homes . . .

The notes below list the nitty-gritty process of touring and looking at homes. I recommend you also read Chapter 6, *Properties to Avoid at the Outset*. You won't see many of these potential disasters, but you want to recognize them when you are doing your house-hunting search.

Many agents recommend you bring a camera (or phone) and take pictures and notes when looking at homes. If you are looking at a lot of properties, it may be hard to sort out what each home looked like a few days later unless you have photos. You may not, however, be allowed to take pictures of the inside the home – just the exterior.

A caution: look past the sloppiness and clutter that you may see. Many homes are now 'staged' – which means de-cluttered with just right books sitting on the bedside table and the dining area set up for an elegant dinner party. I'm not knocking this, as it presents the home very nicely. Just realize: all that nice furniture and furnishings won't be there when you move in.

Also, while I have outlined some of the things to be aware of when looking at homes, I would stress that you don't want to go too deeply into evaluating the home's physical condition at this stage. Save that for the home inspection. You don't buy a home based on its condition: you buy it for other reasons.

That said, look at the following when touring homes that are for sale. Note: what follows is the general stuff, with more specifics after this . . .

Do a quick overview of the **neighborhood . . .**

Obviously look to see if the neighboring properties are kept up. Are there a lot of homes for sale in this neighborhood? If so, ask why? Are there any abandoned homes adjacent to this one – or homes that appear they might as well have been abandoned? Are the lawns mowed? Full of debris? Does the house next door appear to be party house? Are there construction or other large vehicles parked on the street or in nearby yards? Just use your eyes. Ask about anything that is a potential concern.

Look at the Overall Exteriors

1. When driving up, does the home show curb appeal? Does it look like it could be attractive with some reasonable amount of work? This is where you 'buy' the potential – not what's there now.
2. Is there anything compelling about the design, siting, etc. – or is too 'cookie cutter' for your tastes? This may matter a lot to you – or not at all.

3. Is the vegetation overgrown? Are there large trees that will need to come down? (This can be expensive!). Landscaping, however, is something you can often improve.
4. Just look at the general condition of the roof and siding. Ask about the roof age. Look at the exterior siding. Has the home been maintained in recent years?
5. Check the driveway. Does the driveway slope toward the house? Is the paving intact? Is there enough room for parking? Very steep, long driveways will involve plowing costs and a deteriorated driveway can be expensive to have repaved. Gravel driveways may not work on slopes, as the gravel runs off in heavy rains.
6. Another consideration you may want to keep in mind: is the home you are looking at functionally obsolete? If the home is very limited and/or has a lot of problems and/or is in an expensive neighborhood, would you be better off tearing the house down and starting over?

Special case: teardowns. In some upscale suburbs – especially in upscale neighborhoods near cities – you will need to assess whether the home may be impacted by teardowns and rebuilds on neighboring properties. In some upscale neighborhoods with older capes, ranches, and split-level homes, the property values have gotten so high that it is considered preferable to tear older properties down and build a larger, more expensive home in its place. When done right, this can make sense as the older homes may be too limited and antiquated for today's lifestyles. It can also be a boon to property values. But sometimes the new, larger homes are too big for the lots they are set on. What you don't want is to own a small cape or ranch in the middle of two gargantuan, upscale homes built right adjacent to your home. Very often, unless care was taken, the new large homes are out of scale in a neighborhood of smaller, older homes.

Looking at the home on the inside:

1. Note the general condition of the walls, ceilings, and floors. Just how bad does it need updating?
2. Are the interior surfaces basically intact? If extensive cracking is present, your inspector can evaluate this further. Also ask: can you live in the home while you remodel? Have the interiors been given a quick paint job – but not much else has been done to the home?

3. Check to see if the floors are hardwood. Are they stained or need refinishing? Any post mid-60s homes with carpeting will typically have plywood underneath, not hardwood. Are the vinyl floors lifting? Is the carpeting older?
4. Look at ceiling heights. While I love antique homes, the ceiling heights are sometimes too low for many people. Conversely, homes with soaring vaulted ceilings can be hard to heat or keep comfortable. They may work in Texas – but not in New England or other areas with cold winters.
5. Look carefully for any water stains and ask the real estate agents to get a history on these. Beyond that, let the inspector evaluate them further. In most states, sellers are required to fill out a Seller's Disclosure form. These may tell you when systems were replaced and what repairs were done to deal with water leakage or other problems. Not all states (for instance, Massachusetts) require these. Try to get one, if available.

Kitchen

1. Note the general condition. A kitchen that has been tastefully renovated should be regarded as a large plus. (Kitchen renovations are expensive!).
2. Cabinets and countertops. Other than functionality, these are not really inspection concerns. Again, nicely done cabinets or countertops are a plus. Consider your storage needs. Updated kitchens will be reflected in the listing price.
3. Age and condition of appliances. The quality of the appliances is difficult to evaluate. Most have an expected life of 6 to 10 years. Some will last 20 years (who knows?) Newer appliances would be a plus. Plan to replace 'older' ones. Some newer appliances – especially refrigerators – are far more efficient than older units.
4. The overall design and layout of the kitchen. Decide what you can live with. An antiquated or poorly laid out kitchen can be very expensive to remedy. If the kitchen just doesn't work and this is important to you, bring out a kitchen designer or architect – or take lots of photos and measurements for them to see – and determine ahead of the inspection if you can economically make changes you feel are critical.

Bathrooms

1. Look at the number of bathrooms present. Most single-family homes have one and one-half bathrooms. Larger homes may have more. A home with four bedrooms and just one bathroom will not do well at resale. Conversely, small households may do fine with one bathroom. If you have just one bath and will really need a second, try to determine if a second bathroom can be added.

2. Size and layout. You may not need a 'grand bathroom' unless it's an upscale home. Again, it's what you can live with. Decent sized, renovated bathrooms are a plus! Small, antiquated bathrooms will generally be expensive to remodel, if you find them unacceptable – which you may not. On the plus side, renovations are very often deferrable and will add value to the home when done.
3. Are there medicine cabinets (often not present) and adequate storage?
4. Is the lighting adequate and well positioned? This can be updated, often inexpensively.
5. Distressed surfaces due to excessive moisture? Is there an exhaust fan? These are highly desirable for full baths and are desirable for half-baths. Is there mold on the ceiling? Is this just surface mold that can be cleaned off easily?
6. Is a whirlpool (sometimes referred to a Jacuzzi bathtub) present? These were popular in the 90s, especially in McMansions. Few people use them today and, if not a negative, they should not be regarded as a plus. These units are prone to leakage, often need repairs, and they add a lot of moisture to the air. They are a negative when located in the bedroom or open living space. The larger ones are expensive to fill with hot water. Lastly, unless diligently maintained by cleaning and disinfectant procedures, these units develop biofilms that are unhealthy. One study found that the aerosols produced when the jets were running produced high levels of biological contaminants into the air.

Bedrooms and Interior Rooms

1. Note the general size and number of bedrooms. Bedrooms don't have to be large to work! Bedrooms are for sleeping in. With good design, moderately sized bedrooms can work fine and small bedrooms can be much cozier for kids. That said, you may really like having a large master bedroom.
2. The bedrooms should be able to house your current furniture. Buying new furniture is expensive and you don't want to spend money (that you may not have) after closing on the home.
3. Look at the closet space. Older homes will have less. Sometimes you can usually work around this. It depends on how much stuff you have and just how limited the closet and storage space may be.
4. Look at the floor coverings. Old wall-to-wall carpeting can be a source of allergens. Assume plywood is under the floor coverings, unless proven otherwise.
5. Don't assume that overhead lighting will be present; most homes do not have overhead fixtures on the upper floors. Downlights are wonderful – unless there are too many of them, which I now commonly see. They can usually be added.

6. If you need office space, work out rooms, etc., is there someplace you can put these?

Quality of construction

7. The quality of the construction is difficult to evaluate, but be careful if the home appears to have had just a quick redo and paint job – and not much else. You see this in 'flips' a lot of the time.

Fireplaces

1. A fireplace is still regarded as an attractive feature – even though, from an energy perspective, they are a major heat loser. If present, plan on having a chimney sweep examine the flues, as they are formally excluded from the home inspection (see Chapter 14).
2. Gas fireplaces are regarded as a plus. Same with pellet stoves. Woodstoves? Some people love them and others do not want the work and mess they can entail. It's a matter of personal preference. Unless you have access to an inexpensive wood supply, you may not save a lot of money using a woodstove. This may change if fuel costs rise. A woodstove can slightly increase your insurance costs. You must have a place to store the wood so it stays dry (and comes in dry) or you risk an insect infestation.

Front Door and Entryways

1. Does the front entry have curb appeal? A nice entryway adds value to the home. A deteriorated set of brick stairs is not only a safety issue, but it lessens the home's attractiveness. Brick stairs are expensive to replace and may be an issue for your financing company, especially if you are getting an FHA mortgage. The FHA inspector will typically look at safety issues, and unsafe conditions may need to be corrected before the mortgage is approved. Look for the potential to add curb appeal.
2. Note antiquated sliding glass doors or banged up exterior doors. Interior doors are easily replaceable. Old sliders not only look ugly but they can be a safety and maintenance issue. Exterior doors are far more expensive to replace than interior doors.

Windows

1. These are hard to evaluate at this stage, but note if they are extremely distressed. Many windows that look nice perform poorly and vice versa. Many replacement windows do not go well with older homes – but they are energy efficient. Your home inspector does not comment on how

73

they look, but still, cheap replacement windows are not a plus, in my opinion. In general, most single-glazed windows with nice architectural features can be weather-stripped and made viable. Having tilt-in windows for cleaning is a luxury, not a necessity.

Basement

1. Use caution when viewing the basement for the first time. The lack of headroom, narrow stairs, uneven rises, and a lack of hand and guard rails can pose safety hazards. Numerous safety issues are typically present.
2. Look at the foundation. A poured concrete foundation is best. Cement block can be ok. Additions may be on piers. This can be o.k. or not o.k. – let the inspector evaluate this. Mortared stone foundations may be fine or a problem. In most cases, you'll simply have the inspector look at it. Un-mortared stone, rubble, or cottage foundations may be substandard and could be a source of concern. For homes set on piers, these may be fine but you will want to research how these were done and whether they were 'engineered' for the site and soil conditions. (Check on building permits and any documentation the seller may have. Where a concern, plan on having a structural engineer evaluate them further).
3. Look for foundation cracks. Hairline cracks are typical. Really large cracks or a large number of cracks could indicate a problem. Have your inspector and/or a structural engineer evaluate them further.
4. Evidence of water in the basement. Get the sellers disclaimer, if provided. Have your inspector look at this. Be careful if the basement was just finished or was recently painted. Painting the walls may be good faith effort by the seller to make the home look nice for the sale – but it will also hide evidence of past water intrusions. A lot of finished basements show no evidence of problems in terms of water staining or mold, but the work to finish the basement has been done in recent years, so the visible record is misleading. The evidence of past flooding or water intrusion is now missing.
5. If you have a finished basement, you want to be more careful. A nicely finished basement that will not be subject to water intrusion could be nice plus. A basement with a walk-out entry or a basement with a sub-slab French drain system may fit this description. Unfortunately, many finished basements have hidden mold problems. Read chapter 15 for more on mold concerns.

Crawlspaces

Note if crawlspaces are present. Crawlspaces are less desirable than full basements, but they are the norm in many areas of the country. They are also commonly found in older homes. Let the inspector evaluate these. (Do you really want to crawl around on a dirt floor?). Don't go in – but obvious problems would be:

1. Visible rot, mold. Debris on the floor.
2. Insulation hanging down. Note: this may make the space un-inspectable, as home inspectors will not crawl through piles of fiberglass batts. Ask the seller to have this remedied prior to the inspection so that the inspector can enter the space
3. Wires hanging down indicate likely homeowner work with no permit. Consider bringing out an electrician with the home inspector.
4. Rudimentary supports, foundation. Have your inspector examine, or – where the conditions appear to be clearly substandard – plan to bring out a structural engineer in addition to the home inspector. Your inspector may end up recommending an engineer or foundation contractor for a further evaluation in these situations.

Heating and Cooling Systems

1. Note the type and general age. Ask if the system has been serviced in the last year and for any history of problems.
2. Look for evidence that the system is currently operable and has been maintained.
3. If central air conditioning is present, ask about its age and servicing history. Air conditioning systems cannot be operated during cold weather, so you are 'flying blind' on these much of the year.

Plumbing

Let the home inspector evaluate the plumbing. But find out:

1. Is the home served by a public sewage system or does it have a private waste disposal system? (See Chapter 17 on evaluating these). The MLS sheets will have information on the type of water supply and sewage disposal. Homes on a 'tight tank,' where all of the water and effluent goes into one large tank that will need to be pumped out regularly, are less desirable. (These are sometimes found at lakeside sites or sites next to marshes).
2. Ask about any local problems. A barrier island near me had its public sewage system fail a couple of winters ago due to faulty design and an extreme cold snap. This has been repaired – but it was a real pain for those who lost their ability to flush the toilet or take a shower.

Attic

Unless you can walk into the attic or access it by pull-down stairs, don't go into the space. Let the inspector do this. You could view the attic from the pull-down stairwell opening – but be careful: some units have been minimally secured or are damaged and are not safe to use.

If you can see the roof sheathing, look for areas of black spotting or other obvious signs of mold. At the minimum, this will need a further evaluation. Try to do this prior to the home inspection. If the roof sheathing is soaking wet and black – maybe just walk away. In most cases, however, mold remediations are paid for by the seller. Reputable mold remediation companies should also implement measures to prevent future mold problems – but this will need further discussion.

Evaluating the lot and usability of the land

A nice yard is, well . . . nice. I won't go into how nice or what is important to you. Some people want a big yard and others want a small yard with as little maintenance as possible. A big yard and nice landscaping is overall a plus – but it may require a lot of work to keep up. You may love this; others may not want the work. Plan on getting a landscape company to do the mowing, raking, and other tasks – unless you have the time and inclination to do this.

One thing to think about is how usable is the land. Some properties with a big lot may be so wet, rocky, or otherwise unable that the larger lot size has no added value. Square lots are more usable and desirable than narrow or oddly shaped lots. Really steep slopes may be unusable – but that can be o.k. too, if you don't want more lawn. Just ask how usable is the outdoor space? Forget the lot size, unless you can put it to good use (or if it offers added privacy). Good land is valuable, as it can be used for gardens, animals, or just a nice outdoor space.

Just keep in mind that, no matter how desirable the land – and even how large a lot – *the appraisal of the property does not assign a value to this.* You may want to have a nice lot or large acreage, but mortgage lenders will not give you more money for this. Really, only the house and the location (town, neighborhood) matter in terms of current values.

If available, look at a plot plan to see if what you think you are getting conforms to what is on the plan. Importantly, sometimes it doesn't.

The outdoor living space

Having a nice deck is a plus – but a nice deck is almost always a newer deck. A small deck may not be a major negative, but you may need to expand it for it to be an attractive feature. Your home inspector is typically looking at structural and safety concerns with the deck – not whether it is large enough to be comfortably used! Decks over 15 years old should often be considered 'fully depreciated,' so plan on a new deck if the flooring and rails are splintery and 'beat.' Balconies or high decks off bedrooms may look nice – but most are never used. Screened porches are highly desirable, in my opinion, as decks may not be usable when the sun goes down.

Seasonal pitfalls . . . You may be looking at homes in the spring or summer – when properties may be extremely attractive due to the site or the nice outdoor space. These things are a definite plus – just don't let them sway you too much if the home has a lot of other 'issues.' Having nice outside space is great – but you basically live 'inside' the home.

Think about winter . . . While nice outdoor space is a plus you may only use it for a few months out of the year and you should be buying the property more for the home than for the outdoor features. Long driveways will need to be plowed during the winter. Also, being able to walk directly from your garage into the home is a plus for the winter months. This is not a necessity – but it is nice. In warmer regions this is less critical.

Think about summer . . . Properties in New England (and elsewhere) look nicer in the warmer months. A few of the potential negatives:

- Bugs: homes along marshes can be intolerable due to various woodland biting insects during the summer. In my area of New England, there are biting flies (called 'greenheads') that make outdoor activities near coastal marshes difficult during the month of July. 'No see-ums,' a type of small biting fly that fit through screens, can also be a nuisance along marshy areas during a wet summer. These are not insurmountable diffi- culties, but they do impact how much one can use the outdoors during the early summer months.
- No way to enjoy the outdoors at the site. I've seen homes where, due to traffic and the 'lay of the land,' you simply would not be able to do anything outside with any privacy during the warmer months. One property I drive by is set well below a well-traveled road. The in-ground pool may be usable – but not with any privacy.
- Homes with too much direct sun, a lack of trees, or that are just poorly insulated may require extensive air conditioning to be tolerable in the summer. This could be true for a lot of the homes in the south and southwest. Having shaded areas is important. Homes with no shade just 'bake' in the summer.

Garages and Outbuildings

1. Look at detached structures and barns. These may or may not be covered by the home inspection. Usually they would be – at added cost. You don't want to get into a lot of detail in assessing their condition at your showings, but you should think about whether these spaces are something you need or can use. If the structures are deteriorated, they may not worth saving. The critical thing to realize with detached structures is that you will either need to put money into them or they will (eventually) need to be torn down. If unsalvageable, realize that there will be tear-down costs.

    I've inspected properties with large detached structures that were a major attraction to the buyer, but they really had no practical use for them. (Don't pay for what you cannot use!).

2. If you want to replace the garage, do you have room on the lot to do this? Old garages may be right up against the lot line. This may have been allowed in the past – but any new structure will need to meet the 'setback' zoning requirements currently in effect.

Small stuff

1. Smoke detectors (important). These are not a reason to buy or not buy – just plan on installing new ones after you take possession and before you move in. Having operable and properly located detectors may be the seller's responsibility in some states. In Massachusetts, it is normally the seller's responsibility to have a compliance certificate from the fire department regarding the type, location, condition, and age of the smoke AND carbon monoxide detectors. No closing can take place until the closing attorneys have this certificate. Note: for some types of transactions, such as foreclosures and short sales, the buyer may be responsible for getting the compliance permit.
2. Cell phone coverage. This is seldom a problem today in most areas. Still, it could be. Various booster devices can reputedly improve your cell phone reception. Look at your cell phone bars when at the home and this will give you a good idea.

Intangibles

This sounds vague but is actually important. Some homes are very comfortable to live in and work well for the occupants. Others simply are not. It is something that you don't always think about when looking at a home. I am not an architect, but I can almost always tell when I am in an architect-designed home, as things just seem to flow better. Think about how important the layout and 'flow' of the interior space means to you.

A few of these considerations are . . .

1. Does the living space have a cramped feel? When you enter the main living areas, do you feel like that the space just doesn't work? Small or unusually shaped rooms can be the problem – especially when they form the main living space. *This is not always correctible!*
2. Is the interior space too wide open? Sometimes large rooms are just not comfortable. No one ever goes into them, except at large social gatherings. Big family rooms with high vaulted ceilings were popular in older McMansions, and family room additions often are like this. These spaces can be o.k., but you will need some enclosed, comfortable spaces as well.
3. Is the living room divided from the entryway or front hallway? You don't want to have the main entry door open into the living space. My current home had the hallway at the main entry open to the living room for many years. The room never felt comfortable until we had this altered.
4. Is the kitchen remote from the other rooms? Everyone today wants a kitchen that is open to the living space, especially a family room where young children can be watched. Also, for social gatherings, no one wants to be stuck in a secluded kitchen away from the areas where the guests are.

Note: Open floor plans are preferred today. In general, open floor plans are nice when you have young children. Done right, an open floor plan can be great. However, I also see a lot of homes where the walls were removed between rooms without thought and the home becomes one giant 'undefined' space. Sometimes there is no wall space left to place furniture or cabinets. There may also be no private space. Rooms have different functions, and some type of room definition is necessary, even if largely open.

5. Don't just buy 'space' . . . One of those things I see commonly is homes where additions have been made that add space that is basically unusable or has no function. It then becomes a collection area for stored goods (junk). Homeowner additions done without design help often fall into this category. The front porches on older homes that have been enclosed – something we see commonly in New England – often become unused space filled with rarely used items. A front porch was designed to be a porch, not a habitable room. Some are no longer usable as porches. That may or may not be okay; it's not a walk-away factor.

6. Teenagers need remote family rooms or other areas to hang out. Some open floor plans are not suitable for anyone but adults. Any loud music played, for instance, will reverberate through the entire home. Everyone in the family needs space to work, relax, and entertain. Older kids need a certain amount of space. This is important: as family dynamics change, so will the use of the space.

7. Too much space: how many rooms can you live in? Many larger homes, and especially the mega-mansions, have multiple rooms that never get used. This may be o.k., as long as it doesn't affect the overall usability of the living space that does get used. The current trend is to simplify and de-clutter – although the efforts (mine included) don't always match the intentions.

8. Bizarre additions. Homeowners sometimes add on without any thought as to the design of the exterior or interior space. Maybe you could live with this, maybe you can't – but these types of additions should not be regarded as a plus or something that adds value to the home.

9. Old homes should not be architecturally butchered. Avoid buying an antique home if you cannot respect its design when adding on or improving. Avoid ones that have been butchered.

10. Porches, decks, and patios should ideally be accessible from the kitchen or other close-by living areas. In my area, builders tend to stick small porches on the front of the home. Many are too small to sit on and are remote from any living space. Essentially, they look nice – but they never get used. Even on my own home, we had a patio that was off the end of the garage; it was seldom used as it was too far from the kitchen.

Now, in a broader sense, you may need to ask: is the home functionally obsolete?

What about Feng Shui?

Feng Shui is an ancient art and science from China that looks at a home in terms of balancing energy flows to ensure the good fortune for those inhabiting the home. I know very little about this, but a few of its central tenets are that spaces carry energies (chi) that could be detrimental or positive, depending on how they are configured. There is an emphasis on good light, lack of clutter, proper placement of beds and furniture in relation to doorways, and where water may be flowing out of the home (as this is reputedly draining energy from the space).

I had a client who had his Feng Shui specialist look at the home while were doing the inspection. About half-way through the inspection, my client told me he was not buying the home due to problems indicated by the Feng Shui practitioner. She said that the energy flows probably indicated past owners had financial problems. I thought the whole thing was a bit 'over the top,' but the funny thing was, a lot of what she said made sense when I got the history of the previous owners.

Now stop . . . This will pertain to only a small percentage of homes, but it is still important. Is the home you are looking at so limited or is it in such poor condition (i.e., does it have such intractable problems) that it simply is not worth saving? Assuming you can afford to do this, would you be better off buying the property and tearing the house down and starting over? For building contractors, this may be an attractive option. As noted earlier, teardowns may make the most (economic) sense in upscale towns, where the building lots are worth more without the homes on them. I've had young first-time buyers purchase homes (despite everything I could do to dissuade them) that I really think would have been better off torn down. If you wonder why they went ahead, it was usually because the homes were a combination of a low price, a great site, or a great neighborhood. If you are in this position – and assuming that the home you are looking at would be safe and healthy to live in – think about living in the home for some years, giving it some paint and inexpensivefix-ups to make the place comfortable, and then tearing it down and rebuilding when you are financially ready.

CHAPTER 6

Homes to Rule Out at the Outset: Preliminary Investigations . . .

What this chapter covers . . .

- How to identify and avoid homes with inherent problems . . .
- Assessing risks that may come with the property . . .
- Assessing whether expansion is possible . . .
- What investigations you should do <u>before</u> the home inspection . . .
- Types of properties where you need to be cautious . . .

While I don't want to overwhelm you at the start of your house hunting search, I want you avoid the 'big mistake' when buying a home. In this chapter, I'll go over a few of potential problems that may lead you to move on to another property before you get too far into the process and spend a lot of money on inspections, appraisals, and other costs. I'll briefly note some of the conditions that should send you 'running for the hills,' so to speak, 'before you get your feet wet' (two bad idioms in one sentence!). The second section of this chapter will cover the investigations you can do prior to the home inspection. I should note that the issues I cover in this chapter may not apply to most of the homes you may be looking at. They represent the outliers that can still bring about financial ruin – or just a lot of extra work and lack of resale value.

What you want to do is rule out homes and properties with severe or intractable problems <u>before you make an offer</u> or have the home inspected. These issues could impact your decision to purchase a property (at least at the price offered). A lot of these concerns, I should note, would come up at your home inspection

These 'problem' homes would include, in no particular order:

#1 *Homes with <u>serious</u> mold problems or air quality issues.*

Mold is the hot-button issue of the last ten years, and many homes show evidence of mold in one area or another. Just distinguish between the situations where the mold can be cleaned (bathroom ceilings) or remediated (most attic mold), and the serious mold problems that would make the home unhealthy to live in. (Please note that Chapter 15 covers mold and indoor air quality issues in more detail). Don't be put off by seeing areas of suspected mold in the attic. Most of the time this can be remediated and, in most real estate transactions, the seller will take care of this. (Note: this isn't written in stone.) However, when the roof sheathing is completely black, the finished basement shows extensive water staining, or when there is evidence of burst pipes, I would be very careful. If you are still interested in the property, get estimates on a mold remediation prior to the home inspection and prior to your commitment. Very often, however, you will do this after your home inspection reveals these problems. In the most severe cases, such as when the home has been flooded or had burst pipes, get estimates from a contractor on the cost to gut the home and (largely) start over.

#2 *Avoid homes at high risk of flooding . . . (obviously!)*

As noted in Chapter 3, assess the flood risk for homes set near the coast or coastal waterways – or any river or stream, for that matter, where there is a history of flooding. Coastal communities or entire regions may be impacted by the projected sea level rises. Any home that is not elevated above nearby streams and rivers is also at risk. Increased flooding is likely to occur due to increasing severity of storms, sea level rises, and the increase in major rain events. Predicting where flooding may occur in all cases, however, is impossible. In 2012, in Vermont, homes that had sat next to small creeks for the last 150 years were destroyed by the rains and resultant flooding from Hurricane Irene.

Homes near the water but on higher ground may not have problems; properties right on the water or at limited elevations above the floodplain are obviously are at risk. If you are in a FEMA flood zone, look closely at the past history of floods. You may find the risks are minimal to non-existent – or are significant. Obviously, be careful with homes that have previously flooded. Unless the home was gutted and/or properly dried, you may have concealed mold in the walls.

#3 *Avoid homes built with Exterior Insulation and Finish Systems (EIFS) – unless you can verify that the EIF system used <u>was not</u> a 'face sealed' system.*

You may ask: what is EIFS and why should you avoid most of the homes that have it? Very briefly, EIF stands for Exterior Insulation and Finishing system. This was a type of siding/wall cladding that was developed back in the 1980s and was used on thousands of single-family homes and multi-story buildings throughout the

80s and 90s – until it became apparent that extensive decay was occurring within the walls. EIF siding was extensively used in the Mid-Atlantic, Midwest, and Southern states. In Vancouver, entire communities of apartment buildings and condos built with EIF finish experienced a total failure of the siding. Interestingly, it was rarely used in New England and when it was, it was usually on McMansion type homes. Homes with a stone veneer have suffered similar fates when no weep holes were installed and the water management system was faulty.

Unlike traditional stucco, where a lime-based cement plaster is installed in layers over masonry or a wire mesh substrate with open wall cavities on the inside, the EIF cladding systems consists of a polymer coating applied over a foam board sheathing, usually with some type of weather-resistant coating to seal the seams. The foam board usually covers an underlying plywood or oriented strand board wall sheathing. The wall cavity is filled with insulation, with drywall installed on the interior.

The problem with this system is that it depends on having a perfect seal on the exterior, with no water entry anywhere. Unfortunately, this is impossible: all walls leak. Wood-sided walls leak; vinyl leaks, brick leaks. All buildings shrink and may expand with seasonal moisture and temperature fluctuations, and they will move, so you can't get a perfect weather-tight seal. Traditional stucco – and, really, all successful siding systems – allows for leakage by allowing the walls to dry. The walls with a face-sealed EIF finish do not allow drying, with the result that these homes may suffer massive decay under the foam board covering when water inevitably penetrates through the surface finish.

The following websites have good information on Exterior Insulation Finish problems. [If you are reading this in the book version I have posted all of the links in a web site HomeBuyersdHbook.com.]

https://buildingscience.com/documents/digests/bsd-146-eifs-problems-and-solutions

https://www.exterior-design-inst.com/eifs-moisture-intrusion-problems.html

https://www.youtube.com/watch?v=BD9qIMlz_8s

Now, it is important to note that there are EIF systems that utilize a drainage barrier, whereby water that gets through the surface barrier can drain out. This allows the walls to dry out. These systems, when properly installed, should (might?) work. Many of the 'face-sealed' EIF installations were changed to a draining type system, so these may also be okay. Also, for homes built in the southwest or desert areas, the face-sealed EIF systems reportedly work fine as, unlike the eastern half of the country, there simply is not a heavy water load that will saturate the walls and keep them from drying out. The high temperatures of the southwest also help.

I won't go into further detail on this here (or you'll never get through this book), but just be aware of the potential problems should you be looking home built after 1980 that appears to have a stucco finish on the exterior. Avoid these homes unless you can determine that this is not a 'face sealed' system AND that no moisture problems are present within the walls. There are EIF inspectors who use specialized moisture meters and training. Hire one – or just avoid these homes. See the links below (or, for book readers, the links provided at HomeBuyersHbook.com) for what this siding looks like and for more information). Older types of stucco, as noted, usually will do fine (although these exteriors could have different problems). While not all homes with EIF finishes have damage due to water intrusion, neither you nor your inspector can tell what is going on inside the walls.

#4 Avoid homes with <u>extreme</u> termite damage.

Again, distinguish between what may be a limited infestation and damage versus a case where everything appears riddled or where there is a high risk of concealed damage. Lots of homes – most in some regions – will have had termite activity at some point. It is rarely a reason to walk away, in my opinion. (See later advice on how to deal with this issue). However, if you see evidence of extensive termite activity (i.e., the framing appears to be visibly riddled AND you can't you can't tell the extent of the damage), then be very careful. If the home has inaccessible crawlspaces, a finished lower level, or is built on a slab, you (and your inspector) *can't tell how much concealed damage may be present.* Although this doesn't happen often, I've done inspections where the buyer requested that walls and ceilings be opened up to determine if serious damage is present. This is not something you can usually get a seller to do – but I have seen it done. (See Chapter 13 for more on this). In any case, if there is evidence of major damage and you can't determine the extent of the damage, either walk away – or understand that you could face extensive repairs. (These would involve removing the interior or exterior sheathings, doing the structural repairs, and then reinstalling the sheathings and finished materials you removed).

Caution: When it is reported that the termite *infestation* has been treated and a warranty exists, that is a plus – but it doesn't tell you anything about the extent of the structural *damage* that may be present. Termite inspectors and treatments deal with *infestations* – not *damage*. If your home inspector does not do termite/wood boring insect inspections (many don't), then have this done by a licensed termite control company.

#5 Avoid functionally obsolete homes, aka money pits . . .

What do money pits look like? As a brief list:

- Homes that have had little or no updating in the last 40–60 (or more) years. Who knows, maybe they are potential gems – but only if the home was originally well built and has some architectural value. I see a lot of homes that were originally cottages that have been extensively expanded and 'improved' over the years. Many are money pits. Homes that were never well built or are extremely limited are candidates for a teardown and rebuild. You are better off starting over.

- A functionally obsolete home could be a home that needs so much work to bring it up to modern standards and ways of living that it simply isn't worth it. Look for homes that no one has ever put 'a dime' into.
- Homes with a <u>minimal or failing</u> foundation (sometimes just loose stone or rubble in New England), inaccessible crawlspaces, severely substandard construction, poor or bizarre interior layouts, etc., may also be functionally obsolete.

#6 Be careful with amateur design and construction . . .

This is one of those things that keeps home inspectors in business. While I understand that many homeowners cannot afford contractors or tradespeople, the do-it-yourself craze in our country has its drawbacks. I frequently see homes where the homeowner has done extensive work on the home – and *everything* has been done wrong. You may be able to fix these homes – but it will cost you in both time and money. On the other hand, you may find homes, especially in rural areas that were homeowner built and that, while unorthodox, are still livable (and saleable) as long as they were competently built.

As a special case, in the 1970s, there was a lot of interest in building your own home, unfortunately, no matter what one's skill level. I only see these houses occasionally, as most have been torn down. While some may be okay, many are disasters or are functionally obsolete (see above). Look for bizarre exterior design or non-functional interior layouts to recognize these.

Idiosyncratic (unusual) homes may or may not make this list. Some are quite interesting (geodesic domes, <u>some</u> passive solar homes), as long as you know there is a market for these homes when you go to sell. The solar homes from the 1970s almost always need drastic alterations due to the faulty premise that maximizing solar gain on the south and west sides is the best way to heat the home without using fossil fuels. Too much glazing led to overheating in these homes. This can be remedied – but you will have to deal with this.

#7 Be careful with fixer-uppers. Do they make sense for you?

I've covered this before, but I'll cover it again. Buying a fixer-upper is something that, in the 60s, 70s, and 80s, was something lots of first-time buyers did. Not so much anymore. I won't say don't buy a fixer-upper if you feel that is the best way to get into the real estate market. You could even end up with a nice home that's worth a lot more than you paid, IF you know what you are doing and are willing to put in the work. You still have two questions you need to ask. First: do you have the skill sets or the resources – or the willingness to learn what you need to do? Most millennials, as opposed to their boomer parents, have little interest in buying a home that needs a lot of hands-on work. Many are more involved in their careers or families. They may be smarter than their parents and realize that the serious renovations are best left to professionals. I don't want you to underestimate what you can do, but don't over-estimate it either.

If you are intent on getting a home that needs a lot of work – or perhaps realize that, in some markets, these are the only homes you can afford, then go for it. Just be sure you understand the difference between the (potentially) nice solid houses that just need serious updating versus homes that were: #1 poorly built to begin with; #2 may have serious structural or other flaws; #3 are functionally obsolete; #4 are in a poor location that can't be changed, or #5 just were so badly let go that fixing them isn't worth the effort. A second problem is that, at least in my area, the 'good' fixer-upper candidates are largely gone. Most have been purchased and already fixed up. The ones that I do see are over-priced for the amount of work they require.

It is especially important with a fixer-upper to get a thorough home inspection, do the other investigations I've noted, and figure out how much you will need to spend to get the home to the point you would like to get it to. In many cases, you will be better off spending more to buy a nicer house that you don't have to do much to, than buying a money pit that requires untold money and time to make it right. Save yourself the aggravation! To repeat what I noted earlier:

> the true price of the home is not what you spend to purchase it, it's the cost to purchase it AND the costs you will incur for repairs, system replacements, maintenance, and renovations.

#8 Don't avoid – but be careful with antique homes, if:

The home dates from before 1850 and has never had a structural renovation. While most antique homes I inspect have had extensive repairs and renovations over time, occasionally I run into a home that has its old rotting wood posts for supports, bad framing, suspected concealed damage, and no evidence that a structural renovation has been done. Please recognize that walls, windows, and doorways that show sags and settling may indicate *concealed structural damage*. The floor structure may be open to assessment by a home inspector, structural engineer, and qualified carpenter – but the wall cavities are not visible and the framing in basements and crawlspaces may also be concealed from view.

Story: For years, I passed by what appeared to be a nice but very old two-family home on my street. One day, I rode by and the home was gone. It turns out that when a contractor went to do some limited repairs in the basement, he found that basically there was nothing there. The home sat on the ground and everything had rotted away. In this case, there was nothing solid to work with under the first floor, so the home was simply taken down.

Also, be careful with older homes that have been butchered beyond recognition. Most older homes have a degree of architectural integrity that modern homes do not have. Unfortunately, people do bizarre things to these homes, such as replacing the original windows with out of character and misshapen units, obliterating the architectural trim when installing siding, doing incompatible additions, etc. My advice is: don't buy an older home if you can't respect the good work and integrity that may have gone into it (assuming it warrants this).

Most older homes are worth saving, in my opinion – but some are so functionally obsolete or worn out that even they warrant a teardown.

Lastly, realize that most older homes will contain lead-based paint – at least on the older woodwork that has not been replaced. Basic cautions, in my opinion, should enable you to avoid a significant risk of lead poisoning, but you may want to avoid older homes for just this reason if you have (or will have) young kids living there.

#9 Understand: some homes you can add onto or expand – and others you can't . . .

This falls partially under the concerns with the building codes and zoning, covered in Chapter 14. But it goes beyond this. You may be planning to buy a home that you can expand to meet your future needs. The problem is, while existing homes don't necessarily have to meet current code standards, new construction does, and you can't always build onto an older home – at least not easily. Older foundations and framing may be fine for the existing home but will not meet current requirements of the building code for a second-floor addition. This would not be revealed by the home inspection. Building *onto* the home is usually possible, assuming enough land with setbacks is present.

I had clients some years ago who assumed they could put a second floor on when, in fact, the home had an older, cottage type stone foundation that couldn't support anything more than what was there. For the existing structure, the foundation was serviceable, but not for the addition. They had to 'walk away' from the property when they looked into this, as they didn't have the money to lift the house and install a new foundation. I should note that if they hadn't brought their plans for expansion up, I would not have told them to investigate this further. Please realize that many older foundations, whether stone, concrete, block, or whatever, were not sized to support anything more than the existing structure. Even the wall framing in a few older homes (such as many of the Sears kit houses) consisted of 2×3 framing – not 2×4s.

If you are planning on expanding the home, you will need to talk to a building contractor AND the local municipal inspector. Input from an architect or structural engineer may also be critical. You don't just want to get input from one person.

One last note on expanding a home: if you expand a home, you may need to upgrade the septic system (if you have one) or meet requirements to bring the rest of the home up to current standards. Lots to consider – <u>all beyond the scope of the home inspection</u>.

#10 On a different tack: avoid paying for what you don't want or can't use.

Sometimes you will be looking at a large home or a property that has added structures. If you had them built today, it would cost you a small fortune. By this measure, the properties appear to be screaming deals. Perhaps they are, and perhaps you can find a way to use these structures. But sometimes you will have no use for the extra space or accessory buildings. Try to think ahead on this issue. Maybe you could rent out the space? The problem is that all buildings require upkeep and periodic repairs and replacement of major systems if you want to keep them standing. In a similar vein, you will also find homes with expensive renovations done by the current owner. The problem is: if you can't stand any-thing they did, you will rip it all out. Go ahead and buy: just don't pay a premium for work that you can't stand.

#11 Be careful with 'flipped' homes . . .

'Flips' are the term for homes that have been brought at foreclosures or short sales by a contractor or speculator. As heart-rending as it must be to lose a home to foreclosure or a forced sale, it happens. Due to the financial difficulties of the homeowners, these homes very often have not had proper repairs or renovations for some time. Some homeowners will even damage the home on their way out. Other homes that sit unoccupied may also have mold problems – especially if there have been burst pipes.

In many cases, the companies who specialize in 'flipping' the homes will do the necessary work. They will replace the old heating system, rewire the building (where necessary), put in new bathrooms and kitchens, and do a good job. This is why it is hard to warn you off on flips. Reputable companies or builders that specialize in doing flips will get the necessary work done cheaper than you could. Be careful, however, when the flipper just paints the interior and puts in granite countertops in the new kitchen – and doesn't do much else. (The term, used else-where, is 'putting lipstick on a pig'.) In general, I've found that most flippers won't get into crawlspaces to assess and fix nasty conditions, some may not rewire or re-plumb where needed, and many will not go out of the way to disclose (much less fix) conditions that may be important but that aren't readily apparent to prospective buyers. I've inspected properties where the flipper spiffed up the living spaces (most will do that) but left a decrepit 40-year-old heating system in place; hid evidence of water penetrations into the basement; sealed the access to a large crawlspace so entry was not possible; and left the perimeter of the crawlspace open to the winter winds. The list goes on.

Make sure you get a competent home inspector when you do your inspection. Also, <u>check for permits with the building department on the work done</u>. If none exist, be extremely careful. I've had buyers who requested that the person flip-ping the house get permits on the major items where they would have been required. The other option is just to walk away.

#12 Be careful with 'For sale by Owner' (FISBO) properties.

In my opinion, you have less chance of getting accurate information on a 'For sale by Owner' property than when the home is listed with a real estate agent. Most people are basically honest – but the operative words are 'most' and 'basically.' When it comes to selling a home and the amount of money involved . . . well, let's just say there's a huge incentive to either hide or minimize poten-tial problems. The sellers certainly aren't going to offer information they are not required to provide. Also – and just as common – people live with things that you or another new owner would find intolerable. Examples would include poor hot water capacity; limited water from wells in the summer; a septic system that works but can't stand too much use; ovens that work but don't heat accurately; etc. Very often, the evidence of problems will get covered over or dealt with in the cheapest manner. You have to be a bit more careful with 'For Sale by Owner' homes. Having a home listed by a real estate agent provides a degree of extra protection. I know of properties where the local real estate agents were aware of problems and refused to take the listing until the conditions were fixed or disclosed. Homeowners in these situations often just sell the property on their own.

Even if you are buying a For Sale by Owner property, you can hire a real estate agent to guide you through the transaction and act as your buyer's broker. A good lawyer is a must. The buyer's agent can advise you on whether the property is worth what you are paying and can help in negotiations. It's a truism – but true – that while many homeowners view their home as a 'castle,' most are totally unrealistic about the problems or limitations of their property. You don't want to tell them their home is a money pit; it's easier to have your agent convey this (but in gentle terms). Otherwise, you may just get in a shouting match with the owner.

#13 Be careful with <u>new</u> homes built on steep slopes. See Chapter 19, on new construction.

#14 In general terms, perhaps avoid homes where the risk of a problem may be low – but the consequence of a system failing would be extremely high.

I've had buyers walk away from a property when they found out the cost of replacing the septic system on that site, IF it failed – which it hadn't to that point – would be exorbitant. The consequences of the system failing were just too high as the cost for system replacement would be in the tens of thousands of dollars

#15 Cautions with condexes and duplex condos

As a special case, if you are buying a condex, which is really just two side-by-side homes where each owner's property ends at the dividing line between the homes, try to meet (or find out about) the person who owns the other side. The same may be true of a side-by-side condominium, but at least there you may have bylaws that impose some basic, minimum requirements on the owners.

In many areas, you can't find a builder who will put up a single-family home if they can get a condex approved. Many of the new condexes I see are well built and they look nice – but I still think they are less desirable than single-family homes. The problem often comes not after the homes were constructed but years later, when things start to wear out. Very often, one unit owner is meticulous about maintaining their side of the home; the neighbor less so, very often due to financial problems. Another point is that you may not exactly share the same lifestyle and values of your close neighbor.

Condominiums have less of a problem in this regard, as the association will have lots of bylaws and will not allow someone to let their property go. In most cases, condo associations are proactive about repairs and upkeep.

I'll cover condominium issues in a later chapter.

Part 2 Doing pre-inspection investigations . . .

It may or may not be possible to do these investigations and they may not be relevant to the home you are purchasing, but I'll note a few ways you can save you a lot of time, money, and wasted effort. Only one or two of these efforts may be warranted in any given sale. Also, some may be done after the home inspection

#1 *Have knowledgeable friends or relatives go with you for the second showing . . .*

This isn't always possible, but if you are buying a fixer-upper or a home that appears be in moderate to severe distress, bring out knowledgeable parties to look at the home prior to your making an offer. This can save you a lot of aggravation and may save you from spending money on an inspection (plus appraisal fees, title searches, and other up-front costs), where you suspect the home has serious issues that would cause you to walk away. By doing this, you may realize the home has way too much work – or just doesn't meet your needs. Bring out parents or other relatives who are *experienced* homeowners, especially if they have renovated homes themselves. As an example, I had one young client, a son of friends, who looked at two awful (but cheap) properties, both of which he 'walked away' from after the inspection. I advised him to bring his parents (who had renovated several older homes) to look at the next home before making an offer – with the condition that if they believed it was worth going ahead, then proceed with the inspection. Fortunately, the third home was better and they advised going ahead. The inspection certainly went a lot better than the first two. Note: If you think your parents/relatives/others are not going to be helpful, obviously keep them away.

#2 *Bring out a contractor or architect, other trade professionals*

I've noted this before, but for homes that need a lot of work. or when you will want to expand or thoroughly renovate the home, bring out a building contractor or architect that you trust. Have them walk-through the home with you prior to having it inspected. Two cautions are in order, however.

First: a few (but not most!) contractors may look at a fixer-upper as long-term guaranteed employment. It's the exception, but I have had situations where I simply couldn't get a buyer to 'walk away' from what, to me, is obvious money pit, only to have their contractor come in and provide estimates to fix a few of the glaring problems while ignoring the basic fact that the home needed vastly more work. Your home inspector is providing an objective evaluation and you are paying them just for their opinion. A contractor may have an interest other than yours.

As a second caution, having a contractor look at the home is not a substitute for a home inspection, no matter how knowledgeable they are about their own area of expertise. They are not doing a detailed, systematic inspection of the home's systems and structures and are not documenting the findings. But if they are working in your interest and know what they are looking at, they may be able to tell you that the home just needs too much work or the cost of repairs will be far beyond what you expected. You can then 'walk away' early in the process. Note: a home inspector will not do this. A 'pre-inspection' would be comparable to a 'drive by' inspection, with no depth, no systematic evaluation, and no report. It really doesn't help you, and it is way too much legal liability for the inspector. When my son and his wife were looking to purchase a condominium, I did a brief walkthrough with them on a property they were considering – and the property seemed okay. But I then went back to do a full inspection once they had made an offer. This inspection revealed serious problems and they moved on to something else.

Architects who deal with residential construction can often give you a good idea about whether an intended renovations or expansion is possible and what it will cost.

#3 *Check to see the history of building permits on the property; variances . . .*

Go to the municipal building inspector's office to check on whether permits were pulled on work that was done. In some cases, your buyer's agent will do this.

Work done without permits should raise red flags. Very often, however, quality work has been done without code oversight; many homeowners do not get permits for limited repairs. You may not want to get too alarmed about every bit of uninspected work – unless it was a major project or appears to be grossly substandard. Conversely, you really don't know if the work met minimum code standards unless it was inspected and approved by the local building inspector. All the possible problems are now hidden within the walls. You'll find out about them – in time – but not quickly enough to do you any good.

Local building inspectors may also know about problems with specific properties or an entire neighborhood. For instance, are the septic systems on that street failing or was the developer a hack? I just was told of a street in a nice town where the soils are a problem and the homes are beginning to settle. These types of conditions may or may not be apparent at the particular home inspected; they could be covered up. The town (and neighbors), however, may know about local conditions.

Check with the local zoning board on matters relating to the status of variances that may be in effect. Some variances carry a time limit and may go with the 'owner' and not the property. As a former member of my city's appeals board, we would sometime issue a variance for the owner of a property to add a living unit for a disabled or elderly relative, but this would expire with their passing or would require a renewal of the variance after five years. In other words, the in-law apartment in the home may not actually be a legal rental unit.

#4 *Be careful with zoning restrictions . . .*

See Chapter 4, #15 for more on this issue.

#5 Check on wetlands issues, where relevant . . .

If the home appears to be in or near wetlands, check with any local conservation officers (or state agencies if a local conservation person is not available) about whether you can undertake planned expansions of the home or other alterations of the property. I should note that lots of homes are sited near wetlands, where higher ground is present for additions or other structures. Just realize that you can't build over wetlands or within specified distances – at least for permanent structures. You certainly can't fill anything in or alter the wetland in any way. This concern is most relevant if you plan to expand the home or have other structures built – or if the home appears to have already been built in a wetland! In-ground pools do not work in a wet site.

#6 Look at any disclosure form filled out by the owner.

Most of the time, these won't tell you a lot; I will look at them but don't rely on them. These are required in most states, but not all. I've provided a sample disclosure form at the end and via the link provided. A few cautions are in order. First, with bank owned and estate properties, homes with elderly owners, or homes that have not recently been occupied, you may not have an owner who can provide useful information. Second, you will see a lot of the questions filled out as 'unknown.' That doesn't mean they are hiding something. If the owner has not tested for lead paint, for instance, they cannot indicate whether lead is or is not present – even if most likely is. Third, what has worked for or been acceptable to them may not be to you. Limited hot water flows from a tankless system come to mind. I don't know how some homeowners have tolerated this, but they have and it isn't a problem to them. You may not be able to live with things they have lived with. Fourth: read between the lines on a Seller's Disclosure form. The owner may note the roof is 'older.' This can simply mean that roof shingles are simply older but still functional – in which case you should budget for roof surface replacement. But if your inspection reveals that the roof is totally failed and about to leak, this is not, in my opinion, the same as the roof just being 'older.'

And lastly, while most people are honest, they could lie or simply withhold information (which is why you need to do these investigations and get the home inspected!).

#7 Talk to neighbors (well, sometimes) . . .

Another avenue for investigations is neighbors or others who may have knowledge about the homeowner or neighborhood. Obviously, one must be careful here. You can't just go knocking on neighbors' doors to get information. Well, sometimes you can. That said, if you already know someone in the neighborhood, you can sometimes get information about the property that could be useful. Who gets water in the basement very often is common knowledge around the neighborhood. When the home is vacant and possibly in disrepair, strolling over to talk to neighbors who are watering their lawn could prove useful.

#8 Understand what has to be disclosed and what doesn't . . .

See the list provided in Chapter 2.

#9 Determine if you need to have a survey done.

You will want to determine where the property lines are located. I will note that a survey is not done in most real estate transactions. Usually the 'plot plan' will indicate the location of the lot lines and doing a survey is not warranted. It is an extra expense. Where the information on the lot boundaries is sketchy or in dispute, however, you will want to have a survey done. Also, if you get feedback from the owner, your attorney's review of the deed, or the town that there are potential issues with the property boundaries, you will need to resolve these. New construction also has the potential for problems, as what is sometimes indicated on the plot plan is not what you are actually getting. Boundaries that are not marked could also be a problem. I read of a case where common pathways from an adjacent recreation area ran through the newly subdivided lot – and still carried legal rights for use. This was not a disclosed easement.

Another example of how this issue could come into play: I did an inspection where a number of large trees were present along *what appeared to be* the boundary of the property. These were hanging toward a row of neighboring homes. These trees were a definite liability for whoever owned them – which my client decided was not going to be him. He refused to go forward with the purchase unless the seller was able to determine that the trees were not on the property being sold. In this case, the seller had a survey to show that the trees were not on the property line. Occasionally, it will be important to know the exact boundaries – especially if they are in dispute or you need every bit of land for some intended use.

CHAPTER 7
Tips and Strategies

when Making an offer ...Getting the best price...

What this chapter covers...

- **Danger of moving too fast...**
- **Danger of moving too slow...**
- **Strategies on getting your offer accepted...**
- **Using inspection contingency clause...**
- **Other contingency clauses to use...**
- **Cautions when buying from relatives or friends...**

Okay, you've been looking at homes and have found the property that you find either meets your needs - or, at least, is the closest you can get to what you want in the community you want to live in. It can also happen that you have fallen in love with a home for one or another reason that have nothing to do with your wish list or what you thought you wanted when starting out.

In any case, you still need to get your offer accepted. In this chapter I've provided a few brief tips on how to do this and hopefully, get the best deal that may be possible.

In terms of your time frame for buying a home, you have risks of moving too fast or too slow. I've seen both be a problem.

Moving too fast can be a problem if:

#1 You don't get to look at enough houses (or communities) to understand what is out there for homes on the market in given price ranges.

#2 You 'settle' for a home that is okay but you are not crazy about. You could also choose a home that simply doesn't meet your needs a few years down the road.

#3 You overlook some of the critical negatives and risk factors that I discuss in this book in terms of neighborhoods, problem houses, risks to avoid, etc.

#4 You stretch to buy a home at the top of your budget, putting yourself at financial risk.

#5 You make an offer but you have major concerns about the property. There is no way to avoid this if you have to move quickly. It is critical in this situation to use your inspection contingency period to do the home inspection AND other investigations I've outlined. This should allow you to 'walk away' (or renegotiate) before you are legally committed to buying the property.

Moving too slowly:

1. You find a home you really like that is fairly priced in a busy market. Unless you move quickly you will lose out to other buyers.

2. In 'hot' markets (which often means 'tight' markets with not a lot of homes for sale) or with highly desired properties you may need to move really fast.

3. You become a 'looker' who can't pull the trigger and actually purchase a home. There is nothing wrong with looking at a lot of houses but at some point you either need to step up or step back. Some prospective buyers look at dozens of homes and even go through multiple inspections -- but keep rejecting the properties for one reason or another. These clients may be good for home inspectors – but they are terrible for the agents who spend months or years showing properties that their clients will never buy. They also aren't so good for you as a buyer. As noted, if you are in the market sometimes you will eventually have to pull the trigger and actually buy something.

Getting your offer accepted...

In terms of getting your offer accepted and getting the best deal try the following.

1# Decide ahead how high you can go and want to go in your bid. A lot goes into this (which I've covered om the chapter on Financing) but there are times to 'stretch' and times to be cautious. On a related basis, it is important to get an idea of the real market value of a home you may be making an offer on. The listing price of a property is sometimes a fantasy of the homeowner. I've heard the charge that real estate agents will tell a seller that the home should list for a high price to get the listing, and I could be wrong, but I just don't see this in the current seller's market. (For the last few years the prices are high enough as is and the sales prices are often higher than anyone thought they would be). I'm sure it happens, though. Just business...

#2 In terms of negotiations, try to get the best price up front. The most important negotiation is the one when you making your offer and getting your offer accepted. If you get a substantial price reduction (from the actual fair market value (and not just from a possibly inflated listing price) -- and believe you've gotten a fair deal, you can be a lot more forgiving about what comes up at the inspection. The inspection and other evaluations should still give you an 'out' if serious problems are found. To reiterate: You may sometimes be able to renegotiate if previously unknown problems are revealed by the home inspection – but *in a normal or buyer's market* the larger price concessions are realized when you make your offer. If you get a good deal then you should not worry about the 'smaller' defects and routine problems that are revealed by the inspection. Depending on the market and the seller's situation -- such as if they need a quick sale -- you may get a home for less than the listing price.

#3 Just as with any post-inspection negotiations, look at the seller's situation to decide your strategy. Homes that have been on the market for a while may be overpriced (or have serious defects?) but they also may be amenable to price reductions. Homes that are going into foreclosure may be available at an attractive price. Divorce situations or situations where the owner has to move by a certain date give you more leverage.

#4 Your offer may have multiple contingency clauses – not just for the right to do a home inspection. This is important. A few of these would be

- A financing contingency. If you can't get financing this releases you from the contract to purchase. The appraised value of the property should also justify and hopefully meet the sales price if you are going to have a mortgage.
- A home sale contingency that makes your offer to buy this home dependent on the sale of your existing home.
- Under EPA regulations the buyers of homes built before 1978 are legally provided with the right to have the home tested for lead paint during their inspection contingency period. Although this is very often waived, this is another contingency.
- Spousal approval if one of the parties has not been able to see the home
- A contingency that allows you to withdraw if certain conditions are not met, such as a permit to build or a removal of legal restrictions on the property.

- The removal or continued presence of structures or household items that you may cherish or not want to be present.
- You may also have a contingency relating to radon or well water testing when you cannot get the results within the allotted inspection period. This is routinely done and is usually acceptable to the homeowner and listing agents.

This is just a partial list of possible contingencies you may need to include in your offer. Consult your agent and attorney about your particular situation.

#5 Don't allow any restrictions in your contingency clauses. This needs clarification. Your inspection contingency clause, as written in most states, gives you the right to walk away from the deal within a specified time frame -- usually 7 to 10 days in Massachusetts – but it's whatever time limit you negotiate when getting your offer accepted. (In a seller's market or 'hot property' you may only get five days. What you want is the right to 'walk away' if the inspection or other investigations reveal conditions that *are not acceptable to you*. You shouldn't have to justify why you are walking away from the deal. Again, the desirable clause is 'what is acceptable to you'. In the past, listing agents or builders would put in clauses to the effect that you could only walk away from a signed offer only if structural problems or other defects that would cost over a certain dollar threshold were found. Note: In new construction you may sometimes have to accept limitations on your right to walk away from the deal. (Consult your attorney).

In the 1980's I had a client who could not back out of the offer unless the inspection revealed over $10,000 in structural repairs. How many homes have this degree of structural deficiencies? Not many. You could have $100,000 in repair costs but not reach this threshold in structural repairs. Fortunately, I haven't seen these clauses in years – but I can't speak for every area. To repeat: you do not want to have any restriction on your right to walk away from the sale during the inspection contingency period. Importantly, if you are withdrawing from the transaction it is critical to inform the listing agent or seller <u>in writing</u> before your contingency clause has ended.

On the other hand, your offer to purchase may include a clause that says you will <u>not</u> renegotiate the price due to the inspection findings. Sometimes you need to do this when you have gotten a price reduction up front or, in a seller's market, just to get your offer accepted. In the hot real estate market of 2017-2018, many buyers have had to agree to this 'no negotiation clause'. But you still should have the right to walk away if the inspection reveals significant problems or issues you don't want to deal with. You just won't go back to renegotiate the price or terms, as you could in a 'normal' or 'buyer's' market.

#6 Getting a seller to accept your offer may not come down to offering the most money. The _terms_ may be just as important: whether you can close quickly, whether your offer is contingent upon your existing home selling, whether you can give the seller additional time before you take possession, etc. All cash offers are looked upon fondly. Your agent or attorney can probably provide a lot more examples.

One possible approach – that only works with older sellers and young buyers – is to use a personal letter that expresses a genuine love of the property and how much you would like their consideration of your (probably lower) offer. This may work if: it is a genuine feeling, if you are a first-time buyer, the property has been owned by the seller for a long time, ideally you have met the owners and established a relationship with them, and lastly, have owners who want someone to love their home as much as they did. If these conditions do not hold, don't bother with this strategy. It can even backfire if used inappropriately.

#7 Know who are negotiating with. Again, your agent should be helpful here. Many homeowners are extremely difficult to deal with, so you will want to avoid face-to-face negotiations – and sometimes even contacts. A listing agent may wisely steer you away from interactions with a 'difficult' client. You would think that estate sales, where several family members are selling the home of the parents, would be easy to negotiate with as it's all 'free money' for the estate inheritors. Not so: when you have several family members there is always one or two who are totally unrealistic about the value of the home and market conditions. Dealing with estate sales, I gather, is like pulling teeth.

In most cases, avoid dealing directly with the seller. Some people can keep things civil, but it's hard to say to an owner that the home is an ugly mess or severely overpriced without them taking offense. Many people are very uncomfortable with face to face negotiations. Some people can do this and keep things civil – but it is not easy. This is why you have real estate agents.

#8 Don't let the selling side know too much. The seller and listing agent shouldn't know what your income is how much of a mortgage you may qualify for, or even what your skills are. You may qualify for a mortgage that will allow you to easily buy a specific property – but you simply don't want to spend that amount on your mortgage. (You may also just believe you can get the home for less money).

Also, as noted in the chapter on *Post-Inspection Negotiations*, if you announce for all to hear during the inspection that you have the ability to fix every problem then you may not have recourse to negotiations that would perhaps have otherwise occurred. Don't let the selling side (owner and listing agents) know about your ability to get any of the needed work done cheaply by, for example, your contractor father, the cousin who is an electrician, etc.

A related problem that has recently come up: homeowners sometimes will have security cameras that will record what prospective buyers are saying as they view the home. Comments to the effect that you want the home and will pay over the asking price could be used against you. Keep silent during your visits to properties that may have some type of security system present.

#8 Use your contingency clause to allow you time to do not just a home inspection but other tests and investigations that are relevant. These would include, briefly: radon testing, well water testing, termite inspections, lead paint testing, and evaluations by contractors, engineers, or tradespeople on specific systems and areas of concern. Again, you may not have the ability to negotiate based on these issues (I'll note which are typically negotiable concerns in Chapter 13) but you want the right to at least evaluate these concerns, when called for.

#9 **A caution when you are buying from relatives or friends....** Buying a home from a relation or close friends can be a great deal. Lots of buyers get their first home by having a parent or other relation that sells them the home for less than what the parties believe is the market value. Usually, the homeowner, very often elderly, is happy when they can pass down the house to someone they know.

Most of the time this a great way to go. But not always... I did an inspection recently for a buyer who was purchasing the home of a relative. Unfortunately, the condition and limitations of the home really didn't justify what they were paying for it. The problem was, it was hard for them to pull out of the deal or seriously negotiate the price. Face-to-face negotiations are difficult enough, but it's tougher when you are close to the person on the other side of the table. In this situation, you may end up buying something 'as is' that any other buyer would negotiate a lower price on or would just 'walk' away from. No one wants grandma to feel bad...

To avoid this: if you are buying from a relation or someone you know well, always tell the owner you will be doing a home inspection and may have a contractor, architect, or other professional look at the house. Just leave a bit of uncertainty about whether you will be proceeding with the purchase in case you really don't want to go ahead (at least at the price they are looking for). Most homeowners think their homes are worth far more than they are. They just haven't found out yet that the home is really a money pit as they haven't had their home rejected by prospective buyers due to over-pricing or inspection concerns. Lastly, always do the home inspection even if you are dead certain you will buy the home. You never know what you will find; you'll want to know what you are getting into, in any case.

Not to go on too much about this, but if you are buying a limited home from a relation and you plan on expanding it, it is especially important to research if your plans are feasible and what they will cost. It may or may not be worth it.

#9 Ask the questions noted in chapter 7 about any water stains or other obvious defects. Get a history of leakage and repairs. Ask for a Seller's Disclosure statement and read this. Expect that most of the items will be checked as "unknown" Sometimes, however, you will get a seller who provides information on problems they have had and repairs that were made.

Briefly, a few pitfalls when making your offer...

> A buyer who offers to forgo their inspection to get their offer accepted is great for the seller as, for them, it's a done deal. For you, the buyer, however, foregoing the home inspection leaves YOU WITH NO WAY OUT once you make your offer. Basically, you are 'flying blind' with no way to discover if the property has problems – and no recourse *even if* you find out the home has serious problems or issues.

- Being so enamored with some aspects of the property (views, location, next to water, has a great yard) that you ignore the other important concerns and don't follow up with an inspection or further investigations.
- You get emotionally attached to the property. You may get the property – but maybe not. You may accept conditions that will be prohibitively expensive to correct. I've had buyers break down and cry when they found that their dream home overlooking a lake was completely (and I mean completely) termite riddled underneath.
- You get rushed to buy in a seller's market – or conversely, taking too long to deciding to make an offer for a home that will attract a lot of potential buyers.
- You forego the home inspection. This has become common in the seller's market of 2016-18, as buyers offer to pass on the home inspection to get their offers accepted. A buyer who offers to forgo their inspection to get their offer accepted is great for the seller as, for them, it's a done deal. For you, the buyer, however, foregoing the home inspection leaves YOU WITH NO WAY OUT once you make your offer. Basically, you are 'flying blind' with no way to discover if the property has problems – and no recourse *even if* you find that home property has serious problems.
- Assuming the listing price always represents the real fair market value of the home. The represented "fair market value" of the home may sometimes have little relation to what the home is actually worth. The actual selling price could be much lower or higher, depending on market conditions and the desires of the homeowner. Sometimes the listing

price will be too low in the effort to create a bidding war. When this happens the property often ends up selling for more than it was listed for.

- Putting a value on features that your bank or mortgage company will not assign any value to. See the section on Appraisals in Chapter 9, on Financing. Neither you nor the seller may not like this, but appraisers do not assign a value to a number of things you may be buying the property for. A few of these include pools, the landscaping, energy efficient construction, or leased solar panels.
- Underestimating or overestimating your abilities to take on a fixer-upper
- Lastly, NOT reading *The Homebuyer's Handbook* and highlighting topics relevant to your situation.

CHAPTER 8

Legal Issues, Property Insurance Issues

What this chapter covers . . .

- *How variances, liens, and other encumbrances can affect the purchase – and your ownership . . .*
- *What is a 'good' title and what you need to know about this . . .*
- *How the type of ownership you choose can matter . . .*
- *How an attorney can look out for your interests . . .*

Legal issues permeate the whole process of buying a home and, as a non-lawyer, I can only touch on these. This is why you will want to have a qualified attorney who will look out for your interests. What I can do is provide some guidance on the pitfalls that await those who do not do their 'due diligence' (and attorneys who do the same). Knowing how and when to utilize their services is important. You also want to understand the legal issues that could impact your ability to use and enjoy your future home.

In most cases, buyers use the attorney provided by their lender. This will usually be okay. Your bank or mortgage company has a genuine interest in making sure that the property they are providing a mortgage on has a clear title. In other words, they don't want to lend money on a home that they can't sell if you are unable to pay your mortgage. This is one area where your interest and the bank/ mortgage lender's interests are largely one and the same. Banks will typically have a list of attorneys that they have worked with and you can use. When buying a home in a new development where they are arranging the financing, however, I would be cautious about using the attorney they provide. The purchase and sales documents may contain provisions that protect the developer's interests more than your own. In this case, you will want to have your attorney at least review the documents so that you don't sign anything that will work against you.

The optimal scenario, however, is to get the name of attorney from your buyer's agent or even your financing person (assuming they have been helpful up to this point). One could argue that perhaps they would get some type of kickback for this referral, but really, all the agents want is someone who can do the job right (provide 'due diligence') and not screw up the deal unnecessarily (which does happen). So, I have no problem with going with the attorney provided by your buyer's agent. You may know a real estate attorney or have friends or associates with recommendations. That can be fine. Just make sure they are on the bank's/financing company's list of approved attorneys. If not, they can't do the deal.

When does the attorney enter the picture? In most cases, the attorney involvement starts when there is an accepted offer on the table. Why run up the bill if no one knows if there will be a sale? Legal issues pertaining to your situation could, of course, mandate an earlier engagement of an attorney. Issues relating to property boundaries and surveys may also need to be handled during the inspection contingency stage.

If you want to choose your own attorney, you can always do your research and make your choice. In many states, you can get a list of closing attorneys. Lawyers. com or state-run sites will typically have names you can use. Just be sure that you get a real estate attorney and not an attorney who specializes in litigation or even tenant's rights. As noted, *make sure the attorney is approved by your bank or financing company.*

What are a few of the legal pitfalls you need to be aware of?

First, not getting an attorney to oversee the transaction. Many states do not require that a licensed attorney oversee the transaction and be present at the closing. Other states (referred to as 'attorney states') – which includes Massachusetts, Alabama, Connecticut, Delaware, Maine, and numerous others – require an attorney. I suppose it is possible to forego the services of an attorney if you are not in an 'attorney state' or will not have a mortgage, but why anyone would want to do this is beyond me.

A second pitfall: you may have a friend or relation who is an attorney and you want them to handle the legal aspects of the transaction. Lots of bad things can happen when you get an attorney who does not specialize in real estate. Litigators will generally want to find something to litigate. Obviously, there are times you need one of these attorneys – but not during a 'normal' real estate transaction – which, most of the time, are fairly straightforward (which doesn't mean simple).

What are the most basic services that an attorney provides?

First, the attorney needs to ensure that you can obtain a clear title on the property. To use a definition from Investopedia: *'**Clear title** is the phrase used to state that the owner of <u>real property</u> owns it free and clear of <u>encumbrances</u>. In a more limited sense, it is used to state that, although the owner does not own clear title, it is nevertheless within the power of the owner to convey a clear title. For example, a property may be encumbered by a mortgage. This encumbrance means that no one has clear title to the property. However, standard terms in a mortgage require the mortgage holder to release the mortgage if a certain amount of money is paid. Therefore, a buyer with enough money to satisfy both the mortgage and the current owner can get clear title.*

In other words, no one else should be able make a valid legal claim on the property if you have a clear title.

What are some of the most common types of encumbrances that, until cleared, will prevent you (or any buyer) from taking possession of a property?

#1 Any existing mortgages on the property that the property owner has not paid off. In most cases, the discharge of the existing mortgage is straightforward. The monies paid by you (in most cases, the money provided to you in a mortgage from the bank or financing company) will be used to pay off existing mortgage holders. This gets a bit more complicated, however, when there is a second mortgage on the property, as sometimes the current owner does not have the money to pay this off. As the buyer, you probably do not want to assume this debt. This is where attorneys – or, in some cases, your financing professional – may (try to) convince the holders of a second mortgage that is in arrears to accept a partial payment (See Chapter 8 on financing).

When the home is a 'short sale' – which typically means that the homeowner is not paying their mortgage and what they can sell the home for is not enough to pay off the mortgage, an agreement will have been reached so that their bank or mortgage company will allow the sale to proceed without a full payment of the debt. Your attorney will be involved with this, but normally the seller (homeowner) will have gotten their bank to accept a short sale before the home goes on the market.

#2 Liens would be a claim by another party on the property, for instance, due to an unpaid bill. A lien could exist from a tradesman or contractor who did work on the property and who did not get paid. Subcontractors for the contractor could possibly also file a lien if they were not paid for the work they did. More common are tax liens, filed by the town or city for unpaid property taxes.

Other liens could be placed on the property from a court judgment in a lawsuit brought against the owner of the property. Money owed by the property owner for alimony or child support payments that have not been paid in full could also result in a lien on the property.

For your purposes, as the buyer, you will normally have your attorney research the deed to determine that there are no remaining liens on the property. If there are, you would normally have the homeowner take steps to remove these prior to the sale. In some cases, it may be necessary to have the liens paid off as part of the sales transaction.

#3 Easements. Easements can be routine or, in some cases, a bit more of an issue. An easement gives the right for some party to use your property for a specific purpose. Common easements include rights someone may have to cross your property to gain access to their own property. Utility easements are common and would include the rights of a utility company to have sewer piping or electrical or gas lines running over or under your property. There are literally dozens of types of easements and a number of ways that easements can be created. Your attorney needs to know these; we don't.

A few common easements, however, in addition to those mentioned above, Include:

Sidewalk easements. Even if no sidewalks are present, most towns and cities have limited rights to a specified number of feet of your land along the roadway your property fronts on.

Driveway easements (known as an easement of access). This could also include walkways needed to access a portion of your property, for instance, if the homes are too close together to allow a second walkway. An easement could give someone else the right to cross your property; you could have an easement that gives you the right to cross someone else's property (assuming this easement exists on their deed also).

'Rights to Light,' or *solar easements*.

Beach access easements, which could provide your property with legal rights, possibly exclusive, to access a beach – or conversely, they could also allow some other party (for instance, the public) to cross your land to reach the beach.

View easement (this prevents someone from blocking the view of the easement owner or permits the owner to cut the blocking vegetation on the land of another)

Recreational easements. Historic preservation easements, which provide the right for a historical preservation organization to enforce restrictions on alterations to your home, building, or land.

107

In most cases, the easements will be disclosed up front. If not, they should be listed on the deed. You want to make sure that you have clear title or that you know what easements exist and what their ramifications are. Lots of homes have easements; most are no big deal. I had a driveway easement on my first home, as I had to cross a small section of my neighbor's land to reach my property. At my current home, a private driveway to homes in back crosses a corner of my 'property,' with no adverse consequences.

Conversely, some easements might require a closer look. For instance, a utility easement for an existing or possibly major underground gas pipeline that would run close to the house could be something you would want to know about. An easement to allow a roadway or a driveway across your land would be undesirable if it will lead to development behind your property. In areas where you have drilling for natural gas or where coal is mined, you could have mineral easements, which separate the 'surface' rights of the property owner from the rights of a corporation to drill or mine for resources lying underground. These are commonly found in West Virginia and many Western states with a history of fossil fuel extraction. I think you would like to know about these, to put it mildly . . .

Inserting and using contingencies . . .

As contingencies come up when making your offer, I've included these in Chapter 7. As I noted, you can include in your Offer to Purchase a number of contingencies, including an inspection contingency, a financing contingency, and several others. See the previous comments on the importance of an unrestricted contingency clause.

What type of ownership best serves your needs?

This is a financing issue masquerading as a legal issue . . . or maybe it is the opposite? I'm not sure – but it can be important. The issue comes up when you are buying a property with another person, usually a spouse – but as young couples often buy the home before they tie the knot, it may be your fiancé/e or boy/girlfriend. What you should understand is that you can own the home *jointly* or *in common*. When you own a home *jointly,* then, if one party dies, the other party inherits the home free and clear. If you own the home *in common*, then the deceased owner's share would go to their estate and not the other owner. Siblings who inherit real estate from parents usually will own shares of the home 'in common.' This can get sticky when one party wants to sell and the other doesn't – but that is not a matter for us here.

In cases where you will be buying a home with a partner and there is one party that is contributing the down payment and perhaps most of the mortgage payment, whoever is providing the bulk of the money for the down payment may want the mortgage and ownership to go solely in their name. You will simply need to decide between yourself and other party what way to go. Joint owner-ship is the norm and implies the greatest trust for parties starting out, but there are times it may not be appropriate: for instance, when, as noted, the family of one party is largely paying for the home or will be responsible for the mortgage.

Cautions on Legal Matters

First, many states use 'closing companies' to handle the paperwork and the closing, with no attorneys involved. Other states, as noted, require that an attorney handle the closing. While not having an attorney oversee the transac-tion may be standard practice in some states and will usually work out okay, I would be careful. I once heard that you only really need an attorney in about 20 percent of the home sales – but when you need them, you *really* need them.

Second, while using the bank's attorney will usually work out okay, try to use the attorney recommended by your buyer's agent or other parties you trust, again, assuming they are also approved by the bank. Buyer's agents want their clients to have an attorney who knows what they are doing, but they also need know that things will get done in a timely manner. I've read the complaint that some attorneys don't do the title search until the financing and other commitments have been satisfied. This would be desirable cost-wise, except that the title search very often then doesn't get done in time, or it reveals problems that would have shut down the deal before the other expenses were incurred.

Third, it still pays to be careful, even when you have an attorney doing the title search, as I'm not sure all attorneys do the proper research. With properties that have had past transfers of ownership, there may be a tendency to assume that, if nothing came up in past title searches, then everything is probably okay with the title; therefore, they may not dig too deeply. I had a client who related that, when he was buying a large piece of land to put a house on in the Pacific Northwest, he did his own research and read the legal documents relating to the deed. (Note: he was a scientist who didn't mind reading through pages of legal documents.) He found there was a large right of way down the middle of the land that was not picked up by his attorney's title search. A second example I know of personally: a friend of my wife purchased a new home at the base of the subdivision. Her lawyer missed the fact that the developer had designated her backyard as the retention pond for the development. Another example: I recently had clients doing a second inspection who related how, when they went to the closing for the home they were selling, they looked at the plot plan and found that what they thought was their land *was not* really theirs. The land had been subdivided without their understanding in a prior land transaction. This took several months, plus money paid to their buyer, to work this out. They also had to 'walk away' from the first house I inspected as they couldn't close until the land issue was resolved.

Fourth, as I noted, easements are common (sidewalks, utility lines, right of ways that existed over time). Most will not affect the value or use of the property, but (and that's a big BUT) be careful with the exceptions and think through what may be allowed by the easement. Easements that allow someone to use a portion of your property for access can be harmless – or can lead to an unhappy situation. I read of one instance where an easement for a driveway was provided to a party who owned land in back of their property so that he would have easier access to his land. The problem was: the owner of the rear lot cut down the trees lining the driveway that formerly provided a visual barrier. Granting this easement actually reduced the value of the grantor's property.

I would, in fact, be careful with granting any easement without thinking through the consequences. Maybe your neighbor who needs or desires the easement will not abuse it – but will the next person? I won't get into legal advice, but you could possibly grant an easement with a lot of detailed restrictions or just provide a license to the current neighbor to use the access way without creating a legal right to use the land. Talk to your attorney.

Fifth, be careful with adverse possession issues. Adverse possession is something that comes out of British legal tradition. In layman's terms, it means that someone who is using someone else's land openly and notoriously for a set number of years can then lay legal claim to that land.

To quote WikiLeaks: 'The adverse possessor is usually required to prove non-permissive use which is actual, open, and notorious, exclusive, adverse, and continuous for the statutory period. If a claim to title by adverse possession is successful, title is acquired without compensation.'

While rare, how could this be a problem? I was told by a reliable source of two instances they were aware of where adverse possession affected someone's ownership of their property. In the first case, a family they knew owned a sizeable property bordering a lake. Many years ago, this family had been asked by a neighbor without water frontage if that family could use a portion of the land to access the lake. In a spirit of neighborliness, this was verbally granted. Unfortunately for the family owning the land, after a number of years, they received notice that the neighbor had been granted possession of a substantial portion of their land by filing for ownership via adverse possession. The land they planned to give to their kids was no longer theirs.

A second instance related to another nearby lakefront property. The owners of the property with lake frontage, again, in a spirit of being neighborly, had allowed a family without lake access to create and use a driveway down to the lake. This went on for years – until they were informed about how the property owner noted above had lost their legal rights to their land due to an informal permission granted in the past. These homeowners went to an attorney who sent a legal notice to the neighbor stating that their right to cross the land did not include any legal right to the property. Just doing this prevented any future claim of adverse possession by the neighbor. Interestingly, that neighbor, who did not have that many years left before they could claim possession, quickly sold their property and moved on. No permanent and free lakefront property was going to come their way.

I should note that the years required for someone using the land to file for ownership by adverse possession varies from state to state. For some states, it is over 20 years; others allow a _much_ shorter time for this to affect your ownership.

This type of problem is unusual, but just be aware if you buy a property where some other party has been using your property for their own use you may need to clarify and make known your ownership rights to this party. Talk to your attorney!

Other legal areas where you need an attorney . . .

#1 First: variances. Can you do what you want with the property if it doesn't meet existing zoning requirements? An example would be when you need to add on an in-law unit where this is not allowed under the current zoning. You may need to file for a variance with the local appeals board to allow this. Although not commonly needed, it is also possible that the purchase of the property you are buying will be contingent on a variance being issued that will allow a change of use in the current zoning. I've seen this with urban properties. If you have neighbors who object to the variance, I should note, you very often will not get it. Some municipalities routinely grant variances, while others almost never grant them. Do not assume anything. Also, variances may be granted for a limited time. For instance, when I was on the local appeals board, we would sometimes grant a variance to a petitioner who needed to create an in-law for a disabled or elderly relative. The variance was issued, however, for a specific period of time. It was supposed to be reviewed every five years or so to see if the conditions requiring the variance were still present. (No one went back to enforce these time restrictions in my city – but it could happen).

This subject would take a lot more time than justified in this overview, but the point is: if you will need a variance to make the property work for you, you will need to talk to an attorney first and do your due diligence with the town and even the neighbors. If you intend to use the land for agricultural purposes, where neighbors may object to manure smells and the like, find out if you will need a variance and the likelihood that it would be granted.

111

If you are looking to change the use of the property, this will require a variance. Say you want to make a small hairdressing salon in your garage. Don't assume you can do this – or anything – that requires a change in use according to the relevant zoning. In my region, New Hampshire tends to be fairly open to changes in use. Massachusetts, on the other hand, tends to be fairly strict. In many areas of the country, I should note, there is little in the way of zoning or the zoning is very permissive.

#2 Reviewing inspection reports? This can be done and may be necessary in complicated or specific types of transactions – but most of the time you will NOT typically bring the attorney into the negotiations arising out of the inspection findings. This is where you would utilize the buyer's broker (assuming you have a good buyer's agent who knows what they are doing). The buyer's agent should have an understanding of what, in any specific situation, is 'doable' in negotiations and what isn't. Your attorney really doesn't know the intricacies of the local market, the nature of the seller, and even what you care about. Even the attorneys I talked to admit that they generally stay out of these negotiations unless their guidance is sought. Occasionally, you may need your attorney when you have decided to walk away from the property and the seller (or the listing agency) is balky about returning your down payment. (As noted previously, you need to let the seller or seller's agent know in writing and <u>within</u> the contingency period if you are withdrawing your offer to purchase the property).

#3 Reviewing condominium documents. I'll cover buying a condominium in Chapter 20. When buying a condominium, your concern is not only with your unit but the legal and financial condition of the entire complex. Questions will need to be asked about pending assessments by the condominium association for repairs or possible legal impairments (such as the condominium association being sued).

Please note that condominium refers to the nature of the legal ownership – not the type of dwelling. Condominiums can be single family dwellings in a development, a duplex of just two units, a complex of dwellings of various types, or a unit in a multi-story building or high rise. The nature of the legal concerns are often similar to single family homes – but are also different in several respects.

#4 New construction. While things can sometimes go smoothly, there can be a whole separate set of concerns, legal and otherwise, that are more relevant to new construction than to existing single-family homes. I'll <u>briefly</u> review some of these in Chapter 17.

#5 Tenant and possession Issues. In cases where you are buying a property, whether a multifamily or a single family, that is being rented, you may have tenants that you don't want as you need to use their space – or you just don't want: period. I suppose you could even have an owner who refuses to move or can't afford to move (although unusual, I have had clients who had this happen). This is where you need an attorney. In some states, the tenant's rights are stronger than the rights of the owner, so you need to be careful. While legal evictions may be possible, they take time and money. Attorneys will sometimes advise that you simply pay the tenants or former owners to leave.

#6 Handling the closing. Beyond making sure that the mortgage and legal documents are signed – and by the 'right' parties – the attorney is needed to tie up loose ends. These could be:

- Did the final walk-through inspection done just prior to the closing turn up anything that needs resolution?
- Did the homeowner remove cabinets or other attached items?
- Did they trash the place on their way out (This may happen with bank-owned properties)?
- Are there systems that have failed between the time of the inspection and the closing, or have damaged systems or components been observed at the walk-through inspection that were not visible (or present) at the home inspection? Water heaters that were functional at the time of the inspection occasionally will fail prior to the walk-through inspection. In this case, the homeowner will normally have a new unit installed or provide an allowance for a new unit.
- Did the seller clear the property of debris and owner's goods? Clearing a property when large amount of debris or owner's goods have been left behind can be expensive and is a general pain to deal with. I inspected a home years ago where the owner left so much stuff behind the buyers needed several dumpsters to remove the abandoned materials (at a cost of several thousand dollars). Assuming that the transaction is allowed to continue, the closing attorney will very often have monies escrowed, or put aside, (usually well in excess of the expected cost) to pay for a removal of the owner's personal goods and, in some cases, to pay for needed repairs. Note: if you are buying a property from a hoarder, this is a whole another 'ballgame.' You very often will have unsanitary conditions; it may also have been difficult to do a proper inspection with all of the stuff present.
- Is the person who shows up at the closing really the owner? This sounds ridiculous, but the parties have to show identification at the closing to prove who they are. In the past, there have been instances where the couple closing was not the husband and wife who owned the property, but husband and girlfriend posing as the wife. I had clients who I did a second inspection for who disclosed that they had to walk away from the first property as the supposed owner of the first home I inspected

was actually the son of the owner who shared the same name as the father. (The father did not intend to sell).

#7 Issues relating to photovoltaic systems installed on the home . . . This is an interesting problem that is just now coming up. More and more homes have photovoltaic panels on the roof. With the tax credits available, these can be a great investment. In terms of legal issues, you need to be aware of whether the panels are owned by the homeowner or whether the system is owned by the solar company, in which case you lease the equipment. The cost of an owned PV system would be included in the sale price for the home. This is straightforward. If leased, however, the system cannot be included in the mortgage. In this case, your attorney may need to write a personal property mortgage pertaining just to the solar panels and the lease agreement.

#8 Property lines . . . Having a survey done and the possible ramifications of this fall under legal concerns. Where the results of the survey would indicate a possible need to walk away from the property or would affect what you would be willing to pay for the home, you would want the survey contingency put into the original offer. See more on surveys in chapter 6.

Buying a foreclosure or short sale . . .

A foreclosure, as you probably know, occurs when the homeowner has stopped paying their mortgage and the bank has been forced to repossess the home. A property can also be taken by the municipality due to unpaid real estate taxes. A court judgment could also result in a forced sale or change of ownership. A short sale occurs when a homeowner cannot make the payments on their mortgage and they reach an agreement with their bank or financing company to allow them to sell the property for less money than their remaining mortgage amount. This very often allows them to live there until the property is sold.

Buying a foreclosure or short sale can often seem like an attractive option – and it can be, in some cases, especially when it's a short sale. It can also be a nightmare. Foreclosed homes, where the bank or financing company has taken possession of the home, will typically be priced lower than comparable homes – or they may appear to be priced lower as long as you don't look too hard at all of the work they may need. Banks and the real estate companies they employ to sell the homes don't usually sell for pennies on the dollar, by the way; they typically try to get as much money as they can on the sale. Don't expect to be getting a property for 50 percent of what the home is worth; it rarely happens.

Getting a mortgage on a foreclosed home in a distressed neighborhood can also be a challenge. Foreclosed properties are often sold to investors who can buy the homes with cash, so they don't have this difficulty.

There are a few things that you need to be especially careful of when buying a foreclosure.

First, foreclosed properties often have suffered abuse and neglect. Some home-owners losing their home will trash the place on the way out. The fact that they did not have the money to pay the mortgage, moreover, probably also meant that they didn't have any money to put into the home. Repairs, mainte-nance, and the renovations that may have made the home more valuable very often didn't get done. For the work that was done, it was probably not permit approved. Some foreclosed homes are mold-infested, especially if the pipes burst when the heat was shut off. In some cases, the homes will have been vandalized; you may be dealing with broken windows, graffiti, and debris left by the owner or squatters. As cautioned earlier, a run down or foreclosed property is not a bargain when the cost of the repairs and the needed renovations, com-bined with what you are paying for the home, exceeds the value of what the property will be worth at the end of your efforts (not to mention how much of your time and energy may have gone into renovating the property).

When buying a foreclosed or short sale – or any distressed – property, you will need to not only have a thorough inspection done, but you'll need to look long and hard at the work and costs in making the property not only 'right' but what you would happy living in. *IF* you can get the property at the right price, *IF* you have the skills and willingness to do the work needed, and *IF* the nature of the property warrants putting this amount of work into it, the purchase can work – but that's a lot IF'S.

A second problem that was a huge problem after the 2008 financial crisis was that no one could figure out who even owned the property. The brilliant financial minds of the post-2000 era actually sliced up the income streams from mort-gages, packaged them into tranches of bonds given various ratings (mostly 'A' rated even though garbage), and then sold them to investors. The problem was, no one could figure out who owned the mortgages or could untangle the various claims that would exist on each property. I had clients who waited months, and in one case, over a year, in the hopes that someone could figure out where own-ership lay so that they go ahead with the purchase. In the end, they had to simply walk away from the property as they couldn't get legal ownership. This may have been more of a problem in the past, as the securitization of mortgages has fallen under much tighter regulation thanks to the Consumer Protection legislation enacted after 2008 – legislation which the current administration is intent on doing away with.

What about buying a home at a foreclosure auction? This sounds especially attractive, as it holds the promise of getting a super bargain. I must confess that I heard of people getting unbelievable deals on foreclosed homes after the real estate collapse in the early 90s in New England. The problem is: you really don't know what you are getting; you are 'flying blind,' as the saying goes. As an example: many years ago, I inspected a property an investor had purchased at an auction for what she thought was a great price. Unfortunately, the post-purchase inspection revealed that the foundation for the rear section had completely failed

What can you do if you want to purchase a home at an auction? Unless you are a savvy investor with a good attorney – and can stand to take a loss on an individual property – avoid buying a home at an auction. Second, if you do go this route, have your attorney research whether there are any liens or other encumbrances on the property. Do the investigations noted in the Handbook. Third, don't go near the properties where that really look like they are a disaster; they probably are. Fourth, in some cases, the bank will allow you to do a walk-through inspection on the property prior to the auction. This at least gives you some idea of the conditions you will face. You could bring out a home inspector or qualified contractor with you. This is not a full home inspection, and the inspector could incur a lot of liability when doing these, so many will 'take a pass.' Some states, Massachusetts included, do not formally allow partial inspections or walkthroughs (although this may be changing). Most inspectors prefer to do a full inspection and get paid a normal inspection fee. I never get a call to do inspections prior to the auction – but they could be done. You really can't call them a full 'home inspection,' however. You may need to do an inspection after the purchase just to find out what you've bought.

CHAPTER 9
Avoiding Financing Pitfalls . . .

What you'll learn in this chapter . . .

- *How the right financing professional can save you money . . .*
- *Getting pre-qualified . . . what matters . . .*
- *What you need to do to get the best rate . . .*
- *FHA and VA mortgages versus a conventional mortgage . . .*
- *Special mortgage programs may be available . . .*
- *How an appraisal can affect the sale . . .*
- *What you need to know about Homeowner's Insurance . . .*

This chapter will provide a brief overview of the financing process – and the critical pitfalls to avoid when getting a mortgage. We will not, however, cover every bit of information relating to financing. Instead, I'll try to give you what you need to know when applying for a mortgage. I'll also cover how the appraisal process works, so you won't get blindsided when the appraisal does not come up with a high enough value for the property to justify the mortgage you need to buy the home. I'll also include several articles and handouts in the addendum, plus links to information provided by the FTC and the Consumer Financial Protection Bureau on what to look out for when shopping for a mortgage. (As noted earlier, the links are present on the website HomeBuyersHB.com, should you be reading this as a book and not with a Kindle or Nook). These links provide access to lots of useful information on financing. Preferably, however, you won't handle the financing issues on your own.

And that relates to this. This chapter – and the information I've reprinted (or provided links for) in the Addendum – provides great advice, but it's all about doing everything yourself: understanding how to establish good credit, getting a commitment from a bank or mortgage company, and determining the best type of mortgage. You can do lots of research and shop around for a mortgage to get the best rate and, in all likelihood, you won't get the optimal results if you

117

don't have a knowledgeable person do your financing. Just like you need a buyer's agent who will guide you and look out for your interests, a qualified home inspector, and a good real estate attorney, you also need a financing person who knows the 'ins and outs' of home financing and *will act as your advocate* during the entire buying process.

Financing issues are complicated to the extent that you and I as laymen will never know (nor need to know, really). You want to get the financing option that will work best for you. The reality is: each person's financial situation is different, the mortgage programs and terms can vary widely, and the options can vary according to each buyer's situation. Add to that the fact that rates and programs are constantly changing, making it difficult for anyone to navigate this process on their own.

Note: as a special case, it can be important to talk to a financing person regarding any 'roll overs' of monies from the sale of another property. You can get hit with a large tax on the profits made from selling another property if you don't invest it in another property within a set amount of time.

To find a good financing professional, most buyer's agents have financing professionals (and I may use the terms 'financing professionals,' 'loan officers,' or 'mortgage specialists' interchangeably) whom they trust. You can also get a qualified mortgage lending professional who will look out for your interests from a personal referral.

Financing overview . . .

As noted previously, one of the first things you will do when you start your home buying effort a home is get prequalified – or even better, pre-approved. Prequalification means you have been determined to be qualified to get a mortgage up to a certain amount. Pre-approval means the bank or finance company is ready to write the loan as soon as you have an accepted offer (with conditions, of course). You can't really go and look at homes if you have no idea what you can afford and what mortgage you may qualify for given your financial assets and profile. Buyer's agents say they won't even 'let the buyer in the car' to look at homes until they have been prequalified. If you don't know what you can afford and how much you need for a down payment or income to buy in your local market, then you are wasting your – and your agent's – time. I don't know how they do things in other areas of the country, but buyer's agents in my area will not even attempt to prequalify buyers. Instead, they send them to qualified lending professionals.

Another point to clarify: you can either go to a bank or mortgage company and deal with them directly or, you can go to a mortgage broker who will shop around for the best deal. Using a broker could be an option, but agents I've talked to recommend you go directly to specific bank or mortgage companies that have handled previous transactions quickly and fairly. Mortgage brokers are an option, but they have their own fees that may get added onto whatever the mortgage company is offering. I've had buyer's agents state that mortgage brokers don't always know the ins and outs of what they are selling as much as a bank or mortgage company that is doing its own underwriting.

How much can you spend?
Getting prequalified/preapproved . . .

To get prequalified, the loan officer will look at your income, your assets, your credit history, and other relevant information to determine how much money you can afford to spend on a property based on how much you qualify to borrow. To do this, they will normally need to look at:

a. your pay stubs and documentation of your work history
b. your credit history (and credit score)
c. your tax returns, possibly for two years prior, especially if you are self-employed
d. monthly reoccurring costs or income, such as child care, alimony, credit card bills, car payments
e. second mortgages,
f. documentation of your identity
g. ALL of your bank accounts and stock statements, if any.
h. other assets you may have that will buttress your financial position, including IRA or other retirement assets.
i. your credit report (which will be obtained by your financing company)
j. And lastly, ALL extenuating circumstances or history that will affect your ability to pay the mortgage. This can include a lot of stuff, including possible changes in income, legal matters, questionable past history, etc.

The advice commonly provided to buyers is to clean up your finances and save money prior to starting your home search. This is certainly good advice, but it is in your interest to talk to a mortgage professional *early in the process.* Don't assume anything. It happens that things you think are going to keep you from getting a mortgage can often be worked around. In one instance I'm familiar with, a buyer thought that an unpaid second mortgage on their current property would prevent him from getting a mortgage for a new home. The mortgage officer was able to counsel him on how to get the second mortgage balance substantially reduced so he could then move forward to purchase the home he wanted. (The second mortgage was in arrears, so the bank holding the second mortgage was happy to get at least part of their money back). Not everything you think matters will matter to the lender – while some things matter more than you think.

119

A financing professional can also advise you on what to do and what not to do to keep or improve your credit rating. Typical advice would include: don't take out new credit cards, don't spend money or increase the balance on your existing credit cards, don't pay off your credit cards (I'm not sure why, but this can negatively affect your credit score); no new car loans, etc. Saving money is always a good idea. There's a lot more to this, obviously.

The prequalification/preapproval process will determine how large a mortgage you qualify for and thereby what price range of homes you can be looking at. The financing professional can also determine how much you will need as a down payment, depending on the type of the mortgage you will be getting. Obviously, the size of the mortgage you qualify for will determine what you can afford to spend. The lending professional can also determine if you are eligible for any special mortgage program, any down-payment assistance programs that may be available, whether, given your credit rating and income, it will be better to have an FHA or conventional mortgage; AND lastly, whether a fixed or variable rate makes the most sense (see more on this later).

One valuable piece of advice you will get once you have been approved for a mortgage is:

Don't spend money on anything discretionary . . .

If you go out and spend a lot of money after you have been approved but before the closing, it will completely change your financial profile and may interfere with getting the loan to close. Although this advice is mainly for first-time borrowers, it could apply to anyone who is putting the minimum down for a down payment. In other words, don't go out and purchase new furniture for the home or put anything on your credit card. No trips to the Caribbean to celebrate getting a new home. (I've heard of someone doing this!)

Now, before we get into the details of the financing process, please understand that a mortgage is a loan in which your house functions as the collateral. The bank or lender loans you a large chunk of money (very often 80 to 90 percent of the price of the home), which you must pay back – with interest – over a set period of time. If you fail to pay this back, the lender can take the home back through the legal process of foreclosure. You do not want this to happen – ever.

How much can you afford to spend . . .

Assuming you have gone through the pre-approval process and you know what you can afford in a home: what next? Well, before you start looking at homes in the price range you can afford, I recommend stepping back and asking yourself:

How much do I have to spend in this market to get what I want? And second: How much do I <u>want</u> to spend? These can be two different things.

For an FHA loan *at this time*, the sum of your monthly mortgage and real estate tax payments must be less than 31% of your gross (pre-taxes) monthly salary. This may – or may not– include your partner/spouse's income or whoever else will go on the mortgage application. The sum of ALL of your monthly debt payments must be less than 43% of your gross (pre-tax) monthly salary. That is a high limit. <u>It may not be what you want to spend</u>.

Your mortgage payment also includes the monthly portion of your real estate taxes, your homeowner's insurance, and private mortgage insurance (more on this below). The bank needs to ensure that these will be paid, so they collect these from you monthly. This makes sense, as you don't want to have to keep track of your real estate tax or insurance bills. As noted earlier, this is just a portion of your homeownership costs.

The question you should have figured out by this point is not what you can afford to spend (and, therefore, how much home can you buy), but how much you are willing to put out and much do you have to spend to buy in your real estate market. Obviously, if you are paying lots of money for rent, you may be better off putting the money toward building equity in a home. If the rents are high in your area, this will make buying more attractive, but you still may need to take a bigger mortgage than you'd like. This may sometimes be a necessity. (Note: Rental costs at the time this was written have gone up significantly across much of the country). You could also choose to get a less expensive property or look in a less expensive area so that you can avoid being mortgage poor. There are times renting makes sense also, particularly when you need to save and establish your credit or if you may have to move in the next year or two.

What type of mortgage will work best for you?

There is no simple answer for this, but a few of the options you will look at with your financing professional include conventional mortgages offered by your bank or mortgage company, and FHA and VA loans. Special loan programs may also be options.

FHA Loans . . .

The Federal Housing Administration and Veterans Administration offers loan programs with much lower down payments than those required by conventional mortgages. Many FHA loans only require 3.5 percent of the purchase price for a down payment, with the FHA mortgage financing the rest of the purchase. FHA lenders may accept borrowers that have a lower credit rating or have been in bankruptcy or foreclosure – something most conventional lenders will not do.

For first time buyers who qualify, these often are the loans of choice – and they may be the only loan you can get. Lenders do not take a risk with a borrower who chooses an FHA mortgage, as the FHA agency itself insures the loan. This allows them to offer a loan with a low down payment of only 3.5%. For first-time home buyers who have trouble saving, the FHA or VA mortgage is an attractive option.

Another possible advantage of an FHA loan is that, unlike conventional private mortgages, the loan may be assumable by a house purchaser. This is potentially a benefit when you sell your home – especially if market interest rates are significantly higher than when you borrowed the money to buy it. A prospective buyer who is qualified under FHA standards may be able to assume (take over) the mortgage at a lower interest rate than they would pay today. This would benefit both the seller and the buyer. By contrast, conventional mortgages typically contain a 'due-on-sale' clause that means that the loan balance must be repaid when the property is sold. Lenders may allow assumptions, but only at the current market price.

There are some major hurdles to having a mortgage that a buyer can assume when you go to sell, but I won't get too deeply into that here (the buyer may need to come up with a larger down payment, as you would have paid off a portion of the loan and the home may have appreciated in value). But still, when interest rates are rising, having a mortgage that a new buyer can assume could be of value.

Here are some other benefits of an FHA loan:

- Mortgage insurance can be added onto the loan instead of paid out of pocket in private mortgage insurance (as done with traditional loans).
- Debt ratios can be higher than with other loans.
- Anyone can get an FHA loan, even though they are usually the choice of first-time buyers or those with low or moderate income levels.
- There is no income limit.
- No prepayment penalty.
- Easier for the borrower to use gifts and other special funding for closing costs and down payments.
- Possible funding for home improvements

The negatives of an FHA loan could be:

- A higher loan interest rate than with a conventional (private) loan. For buyers with a large down payment, a conventional loan will very often be the better option.
- Higher mortgage insurance than with private insurance.

- Lower loan limits. FHA loans put limits on how much a person can borrow based on the area where they live. They are usually determined by the average price of a moderate home in that area.

VA Loans . . .

VA loans have been available to veterans ever since Congress created the program in 1944 to help World War II veterans achieve homeownership. Since then, these loans have helped millions of ex-servicemen and women become homeowners. Lenders that are approved to offer VA loans are protected with the guarantee that a fourth of the loan will be repaid if a borrower should default. This guarantee allows lenders to offer more competitive rates than with other special programs.

Numerous benefits make this an excellent loan option for anyone that has served in the military. These include:

- No down payment is required.
- No mortgage insurance is required, which lowers the monthly payments.
- Lower requirements to qualify for the loan. In fact, it is estimated that up to eighty percent of those with a VA loan would not qualify for any other loan.
- Interest rates are competitive with other types of loans and may often be lower.
- No prepayment penalties.
- Sellers can pay up to six percent of the closing costs, which further reduces the amount of cash needed to purchase.
- Higher debt-to-income ratios are allowed.
- No additional underwriting is needed if the owner decides to refinance.

There are two possible disadvantages to choosing VA loans. First, you are limited in terms of the house you can buy. Second, there is an income limit and higher income borrowers will not qualify. This loan was designed for low to moderate income buyers who cannot qualify for other loans because they do not have money to save for a down payment.

Conventional Mortgage Loans

When are conventional mortgages better? There is no simple answer, as numerous factors come into play. For the same property with the same mortgage amount, buyers with higher credit scores are very often better off with a conventional mortgage; those with slightly lower credit score may be better off with an FHA mortgage. In general, when you don't need to finance more than 80 percent of the loan, a conventional mortgage will usually be a better option as it will carry lower rates. Your financing professional can figure out what option will work best for you.

What about Private Mortgage Insurance (PMI)?

PMI is an insurance program that reimburses the lender if the borrower defaults on the loan. PMI is available for conventional mortgages only; the FHA and VA have their own mortgage insurance programs.

The private mortgage insurance paid by home-loan borrowers allows lenders to offer mortgages to many buyers who would not otherwise qualify for a loan. At one time, mortgages carried a minimum down payment, usually 20 percent of the purchase price. The down payment was meant to ensure that the buyer would honor the loan commitment, as defaulting would mean the loss of a large investment. In theory, with at least 20 percent equity in the home from the start of the loan, a lender would be able to recover at least this amount by selling the home, if necessary, after a foreclosure.

PMI came about as a way for potential buyers who had less than a twenty percent down payment buy a home. Most borrowers now pay the PMI premium as part of the monthly mortgage payment. The PMI rate is figured as a percentage, usually around 1 to 2 percent of the outstanding principal amount of the loan, divided into twelve monthly payments. On a loan amounting to $150,000 in principle, the annual premium at the PMI rate of 1 percent is $1,500, or $125 a month.

Once you have paid down a mortgage – or you can prove that the home has appreciated sufficiently in value since you took the mortgage, you can apply to end your PMI payments.

Other Mortgage Decisions: Points . . . fixed versus variable rates . . . the term of the loan . . . interest rates . . .

Other factors that will determine your monthly mortgage costs include:

#1 Whether you will pay 'points' or a percentage of the mortgage up front to bring down the overall payments.

#2 Whether you get a fixed or variable rate. Either could make sense, depending on how long you will be in the property. Variable rates will generally start off lower. They could make sense if you will most likely own the home for a few years. If you are buying when rates are high, it is possible that you come out ahead when the rates drop lower. (You may simply want to just refinance the property with a new mortgage, however, in that case).

#3 The length of the mortgage term . . .
From talking to mortgage professionals, it seems like the standard loan these days is a 30-year fixed mortgage. But is having a 30-year mortgage always the way to go? While you will pay less each month than with a shorter-term mortgage, with a 20 or 15 year mortgage you will build equity and pay off the loan much faster. The critical issue is: can you afford the higher payment? Your age may be a factor: do you want to be paying a mortgage in your 60s or 70s? Your need for tax write-offs could enter the calculation. You may want to have the mortgage paid up at some point and not have to worry about having to make endless payments. I recommend talking to your financing professional to compare the monthly costs of a 20-year mortgage term versus a 30-year mortgage.

#4 The current interest rates . . . When the interest rates are high, your mortgage will be higher due to the added interest expense. When interest rates are rising, fewer potential buyers may qualify for a mort-gage. At some point, this affects the prices of real estate in that market. This can take a while to play out, however.

Other Special Mortgage Programs

The US Department of Agriculture offers a similar program to the FHA and VA, designed for **low- and moderate-income borrowers in rural areas**.

USDA loans can be a good option for borrowers who have little available sav-ings. They offer **zero down payments** and are usually cheaper than FHA loans. Borrowers will pay an upfront fee, as well as ongoing mortgage premiums to the USDA.

Another financing option that may be possible is one of the special mortgage pro-grams or down payment assistance programs run by the states. These are mainly for low and moderate income buyers or buyers with limited money available for down payments. I won't list the programs that may be available. Massachusetts, where I reside, has a number of programs designed to assist and advise first time homebuyers. See http://www.mass.gov/hed/housing/affordable-own/first-time-home-buyer-fthb.html

New Hampshire has a loan assistance program also; contact them at https://gonewhampshirehousing.com

In Maine, see the information at the MaineHousing.org website. http://www.mainehousing.org/programs-services/homebuyer/homebuyerdetail/firsthome

Rather than get too much into the specifics, I suggest you do a Google search in the state you may be buying in. Just Google 'special mortgage programs' and the name of your state.

Rehab loans, called 203K loans, are also available from the FHA. These are an option if you are looking at a home that is seriously run down or damaged but is still worth salvaging. Foreclosed properties come to mind. These loans, very simply, allow you access to the money you may need to make the home habitable and safe. I won't spend a lot of time discussing these. I rarely see them done – but that doesn't mean they can't be a good option in some cases.

A visit to the HUD website's 203(k) page is a good starting point for more information on the program. The resources include a detailed description of eligible properties and improvements. While 203(k) loans cannot be used for luxury items or improvements that do not become a permanent part of the property, items such as painting, room additions, and decks may be allowed. Information on maximum mortgage amounts, fees, and the application process can also be found at that site or by phone at (800) CALL-FHA.

Jumbo mortgages

A **jumbo** mortgage is a home **loan** for an amount that exceeds conforming **loan** limits established by regulation. At the time this was written, the **jumbo loan** limit is $417,000 in most of the United States and $625,500 in the highest-cost areas. These loans, often more than half a million dollars and up, are designed to finance luxury properties and homes in highly competitive local real estate markets. They come with unique underwriting requirements and tax implications. Talk to your financing professional, as, again, there are many banks and mortgage that do jumbo loans, with different programs that may work for you.

Take back mortgages

A take-back mortgage would be where the property owner is essentially acting as the bank. This type of transaction has a number of potential pitfalls for both the buyer and the seller. As you don't see this type of mortgage financing too often, I won't get into this here. If done, this type of seller financing needs to be properly structured by real estate attorneys. Besides the potential legal issues with take-back mortgages, I would be concerned that, if this is the only way a property can be financed, are there are some inherent problems with the property or your income or assets that would make this the only option? The potential for fraud and lawsuits is endless.

One example: if the seller does not own the property being sold free and clear of any mortgage or trust deed and the buyer cannot get a loan to pay off the existing mortgage, the buyer obtaining a mortgage from the seller may be taking title subject to the seller's existing loans that have the property as collateral.

Should that happen, the buyer will have to pay on this loan just like the seller was doing. The same is if there are undisclosed liens on the property. Another problem that could arise for the buyer is that the loan in place may not be assumable. If this is the case, the transfer of title to a new owner of the property may very well trigger a due on sales clause in the existing mortgage, where the lender refuses to accept payments from the new owner. This will force the new buyer to scramble to get a new loan, assuming one is available. If not, the new buyer could lose the home in a foreclosure. If a foreclosure proceeding happens in such a scenario, the seller will be forced to service the loan that is in place or risk losing the equity in the property. As you can imagine, the above situation invariably leads to litigation by the seller against the buyer.

If you are in an owner financing situation and an existing mortgage exists, it is imperative that the seller disclose this fact to the buyers. You would need to ascertain whether or not the loan secured by the mortgage is assumable or not.

Shopping for a loan when you are on your own . . .

While I have recommended finding a mortgage professional to whom you have been referred by someone you trust to look out for your interests, you may also be looking at the listed rates for a number of mortgage companies; you may also have a mortgage broker. This can work – but I've been told that it's difficult to compare what you will pay when just looking at the advertised rates; the same is true for what you will get for service. There are loads of fees and expenses that are part of the financing process. Be careful: ask a lot of questions. Use the Good Faith Estimate form to compare what your financing will cost from different vendors. Get feedback on which fees may be waivable and which aren't. In general, I've been told that the mortgage origination and other financing costs should come to around $3000 on a $100000 loan. I'm sure this varies – and larger mortgages may not have proportionally higher fees. Do a Google search on the financing company to look for red flags. I would avoid companies that operate over the internet only. I've overheard complaints from buyers about companies not being able to close when promised, as the companies did not get the paperwork and legal paperwork done in time. At one inspection, I overheard my client yelling over the phone at his mortgage company because they had changed the terms – after it was too late for him to do anything about it. (Changes in the lending standards make it more difficult for this to occur today, I should note).

Fortunately, there are a number of clearly written guides put out by the FTC and the Consumer Financial Protection Bureau (set up after the fraud and resulting collapse of the financial system in 2007–2008) on how to get through the whole financing process unscathed. I'll list these at the end of this chapter. (You can also find these links at the Handbook's accompanying web site, HomeBuyersHBook. com). Reading these is especially valuable if you are making financing choices on your own. If the program has not been gutted yet, you may be able to get a HUD housing counselor to advise you. Many agencies assisting first time buyers have courses you can take to qualify for an FHA or down payment assistance loans. I've included a list of these at the end of the chapter (with links for those who are downloading a copy of this book).

What you need to know about closing costs . . .

The closing costs are all the costs you will have to pay when you 'close' the deal and take legal possession of the home. Fortunately, this is a one-time expense. Unfortunately, closing costs can add up. I'll discuss briefly below a number of the expenses that go into your closing costs. To keep these costs down, some can be wrapped into your mortgage amount so you will be paying for them over time. As noted, your mortgage, real estate taxes, and homeowner's insurance will be ongoing costs of home ownership.

Basic closing costs include:

- The appraisal fee
- The mortgage origination fees (how the bank makes its money)
- Transfer taxes
- Government recording charges (such as filing fees for the deed)
- Title insurance. This is discussed more in the Legal issues chapter. Basically, title insurance is provided by title insurance companies who have qualified real estate attorneys review the title to make sure there are no encumbrances, unrecognized easements, liens, or other claims on the property.
- Homeowner's insurance, prorated for next month
- Lender and attorney fees
- Upfront payment of the first month's interest
- Prepayment of real estate taxes, pro-rated
- Possible Homeowners' Association fees (usually prorated to include first month's payment)
- Possible flood insurance –see more below
- Possible fuel adjustment charges (for instance, for the value of the oil left in the oil tank)

You need to look at what will be included. Most of the fees are not waivable; some other fees could possibly be (such as the fuel adjustment fee, depending on the seller). Importantly, as the closing costs can be considerable, especially when you are struggling to come up with a down payment, the closing costs in some cases are paid for by the seller. This often occurs as part of either the initial negotiations or when problems are identified by the home inspection. Rather than put money toward repairs, the seller may agree to pay the closing costs for the buyer. When done, this reduces the amount of money you need to come up with at the time of the purchase. It is to your benefit to have the seller pay the closing costs rather than get a reduction in the price of the home, as it puts more money in your pocket. You won't be cash short. I should note that there is no requirement that a seller do this.

As noted earlier, you will want to look at the 'Good faith Estimate,' a 3-page form that summarizes the loan terms and settlement charges. It explains what you will pay if you go forward with the loan process and are approved for the loan. I've included a copy in the Addendum.

How can an appraisal affect the transaction?

The appraisal is the process to determine the market value of a home (or other property). The appraiser compares the property being sold to similar properties in that area to determine its 'fair market value.' Essentially, your bank or financing company needs to know the value is present for what they are lending on should they need to take the property back due through a foreclosure. The appraisal is something that you will pay for as part of the closing costs. I'd like to say that the appraisal provides you with some assurance that you will not grossly overpay for a property. Unfortunately, in a 'hot' market, all homes and properties may be selling for top dollar, so it only assures the bank that your property is no more inflated than the rest of the homes being sold.

In any case, once you have an accepted offer, you will typically have a set period of time to do the home inspection – as well as the other tests and investigations you want to do. Usually, the appraisal will be done once the financing company (or bank) knows you will not be withdrawing due to problems revealed by the home inspection. The appraiser is typically chosen from an approved list at the bank/mortgage company doing the financing. If the appraiser at the top of the rotating list decides to pass on that job, the option to do the appraisal is offered to the next in line at the list. They also can refuse it if they are busy or don't want that particular job. To avoid any conflicts of interest, neither you, the listing agent, the buyer's agent, nor the seller has any input on who does the appraisal. Nor are these parties allowed to have any input on the appraiser's 'opinion' – and it is an opinion based on guidelines to determine the value of the home. When possible, delay having the appraisal done until after the home inspection has been done. Occasionally, I see a situation where the buyer 'walks away' from the home after finding serious problems with the property (or for other reasons), but they have already spent money on having the bank do the appraisal.

Conversely, things need to move quickly, so banks will normally order an appraisal on the property once they know the inspection has been done. Getting this done in a timely manner can be an issue for financing companies you find on the internet, by the way, as they just don't always have the local connections to get the appraisal done quickly.

An appraisal, as you probably realize, is not a home inspection. The home inspection is an evaluation of the structural, mechanical, and functional condition of the property. Home inspectors do not care about the location of the home; the quality or features of the town or neighborhood; the square footage of the home and property; how attractive things look; the number of bedrooms or bathrooms; whether the kitchen or bathrooms are exquisite or just functional; the presence of a garage; amenities such as pools and nice landscaping; detractions, such a dilapidated neighboring property; whether the home is on a busy street or next to a highway – in sum: all the things that determine the value of the home – and why you may want to buy it. These are all appraisal concerns. The home inspection doesn't determine value: it just gives you an objective picture of the physical condition of the home so that (hopefully) you don't get stuck with expenses that you did not plan for.

The appraisal determines how much the bank is willing to offer to lend you for a mortgage. For a conventional loan, for instance, the bank may be willing to offer a mortgage for 80 percent of the fair market value (usually this is a greater percent due to private mortgage insurance, but we'll keep it simple here). For a home with an appraised value of $400,000, the bank would be willing to provide a $320,000 mortgage.

Which features do not count for value in the appraisal?

A home may be valued at a price that you feel you are happy to pay – but the appraiser may not agree. This may affect the homeowner more than you, as they may need to lower the price of the home in order to sell it. But if it is a 'desirable' property with a lot of buyer interest, then you may need to come up with more money for the down payment. A problem arises, however, due to the fact that appraisers do not value a lot of things that you would think would add value. A few of these are:

- Finished basements. Finished basements very often will not count as living space, especially if they are largely below ground, lack a bathroom, or are not heated. Walk-out basements may be regarded differently.
- The size and value of the lot.
- The beautiful landscaping that may be present is not counted in the appraisal.
- Pools are not included in the appraised value.
- Guesthouses do not get full value as living space.
- Leased solar panels. (Panels that are owned by the homeowner may partially count in the appraisal).

- Garage apartments may not get full value as living space.
- Limited or substandard stand-alone garages may not be valued – or not for much.
- Enclosed porches are generally not counted as living space.
- The energy efficiency of the property (although this is changing as newer, energy-efficient homes are recognized as a superior investment. Homes with low energy costs mean more money can go for the mortgage).

All of the above things could be reasons why you are buying the home – but they don't formally add value as far as the bank is concerned. Whether this is wrong or right doesn't matter – these aren't things the bank can lend money on. You need to be aware of this as the appraised value may come in lower than what you need to get a mortgage to buy the property. As noted, in this case, either the seller would need to drop the price (perhaps in a buyer's market but less tenable in a seller's market) – or you would have to come up with money for the down payment. Just be aware of this issue, so you don't get blindsided.

How often does the appraisal affect the sale?

How often does the home not appraise for as much as the home is selling for? From what I hear: it does happen, but not a lot. There are reasons for this. First, the listing agent and seller normally know that putting an exorbitant price on the property – one that is far beyond what any honest appraiser would value the property at – means the property simply will not qualify for financing, at least not at that price. While the property owners would certainly like to get the most they can, the listing agent normally just wants the deal to go through (so they can get paid). Fair enough. Also, experienced agents will have a pretty good idea of what the appraised value of the home should be.

Appraisal Fraud . . .

But what about appraisal fraud? This is not as much of a problem as it was in the mid-2000s, as most lending institutions have implemented safeguards against appraisal fraud. Federal guidelines now require banks to have a firewall between the lenders and appraisers to prevent the types of collusion that occurred in the 2003–2007 period. The way the process works now is that lending institutions, lenders, or real estate agencies go through Appraisal Management Companies (AMCs) who maintain a list of qualified appraisers. As noted, the lenders have no choice about who actually does the appraisal. This is to prevent collusion with an appraiser to inflate the value of a home to the benefit of the seller. An automated underwriting system has a lot of checks and balances. Each loan is normally reviewed by the AMC for discrepancies, and loan officers not only cannot choose the appraiser but they are not allowed to have contact with an appraiser doing the job. This system may not be in place everywhere, but this is how it generally works.

What you need to know about property insurance . . .

Another thing you will need to do when buying a home is obtain homeowner's insurance. This will normally be included in your monthly mortgage payment to the bank. This is easier for you (one less bill to take of) and necessary for the bank, as they will require that you keep the property fully insured.

Homeowner's insurance gives you basic protection should your home burn down or suffer damage from specific types of incidents, such as fire, tornadoes, or theft. Most will also provide liability coverage for accidents that may occur at your property. I won't get into the details on homeowners insurance, except to note a few points:

First: the standard HO-3 policy protects your home against damage caused by 'named perils,' such as fire, lightning strikes, hail, extreme winds and rains, tornadoes, or theft. Homeowner policies may include coverage of your personal property – *but only for items and risks that are explicitly defined*. An HO-5 policy, if offered, may include personal property, but this policy will cost more and there are both limits and exclusions.

Second, policies can be written to provide cash value or replacement value coverage. Cash value would pay for repairs or replacements, but only for the depreciated value of the item. Replacing an older heating system, for instance, that suffered damage due to flooding (or other 'named perils') may only provide a fraction of the replacement cost, as the system was already largely depreciated. With replacement coverage, the cost of a new heating system would be provided.

Third, your homeowner's insurance should also include a general liability policy that covers you (up to a certain dollar amount) should someone injure them-selves while at your property. Your personal possessions would also normally be covered – but many types of items are excluded and others come with coverage limits or caps. Discuss this with your insurance agent. High-value items, such as jewelry, musical instruments, etc., may require 'riders' with additional costs.

Fourth, your coverage is based on the value of the home. You don't include the value of the land, as this would just raise your costs unnecessarily. (If your land falls into the ocean, by the way, your insurance will not cover this loss.)

Fifth, your homeowner's insurance does not necessarily cover every type of natural disaster. As noted, policies normally state that the damage must arise from something 'sudden and accidental' (a 'named peril'). The damage that occurs from a lack of maintenance, homeowner negligence, improper construction, or just age is not covered. Examples of non-covered items would be: damage from a leaky faucet that you did not fix, damage from burst pipes that occurred because you failed to keep the heat on during the winter, or the normal wear and tear from a worn-out roof or siding. The replacement of a water heater or heating system will not be covered if they simply fail due to their age. (The damage that occurs from their failure, however, may be covered). Problems due to faulty workmanship <u>are not covered</u>. Your homeowner's policy will not cover damage that occurred to flooding from rising groundwater, as may occur in a finished basement when water enters the basement after a heavy rain. Most importantly, perhaps, <u>your homeowner's insurance will not cover anything to do with MOLD or indoor air quality</u>. If you have flood insurance, it may cover the removal of moldy materials that resulted from the flooding – but not the mold that may arise from this or other sources.

Homeowner's insurance does not cover flood damage; flood insurance has to be purchased separately. If the home you are buying is in a designated 'special flood hazard area,' a mortgage lender cannot legally provide a loan unless government-mandated flood insurance is purchased. In this case, the purchase of flood insurance will be required by the lender and therefore included in the escrow account and payments. Flood insurance can be purchased on a home not located in an SFHA, but in that case, the insurance is not required by either the mortgage company or the law. You can research this at floodsmart.gov. As noted earlier, if you will not have a mortgage on the property, you may not be required to have flood insurance even if the home is in a designated flood zone. Obviously, it is important that you get this.

Sixth, homeowner's insurance policies do not cover back-ups from sewer pipes (including those that run to septic systems). Nor do they cover the damage caused by toilet overflows or sump pump failures. All these are considered preventable conditions with proper maintenance and precautionary repairs. For sewer pipes, for instance, it may have been possible to have had a back-flow valve installed that would have let the effluent out but not back in. You may, however, be able to get coverage from a sewer back up as an 'add-on' to your standard policy. (Given the costs involved when the sewage backs up, this would be a good idea). This would not cover the actual replacement of cracked sewer or waste pipes. Consult your insurance agent.

Seventh, **homeowner's insurance does not cover flood damage; flood insurance has to be purchased separately**. If the home you are buying is in a designated 'special flood hazard area' (SFHA), a mortgage lender cannot legally provide a loan unless government-mandated flood insurance is purchased. In this case, the purchase of flood insurance will be required by the lender and therefore included in the escrow account and payments. Flood insurance can be purchased on a home not located in an SFHA, but in that case, the insurance is not required by either the mortgage company or the law. You can research this at floodsmart.gov. As noted earlier, if you will not have a mortgage on the property, you may not be required to have flood insurance even if the home is in a designated flood zone. Obviously, it is important that you still get this.

Eighth, *earthquake damage is not covered*. You can buy this as a separate policy in most states. California requires that insurers offer policies that cover earthquake damage, but it does not require that homeowners buy this. Interestingly, most California homeowners (and renters) do not have earthquake insurance. Unfortunately, this insurance is expensive and it carries a large (15) percent deductible. On a home with $500,000 in damage (such as could occur from a total loss), the deductible would be $75,000. Note: you will want to talk to your insurer as policies may be available under better terms – or not at all.

Many people do not get earthquake insurance, as they have the misconception that the federal government problems will make things right. This is not the case. FEMA notes on their website that disaster assistance 'is meant to help you with critical expenses that cannot be covered in other ways. This assistance is not intended to restore your damaged property to its condition before the disaster.' FEMA may help provide temporary shelter and food, but most of the assistance FEMA provides is provided in low-cost loans that you pay back.

Caution: If you are buying the home without a mortgage, then there may no requirement to have the homeowner's insurance set up prior to purchase. Excepting your attorney, no one may be advising you on this. You need to do this, however, should the property suffer damage that would be covered or if a lawsuit was filed due to someone getting injured on your property.

I've also included a blog from a very good authority on insurance, as she covers this topic very clearly. You can also follow the link at **https://www.huffington-post.com/laura-adams/post_13579_b_12887288.html**

Resources

Consumer Financial Protection Bureau

https://www.consumerfinance.gov/owning-a-home/
28 page Guide to owning a home: https://s3.amazonaws.com/files.consumerfinance.gov/f/201503_cfpb_your-home-loan-toolkit-web.pdf
https://www.consumerfinance.gov/documents/2233/201701_cfpb_Credit-report-review-checklist.pdf
https://www.consumerfinance.gov/documents/1643/Spending-Tracker_Owning-a-Home_CFPB.pdf
https://www.consumerfinance.gov/find-a-housing-counselor/
https://www.mtgprofessor.com/Mistakes/mistakes_buying_a_house.html
https://www.mtgprofessor.com/home.aspx This guy provides wonderful, consumer protective advice on everything to do with mortgages. Check out his site.
https://www.maxrealestateexposure.com/how-to-avoid-overpaying-for-a-mortgage/

CHAPTER 10
Getting the Most from Your Home Inspection . . .

What you will get out of this chapter:

- How to find a qualified home inspector who will work hard for you . . .
- What matters when choosing an inspector; what doesn't . . .
- What the inspection won't tell you – and how you can work around these limitations . . .
- What the inspection covers – and what it doesn't . . .
- When to follow up with specialists. Who you can utilize and when . . .

Choosing a home inspector . . .

So, you have had your offer accepted and it's time for the home inspection. In terms of who you choose to do the inspection, I'll provide some guidelines below. The fact is: not all home inspections are done to the same standard and not all home inspectors bring the same dedication and experience to the job. And even when you get a qualified inspector, home inspections have limitations that you need to understand so you can act appropriately on the findings and not be disappointed with what the inspection can't do for you.

It is important to realize that choosing a home inspector who goes easy on the home or doesn't take the time to do a proper job can cost you a few thousand dollars, or occasionally tens of thousands of dollars in repair costs or lost value over the period you own the home. You want to find an inspector who takes the time to give you a thorough education on the home, including how you should maintain it, as opposed to an inspector who gets in and out quickly so they can go to their next inspection.

I've inspected numerous homes where the previous inspector failed to find or properly evaluate conditions that ended up costing the owner thousands and sometimes tens of thousands of dollars to remedy. In other cases, the things they weren't told greatly reduced the value of the property when they went to sell.

So, how do you find a qualified inspector who you can trust? Your buyer's agent may recommend an inspector or provide you with a list of home inspectors they have worked with. This works when they are providing you with inspectors who are competent, uncompromised, and experienced. It's not okay if they screen out inspectors who they feel take too long at the inspection or are too critical. I've seen both types of lists. In my area, many buyer's agents actually screen out the 'fly-by-night' inspectors or those inspectors who don't know what they are talking about. But I must confess: these are the agents I work with. I don't hear from those who want a 'quick' inspection.

I should also note that you may be to trust the referral you get from a buyer's agent simply because they have a fiduciary relationship that requires they work in your best interest. A referral from a 'selling agent' would not carry the same requirement of care. In the state I do most of my work in (Massachusetts), listing and selling agents are legally prohibited from recommending the names of home inspectors due to the potential conflict of interest.

As buyer's agents know who is a 'good inspector' and does right by their clients, I think you are usually better off taking their recommendation than finding someone on your own. (That, again, assumes you have a buyer's agent who is working hard for you). But another good avenue to finding an inspector is to ask family, friends, and co-workers for the names of inspectors they have used and been happy with. My caution is that these buyers don't have anything to compare their inspection to. Unless they have been on a bunch of inspections, it's hard to tell a mediocre but okay inspection from a great inspection.

What else could you look at to make your decision?

#1 First, whenever possible, get someone who is a member of the American Society of Home Inspectors (ASHI). ASHI is the original and most reputable home inspection professional association. ASHI was at the forefront in establishing Standards of Practice and a Code of Ethics for home inspectors and in requiring its members to obtain member-ship educational credits each year by attending seminars, taking rele-vant courses, and by other means upgrade their knowledge each year. Becoming an ASHI member requires extensive experience and passing a difficult national exam. Other associations exist, specifically InterNACHI (International Association of Certified Inspectors). NACHI has wonderful educational tools for their members and offers a lot of resources – but becoming a member, the last time I looked, required little more than paying your dues and passing an exam that my grandson could pass

137

(and he's only five). Many NACHI inspectors are well qualified and do a great job – but I would stick with an ASHI member when possible. (Go to http://www.homeinspector.org/ and hit 'Finding an Inspector' for a list of ASHI inspectors in your area. In New England, I recommend finding an inspector at ashinewengland.org. Where you can, get inspectors who are members of a local chapter, as these inspectors tend to be more involved in educational seminars and training.

#2 Ask how long the inspector spends at the inspection. This is critical. *Short inspections shortchange you.* You don't need four hours to inspect most homes (unless they are in really bad shape), but depending on the nature of the housing stock where you are buying (and the size, age, and condition of the home), your inspector should take 2 to 3 hours for most homes – and that <u>does not </u>include the time writing the report. In New England, with its old homes and sometimes complex systems, many single-family homes require 3 to 4 hours to inspect properly. Large homes, homes with multiple buildings, or estates can take 5 to 10 hours – or full days. Condos require less time – but townhouse condominiums will sometimes require 2 to 3 hours; small garden style condominiums, however, may only require 1 to 1 1/2 hours maximum – but your inspector had better allot more time, just to be sure. Also, the time spent on-site shouldn't include the time writing up the report when the inspector is doing an on-site report. Note: having two inspectors from the same company do the inspection together speeds up the process and is not a negative, in my opinion.

Also, your home inspector should provide you with an education on the home – and you can't do this if the inspection is rushed. In one instance, I was hired to do a second inspection – not because the first inspector did a bad job – but just because they didn't slow down to explain anything to the buyer. *The more time the inspector spends with you (up to a point), the more you will learn about the home.*

My advice? If you get a one-hour inspection on a single-family home or you feel you didn't learn anything, get another inspection done. You are about to make the largest investment you will probably ever make in your life. You want the inspection done right.

#3 What type of report you get can be important. Narrative reports sent by email provide the most information and are *usually* the best choice if the home is complex or has a lot of 'issues'. That said, my opinion on reports has changed. Many on-site reports are quite good, and they work well for most properties.

138

Office-generated reports have downsides too: they take longer (meaning, you will pay more), they sometimes contain too much information (so you can't figure out what is important and what isn't), and you won't get them as quickly. I've seen some reports that just contain a lot of boiler-plate mush. The problem with 80-page reports is that no one reads them and the important stuff from the inspection tends to get buried. With this type of report, I suggest you go through with a highlighter and mark up those items that are of greatest concern. These will typically either be safety-related issues or problems with potentially large repair costs.

Many on-site reports are quite good – but some checklist reports can be difficult to negotiate from, as they may not clearly describe the problem and what action needs to be taken. Also, everyone likes photos in their report. They have a value – but photos show some types of problems well, while subtle but important problems won't show up at all in photos. You need to read the written comments. I use photos but there use can be over-rated.

Lastly, and this may sound contradictory, but I've seen handwritten reports on condominiums and small houses where the (very experienced) inspector basically 'nailed' the conditions. In general, however, avoid handwritten reports.

#4 Does size (of the inspection company) matter? I used to feel that smaller inspection companies were always better than large companies. But much as I'd like to say this as a sole proprietor/future two-inspector company, many multi-inspector companies do a fine job. Multi-inspector companies may also bring more resources 'to the table' than a single person operation. Unfortunately, unless you get to choose the specific inspector who may have been recommended, you may end up with someone who many not give you the same level of service. Also, the small or sole proprietor companies very often will depend on the satisfaction of their clients for their referrals – whereas larger companies (out of necessity) are marketing driven for their business.

In my region, there is one very large company employing dozens of inspectors who each do 10–15 inspections a week. While they have some qualified inspectors, you never know who you will get or how much time they will spend doing the inspection. At least in the past, this company put time limits on how long their inspectors could spend at the inspection. When the home is complex or has a lot of problems – or you'd just like your inspector to spend time explaining everything – you may not get the inspection that you need.

#5 This goes along with the previous advice – but avoid ultra cheap prices. That said, the going rate for inspections tends to vary depending on where you are buying and the nature of the real estate market. Where the real estate prices are high, such as around metro Boston and metro New York, the inspection fees tend to be quite high. In many rural or less well-off areas, however, the inspection fees are much lower. I recently talked with an inspector from an economically depressed area in western Massachusetts, where the average fee for an inspection is $350 to $400. Around Boston and other metro areas, you could pay double that (but the homes are bigger and more complex). The risk of *extremely* low prices is that the inspection company has a business model whereby they do a lot of inspections to make up for their lower prices – and they may not take enough time to do the job right. In most areas, expect to pay anywhere from $450 to $675 for an inspection of a single-family home, depending on the area and local pricing. Larger homes or properties with additional buildings will have additional fees. Extra services, such as wood destroying insect inspections, radon testing, or water quality testing, would have their own fees. Inspections of homes with multiple heating or cooling systems, crawlspaces, or that are located a long distance from the inspector's home office may also cost more.

Unfortunately, cheap inspections can be very expensive. As just a couple of examples (out of dozens I could cite):

I did an inspection on an upscale contemporary home a few years back. It was a nice home and well built, in many respects, but it had huge stone entryways that were butted to the house without the benefit of flashing along this seam. Major structural damage was present on the framing behind these entryways. Repairs would require removal of the stonework and extensive carpentry repairs. Other serious problems were present. When these were disclosed to the listing agent, she questioned me, stating 'the seller had the home inspected just two years ago and none of this was found.' Believe me, these conditions were there to see. The repair costs, I estimated, would run well over $40,000 then and $60,000 now.

I used to find this type of stuff all the time – less so, now. The quality of the inspections is much higher than in the past. Even many of the lower cost, multi-inspector firms generally provide quality inspections. However, I also see homes where the inspectors were in such a rush that they simply did not take the time to inform the clients about the need for critical maintenance and what they should expect. In some cases, prompt attention and maintenance could have helped the homeowner avoid large repair costs in the future.

140

About climbing roofs and entering crawlspaces . . .

Roofs. Most home inspectors don't climb roofs. Almost all pitched roofs can be adequately viewed from the ground with binoculars or by using a camera (zooming in). Steeply-pitched roofs are unsafe to climb and most can be clearly viewed from the ground. Drones can help – but the actual percentage of roofs you need these on is very small. The operator also must be licensed by the FCC.

Crawlspaces. If the property you are looking to buy has crawlspaces, make sure the inspector is able to enter these areas and is willing to do so. Most inspectors can, but some inspectors may have physical limitations that prohibit this. I recently heard of an inspection where the inspector couldn't get into a crawlspace in an older home. This space ended up being termite riddled and a significant problem. Some crawlspaces, I should note, are not safely accessible and no inspector will enter crawlspaces with insect or rodent feces on the floor, damp floors, asbestos lying on the ground, fiberglass insulation hanging down, less than 18 inches clearance to the floor, etc. *Concealed crawlspaces, where no means of ready access or viewing was found, may have serious problems.* I recommend that you have your buyer's agent request, prior to the inspection, that the seller provide safe access to crawlspaces and attic areas. You could put this in your offer. Much of the time, however, your inspector will find that the crawlspaces are not 'readily accessible.' In this case, you may even want to request that the space be cleaned out so they can be entered – and then request a return visit by the inspector. As this will involve extra fees, you may want to verify that the crawlspace was cleared in the first place.

No inspector will enter crawl-spaces with insect or rodent feces on the floor, damp floors, asbestos lying on the ground, fiberglass insulation hanging down, less than 18 inches clearance to the floor, etc. Concealed crawlspaces, where no means of ready access or viewing was found, may have serious problems. I recommend that you have your buyer's agent request prior to the inspection that the seller provide safe access to crawlspaces and attic areas. You could put this in your offer.

Part B Pitfalls to avoid . . .

Pitfall #1 Skipping the inspection . . .

People skip inspections for a bunch of reasons. Sometimes they feel that the home is in such good condition that an inspection will not tell them much. While occasionally this is the case, every inspector sees homes that 'look' perfect but that turn out to have serious, previously unknown problems. Even when the home is in overall good condition, an inspection should provide you with objective, professional advice on home repairs and renovations. The home inspector is not there to 'sell you anything,' so the feedback you get – for instance, on installing gutters, siding the home, replacing windows, resurfacing the roof, repairing vs. replacing heating or cooling systems, etc. – is something that you may not get from a contractor or tradesperson who has an interest in doing the work.

This bears repeating: the home inspection is the one time you will have a construction professional provide you with advice and information that is intended *for your interest only.* The home inspector is not a contractor, window salesman, roofer, etc. who has a financial interest in what you choose to do. (This is why more homeowners should have a periodic inspection of their home to identify what problems are developing, what items need to be done soon versus what can be deferred, and where maintenance is needed. Few homeowners do this, however).

In a seller's market, people will skip the inspection, using this as a negotiating tool to get their offer accepted when there are multiple bids on the property. Competing offers will drive buyers to forgo the inspection. A seller loves it when you don't have an inspection, as they know you cannot withdraw your offer once it has been made. This can be an absolute disaster, as you may have no idea of what you are really getting. (I've covered this more in the chapter on Post Inspection Negotiations).

A third reason why people skip the inspection is that they feel they are well equipped to deal with any issues. Perhaps, in a few cases, they are, but wouldn't you like to know what you are dealing with?

Lastly, some buyers may not want to spend the money. If you can't afford a home inspection, you shouldn't be buying a home.

Pitfall #2 Getting a friend in construction, father-in-law, etc., to do the inspection . . .

While I support the idea of having friends or relatives who are knowledgeable about construction also look at the home and even attend the inspection, the input they provide is still not an inspection. Doing an inspection is a systematic process covering numerous systems and structures. You can get the most knowledgeable construction professional in the world, but they wouldn't know how to properly inspect a home unless they are trained how to do this. They also can't legally function as a home inspector and provide a report that you can negotiate from. That said, the more knowledgeable people you have looking out for your interests, the better. They may have valuable input on whether the home is too small, poorly designed, or is just not the right home for you. These are NOT specifically inspection concerns. Very often, young buyers bring out one or more of their parents. This is usually fine – and it's a good time for them to view the property – but limit your parent's involvement if you don't feel it will be helpful.

Pitfall #3 Doing the inspection after the contingency period has ended . . .

Earlier, I noted the importance of getting the inspection done within the inspection contingency period – and, ideally, early in the allotted time so that you can follow up with contractors or specialists should the inspection identify potentially serious concerns. Very occasionally, I've had buyers contact me to do an inspection after their contingency period has ended. Essentially, they've already 'bought the property.'

While this can be a valuable learning experience – and is better than not doing an inspection at all – you are without recourse on problems found by the inspection. I can think of at least one home I inspected after the buyers had let their inspection contingency period lapse. The home had been completely renovated from the first floor up and was quite attractive. Unfortunately, the house was held up a bunch of rotting pilings and would need a completely new support structure.

In the current seller's market (when this was written), buyers very often are forgoing the inspection to get their offer accepted. I do not recommend this – but if you have to go this route, at least have an inspection after you take possession so that you understand what the home requires for maintenance and upkeep – and to find out what you've just purchased!

Pitfall #4 Failing to follow up on the inspection findings with additional investigations.

This is important. The inspection covers dozens of systems, hundreds of components, thousands of square feet of surface area, and utilizes knowledge from dozens of trades and professions. Importantly, your inspector can't do the more in-depth technical evaluation that is sometimes needed. They can't dissemble heating systems, can't take apart walls or ceilings, and cannot provide cost estimates. They can, however, recommend further evaluations by certified professionals. See the list of trade and other professionals you could utilize in the next chapter.

Pitfall #5 Having UNREALISTIC EXPECTATIONS about what the inspection can accomplish . . .

A popular TV show, called 'Holmes on Homes,' features a professed home inspector (actually a contractor) who goes to properties where the homeowners have purchased the home in the last year or so and are having lots of problems. He finds deficient conditions that were not revealed by the home inspection and makes himself into a hero by 'rescuing' the poor homeowner. While the previous home inspector may, in some cases, have missed evidence of problems, more often than not no home inspector could ever find what he finds as he rips out walls and ceilings, digs up the yard, and utilizes specialized equipment to identify hidden problems. A real home inspector cannot do any type of destructive testing without paying for repairs to restore the surfaces to their original condition (or better). Nobody does this. But opening up ceilings, walls, or floors – what we term 'destructive testing' – may reveal larger damage and problems there was no evidence for at the inspection. Canadian home inspectors, I should note, hate this guy. (This show was filmed in Canada.)

The other problem is that the *evidence* of problems that are found on 'Holmes on Homes' usually shows up after the homeowner has lived at the property for a while. The drains stop draining after a few months, water stains show up where none had been. Anyone who has owned a home knows that certain types of problems are not revealed until you have lived in the home. Evidence of leakage from defective flashing, for instance, may show up only after a good hurricane or northeaster. A lot of conditions will show up during seasonal changes or due to the differing lifestyle of the new occupants. Lastly, previous owners or flippers can and do hide conditions by painting walls and covering items. Most people are honest – but certainly not all.

What the inspection covers – and why only these . . .

A partial list of the major components covered by the inspection includes:

roof surfaces, visible flashing	heating system	grading and drainage
chimneys	electrical system	bathroom fixtures
gutters, roof drainage	plumbing system (vis. portions)	kitchen fixtures
siding and trim, walls	basement water problems	kitchen appliances*
fascia, soffits, rakes	windows, doors	Interior walls, ceilings, floors
steps, stairs, stoops, landings	garage doors	garage door operators
central cooling	porches, decks	fireplaces (excluding flues)
wood stove installations attic, walls,	landscaping** foundation attic insulation and ventilation	visible structure: basement, retaining walls**

*This does not include refrigerators, compactors, or laundry equipment.
** As they affect the home

While this may seem to be a limited number, each of these may entail dozens of components or concerns, plus thousands of square feet of surface area. In general, the inspection covers the major components and systems that are subject to a visual, non-technically exhaustive inspection.

What the inspection <u>won't</u> do for you . . . and strategies to overcome these limitations.

Besides the exclusions and limitations noted in Chapter 13, I think it is important to note some of the things a home inspection will not help you with so that you can pursue these concerns further.

#1 The home inspection does not <u>remove</u> the risk of concealed damage . . .

Homes can have damage *within* walls, ceilings, or floors, where the evidence for this is missing, misleading, or inconclusive. Very often, the damage is due to water intrusion into the walls from the exterior. Damage may also be present from past or current termite infestations.

The damage is concealed on the exterior due to the siding and is concealed on the inside due to interior sheathings or insulation – or in other cases, just a lack of access to the spot showing the evidence. Concealed damage could be occurring now – or the damage could have occurred well in the past and was simply never visible. While the evidence of problems could have been hidden by the current homeowner, more often than not, I find that the current homeowner is oblivious to what is going on with their homes.

<u>Concealed damage can be present with little or no evidence of its presence.</u> A couple of examples . . .

I own an older (1860s) home with an east-facing clapboard sided wall. This wall gets a lot of wind-driven rain from northeasters (the type of storm we get in New England). About twenty years ago, I noticed decay on a window casing on that side. I went out one weekend to do the repairs, removing the storm window and pulling off the damaged trim. The problem was: as soon as I pulled off the trim, I found that the underlying board sheathing was extensively damaged. The further I went in pulling off the siding, the more damage I found. The cedar siding, however, looked perfect (as cedar siding does not readily decay). As there was a hurricane coming, I had to seal up the wall and wait until I could hire a carpenter to lay up scaffolding and assist me.

As it turns out, we ended up stripping off about fifty percent of the siding and replacing the sheathings and siding. This repair lasted for some time,

---

but years later, I had to have a builder strip the entire wall, re-flash it, and build the wall out using a 'rain screen' design, where the siding was set off the wall. This was the only way that I could keep water out. The wall always <u>looked</u> perfect, however.

Now, you may ask, how could this have not been visible? The problem is that most wood clapboard and shingle sidings are red cedar, and these materials just do not easily decay. But all of the material <u>behind</u> the siding decayed. Vinyl siding, similarly, will hide what is going on as the vinyl itself will always look perfect – even if the wall behind it is badly damaged. Damage due to past water penetrations is common and perhaps routinely present in antique homes, in homes that have been 'let go' for years, or homes where the flashing was improperly installed. <u>This can include new homes</u> – and probably a high percentage of homes built in the last 40 years.

Similarly, damage from termites is also something that may not be easily visible, especially when the basement walls or ceilings are finished, covered with insulation, or are otherwise not readily accessible. Slab-on-grade homes are particularly at risk, as the termites can come up into the walls completely unseen. Having a termite/wood destroying insect inspection done at the time of the inspection will reduce your risk of unknown infestations – but not from concealed damage.

Unfortunately, home inspectors, unless they have X-ray vision, can't see what is going on within the enclosed walls, ceilings, and floors. Very often, the visible evidence is misleading. Inspectors routinely see water stains on walls or ceilings or decay on exterior woodwork. Most of the time there will be little or no concealed damage – so you can't get alarmed about these unless you have evidence of further damage. But there are no absolutes on any of this. Your inspector can recommend further evaluation and invasive testing on everything – but you really have to 'pick and choose' when additional investigations are warranted.

A final note: unless you own the home, your home inspector can't move stored items, look below carpeting, move furniture, furnishings, or insulation. Stuff stays hidden.

What should you do when damage is suspected . . .

The best option, when there is evidence of *likely and significant* concealed damage, based on the visible evidence, is to request that the walls or ceilings be opened up for further evaluation. I've advised this on a couple of occasions where there was a high risk of concealed damage – but I have to tell you, doing this is usually not feasible. Opening up a wall to look at what is inside itself causes damage. On the rare occasion that a homeowner does allow this, they will normally stipulate that the removed interior sheathing (usually drywall or plaster) or exterior siding be put back in its original condition. Neither you nor your home inspector will want to bear this expense. The times when home-owners will allow this are when there is strong evidence of serious damage and neither you (nor any buyer) is likely to purchase the home without resolving the extent of the problem.

When is it most likely that you will have interior sheathings or exterior siding removed? Probably with termite activity, as you can't see how far the damage is without removing the siding or interior drywall/plaster/paneling. Evidence of sig-nificant termite damage could be such a concern that the seller may not have a choice about allowing further invasive (and possibly 'destructive') testing if they want to sell the home. Sometimes these investigations will be fruitful, sometimes not. I had one home where I found termites on a piece of wood right next to the foundation; this was an area with a lot of termite activity. I recommended that the paneling in the basement be removed, as there was a high likelihood of finding termite activity on the enclosed framing. As it turns out, there were no termites inside the home, but the opening of the wall satisfied my client and the sale could then proceed. He would not buy the home, however, with the potential for concealed termite activity present.

> *When you have evidence of likely concealed damage (which doesn't mean just a water stain on the ceiling or wall), where it is likely that this is a 'significant' condition, you may need to have a carpenter/contractor determine the extent of the damage. If this can't be done, then you need to either accept the risk – or walk away from the deal.*

I should also note that, with antique homes or cottage type structures, walls that are not straight (or plumb) may indicate damage to the concealed framing. The homes _were not_ built with those conditions. Framing and structural repairs may have been done – but you really can't verify this until the walls are opened up. Homes with dips and sags in the walls are a 'red flag' for concealed damage. Caveat emptor (buyer beware).

#2 Home inspectors lack the power of enforceability . . .

I sometimes tell my clients that I can recommend that something be repaired, but no one grants us any powers of enforceability. A municipal code official can *require* repairs on new work that is not code compliant. They can also require a tear out of existing work where no permit was pulled for the work. This may be done in a few states or municipalities but is rarely done in most. Municipal code officials are most likely to condemn existing work if it represents a gross safety hazard or when an addition didn't follow the zoning requirements for setbacks or permits. An FHA or VA inspector can require specific repairs, as they hold the power of not approving the mortgage. Unfortunately, they provide only a limited inspection. In any case, your inspector can recommend repairs or call something grossly deficient or unsafe – but they can't <u>make</u> anyone do anything. (That's up to you). In terms of work done by the homeowner, you need to do 'due diligence' and check for permits on major repairs and renovations. Work done without permits should raise red flags.

#3 Seasonal limitations are important . . .

Seasonal limitations present problems. First, many homebuyers purchase a home in the spring or summer, when the landscaping is lush and beautiful. What gets overlooked are the issues relating to ice and snow. For instance, is the driveway negotiable during icy conditions? Is the home hard to heat? Do the windows show excessive air infiltration?

Conversely, when inspecting during the colder months (which may begin early in the fall in some areas), the central air conditioning system cannot be tested. Ice and snow make it difficult to view the roof surfaces, decks, walkways, and lot grading. Decayed wood will be hard as a rock during freezing conditions. Inspecting the septic system is difficult. A failed system could be present beneath the deep snow (see more on septic inspections in Chapter 17). Bee activity won't be visible when it is cold <u>or</u> raining.

In Southern states, the unrecognized seasonal concerns would be: first, just how 'leaky' and poorly insulated many of these homes are – and how exposed the piping is to 'freeze ups' during those 'rare' periods of extreme cold.

Another problem, covered in Chapter 13, is that certain types of deficiencies in the heating and cooling systems may only show up during maximum output conditions. Comfort levels during weather extremes similarly can't be ascertained by the home inspection. This is important! If the home is new or is newly renovated, can the new, minimally sized heating system really heat the home?

#4 Home inspectors look for functionality and safety. The home inspection is evaluating the structural, functional, and mechanical condition of the home – and not what you may expect or desire in terms of its appearance, age, or potential for upgrading. Your home inspector will not make value judgments, for instance, on a dated kitchen. I've had clients who have said they had no problem with a decrepit kitchen that most people would rip out immediately. Everyone has their own standards and their own time frame for renovations. Not everything gets done tomorrow (although most younger buyers do not accept this!).

The home inspection is an evaluation of the structural, mechanical, electrical, and 'functional' condition of the property, nothing more. (Well, a bit more to qualify that: a good inspector should also give you an overview of some of the risks, as well as the maintenance concerns, that come with the home and what you can do to make it more livable and energy efficient).

#5 The home inspector cannot predict the future nor find every problem. This may be obvious, but the unfortunate fact is that a small percentage of home-buyers will have the misfortune of having to unexpectedly spend a lot of money on repairs within a few months of moving in. This happens. It happened to me with my first house (long ago). The inspection is not a warranty or guarantee, as the inspection contracts like to say. Home inspections should be regarded as a 'value added' service where, for a limited amount of money, the inspector looks at dozens of systems, hundreds of components, and tens of thousands of square feet of surface area, under many restrictions and limitations, for a brief amount of time, with weather, access, and viewing limitations. Home inspections were not designed to remove the risk of buying and owning a home. Some trades-people love to 'throw the inspectors under the bus,' stating they should have found this and found that. Occasionally, they are right. More often, the problem simply couldn't be determined from the evidence visible at the inspection.

#6 The home inspection will not provide costs for repair or replacements. The states I work in, Massachusetts and New Hampshire, do not allow home inspec-tors to quote costs, with the potential for fines or license suspension if they do so. Even in states where an inspector can – and is willing – to provide 'cost to repair' estimates, you shouldn't completely rely on these, in my opinion, unless they are the contractor who is bidding the job (and if they are bidding the job, they are not a home inspector).

That said, sometimes you will want to get at least a ballpark estimate from your inspector. I sometimes find that what my client thinks is a $5000 problem is really a $400 problem – and vice versa – so I at least need get them on the right page. Some types of costs are very easy to estimate, such as the cost to replace an electrical panel. Most of the time, you would like to get estimates from contrac-tors on conditions that carry significant repair costs. The problem – and this is important – is that you usually can't get contractors in to look at the home in the short period left after the inspection has been done. You may have just a few days to do this. When you know or suspect that the home will need serious repairs or updating, you should try line up the appropriate contractor to look at the home *at the time of the home inspection – or before, when possible.* At least (try) to do this within your contingency period. Very often, when the inspection reveals a lot of problems, a lump sum reduction is thrown at the buyer. This may or may not be adequate to take care of the problems, but sometimes it is the best you can do.

I should note that another reason your home inspector won't provide cost data is the fact that estimated costs will vary widely: for the same work, we sometimes see estimates vary by a factor of three. While this may be due to the quality of the work, it can also reflect the contractor's work schedule, how good a salesperson they are, and whether they are free or booked up for the next six months. Lastly, for reconstruction estimates, finding concealed damage or additional problems after the work has started will push up the costs greatly. Just watch the HGTV renovation shows. They always find conditions needing expensive, unanticipated repairs after the project has begun.

This is called the 'mushroom factor,' meaning that every repair or alteration very often leads to more items needing correction or replacement. (This is more the case, however, for older than newer homes). As an example, I had a client who relayed to me (laughing about it, no less) how he spent several thousand dollars in repairs when he went to replace an old toilet. Nothing matched, so he ended up redoing the whole waste plumbing system.

Another problem with costs is that you have a range of options for dealing with a potential problem – say, for instance, an aged heating or cooling system. You could be looking at a complete replacement of the unit, 'repairs or replacement' of non-working or problematic components, or simply a servicing and 'watch and wait' until the system fails. Whichever is appropriate may depend in some cases on your budget and your risk tolerance – and the feedback from your serviceperson or contractor.

A final problem with a home inspector offering cost estimates is that they must be provided in such a broad range that they may not be useful in negotiations. My telling a client that the roof surfaces will need replacement at $9,000 to $12,000 is a lot less useful in negotiations than a roofer's estimates of, say, $10,400.

More advice on repair costs . . .

For items needing urgent repairs, such as a leaking pipe where more damage will occur if this is not fixed now, you may want to simply request the seller have the item repaired. If the heating system shows a lack of a servicing history, it is often possible to ask the seller to have the system serviced. This advice is most pertinent to heating, cooling, and mechanical systems that have not been serviced in the last year or so or that show evidence of problems. In many cases, the problems we find with mechanical systems can be resolved without large repair costs. They just need servicing or component replacements. In 'short' or 'as is' sales, the owner will not do anything.

Important: When the home you are buying has older systems, you may want to not only have repairs or servicing done from a relevant contractor/tradesperson, but you may want to get an idea of what it will cost if the system fails. This can pertain to non-inspection components as well. I once had a client walk away from a property as they found that the septic system, while working at that time, would cost an immense amount of money to replace IF (and when) it failed.

Lastly, if most of the principal systems on the home are old and worn, you better plan on setting aside money to pay for unscheduled repairs and replacements (and this doesn't include 'renovation' costs, such a new bathroom and kitchen).

Setting aside a certain amount of money for emergencies is always a good idea. Some authorities recommend having enough cash or liquid assets to cover your expenses for six months. Good luck with that! Unless you have some type of financial backstop (family money, investments, etc.), however, I would recommend leaving some money off the table when buying a home instead of making a larger down payment. You may need the money for emergencies – or for renovations and basic improvements after you move in.

#7 The home inspection is not a guide to doing a historic restoration. This entails a whole different set of considerations. The 'old house' magazines are filled with these types of properties – and these usually end up as wonderful homes. But, unless you are a skilled craftsperson with a lot of time and expertise to finish the needed work, you will need money to get to the 'end line.' These projects may be doable on less money if you can stretch out the project over a number of years and can live in 'less than optimal' living conditions while the work is being done. While these homes need a good home inspection, the inspection can't be used to determine the scope of the work. You may need a team of talented craftsmen, contractors with expertise in antique homes, and an architect to determine the extent of the work needed.

#8 The home inspection does not determine <u>who</u> does the needed repairs, servicing, or other work.

This is important. The home inspection may indicate that 'a system or component' is worn out or not working – or maybe just old or substandard. What the home inspector does not do – and cannot do legally – is say who is responsible for what. Your inspector should put things in neutral terms, neither assigning needed work to the home seller nor to you, the buyer. That said, there are many conditions that typically 'go with the home' and would be the buyer's responsibility, while other conditions (in a normal market!) would very often fall on the seller to either correct or make allowances on. There are no absolutes, as every buyer (and seller) are different, each situation is different, and everyone has their own feeling about what is 'acceptable' and what isn't. See the next chapter on Post Inspection Negotiations for more advice.

The fact that the home inspector is putting things in neutral terms is confusing for many buyers. The point is: you need to determine what is 'acceptable' to you

AND what is 'doable' in negotiations. You should discuss with your buyer's agent whether some defect or deficiency is something that you can get an allowance on from the seller. Buyers occasionally ask me: who is responsible for repairing defective or less than optimal conditions? This can vary, interestingly, between different states and regions, but in most areas there is **no requirement that a homeowner fix anything**. That doesn't mean you have to accept everything. The 'smaller' stuff, unless it is grossly unsafe, goes with the house. While the inspector may provide you with a lot of valuable information, it is up to you to decide how to use it. (Note: I've been told that, in some states, particularly New Jersey and New York, it is customary to have deficient conditions corrected prior to the sale. Talk to your buyer's agent and/or attorney about local practices).

With new construction, high-end homes, and condominiums, buyers often hold the home's condition to a much higher standard. Caulking the bathtub, a maintenance item on older or less expensive homes, is something some new construction buyers don't feel they should have to do. In my opinion, it should be up to the seller to ensure the basic systems are functional. You don't want to move in and then have to call a plumber to get the sink faucet or dishwasher working. In general, items needing *urgent repairs* or that will cause possible damage if not fixed now will be the items most often put back on the seller to remedy. Most listing agents will not have a problem with this. (See cautions on this in the next chapter).

#9 The home inspector cannot legally advise you to buy or not buy the home.

This is against most state regulations and your inspector could even lose their license if they explicitly advise this. We can say the home has 25 major defects, needs a new foundation, is mold infested, may need to be bulldozed, etc. Occasionally, I simply reiterate to my client that it is against state law for me to advise walking away – and hopefully they get the point.

While we aren't supposed to advise purchase either, I think every inspector has times when we have to reassure buyers who are excessively concerned about some condition that really doesn't warrant that much concern.

#10 Home inspectors will not determine the 'adequacy' of repairs.

Inspectors will not go back to a home to evaluate whether some repair done by a homeowner or their contractor was done 'properly.' Even recent repairs that appear have been done in a workmanlike manner fall into this category. Maybe a now-concealed flashing repair to correct a leak was done properly. Maybe – but you really can't tell this unless you saw the work being done or can verify what the contractor did – and then see if the repair lasts as long as it should.

#11 Your home inspector does not (normally) do the 'walk through' inspection done just prior to the closing.

The walk-through inspection is done just prior to the closing. It consists of walking through the property with your buyer's agent to ensure there are no changes that would warrant delaying the closing – or require final adjustments on the price. A few important items would be:

1. Is the heating system operable? Does it show any signs of failure (such as leaking from a boiler?).
2. Does the central air conditioning come on and produce cooled air? (Only test if the temperature has been above 60 degrees for the last 24 hours AND the power to the unit has been on for the last 24 hours). Do not turn on the power (energize the breaker) and then test the AC – you may ruin the condenser unit. Also, you need to use a laser thermometer to tell if the air is cooling. When the system's fan is running the moving air will feel cool – but it may not be cooling at all.
3. Is the water heater still working and does it show signs of failure? Water heaters do not last forever. Most of the time you know the system is failing when you see leakage under the unit or along the inlet fittings at the top. It is not unheard of for a water heater to fail between the time of the home inspection and the closing!
4. Is there any evidence of burst pipes due to freeze-ups? If the home is cold and has been minimally heated (or not heated at all) will the pipes leak when thawed? If you do not own the home yet, don't turn up the thermostat to thaw the pipes.
5. Did the owner take things they were supposed to leave? Most often this would be appliances, light fixtures, or other things of value.
6. Did the previous owner not take the things they were supposed to have taken? Is the property still full of personal goods, debris, and unwanted materials? This is a common problem. If you will need to get a dumpster and pay someone to remove the items from the premises, this will cost you. In the more egregious situations, your closing attorney may need to get monies set aside to cover the cost of having unwanted items removed.
7. Is there evidence of damage that was not visible at the time of the home inspection? Examples would be: damage due to severe weather conditions. I've seen roofs with blown off shingles from hurricane-level winds where the roofs were otherwise fine (but aging) two months earlier. Another example would be damage that was concealed by the current owner but that is now visible, once their furniture and furnishings are removed. A good example was a story I heard in the 80s about a sale where the owner's kids set up a large puzzle in the middle of the living room that everyone had to step around. At the walk-through inspection it was revealed that the puzzle was hiding a large hole in the floor!

8. Related to the above: did the owner trash the place on their way out? This is a common problem with foreclosures, divorce sales, or embittered tenants. Always assume that some negative 'stuff' will be found; make a list for your attorney when you have significant damage or debris present.
9. Test the plumbing. I know of a case where the owner's kids flushed objects into the waste disposal system; this caused the wastewater to back up for the new owner. (They must have done this on their way out the door). Run the water for a while, flush the toilets; go into the basement and make sure nothing is amiss.

IMPORTANT: Do the walk-through inspection as close to the closing time as possible. I had a client who related that, when he purchased his last home in the Midwest, he did the walk-through inspection the night before. When he got to the house the next day, after the closing, he found that the owner had ripped out the nice kitchen cabinets that morning. Obviously, this is an extreme example, but still . . .

Note: you could have your inspector do the walk-through inspection. You will have to pay for this, however, so figure out if you really need their services. Most of the time, you will simply do this inspection with your buyer's broker – or the listing agent when you don't have a buyer's agent.

#12 Your inspector is not doing a 'quality of component' inspection.

It is difficult to tell the quality of a faucet, for instance, unless one is plumber or remodeler. A lot of cheap faucets work fine – just not as long. Similarly, kitchen cabinets come in a wide array of types, materials, and styles. It is not the home inspector's function to criticize these based on appearance, design, or age, although the inspection may note damaged or non- functional items. This has the most relevance for new construction. If you are buying new construction and want this type of information, you may want to hire a qualified remodeler who has no self-interest in the sale and no 'axe to grind.'

#13 The inspection doesn't cover many of the important systems, components, and concerns that can be a source of problems or expense.

See Chapter 13, 'What Slips through the Cracks' for what to do on these.

#14 Lastly, inspectors are not perfect. Every inspector occasionally misses some-thing. There is so much to look at. Every inspector I know will admit that, when they inspect the same house for a different buyer (after the first buyer didn't proceed with the sale), they will find something else. You should expect a high level of effort – but don't expect perfection.

Why your inspection report can lead you 'dazed and confused' . . .

#1 If you did not attend the inspection, it may be difficult to tell from the report which are the critical items and which aren't. *When you can't be there, try to have a surrogate attend the inspection. Having a post-inspection consultation with your inspector by phone later that day will also help you put the findings in perspective.* Have your inspector verbally 'walk you through' the inspection. The inspection report may be invaluable – but getting the verbal walk-through is just as important.

#2 *Some reports have too much information.* You have to wade through extensive disclosures and background information to find the 'meat' of the inspection. In this case, I recommend that you use a highlighter to emphasize what are the most important issues from the inspection. These could be the items that you think may be subject to negotiation, large cost items, or just items that need urgent attention. The problem is that all deficient conditions are recommended for repair, even though some are less important than others and some repairs could be optional or deferrable.

#3 **READ THE REPORT!!** All too many buyers simply don't read their reports. You may have to wade through a lot of material, but you really need to read the report carefully. Call the inspector about anything that you don't understand or have questions on. Ignore the CYA (cover your ***) comments; they are an unfortunate necessity in today's world.

#4 For any item even remotely related to safety, the inspection report does not tell you the _degree_ of risk for each item. This means that many electrical and stair concerns may be noted as needing 'urgent' or 'immediate' repairs. No assessment of actual risk is – or can be – provided. As an example, a well-built three-step staircase that 'should' (by current codes) have fully compliant hand and guard rails, cannot be given a 'free pass' given the minimal risk of someone tripping or falling. The report will describe these in the same language as a deteriorated, unsafe-for-use staircase that may also be present. The report gives everything the same level of concern, with a recommendation for repairs. You need to figure out what is *grossly* unsafe versus when repairs are not critical or can be deferred. Nothing is given a free pass.

A brief note on inspection contracts . . .

All home inspection companies will provide you with a contract to sign. This is a necessity, given that a few buyers will assume that the home inspector will #1 be looking at all of the components on the property, #2 can see through walls, #3 has no limitations on what they can do and see, #4 will provide a warranty on every system, #5 can tell you how long things will last, #6 will remove the risk of systems failing prematurely, #7 will predict when severe weather events may occur that will impact the home, and so on. (Sorry. This is a bad attempt at humor.) In any case, home inspectors have an absolute need to define what they are doing and the limitations they typically face when doing an inspection (especially given the number of systems and areas they cover in a short time frame). The insurance companies providing Errors and Omissions coverage for home inspectors require a signed contract to enable coverage, so it is to your advantage to sign this, should it be needed. The insurance companies may also specify the contract that will be used and require the inspector to include clauses that limit their liability to the cost of the inspection *if allowed in that state*. (Note: a limitation of liability clause may be prohibited in some states. Massachusetts does not allow an inspector to limit his liability to the cost of the inspection – but other states do allow this.)

CHAPTER 11
Overcoming the Limitations of the Home Inspection . . .

What this chapter covers . . .

- Other professionals you may need to utilize – and when. . .
- Understanding what VA and FHA inspections do. . .

I have noted below the trade professionals and specialists whose expertise you could utilize when purchasing a home. I realize this can get a bit overwhelming, as you may simply ask, 'Why have a home inspection, if I will need to bring in various specialists to evaluate specific areas of concern?' The unfortunate reality is: the home inspection covers so many systems, areas, and concerns that it can't <u>always</u> tell you everything you would like to know. Certain types of problems can't be identified or fully evaluated without specialized equipment or knowledge. There are also important home components (such as chimney flues) that simply <u>are not</u> part of the home inspection. Just realize that your home inspector is providing an overview of dozens of systems and components, while each trade professional is only looking at their own area of expertise.

Recommendations for further inspection can be abused, however, such as when an inspector routinely recommends a further evaluation of every system present. This is a cop-out. But as the home inspector sometimes can't tell you the extent of damage that may be present and the costs of repairs, there will generally be recommendations for 'further evaluation' in the report.

In any case, below are a few of the trade and specialized professionals whose expertise may be relevant to evaluating the condition of the property. I'll try to indicate when their expertise is most critical. Most often, they will <u>NOT</u> be needed – but you want to be aware of when their input may be critical.

Important: When you have strong suspicions that some major system or structure on the property you are looking to buy may be a problem, try to have one or more of the relevant trade professionals come to the inspection. Even bring them before the inspection, as arranging their visit in the short time frame after the inspection is not always feasible.

Other professionals whose services you may need . . .

Chimney sweeps

A further evaluation of the interior of chimneys by a qualified chimney sweep is routinely recommended by home inspectors. In fact, they may be the trade professional most often recommended. The reason is that, while your home inspector can see the exterior of the chimney and the masonry in the fireplace, they can't see much else. Most chimney flues are concealed from view, due to their design, obstructions, or soot coatings. For this reason, *chimney flues are formally excluded from a home inspection*. Many chimneys have flues you can't view. Flues for heating systems, wood stoves, and water heaters are completely concealed. Even where you can view the flue, a soot covering can hide evidence of cracks. Your inspector may look – as sometimes problems are apparent – but do not confuse this with a full chimney inspection; it is a best effort.

Chimney flues are formally excluded from the home inspection. Lots of chimneys have flues you can't look up. Flues for heating systems, wood stoves, and water heaters are completely concealed. Even where you can view the flue, a soot covering can hide evidence of cracks.

Unfortunately, chimney flues are where a lot of problems are found – and the fixes are seldom cheap. Those most at risk include:

1. Chimneys in antique homes. Unless fully retrofitted with flue liners, the fireplaces in antique homes are very often not safely usable. (Note: listing sheets for antique homes often state that the fireplaces are 'usable.' That does not mean 'safely usable.' Two different things). I've seen fires burning in a fireplace where I couldn't figure why the house hadn't burned down yet.

2. Masonry chimneys serving wood stoves, unless retrofitted with a stainless steel metal liner.

3. Block chimneys. Many were installed in the early 1980s and are just worn out.

4. 'Orphaned' chimneys that serve a gas-fired water heater only, with the heating system now direct vented. These should have been retrofitted with an internal liner, as the flue is too large to vent just a water heater.

5. All unlined chimneys – which means most chimneys installed before 1920.

6. Chimneys with terra cotta tile liners – which means most of the chimneys installed over the last 60 years.

In short, chimneys warrant a further evaluation by a chimney sweep. Even the wood box chimneys with metal flues inside pose fire risks. Most inspectors recommend a Level 2 inspection, which involves using a camera to view the entire interior of the chimney. These can get expensive, but chimney repairs are even more expensive. In one relatively newer home I inspected last year, a chimney scan revealed internal problems with the chimney that would cost $20,000 to correct. The flue liners were cracked and needed to be completely replaced.

If the home you are buying has a wood-burning fireplace or chimney, include in your offer that you will have a chimney evaluated. (You should do this for any type of chimney, but those used for wood burning would be at higher risk). For a list of qualified sweeps, contact the Chimney Safety Institute of America (CSIA) at http://www.csia.org/. See more on chimney flues in chapter 13.

Structural Engineers

Structural engineers may be needed for properties with serious foundation or framing deficiencies. Not every structural problem requires a structural engineer. Sometimes, the conditions and the scope and cost of repairs are apparent. Homes with serious or multiple structural issues, known or just suspected, however, should be evaluated by a structural engineer. When engaging a structural engineer, choose someone who specializes in evaluating residential buildings. A good structural engineer can design a proper support system for the home and many will be able to provide cost estimates – which your home inspector cannot do.

Why not just hire a contractor to fix the problem? For many types of framing problems, you can. But sometimes you need to have a qualified structural expert to design the solution – or perhaps to tell you the risks are not worth the effort. As with the home inspector, you are paying them for their information and not for the repairs themselves, so they should have no interest in whether you buy the home. A caution, however: not all structural engineers work at the same level. Some are more used to designing bridges or buildings than dealing with residential structures. I once inspected a home that was sinking, where the engineer's report totally misread the situation. Many inspectors have the names of structural engineers they trust and recommend.

Civil engineers

These would be needed if the home has serious drainage and grading issues that need a designed solution, with cost estimates. A possible example would be waterfront homes that need a designed solution due to flooding concerns. A hillside home that is experiencing drainage problems would be another candidate.

Geotechnical engineers

Most of you won't need to utilize a geotechnical engineer when buying a home. They are more commonly utilized in new construction – and especially for commercial buildings. If the home you are looking at shows evidence of serious foundation issues, you will want to hire a qualified structural engineer or foundation contractor to evaluate the problem. When designing a solution, they may bring in a geotechnical engineer to assess the bearing capacity of the soils under the home.

Geotechnical engineers may also be needed in earthquake-prone regions to determine how well a given home will hold up during a severe quake. The expertise of a geotechnical engineer is often required in areas of the country with expansive soils. Many areas of the upper Plains and southwest have soils that contain Bentonite, a type of clay. This can cause all kinds of problems if the foundation was not properly designed. If you are buying newer construction in Texas or in many western states, be aware of this as a potential problem. Do your research on the development and the type of foundation that will be installed. If you have unanswered questions, hire a geotechnical engineer.

As a specific caution, try to avoid buying a home that was built on filled land – especially if that region is prone to earthquakes. Much of Boston was built on filled land and, with ongoing work to the support structures, the buildings have remained viable. Fortunately, there is not a history of frequent severe earthquakes in this region. You don't want to have a home that was built on 'filled' land (as when a developer filled in a marsh or bay to create more buildable land) when the area has a high risk of earthquakes. In an earthquake, the soil turns to mush and has no bearing capacity. The home (and perhaps you) won't survive.

While determining soil problems is beyond the scope of an inspection, your home inspector will normally look for the evidence of problems that would be caused by soil or drainage deficiencies. Hairline cracks in foundations, I should note, are commonly found and rarely indicate the likelihood of serious soil or foundation issues – at least in New England, where the soils tend to be fairly stable. (That's "tend to be"). That said, *the newer the construction and the newer the crack, the less assurance your inspector can provide*. The small hairline cracks that very often run from window openings to the floor are routinely found and are seldom a problem if they have been there for a while – and are not getting larger. The cracks to be concerned about are those with differential movement vertically, laterally, or horizontally – or any crack that is showing evidence of ongoing settlement, movement, or distress. If serious problems are suspected, you may want to engage a structural engineer and possibly a foundation specialist to assess the conditions more fully. Many problems are subject to engineering solutions (which are often expensive, however).

Masons and Foundation Specialists

Masons should be brought in to assess problems with chimneys, brick stairs, and stone or brick foundations. In my opinion, chimney sweeps can better evaluate the interior of the chimney – but they can't provide the cost of rebuilding a dete-riorated chimney. A foundation contractor would be invaluable for homes with failing, problematic, or just grossly substandard foundations. If the inspector recommends a further evaluation, get this done. Masonry repairs are expensive.

Heating/Ventilation/Air Conditioning (HVAC) contractors for cooling and forced hot air systems

Home inspectors inspect heating and air conditioning systems but it is a limited evaluation – even when the systems can be operated. Most central air condi-tioning systems cannot be run when the temperatures have been below sixty degrees in the last 24 hours, so they are not subject to testing for most of the year in northerly climates. HVAC technicians can go beyond a basic evaluation and can measure efficiency, identify component deficiencies, and determine if the system is showing signs of imminent failure. Old systems that appear to be at the end of their design life or were not working at the inspection, or systems that have not been serviced in the last couple of years, are good candidates for a further evaluation. You may also bring an HVAC contractor if you would like to install central air conditioning in your home and need to look at the options and costs.

Plumbers

Bringing out a plumber will be most valuable when the home has old plumbing, especially older cast iron pipes that are showing signs of significant corrosion. Homes with unconventional or clearly amateur plumbing may warrant further evaluation. A plumber's advice is critical if you are going to be adding a bathroom or will be doing renovations that involve plumbing. Plumbing work is expensive.

Heating/plumbing contractor

Forced hot water and steam systems are installed and repaired by plumbing/ heating contractors. Not all plumbers install and service heating systems. Oil service technicians take care of the oil system components. Steam systems may require an experienced plumber as they require a specialized knowledge to evaluate properly. The newer high-efficiency gas systems require specialized knowledge. Very often the company that installed the system will be needed to service it.

Oil service technicians

The oil burner plus the operating and safety controls on an oil-fired system may need to be evaluated by an oil service technician if the system is malfunctioning or has not been serviced in the last two years. Usually, however, this is something you do after you move in. You could ask that the system be cleaned, serviced, and evaluated if this has not been done in the last couple of years. This is often regarded as a reasonable request by listing agents and is often a 'doable' item in negotiations.

Oil-fired systems need an annual cleaning and tuning by an oil serviceperson. They should also check the condition of oil tanks (but I find this often gets over-looked). See more on Oil tanks in Chapter 12, *What Falls Through the Cracks*.

Electricians

Bring out an electrician for cost estimates when the electrical system will need a major upgrading, such as adding numerous circuits, the removal of knob and tube wiring, redoing homeowner work. Upgrading panels is often desirable – but the costs tend to be fairly consistent so you may not need an on-site visit for a quote. Your home inspector will be looking at these issues – they just can't provide cost estimates. Unless you have a new home, almost every property will 'need' electrical repairs and safety upgrades, so you should plan on having an electrician do this after you move in. Most electrical panels over 25 years old are now regarded as obsolete and will benefit from replacement. Plan to bring an electrician in beforehand if you've got an antiquated system or serious concerns; otherwise, do this when you move in. See more on electrical defects in Chapter 12, *What Falls Through the Cracks*.

Excavation and sewer contractors

While this is seldom has been done in my area unless there was evidence of problems (such as drains backing up), a sewer scan is increasingly being done in many areas of the country. The inspection limitation is the fact that backups from clogged or damaged underground sewer lines very often don't show up until you have lived in the home for a while. Not uncommonly, however, sewer drain pipes are cracked or partially clogged – or were just improperly installed. Sewer scans are desirable for older homes (which, in this case, means any home over 30 years old), given the higher potential for cracked or clogged pipes. Definitely do this if the current owner discloses that they have the sewer line reamed out every couple of years as tree roots are getting in. A failing drain pipe will be costly to correct.

Septic system evaluators

See Chapter 16, *Evaluating Private Waste Disposal Systems*, for more information on evaluating these systems. This subject deserves its own chapter.

Building contractors or carpenters

Bringing out a building contractor will be useful when the home shows the need for repairs to siding, trim, framing, wood stairs, porches, decks, windows, etc. if the damage or deficiencies appear to be substantial. See the previous comments on 'concealed damage.' You may also simply want to know what it will cost to put on a new deck, renovate the home, add on, finish the basement, or do other improvements. Expect to see damaged and decayed trim, as this is routinely found on homes built in the last 50 or so years.

Contractors who specialize in repairing older homes . . .

Carpenters or contractors who specialize in older or antique structures can be very valuable when buying an older home. Contractors who specialize in new construction may not know the options for dealing with the framing in older homes.

Siding and window contractors

Homes with siding that is worn, in need of substantial repairs, or that is clearly near the end of its useful life may be good candidates for residing. Damaged or aged vinyl siding or improperly installed claddings may warrant a further evaluation to assess the time frame and costs for replacement. If you plan on replacing the siding or windows, I recommend that you do your research on the various options before getting estimates from contractors. Vinyl siding can work great on some homes – and is totally inappropriate for others. There are lots of options for new siding. Don't replace existing windows just because they are older – assuming they are attractive and are not worn out. IF the windows are intact, are reasonably tight-fitting, and don't need new storm units, you will save little on your heating costs by replacing them.

Remodelers/Kitchen designers

These would more valuable after moving in – but knowing that you can improve the home in the manner you want can be invaluable. Redesigning a kitchen in your head is fun. Finding out that none of your plans is affordable or practical is not. Due diligence is paramount when you have immediate plans for renovations. Choosing a substandard home with plans to make it your 'perfect' home is risky without verifying that 'perfect' is possible.

Painting contractors

Usually, the paint problems will be apparent to you and the home inspector. Painting a large home, however, can be very pricey, so you may want to get an estimate. You may need to price in siding/trim repairs or replacement if these are needed. Painting costs are considered deferrable and would not typically be subject to renegotiation – with the following exception. If you are getting an FHA or VA mortgage their inspection will flag any peeling paint. (I think a lot of concern is with lead paint – but they flag all peeling paint as an issue). In any case, whether the seller does it – or someone does it – any peeling paint may need to be removed from the exterior (and interior) <u>prior to the sale</u>.

Lead paint testing technicians

You can do lead paint testing during the home inspection period. The safe assumption, however, is that lead paint could be present on any homes built before 1979 – or even newer homes where older architectural woodwork is present. As a practical matter, most homes built in the 1970s will have little if any lead paint. Homes built in the 1960s commonly have lead paint on the exterior trim, less so on the interior. Note: as the assumption is that lead paint will be present on pre-1979 homes, the presence of lead paint is seldom a negotiable issue. You may want to know what you are dealing with, however, and if you plan on renting the home, then you want to know if lead paint is present and what it will cost to make the home compliant with lead paint regulations. This often means new windows, new woodwork, and no peeling paint on the interior or exterior.

Home Energy Raters

This is something relatively new and may not be available in your area, but in some states you can get an energy rating done on the home you are buying. (This may have been done by the seller prior to putting the home on the market.) This may be a required evaluation in the next couple of years. While the current energy rating of the home could have value, what you really want to know is the *potential* to make the home more energy efficient. This may be more important than knowing the home's current energy profile. You can do a lot with some homes; others, not so much.

Energy auditors

Having an energy audit to determine what measures will be cost effective to implement is highly desirable and recommended. You will normally do this, however, after you have moved in. Important: Do not have insulation installed or undertake other energy improvements until you have had the audit, as there may be programs that will subsidize this work. In some states, these are available to every homeowner. To take advantage of these programs, however, you will need to have the audit.

Environmental hazards – see Chapter 13.

Mold Testing – see Chapter 14.

Asbestos abatement contractors

If asbestos is found or suspected, an asbestos abatement contractor could provide the estimates for its removal. See more in chapter 13.

Architects

Bringing in an architect is a great idea if you are looking for ideas to transform a poorly designed or limited home into what you want. Not enough people do this. You may find that, with some alterations, a home with layout or design problems can be altered to work for you – or not.

Landscape contractors

A landscape contractor may be needed to assess the cost of rebuilding retaining walls (which could also require a stonemason), installing or rebuilding walkways, tree removal (although this is not, strictly speaking, their specialty), or dealing with other vegetation problems. These items can be expensive.

Paving contractors

The condition of the driveway should be obvious. This tends to be a discretionary and deferrable item. That said, re-paving a driveway can be expensive. Get further input in extreme situations, such as where the long, winding driveway going up a hill is washing out. You also may want to be aware of future risks and costs – or just what it will cost to pave or re-pave the driveway.

Arborists

Usually, bringing in an arborist will wait until you are in the home – but not always. If you have questions about the viability of one or more trees, an arborist is the person to utilize. Dead, unhealthy, or high-risk trees that fall on your home OR onto neighboring homes (or their cars, fences, kids) may need to be removed – in some cases, immediately. This can be expensive. (My sister spent $9000 having a large willow tree entangled in power lines removed. This was obviously an extreme case . . . but still).

Pool specialists . . .

Most home inspectors <u>do not</u> inspect pools. Above-ground pools are seldom inspected. One concern with all pools is safety: are there barriers separating the pool from the deck, locking gates, alarms on doors leading pool decks, etc.? In-ground pools, as a short list, could have either vinyl liners (that wear out or crack), failing pool 'decks' (concrete or stonework around the pool), failing equipment, etc.

If the pool is older – or you just have concerns with it– hire a pool inspector. Obviously, the older the pool and the less information provided by the current owner, the greater the risk. If you are buying in the winter (or when the pool is shut down), obtain the maintenance record from the seller and ask whoever did the servicing if the system was in 'good working order' at the end of the last pool season. See more on pools in Chapter 12, *What Falls Through the Cracks*.

About VA and FHA Inspections . . .

VA loans require a termite inspection and a *Wood Destroying Insect Report* documenting the presence or absence of wood destroying insects in the home. Both the FHA and VA require specific well water tests when homes are served by private wells. Let your inspector know, if you are getting an FHA or VA mortgage, if the home has a well for the potable water supply as they will need to do a specific water test.

The FHA and VA lenders do their own inspection of the property. This is more of an appraisal than an inspection, although they do look at the physical condition of the property. While the FHA and VA inspections are a good thing and can provide you with a degree of added protection, they cover just a fraction of what a home inspection covers. They tend to look at a few types of problems – especially stair safety and peeling paint. They do provide one advantage over a home inspection: the FHA or VA inspector can request that various conditions be fixed or they won't approve the financing. If the seller wants to sell the home to you, they will need to remedy these items. Your home inspector, on the other hand, does not have any power of enforceability in terms of getting an owner to take care of a problem.

VA loans require a termite inspection and a Wood Destroying Insect Report documenting the presence or absence of wood destroying insects in the home. <u>Both the FHA and VA require specific well water tests when homes are served by private wells.</u> Let your inspector know, if you are getting an FHA or VA mortgage, if the home has a well for the potable water supply as they will need to do a specific water test.

CHAPTER 12
Post-Inspection Negotiations

What you'll learn in this chapter . . .

- Knowing the types of market you are in will determine your negotiating strategy . . .
- Why have an inspection even if you've made a 'no negotiation' offer . . .
- The four choices you have when the inspection reveals problems . . .
- Know when NOT TO negotiate . . .
- Utilizing your buyer's agent . . .
- Follow up on potentially problematic conditions or issues . . .
- What is negotiable – and what isn't . . .
- What specific conditions are often subject to renegotiation, which are sometimes negotiable, and which 'go with the house'

Negotiations can take place not just when making your offer to purchase, but during your inspection contingency period *after* you have had your offer accepted. The home inspection – plus the investigations and testing you can do during your contingency period – may reveal problems or 'issues' that you were not aware of when making your offer to purchase the property.

Unfortunately, no matter how much *information* your home inspection provides, it does not give you a lot of <u>advice</u> on what to do with the findings – and specifically what may be negotiable and when it is feasible to negotiate. It's (largely) up to you – with help from your buyer's agent – to decide what to do when the inspection reveals problems you did not anticipate. In this chapter, I'll try to give you guidelines on what may typically be negotiable and what isn't, as well as advice on getting the best results. A lot of this may come across as 'common sense' – and it is – but there are a lot of pitfalls you need to be aware of – as well as strategies that will help you achieve the best outcome. At the end of this chapter, I'll provide a list of specific issues that typically are – and are not

– subject to post-inspection negotiations. Note: advice regarding post-inspection negotiations has been provided in the last two chapters as well.

Buyer's market, neutral market, or seller's market . . .

Before we get into post-inspection guidelines and strategies, it is important to realize that *whether* and *how aggressively* you can negotiate depends on the state of your local real estate market. When a previous draft of this chapter was written, it was basically a 'neutral' or, I would call, a healthy market, where there were an equal number of people looking to buy and homeowners looking to sell. Before that, in 2008–2009, we had a buyer's market, with more homes for sale than buyers. At the time of this writing, much of the country is in a 'seller's market, where there are far more buyers than homes for sale. This is particularly true along the east coast and in upscale urban and suburban areas. (Note: Conditions may have changed by the time you read this.)

It is important to realize that in a **seller's market**, where there are more buyers than homes for sale – AND in any market with a desirable property that may have lots of interested buyers – you may not be able to renegotiate to have things repaired or get price reductions due to the problems found by at the inspection or other investigations.

In a seller's market, it is often the case that you will make your offer with the provision that the inspection is for 'information only' purposes. Unfortunately, you may need to do this just to get your offer accepted. What you don't want to do is completely waive your right to do an inspection. Buyers will do this when they are in a bidding war for a property, or just to make their offer more attractive.

Sellers love this, as it means that you cannot withdraw your offer and walk away from the purchase due to problems found by the home inspection. You may not even be able to withdraw your offer due to other types of problems that are revealed during the inspection period. Obviously, this could be disastrous to your financial (and mental) health. My advice:

*Always do the inspection, even if you agree to
no post-inspection negotiations.*

The problem with foregoing the inspection is <u>that you simply have no 'out,'</u> or way to walk from the deal that an inspection affords you. (This assumes you have an unrestricted home inspection contingency clause – which you had better have). In a seller's market, you may have to agree that the inspection is for 'information only' purposes, where you agree to not renegotiate based on the inspection findings. But if the inspection reveals serious problems with the property, then you at least have the right to walk away.

Importantly, the inspection period also gives you time to reconsider what you are buying. You may decide that the home is not right for you (too expensive, not really what you want, too many risks). Your inspection then provides you with an 'out.' When you agree to forego doing the inspection, the property is basically yours as soon as your offer is accepted by the seller. If you find out that the home is riddled with termites or it is revealed that there is a toxic waste dump out back: TOO BAD. It's yours. You may only find the bad stuff out after you move in. Importantly, if you don't proceed with the sale, you may forfeit your deposit. Ka-ching – there's potentially tens of thousands you just gave to the seller. (Did I note that you may need to an attorney looking out for your interests?)

Also, properties listed as 'as is' really aren't always sold 'as is.' As an example: I did an inspection last year where the property was 'as is,' with multiple back-up offers. The inspection revealed a structural problem that would be extremely expensive to repair. My client still wanted the home, and the buyer's agent approached the listing agent about the problem. She got the seller to reduce the price by $10,000, rather than deal with other potential buyers who would prob-ably 'walk' or renegotiate after their inspection. Banks always list the foreclosed properties they have taken back as 'as is' – but this doesn't always hold up. When the inspection reveals serious problems (termite damage comes to mind), they sometimes back off. I've seen buyer's agents negotiate successfully with banks for a lower price on 'as is' properties numerous times. This is when the problems found were both serious and were previously unknown

The final reason to do the inspection, even when you are agreeing to purchase the property 'as is,' is just so you know what you need to deal with in your 'new' home. You want to know what needs immediate repairs, what can wait, and what needs critical maintenance. As I noted earlier, the home inspection is the only time you will have someone who can provide an objective, professional source of information look at your home. We are not there to sell you windows, a new deck, new kitchen, etc., so you should be able to trust that the information you get is for your benefit only. You may not always get this from a contractor – and it simply is not their function.

Advice on post inspection negotiations . . .

#1 Realize that you basically have four choices in terms of what to do when the inspection reveals problems that you did not know about previously. You can:

- Accept the conditions as is. This is often appropriate if you got the home for less than fair market value or you already negotiated a lower price for the home – or if the conditions found were just typical for a home of that age, price, and apparent condition. Accepting conditions 'as is' may also be appropriate when you are buying in a 'seller's market,' as your ability to re-negotiate is limited. You may also simply want the property badly enough that you don't want to take a chance on losing it to someone else. If the inspection revealed just minor or deferrable items that were not a surprise to you, be happy with this (as it's not the norm!)

- You can ask for allowances or price reductions due to the conditions revealed by the inspection. You may need to follow up with contractors or specialists to get a firm idea of likely repair options and costs. (Note: some types of costs are easy to estimate; reconstruction costs are difficult – and sometimes impossible). An extension to allow this may be needed. This may be granted in some cases – but not others.

- You can ask the owner to fix something or have suspect problems resolved so you know they will not be an issue going forward. This is appropriate for when there are gross safety issues, such as live wires that are exposed, or for severely deferred maintenance on heating and cooling systems. Sometimes the seller will have these systems serviced (if overdue) or determined to be in 'good working order' by the appropriate serviceperson.

- You can walk away from the deal – or at least withdraw your original offer until you figure out if you still want the property. When the inspection reveals serious problems and you are still interested in the property you may ask for an extension to try to resolve whether expensive repairs or replacements will be necessary – plus their potential costs. Assuming you have an unrestricted contingency clause, you can withdraw your offer.

All of these could be appropriate, depending on the situation.

#2 There are no <u>absolute</u> ground rules in post-inspection negotiations.

Buyers sometimes ask me during an inspection what the seller has to fix. Unless you have statutory requirements (such as the requirement for working smoke detectors, as found in some states). The fact is: the seller doesn't have to correct anything. But there is nothing that says you can't ask for anything. Everything could be negotiable, depending on the situation. However, you have to know what is appropriate, what is 'doable,' and what is the best way to go about things.

Listing agents and builders sometimes say that the inspection is for 'information only.' This could be true in a seller's market, but may not be true for health or safety items. I also have to ask: why would you do an inspection if you are not going to act on the inspection findings when serious or just unacceptable problems are found?

I should note that what is customary in some states is not the norm in others. I've had buyers from New Jersey who were aghast that the sellers would not be 'required' to undertake the repairs of deficient items. That may be the norm in New Jersey but not in most of New England. I recommend researching how things are handled in the state you are purchasing in.

#3 Don't think that you have to negotiate – and know when not to . . .

In my opinion, the most important negotiations are those you do up front, when you are making your offer and are reaching an agreement with the seller. This is where you hope you can get the home you want at the best possible price and at the best possible terms. If you are in a 'normal' or buyer's market and can get the home for under 'market value' (assuming this is a realistic figure), this is where you will realize the biggest savings. When you get the home on attractive terms, moreover, you may not feel the need to renegotiate on the smaller defects and problems that are typically found. Prior to the current seller's market, I'd often find that my clients weren't concerned about problems the inspection revealed as they'd gotten a reduction from the asking price when making their offer. As noted above, seller's markets are different. You have less bargaining power (and sometimes none) when there are multiple offers on the property.

Also, in homes with great positives (for instance, beautiful interiors, renovated kitchens and bathrooms, beautiful land or location, or lots of amenities one doesn't normally see), be more tolerant of the problems that may be found. Weigh the good against the bad (assuming you are not paying an astronomical price for the good stuff). If it's your 'dream house,' just buy it (assuming you can afford to).

#4 Renegotiations

These can arise not just from issues raised by the home inspection. The other investigations and testing you do, such as water quality testing (usually with homes with private wells), radon testing, termite/wood-boring insect inspections, specialist evaluations, lead testing, etc. may reveal problems that you had not known about previously. New information about the property from other sources could even be found during your inspection contingency period that could cause you to reconsider the purchase or the price you are paying. It's not just problems or issues raised by the home inspection that could be important. I've provided advice on specific conditions at the end of this chapter.

#5 Know when to walk away from the deal . . .

The most drastic renegotiation (but not necessarily the hardest) is to simply use your right to withdraw your offer to purchase the property when the inspection reveals severe or widespread problems with the home that are beyond your capacity or willingness to deal with. You may just realize during the inspection contingency period that the home just isn't right for you. In these situations, you will want to get your deposit back and find another property. Again, this is just too big a purchase not to get things right. The important point here is that you need to feel comfortable with what you are buying. You don't need to justify why you are walking away from the deal.

> I had clients do an inspection and where they were satisfied with the home's condition, but they just were not excited about the property either. They continued to look at houses in the next couple of days, found their 'dream home' and were able to withdraw their offer on the first property and buy the one that they desired more. Note: this may be good for your home inspector – but not for everyone else involved in the transaction.

In my area – or at least with the agents I deal with – I don't see problems with agents trying to 'shoehorn' people into properties that buyers want to – or should – be walking away from. But I have seen it occasionally with novice or part-time agents (successful real estate agents don't need any one deal that bad and most understand that this isn't a way to build a business long term). Agent pressure to go ahead with a purchase can occur, however, and may be the norm in some areas of the country. It can also occur if the agent really needs to make the sale to pay their own mortgage! The thing to realize is: it's your money and nobody can make that decision but you. Don't worry about hurting someone's feelings. As far as the agent is concerned, if you feel that they are working hard to find you the 'right' home, let them find you another. If not, drop them.

IMPORTANT: If you decide you do not want the home after the inspection, then you must let the seller know in writing that you are withdrawing your Offer to Purchase (which may be in your Purchase and Sales document) and you must do this within the inspection contingency period. Usually, your buyer's agent and/or attorney will do this. Just make sure that it is done. Again, I am assuming you have an unrestricted contingency clause, so you don't have to have some threshold of damage or certain types of damage to withdraw your offer and get your deposit back.

One last point: when the property is revealed as a disaster, don't get 'brought off' by a seller who may lower the cost by $10,000 or $20,000 if the likely cost for repairs or what you want to do will be much larger. When the home was never built properly to begin with or needs massive repairs or renovations to make the home habitable, ask yourself would you be better off with a building lot (or a different home)? Most homes can be saved . . . some cannot.

#6 That which was disclosed up front is not likely to be subject to negotiation later.

Conversely, a listing that describes the home as a 'fixer-upper' is not telling you how much work may be involved. It may be far more than you expected. In this case, you could possibly renegotiate based on the <u>extent</u> of the repairs or renovations needed and their likely cost. If the seller told you the roof needed replacing, and you made your offer knowing this information, then it's difficult to turn around later and try to renegotiate based on this condition. If they told you the roof is 'older' and it is leaking, you may be able to renegotiate part of the price, but probably not the total replacement cost.

#7 *You have to be careful as to when and how you negotiate*.

Important: If you make a formal request in writing for a reduction in the price of the home or for a seller to fix some problem that was identified by the inspection – or even a demand an extension – the seller may no longer be bound by their acceptance of your original offer. You are making a counter offer. <u>They can turn around and sell the home to someone else.</u> This happens.

This is why (to reiterate) you should have a good buyer's agent and attorney. There are times to negotiate and times when you simply need to accept things 'as is' – or just walk away from the deal. What can also happen, however, is that your buyer's agent may have a 'discussion' with the listing agent after the inspection, when previously unknown problems were revealed. Sometimes the listing agent will convince the seller that it is their interest to make an accommodation on the price rather than lose the sale. (They know the same issue will come up at future inspections). You have not formally made a counter offer, so the seller can't go and sell it someone else. (Consult your attorney!)

Due to the liability that surrounds mold, this is normally corrected prior to the sale. Very often, the same is true for grossly unsafe electrical conditions. Unfortunately, however, the homeowners in a seller's market increasingly will not do anything. Also, understand that homeowners who are underwater financially very often can't do anything. The same is true if they have vacated the home and are living in another area of the country.

I should note that when I see deals go 'down the tube' after the inspection, it's usually due to the seller (homeowner) shooting themselves in the foot. Some sellers just can't accept that their home has problems or deficient conditions that a new owner is not willing to accept. Many homeowners and listing agents squeeze the buyer on the time they have to for the inspection, will not allow follow up by contractors to resolve conditions, and will make no accommodation on anything. Buyers end up getting ticked off and walk from the deal.

#8 Know the limits of your home inspector in negotiations.

As noted, while your home inspector should identify the conditions that need repairs, they are not going to tell you <u>whether</u> to negotiate, <u>what</u> to negotiate, or <u>how</u> to do this. We don't get involved in this. The fact is that, as a home inspector, I don't know what you are paying for the home, what the 'fair market' values in that area are, whether you got a lot of money off up front, whether there are back-up offers on the property, whether the seller is hard to deal with – or even what matters to you. Each situation and each buyer are different. Facing the same problems, some buyers will negotiate aggressively while others will not negotiate at all. I've done inspections where the buyer ignored items that I thought needed serious repairs – and requested that a few minor problems be fixed.

#9 If you are on your own and do not have a buyer's agent or attorney assisting you, decide how comfortable you are with negotiations . . .

Some people are very comfortable negotiating everything, while others prefer to avoid any type of conflict. Most people fall in the middle, but still prefer harmonious relationships over extracting the absolute best deal. As noted, in a normal or buyer's market, I recommend that you try to get the absolute best price you can for the home when making your offer. If you do this, you can ignore the 'smaller' defects that will come up due to the inspection. New construction, condominiums, and expensive homes may be another matter – especially if you paying close to (or over) the full asking price. When you are paying for perfection, you should (you would hope) get something close to it.

You also have to evaluate the seller. Some people are just tough to negotiate with. Also recognize that many older homeowners are proud of their homes and may have spent many years there. In your contacts and negotiations with the owner, you should be sensitive to this – but not so sensitive that you don't pursue your own interests.

> I read of one instance where the buyers decided, after hearing the older sellers rhapsodize about how well they cared for their home and how they had done everything to it, that they decided they didn't need to have an inspection done. The home, it turned out, needed thousands of dollars in structural repairs.

When you are in negotiations, try to keep things civil. This is why you have real estate agents. They are not emotionally involved in the outcome and can act as intermediaries. Good real estate agents, I've found, are accepting of the need to have adjustments made in the price or have conditions repaired or resolved by the owner.

It can be difficult to negotiate directly with a seller when there is no broker involved. Many sellers have an inflated view of the property. Many think their property is worth far more than what they are getting. While some are reasonable and can deal with negotiations fairly and non-emotionally, others are just a pain in the butt. This is a zero-sum game: whatever you win, they lose, so it's hard for many sellers (and buyers) to keep the emotions out of the process. You even need to be careful of getting too close to the homeowners – especially the sweet old couple who have treated you like family – as you may find it harder to back out or renegotiate if problems are found. In one inspection I did, the buyers were so close to the elderly sellers that they couldn't break the news to them that the home was termite riddled (and actually had to be torn down). They left it to me to break the bad news.

Even while always working to get the best deal for yourself, try to maintain a good relationship with the seller, when possible. Even when you are in a buyer's market, there is nothing to be gained by extracting every last possible concession from the owner. The home-buying experience is much more rewarding when you maintain a good relationship with the homeowner. I've known sellers who, antagonized by the petty or inappropriate demands of a buyer, stripped the home clean of everything that they legally could, even though these items would be of little use to them.

#10 Use your buyer's agent and not your attorney when deciding whether to and what to negotiate . . .

Lastly, while attorneys can provide an invaluable service to buyers in many aspects of the transaction, I think it is hard for them to decide what are the critical issues from the inspection unless they were either present – or you go over with them what are the important issues to you. In most cases, the negotiations are best done by you or your buyer's agent. A good real estate attorney can be invaluable in protecting your interest on the legal issues involved. The attorneys I talked to indicated they usually stay out of the post-inspection negotiations unless their assistance was requested.

#10 Follow up when problems are found . . .

Follow up on the inspection with specialists or tradespersons to determine what level of repairs are necessary and the potential costs. Home inspectors do not – and in many states cannot – provide repair costs. They could conceivably lose their inspector's license if they do this. The home inspection is a limited, visual survey of the home. It covers an immense amount of ground in terms of the systems and areas it includes. Your inspector, no matter how well qualified, acts as a generalist. They can't always tell you what caused a particular condition or what the repair costs will be.

To determine the extent of the problem and the likely repair costs, try to bring out one or more of the specialists discussed in the last chapter. For instance, if your inspector finds evidence of decay or substantial damage on the home, they may advise that you bring out a carpenter or building contractor. If the heating system was not working properly or is just extremely aged, request that an HVAC technician examine the system. If the electrical service or wiring is found to be problematic and you will need to upgrade the system, you may want to bring out an electrician to find out what this will involve and what it will cost. This list could go on for several pages, but the point is this:

You need to be diligent about pursuing further investigations on anything where the inspection revealed a problem or where the extent or cost of repairs cost could not be determined.

Unfortunately, there are two problems with the above advice. First, in the real world, you very often <u>cannot get</u> a contractor, electrician, heating specialist, or whomever, out to the home within the contingency inspection period – or quickly enough to do you any good. While your inspector will tell you to get further input and cost estimates, this is not always possible to do in the short time period you have. You can ask for an extension to have a suspected problem further evaluated. Usually this will be acceptable to the seller – but not when there are backup offers.

If you can't get a further evaluation done, you can do one of two things: first, for mechanical systems with no recent maintenance history, you can ask that the system be serviced by a professional who can then attest to the 'good working order' (or repairs or replacement needed) of the system. Ideally, get the receipts showing what was done. When the home inspection reveals a number of previously unknown problems, a 'lump sum' reduction in the price may be offered. This will seldom fully cover the total cost of repairs – but sometimes it is the best you can do.

The second problem I see with having a contractor look at a home that is in disrepair is that they are not an objective source of information. They may provide valuable cost estimates for repairs or renovations in their area of expertise. They simply are not looking at every system or problem. A few (and just a few) may see a decrepit home as a full employment opportunity for the next year.

#10 Ask the homeowners or occupants about problems that may have been repaired.

Have your buyer's agent forward questions to the listing agent where you would like to get a history of conditions found at the inspection. Homeowners, for instance, can often provide information as to when a water stain on a ceiling occurred and what was done to fix it. A homeowner who has been in the property for 30 years obviously can provide a lot more information than a family that inherits the property in an estate.

#11 Be careful with what you say during the inspection – or even prior to making your offer . . .

This is important! Don't give out information that could work against you. Just as during the process of making a bid for a home you don't want to let the listing agent know what you are willing to pay, don't undercut yourself in post-inspection negotiations by stating that, even if the seller makes no concessions, you'll buy the home. Also, when going through the inspection, if the inspector finds something that will need attention, don't state that you 'don't care about this' because you're able to take care of it yourself. As an example, if the home has a substandard or defective electrical system, don't volunteer that your brother-in-law is an electrician whom you will get to do the repairs (after all, your brother-in-law will still charge you and you may find you can't get him for six months). Many first-time buyers do this all the time (before I can shush them up) – saying 'I can fix this and I can fix that.' *You may have the skills to deal with the home's conditions, but no one on the 'selling side' should know this.* But don't overplay your hand either, by over-exaggerating your concern over some fixable item.

Obviously, how much you want the property makes a difference in what you can accept and how aggressively you may be willing to negotiate. With a property that has most everything you want in a home – or you just want it, period – you may be much less willing walk away from it due to problems revealed by the inspection. Falling in love with a home is great, but you've got to stay unemotional until the whole process is over. I've had clients break down and cry when the inspection revealed their dream house to be termite-riddled and structurally unsound. Also, try to not let the listing agent or the seller know how much you love the home, as this may work against you if you need to ask for concessions during the buying process.

#12 Know what is negotiable and what isn't . . .

Look at every defect in terms of the *urgency* (or time frame) for repairs, the *degree of risk* the item poses, and the *seriousness or expense* it will pose. This is a bit of a formal breakdown, but it can be useful. For instance, if the roof surface is aging but still should provide several more years of useful life, you may not be as concerned as if the roof needs immediate replacement.

In terms of items needing urgent repairs, these are less likely to be 'acceptable.' Certainly, if the sink drain is leaking and will cause further damage by the time you move in, you would like to have that item fixed as soon as possible. Major systems that are simply not working represent items that need *urgent* repairs or resolution. For instance, if a heating system is not working or individual zones would not come on, it is critical that the nature of the problem be resolved within the contingency period.

Unless the house is being sold in 'as is' condition and clearly needs major work, you should not have to do a lot of immediate repairs just to make the home habitable – at least, in my opinion. Vacant homes may come with a need for more immediate repairs.

Also examine the *risks* that go with the property. A good example of when you need to evaluate risks is when the probability of there being a problem is small (over some period of time), but the expenses involved in correcting the condition will be enormous. As noted earlier, I had an inspection where the buyers determined that if the septic system failed there would be no way to replace it except by spending tens of thousands of dollars. Even though the septic system was functional at the time of the inspection, the buyers decided they could not live with this risk.

Environmental risks can often be large. For instance, when the home has an underground fuel oil tank, the actual risk of having a failed tank may be small. But if the tank has been leaking, then you may face tens of thousands of dollars in repair costs. It would be prudent to avoid any home with large, unknown risks unless they are completely resolved prior to the sale commitment.

In general, defects that affect the habitability of the home or that represent health or gross safety concerns (usually electrical) are the conditions most readily subject to successful post-inspection negotiation. In other words: systems not working, plumbing leaks, unsafe conditions, etc.

#13 Advice on having the seller fix problems . . .

In many cases, the inspection reveals conditions that need repairs – or just areas of unfinished work. Again, assuming you are in a 'normal' or buyer's market, it may be appropriate to ask that certain conditions be repaired or finished.

In most cases, however, other than doing repairs to items that affect habitability or will cause more damage if not corrected immediately, you may not want the seller finishing work that is half done. This is especially true when the homeowners have done a lot of work themselves and very little was done right. (Unfortunately, these are the homeowners who will readily volunteer to fix the defects brought to their attention!). Be nice about it, but don't let them. I've had clients request that the homeowner stop all renovations, as it is obvious that much of what is being done they will have to undo.

Look at your abilities and those of the seller. If the homeowner you are buying from is an experienced handyman or builder and you are not, it is reasonable to ask that they complete work that has been started or to fix items that need repairs. Conversely, if you have the skills to do home repairs and won't have to pay someone to do everything, then you will want to take care of the routine problems yourself. Much of the time, you will not be able to get a seller to do anything. They just want out.

New construction is different. With new homes or homes that are being completely renovated, it is accepted practice to simply make a punch list of all the items that need finishing or correction. In most cases, the builder will take care of these.

Addendum

Specific problems and issues and how they usually 'play out' in negotiations

There are conditions that commonly result in re-negotiation and, just as important, issues and problems that almost always 'go with the property.' I've noted a number of concerns below and how these usually 'play out.'

*What conditions **ARE NOT** (typically) subject to negotiation . . .*

First, those items that you would normally be aware of when making your offer:

1. **Peeling paint or worn surfaces** on the interior or exterior. These conditions are obvious when making your bid. The exception is with VA and FHA loans, as their inspectors will not accept peeling paint.

2. Easily visible **surface damage to the walls and ceilings**. Same reason as above.

3. **Deteriorated driveways, walkways, and exterior stairs.** These are also obvious when making your offer, unless you are dealing with new construction where these were not finished.

4. **What is present or not present**. Again, this should be obvious when you made your offer. Buyers sometimes find that a nice chandelier is missing – but it was disclosed on the listing sheet and was taken by the seller.

5. **The condition of the landscaping – except for new construction, where the lawn normally may need seeding and gullies filled in due to wintertime or wash-out conditions.**

6. **The attractiveness or utility of the kitchen and bathrooms**. Take note of the condition and what you may need to spend to upgrade the kitchen or bathroom when looking at a home – but this is not something subject to renegotiation. Things that don't work may be subject to negotiation – but not components or systems that are just older or worn.

7. **Older heating or cooling systems** – as long as they are functioning normally. The inspector will commonly note that systems are at the end of their design life or are 'fully depreciated.' This may be true, but in practice these systems can and often do provide years of additional life. I've seen 30-year-old air conditioning units in the last couple of years that were still going strong despite being well past their 'normal' life expectancy. You should plan on

replacing older systems. I advise getting estimates on the potential costs – but as a negotiable issue, if it is working and functional, then you usually won't get a seller to make an accommodation based on a system's age. Usually. This may also not be true if the seller grossly misrepresented the age of a major system.

Also, the home inspection does not fail central air conditioning systems that utilize the older R-22 refrigerant – but it is important to realize that the R-22 refrigerant is being phased out and may no longer be available (or at least 'readily available') after 2020. What this means is that, if you have a central air conditioning unit manufactured before 2008 that uses R-22 refrigerant then you will be looking at replacing the entire HVAC system (which includes both the outside condenser and the air handling unit in the attic or basement) when there is a need to add refrigerant due to leaks or needed repairs. The older R-22 refrigerant will simply not be available.

8. **Code issues.** Your inspector may recommend that stairs be repaired to meet current standards for hand and guard rails, but this is noted as a safety concern and not a code issue. Owners will typically not undertake these repairs, except when an FHA or VA inspection requires it. Any repairs made, however, should meet current code requirements. *Older homes do not have to meet current code standards.*

9. **Code compliance.** This is a tough one. The home inspection is not a code inspection, and older homes and existing work very often will not conform to current standards. Your home inspector will look at components such as decks or stairs in terms of safety and 'serviceability' (durability). A lot of non-approved work is done and much of it is workmanlike; *a lot isn't.* In Massachusetts and New Hampshire, most municipal building inspectors do not require that a new owner have something torn out because a previous owner or their contractor did not pull permits – <u>but it does happen</u>, especially if the work was especially egregious or resulted in unsafe conditions. In most cases, however, the municipal building (code) inspector won't come back on a new homeowner who didn't do the work. As noted, this may not be the case in states where code officials have a stricter standard; they may mandate a tear out of unapproved work. Your home inspector, however, is not there to 'enforce' the code.

You should check the permit history of the home at the local building department early in the process. Work done without permits is a red flag. Talk to the local building/plumbing/electrical inspector, perhaps without identifying the property (you don't want them going out and confronting the current homeowner). Ask how they handle this issue in that locality.

10. **Lead paint.** Lead paint, while a significant concern, is seldom a negotiable issue. Most buyers assume – or should assume – that lead paint could be present on 'older' homes (or on older woodwork of any kind). Lead paint may be present on any home built before 1978 (or where older lead-based paint may have been used). Lead paint is rarely found in 1970s homes, is not commonly found on the interiors in 60s homes, and would not be present on most woodwork with a stain or varnish finish, although there are exceptions. If a home was represented to be lead-free or to meet the standards for compliance in the state you are buying in and you find it isn't, this could be a negotiable issue, but this is rarely the case. Buyers who don't want a home with lead paint should avoid older homes with a lot of old windows, doors, or old painted woodwork. *Anyone buying an investment property should make sure that the home has been completely 'de-leaded' to the appropriate standard,* due to the concern with lawsuits from tenant's kids getting lead poisoned. (You will be sued even if they ingested the lead at another property).

11. **Asbestos-cement siding and many other asbestos-containing materials** (see exception below). Asbestos-cement siding is commonly found in New England. The asbestos in this material is 'bound up' with the cement, so it does not readily become airborne. There is no mandate to remove this type of siding and it is not considered a health hazard. Nevertheless, if removed, it must go to an asbestos dump. Seeing the stuff in a pile in the basement, then, is a different concern than when it is still present for a siding. The presence of asbestos-cement shingles, whether exposed or covered by a vinyl or aluminum siding, is not a negotiable item, from my experience. Similarly, asbestos is commonly present in older composition floor coverings, floor mastics, and literally dozens of building products. Again, these are not considered a significant hazard and you can't tell if asbestos is present without specialized, destructive testing. They 'go with the property.' See the comments below, however, regarding the asbestos insulation found on heating pipes, ducts, and boilers in older homes.

12. **Electrical service levels.** Young buyers, in particular, always seem to be concerned when the home does not have a 200 amp service. Yes, having a 200 amp service may be nice, but most homes do not require 200 amps. One hundred amps, the traditional standard, provides plenty of power – and very often more than enough when the major appliances are gas-fired. The service levels are a capacity issue and rarely a safety issue. Conversely, it is common for homes to need a larger panel to accommodate the number of circuits that are present. This could be an issue if the panel is already well over capacity – but not if it will need upgrading due to new circuits that will be installed. (Note: If upgrading the panel, I recommend upgrading the service to 200 amps. Also, any panel over 25 years old is now considered 'older.'

Installing a new, larger panel or adding a subpanel, may be an upgrade – but if the existing panel already serves more circuits than it was designed for, then this is a safety issue). Sixty amp services (for single family homes), I should note, would be considered antiquated and in need of upgrading. Your bank or mortgage company may even require this.

13. ***Under-framed roofs and floors.*** Assuming no evidence of likely failure or serious distress and reflecting the construction standards when the home was built are not negotiable items. Antique homes often show sags in the floors and roof – and even homes built into the 1960s have roofs that sag due to undersized rafters (by today's standards). Older homes commonly show unorthodox framing. Unless significant distress is evident or likely, this may not be a negotiable concern. Reinforcements, however, may be desirable and may be recommended. Note: exceptions exist, such as when the roof framing shows cracks, severe deflection, or grossly substandard construction.

14. ***Insulation levels and energy costs.*** Energy costs and insulation are not items for renegotiation. The lack of adequate insulation is common. Limited insulation is not typically regarded as a 'defect'; adding more is an 'upgrade.' Older windows will very often be loose-fitting (most don't warrant replacement on energy grounds, however). If a seller has represented the home to be 'fully insulated' and it is not, then this could be an issue. Homes with high fuel or utility costs may be something you will want to look at before making your offer but they are not typically negotiable issues.

15. ***Urea Formaldehyde Foam Insulation (UFFI) . . .*** This was a type of insulation used in the 1970s up to 1982. When improperly installed, the home's occupants were exposed to high levels of formaldehyde. Some became chemically sensitized. This material is no longer regarded as a hazard as the formaldehyde has typically out-gassed long ago. Testing for formaldehyde is no longer considered warranted for UFFI homes.

Problems/conditions that COULD BE negotiable issues . . .

16. **Certain types of code issues.** While many code issues with older homes simply reflect the fact that homes were not built to current standards, there are areas where code related issues are more problematic. These are:

    a. Where decks or other structures were built too close to the property line. Were the required setbacks not followed? I've seen instances where decks had to be removed or partially removed as the homeowner-built deck did not meet the required setback standards.

b. Any filling or covering of wetlands or locating permanent structures built too close to wetlands (as determined by local/state regulations).

c. When the non-conforming structure is unsafe or grossly substandard. This would be a significant concern. The town's building inspectors may not be aware of these problems, but if they are made aware they could intervene to require removal or reconstruction.

d. Local practices. While municipal building inspectors in my area do not routinely require that a homeowner rip out work done by a previous owner (unless it is the type of code issue noted above), this may be different in other states.

e. The degree of the safety concern. Virtually all existing stairs, walkways, and decks do not meet today's safety (code) standards. These conditions may be called 'unsafe' by the inspection – but if the defects are minor or code related then these conditions 'go with the home.' Repairs and upgrading are still needed.

17. ***Loose, friable (crushable) asbestos on steam pipes, especially if deteriorated.*** The presence of the loose, crushable type asbestos-containing insulation commonly found on steam pipes and boilers may or may not be a negotiable issue, depending on a bunch of factors. I should note, first, that home inspectors always refer to asbestos-containing materials as '*suspected* asbestos-containing materials,' as one must do an X-ray spectrometry test to definitively ascertain whether a material is asbestos-containing. For the older, white pipe insulation on boilers and heating pipes, and the older, white paper insulation on ductwork, these will usually contain asbestos.

Whether the presence of asbestos becomes a negotiable issue depends on several things. First is its condition: Is the material largely intact or is loose and deteriorated? Second, how visible was the material and what was its condition when you made your offer to purchase? Third, is it in a space that will remain unfinished and largely unused (such as many basements in older New England homes)? What is the nature and price of the property (the more upscale the home, the more asbestos tends to be an issue). If it's in the basement of a multi-family rental property it is usually ignored. And lastly, how much, very simply, do you care about the presence of asbestos in the home? What I've found is that the level of concern differs widely regarding asbestos-containing materials. Some buyers will not tolerate the presence of any (visible) asbestos-containing materials (ACMs) in the home; others don't care. If largely intact and in an unfinished space, many authorities do not recommend that the material be removed. The risk is not having ACMs present – it's the risk of breathing in air borne particles. ACMs that are intact and are not likely to be damaged represent a minimal risk of exposure. In all cases, however, given that this material is a 'negative,' *it is preferable to not have the material present.*

18. **Water quality issues** ... Many (but not all) water quality issues <u>are not</u> subject to renegotiation. Bad tasting water, water full of minerals, etc. may need a treatment system but these usually fall upon the buyer. Items that affect health, however, particularly arsenic or bacteria in the private well water supply may be subject to negotiation. Bacteria in the well water will typically mandate an immediate disinfectant procedure to shock the well, with post-treatment testing usually done. FHA and VA loans require that well water meet certain standards.

Radon in well water is *usually* not subject to renegotiation due to the fact that there is no national standard of what level warrants a remediation system. Whereas there is a recognized EPA 'action level' for *radon in the air*, there is no EPA standard, or 'action level,' for radon present in the well water. Each state has its own non-binding standard regarding what is 'acceptable' for radon in water. New Hampshire had a recommended maximum contaminant level of 2000 pico-Curies (pCi) of radon in well water (this is being revised however, but the current action level is unclear at this time). Massachusetts's action level for suggested remediation is 10,000 pCi of radon. To repeat: there is no EPA recognized 'acceptable' level, making this a difficult area for negotiation.

That said, really high levels of radon in water COULD BE a negotiable issue as this may not be acceptable to many buyers. Also, many towns are requiring radon in water mitigation systems in new construction when the radon in water levels exceed that state's suggested 'action level.'

19. **Windows** When these are just old, worn, or *moderately* loose-fitting, they usually will not be subject to renegotiation as long as they work. Conversely, windows with damaged hardware that are unsafe for use (such as when they crash down when opened or the lock is released) need urgent attention – and that occasionally means window replacement at significant cost. Many 20- to 30-year-old vinyl windows have damaged hardware that make them unsafe for use. Some can be repaired, but many can't – or it just isn't worth it.

Double-glazed windows commonly show fogging glass due to what is called breached seals. There are no absolutes here. Having a couple of windows showing a slight bit of fogging does not alarm many buyers; repairs may be deferrable and very often the buyer may be anticipating the replacement of these windows. On the other hand, when a high percentage of the windows are fogged up – or just don't work properly – then a complete replacement of the windows may be in order. So, as with everything, it's a matter of degree. Also, the newer, the more expensive, and more (seemingly) perfect the home, the less likely it is that having windows with breached seals will be an acceptable condition. Lastly, having a top sash in an upstairs window minimally fogged is a lot different than having multiple windows or a large picture window fogged up.

20. *Malfunctioning or nonworking appliances* These may be subject to renegotiation, especially things like a leaking dishwasher, non-working burners
on a stove, or a non-functional disposal. If the appliance is older (which for
appliances means over eight years old) and they are clearly beyond their
service life, then they 'go with the property' as most buyers will be planning
to replace these anyhow.

Concerns USUALLY subject to renegotiation . . .

See the cautions noted above. In some cases (bank-owned, properties with
multiple offers, etc.), it may not be possible to do any renegotiations based on
the inspection findings. All the guidelines below (and above) are generalities.
Nothing is written in stone.

1. ***Essential systems not working.*** Unless disclosed prior to the inspection, the
    expectation is that basic mechanical and heating systems, the plumbing, and
    the electricity will work and are viable and safe for use. This is also true for
    central air conditioning, especially in the warmer regions. (In colder regions,
    AC systems are not subject to testing for much of the year). These are basic
    'requirements' for habitability.

2. ***Gross electrical hazards.*** Almost every home inspection will reveal some
    type of electrical hazard – or just conditions that, relative to modern require-
    ments, warrant upgrading or repairs. A lot of the non-critical stuff, such as
    service upgrades, fall to the buyer. Gross hazards, however, such as the
    presence of Federal Pacific electrical panels, exposed splices or live wires,
    knob and tube wiring, or grossly deficient homeowner work, will typically be
    an issue for most buyers – as they should be.

3. ***Mold problems.*** This tends to be something that the seller deals with. Due to
    liability reasons, both the buyer's and listing agents (at least in my coverage
    area) will require a mold remediation be done prior to the sale. The reality is
    that if you 'walk away from the sale,' the problem will have to be disclosed
    to the next buyer (and the next) until the problem is fixed. The potential
    for mold <u>behind</u> the walls in finished basements, while more of a health
    concern than mold in the attic, may be less of a negotiable issue, simply
    because it is not open to view.

4. ***Termite infestations.*** *Active* termite infestations are typically something that
    a seller would take care of. Many banks will not provide a mortgage on a
    home that has an active termite infestation. What gets a bit trickier is when
    you find termite damage on the home during the colder months. As noted
    earlier, termites are not active in the winter. If the home was never treated
    for termites, it is desirable to have this done, as you simply don't know if the

termites will be back in the spring. If the evidence indicates that the termite damage is older, many termite/pest control companies will still recommend a treatment if one has not been done. They obviously have a self-interest in treating, but I can see their point too. They cannot provide any assurance that termites will not show up when warmer weather arrives or next year – and homeowners will blame them for not treating a home where evidence of previous infestations was found. Older damage, however, very often just means you will want to have a yearly termite inspection.

5. ***Extensive structural damage or decay.*** Obviously, if you knew about the extent of the damage prior to the inspection, then the problem is yours. This is rarely the case. A lot depends on whether the damage is a 'surprise' that no one knew about. In homes where the damage appears extensive, or the scope of the repairs can't be determined, or is simply beyond your capacity to deal with, it may be prudent to just walk away from the home. These properties can be better for contractors or very adept homeowners, as they can do the needed work.

Conversely, almost every home will show decayed trim. If not excessive, this may go with the property.

6. ***Radon in the air.*** Radon is a radioactive soil gas that may be present at elevated levels in many homes. (See the later chapter for more information on radon). Statistically, twenty-five percent of New England homes have elevated levels of radon, according to the EPA. I recommend that every home be tested for radon, except for upper story condos with no basements. In older homes with totally unusable basements, this testing to should be done on the first floor living area. The presence of elevated levels of radon is typically a negotiable issue. While there is no *requirement* that a seller correct a radon problem, it is customary that the seller does this – or provides an allowance to the buyer to have this done. The typical cost to correct a radon problem is $1200–1500. A few homes may run much more. Most real estate agents do not have a problem with this, as they know that, should a buyer not buy the home with high radon levels, they must disclose this to any future buyer (who would typically ask for a remediation system). I do not, however, recommend that people walk away from homes with reasonably high radon levels, as this is a correctable problem.

7. ***Unsafe chimney conditions.*** This includes conditions such as cracked flue tiles and are almost always subject to negotiation as they are a big expense. Unsafe woodstove installations, by comparison, are not, as the stove can simply be removed.

8. ***Plumbing leaks.*** Corroded gate valves and supply pipe connections are commonly found and go with the property. *Active* leaks on the supply or waste piping, however, need immediate attention as they will cause more damage if not corrected immediately. With older cast iron waste pipes, there is a fine line between pipes that show incipient corrosion under the pipe (they all show this, in time) and actual drip marks under the pipes or detectable moisture. In the first case, where incipient corrosion is found, the replacement of the pipes will usually fall on the buyer as this may be a deferrable expense. Leaking pipes or severe corrosion, more often than not will be a significant concern and could be a negotiable issue. It's a matter of degree (and other factors).

9. ***Knob and tube wiring . . .*** Knob and tube wiring is an old type of wiring that has separate neutral and hot wires that run through joists within ceramic tubes. This type of wiring was the original wiring type and was widely used in Victorian-era homes up into the 1930s (and occasionally later). We see this type of wiring commonly in antique homes in New England. In areas where the housing stock is newer, you may rarely see this. Your inspector should be able to identify knob and tube wiring if it is present and readily visible (Note: sometimes it isn't!)

Beyond the safety concerns with this type of wiring (it is ungrounded, brittle, you can't enclose it in insulation, and the connections are often suspect), you need to be aware that insurance companies are increasingly unwilling to offer home-owner's insurance when knob and tube wiring is present. In addition, insulation companies will not install insulation if knob and tube wiring is present. For these reasons, *it is now a standard practice to remove and replace existing knob and tube wiring*. Obviously, this can get expensive. You will want to get cost estimates from an electrician if the home you are buying has knob and tube wiring. Many homeowners have had this wiring removed prior to the sale as they know it will be an issue for potential buyers.

10. ***Liquid underground fuel oil tanks (LUSTS).*** These tanks are less commonly found, at least in my area, as most have been removed due to the hazard they pose. If leaking, the site remediation costs can run into the tens – or hundreds of thousands of dollars. Banks and mortgage companies typically will not provide a mortgage on a property with an underground oil tank (assuming they know one is present). Please note that underground pro-pane tanks are common and are not an environmental hazard. Do not buy a home with a liquid underground fuel tank unless it is has been properly removed and all permits are obtained from the state or municipal authority that oversaw the removal of the tank. You don't want the liability.

CHAPTER 13
What Falls Through the Cracks . . .

What you will learn in this chapter . . .

- *This chapter will cover many important systems, components and concerns that <u>are not</u> covered by the home inspection) – but that you may need to follow up on . . .*

If you've read the previous chapters, you've learned how to get a quality inspection and how to follow up on concerns that may be raised by the inspection. Unfortunately, your journey hasn't ended. The fact is: the home inspection does not deal with many important systems and concerns that could be a source of aggravation or expense. You need to be aware of these and follow up, where appropriate.

Please note that, out of the list below, typically only one to as many as seven of these concerns may be relevant to the property you are buying. They are the outliers, the problems or systems not typically found in most homes. Some of these items are included because everyone thinks they are part of the home inspection – but they aren't. Some are excluded, as they may require specialized knowledge, while other are excluded for the opposite reason: they require no special knowledge and any buyer can recognize their condition. Other excluded items, I should note, require invasive procedures. *But all the concerns in this chapter are potentially important and you neglect them at your peril.*

[Note: Some of these concerns may be covered by your home inspector, usually for extra fees.]

Important stuff that the home inspection doesn't cover . . .

(Note: the first four of these concerns have been noted below – but they are covered in separate chapters).

Mold and indoor air quality. This is such a 'hot button' issue today that I've covered this in more detail in a separate chapter (#14). Home inspectors may look for visible mold and comment on it – but the home inspection is not a mold inspection either.

Private wells, water quantity and quality, and water purification systems. These are not inspection concerns – but many inspection companies offer water quality testing. This is especially important for homes with well systems. Due to the numerous issues with wells and water quality in general, I've covered this in a separate chapter. Read this chapter (#15) if the home you are buying has well water – or if you just have a concern about what comes out of the tap.

Environmental issues. This is a long list. See chapter 12 and 13 for concerns to be aware of.

Septic and private waste disposal systems are important and require more discussion. See Chapter 16 for a discussion on how they work, how they fail, and what you can do to properly evaluate the system when buying a home. A failed septic system can entail an enormous expense that you want to avoid – especially in the first few years or after moving in. Note: if the home you are looking at <u>does not</u> have a private septic system, skip this chapter.

Concealed damage. This is sufficiently important that I have covered it in Chapter 9 (*Getting the Most from Your Home Inspection*). Read this.

THINGS NOT COVERED THAT CAN COST YOU A LOT . . .

#1 Chimney flues and the interiors of chimneys

(Note: this repeats advice from chapter 10, but I've provided more information below).

<u>In my opinion, this may be the most important exclusion from the home inspection</u>. The fact is, home inspectors are required to look at the exterior of chimneys and the venting of heating systems and other combustion 'appliances.' The *internal* portions of the chimney (what is called the 'flues'), however, *are very often partially or completely concealed and are thereby listed as excluded items in the Standards of Practice that govern home inspections.* To fully inspect the inside of a chimney, one needs to have the right equipment, remove combustion appliances (woodstoves, heating systems, water heaters, etc.), clean the chimney, and view the concealed areas with a camera. Home inspectors look at the structural issues of a chimney – but they can't inspect them fully.

Most inspectors (at least in my region) recommend having what is called a Level 2 chimney inspection performed by a qualified chimney sweep. This utilizes specialized cameras that does a video scan of the chimney interior. This is most critical for older chimneys, chimneys serving woodstoves, chimneys where you can't see any of the flues from below, or any chimney with evidence of significant structural distress. Level 2 inspections can be expensive to do – but not as expensive as finding the problems after you move in.

What you need to realize is that chimneys and fireplaces are just rife with problems. And while this may be especially true with older homes, a lot of relatively new chimneys also have problems. A few conditions that home inspectors commonly find include:

- No flue liners. Unlined chimneys were the norm up into the 20th century. Lots of unlined flues are still in use. Many are still functional, but all are suspect as they will often deteriorate when there is a change of use with the chimney (for instance, converting from oil to gas). Very often, they will require upgrading by your municipality or utility company when the heating or hot water systems are replaced. Even if not required, upgrading is normally desirable.
- Deteriorated terracotta liners. The clay liners commonly used for the last 80 years routinely crack and fail. Or, the mortar between the sections falls out. Or, they were improperly installed. Or, movement in the chimney causes these the liners to shift. Or, when exposed to the combustion byproducts of gas systems, they simply fall apart. They don't work well for wood stoves and can be problematic for gas-fired systems.

I have to say that a lot of terracotta flues look (and are) fine when the chimney was well built and the flues serve seldom used fireplaces or oil-fired heating systems. But they are also prone to cracks and distress.

- Concealed faults in the installations. Sometimes wood was left as forming under the fireplace or elsewhere. Poor clearances to combustibles are common. Gaps were left around the damper frame. Older, less safe flue installations may or may not be functional – but all will require repairs and upgrading with any change to the system.
- Dampers often are missing, do not work, work poorly, or are very loose-fitting, allowing continual heat losses.
- The metal flues used in manufactured fireplaces (what used to be called 'zero clearance types'), while very often okay, also have been a source of numerous fires.

I could go on, but chimney flues may have serious problems that simply are not visible to a home inspector. The cost of repairs to flues, moreover, can run into the tens of thousands of dollars.

A lot of buyers remark that they will have the chimney cleaned and inspected before they use it. Great – but if the chimney sweep identifies problems that may cost thousands of dollars to fix, would you rather hear about this after you own the home – or before, when the issues may still be subject to negotiation? Also, it is good when a homeowner says that they have had the chimney cleaned – but this doesn't mean they had a full inspection done.

(Just to be fair: most of the metal type B vents used on older and mid-efficiency gas systems do not show problems; the same is true for most of the PVC plastic pipe used for venting high efficiency gas systems. The lined flues serving oil systems are also at lower risk. That's not 'no risk,' though).

#2 Termites and wood boring insects

A termite/wood boring insect inspection may or may not be offered by your home inspection company. If not, I recommend that you have this done by a termite/pest control company. (This assumes that you are in area where termites may be present – which is most of the country, excluding the far northern states and dry/desert areas). This will <u>not</u> typically be a required inspection unless you are getting a VA mortgage or your mortgage lender requires this. <u>Ask your inspection company ahead of time whether they offer this.</u>

Note: if you are getting a **VA mortgage** they will *require* a termite/wood boring insect inspection and report. What is unusual is that they do not allow you (the buyer) to pay for this. In most cases, the seller ends up paying for the termite inspection, although sometimes the fee is simply waived by the inspection company.

Several points: *first,* termites are the most important wood-boring insect. Carpenter ants will do damage, but they usually are far less destructive. They are also harder to find, so even the few termite control companies that provide warranties for termites won't provide them for ants. Ants like to nest in moist or decaying wood, so very often the home with ant infestations really has a moisture problem that needs correction. Ants will also forage, so ants seen in the home may have their actual nest may in the tree stump next to the home. Lastly, ant treatments do not last long. In my opinion most ant treatments, at least on an ongoing basis, are a waste of money. I've found that various borate containing products (such as Terro®) will effectively control carpenter (and other) ants. If the home has a bad infestation, however, an initial 'knock down' treatment could be warranted.

The wood destroying insect/pest inspector may be looking for insect damage but more specifically they look for an *infestation,* the evidence of termite activity. When termite damage is found and there is no history of a recent treatment or warranty, they may recommend that the home be treated even when active termites were not found. In my opinion, this may be warranted, as no one can tell if and when the termites may have left and whether they will return. Sellers hate this, as they feel that are treating their home (at significant expense) even when no live termites are present. Unfortunately, termites are not active in northern areas during the colder months so you can't tell if active termites are present until sometime in April (or later). As no one does escrows anymore (where money is set aside that would pay for a treatment *if* termites are found in the late spring or summer), you are accepting the risk of paying for a treatment if this has not been done already.

Another type of wood boring insect is *powder post beetles*. These are commonly found in the basements of antique homes in northern areas and can encompass several types. They can do a lot of damage – but only over a long time frame. They proliferate in the damp basements of antique homes before the floors were covered with concrete and heating systems were installed. Many antique homes show damage but no current infestations. If significant active infestations are present they should be treated. Minimal infestations could be subject to localized controls. Also, if you dry out the basement they will often disappear.

Important: home inspectors <u>are not</u> required to look for wood-boring insect *infestations* but they should be looking for visible structural *damage:* <u>these are two separate things</u>. The problem with termites, however, is that very often the damage is concealed from view. Every home inspector out there has probed a piece of wood that looks perfect – until they plunge all the way through. Termites can be present behind finished walls and insulation and are simply not visible in all cases. Termites are insidious that way. Also, even when you find activity, you very often can't tell how far the damage extends. This is especially true in finished basements and with slab-on-grade homes. Termite damage and activity may be largely to completely concealed from view.

What can you do? If the home inspector or termite inspector finds evidence of past termite activity and there are suspicions about the extent of the damage, you could request that wall or ceiling sheathings be removed (or holes cut) to determine if the damage is severe. I've seen this done – but it's not easy. Removing sheathings or cutting holes in the finished ceilings or walls in the basement to look at the framing will damage the seller's property and most will not go along with this. You may need to decide where the evidence points to a high risk of significant damage before requesting this.

#3 Other bugs

The home may be filled with cockroaches, Palmetto bugs (these are just giant cockroaches given an exotic name in southern states), and other noxious bugs. Stink bugs are the new problem. While a nuisance, these are not wood destroying insects that will affect the structure. The principal concern is cases where you can't control the infestations due to adjacent living units that have a problem. There are strategies for eliminating or minimizing cockroach activity. (Proper food storage comes to mind). Having the home treated with an effective, non-toxic pesticide may be necessary. (In some cities, you may have to tolerate some pests if you are going to live in older, multi-unit buildings). Spiders are ignored. I suggest you do a bit of research on what brown recluse spiders look like, however, as these can disable you for months if you get bitten. (One home-owner I talked with stated he almost lost his leg after he was bitten.

#4 Pests

While termite control outfits are often called *pest control* companies, pests are a different thing. Many of the creatures listed below warrant removal or control by 'pest control' companies. As with many of the concerns noted in this chapter, home inspectors may report on noxious pests or those that pose a health or safety hazard – assuming they are visible or leave clear evidence of their presence; mouse infestations can be an exception as they are not always apparent. A few pests include:

- Mice. Literally every home (excluding newer and/or tightly built homes) will have mouse infestations, unless controlled. They usually come in during the fall when it starts to get colder. Mice do a lot of damage to fin-ished materials and stored items and their infestations are both unhealthy and bad for the home. They should not be allowed to proliferate, so control mechanisms in the fall months are critical. Insulation that has housed mice will often be urine soaked and will need professional removal.

- Bats. Bats are misunderstood. They are ugly and have all that Dracula thing about them – but they are harmless except for the (very) occasional rabid bat. But you don't want them in your home (and especially not in the living space). Bat guano (or any pest guano), sometimes found in an attic, is not something you want to be exposed to and breathe in. It is best that any significant amount of bat guano be professionally removed. Antique homes have been torn down due to 100 years of bat guano deposits found in their attics. To get rid of bats, pest control companies must find the likely entrance points and put 'one way' exits so the bats can get out but not back in. Bats are a 'protected species,' so you can't just kill them.
- Squirrels. They can do a lot of damage if they get into a home. Usually, they are in attics. They need to be removed with one-way exit screens installed by a pest control company. Open holes in the fascia or siding may need to be sealed and tree branches allowing access to the roof cut back.
- Raccoons. These need to be removed by a pest control specialist. If they are already nesting in the chimney, you sometimes have to wait until they leave with their young.
- Rats. These may be found in both urban and rural (farming) locations. These would need removal by a pest control specialist and blockage of access points. Food sources in the home (such as poorly sealed foodstuffs) would need to be securely stored.

#5 Smoke and carbon monoxide detectors MAY BE excluded

Some states (for instance, Massachusetts) require an inspection and certificate of compliance by the local fire marshal or building inspector that verifies the type, age, location, and operation of the smoke and carbon monoxide detectors. This must be obtained by the seller and the closing cannot proceed without this certificate. In states where sellers must have a compliance certificate for the sale to take place, these detectors are not examined by the home inspector. Other states (for instance, New Hampshire) require that the home inspector observe but not test smoke detectors. Various states could have regulations or Standards of Practice for home inspectors that mandate these units be tested. Many states require hard-wired systems for new construction but do not mandate these for existing homes. States have different requirements for what must be present at the time of the real estate transaction. Some will require interconnected systems and smoke detectors in each bedroom. Other states may have no or few requirements.

In general, testing is problematic as: the units will not stop chirping until the batteries (or detectors themselves) are replaced. Also, you don't know if the battery will be dead (or removed) by the time you move in. The code requirements on these are also regularly upgraded.

My recommendation: Check these before moving in (even if approved or found to be working prior to the sale). Replace any smoke detector unit approaching or over ten years of age. Also, *ionization* type smoke detectors may be allowed but *photoelectric* detectors have been found to be more reliable for smoldering fires. Plan to have a smoke detector within twenty feet of every bedroom and ideally one in each bedroom also. One or more smoke detectors should also be present in the basement, with one on the ceiling at the base of the stairs. As of 2007, all smoke detectors should be interconnected. When one alarm goes off all should sound. These may be hard-wired in new construction, but you will need to get Wi-Fi or RF linked detectors where re-wiring will be difficult. The best option is to have a combination photovoltaic / ionization units. Test monthly.

Carbon monoxide detectors may not be required in many states, but I recommend you install them prior to moving in. Consult your fire department for suggested (or required) locations. Don't put one right next to the heating system. Replace all units over five years of age.

IMPORTANT! Carbon monoxide detectors are intended to prevent people from dying due to high CO levels. Most are designed to go off if the levels rise above 30 PPM (parts per million) for a specified time. What they are not designed to do is detect the lower levels that will seriously affect the health of the home's occupants and possibly leave them with chronic respiratory or other health problems. Why is this? The reason stems from the fact that, due to temperature inversions that occasionally occur, the CO levels in the outside air can, for a short time (a week or so?) exceed 20 ppm. When this happened in Chicago some years back, many of the early generation CO detectors went off and the fire department spent long days responding to calls from homeowners who thought they were being poisoned from *internally* generated CO. Out of necessity, the carbon monoxide detectors now sold to the public will sound alarms only when they detect levels that are higher than possible background levels of CO.

The problem with UL listed alarms then, is that they're meant to offer protection to healthy adults when fairly high levels of CO are present. So how much CO does a UL listed alarm allow you to breathe before it goes off?

Here's what UL standard 2034 allows:

30 ppm for up to 30 days

- 70 ppm for up to 4 hours
- 150 ppm for up to 50 minutes
- 400 ppm for up to 15 minutes

Obviously, you can have a significant exposure before any alarm warning goes off. Chronic exposure to even low levels of carbon monoxide may cause brain damage, anemia, and respiratory problems, such as bronchitis and emphysema. The elderly, pregnant women, and young children are more susceptible to health problems due to exposure to low levels of CO.

What can you do? First, have your heating system serviced annually. If you have direct vented systems, keep all the outside vent hoods clear of ice and snow. Third, be aware of the symptoms of carbon monoxide poisoning, as they are very similar to what people feel when they have a bad flu; if you feel better when you leave the home, something is probably wrong. Lastly, you can purchase 'low alarming CO detectors' that will alert you when low levels are present. These are more expensive than standard CO detectors and you won't find these in stores. One good source is Tru Tech Tools (www.trutechtools.com). For other sources, just Google 'Low-level CO detectors.'

#6 Pools, pool equipment, pool piping, and spas

The inspection of pools is not part of the home inspection. A pool inspection requires a pool specialist. (Note: I don't know about other inspectors, but I will occasionally look at pools as very often I can clearly see that the pool has serious 'issues' – or may not even be viable. But I make no pretense about being a pool inspector.)

One of the problems with inspecting pools is that, in northern areas, they will be winterized and covered over for much of the year. Sometimes the pools have not been in recent use and are shut down. Above-ground pools are often antiquated and are prone to collapse if not properly winterized.

The underground piping to the pool can often be a problem – and leaks can be difficult to detect. Concrete pools (often gunite) can be lovely – but if the tiles or 'plaster' are loosening, repairs would be a major expense. Pools have numerous safety issues. This includes, as a partial list, unblocked access from a deck, gates that are not self-closing, faulty or homeowner wiring to pool equipment, poorly fitting covers that will not keep out a determined child, and diving boards (no longer allowed by many insurance companies). I recommend reviewing these concerns with a pool specialist and doing your own research on pool safety. If you have young children (or grandchildren) or are anticipating having kids, you will need to be especially aware of pool issues. Pools should be made safe for wandering or visiting children – and even wildlife and household pets. <u>Dogs cannot get out of most pools</u>.

#7 Spas (hot tubs) and Saunas

Spas are not required to be inspected under many state standards. In practice, I find they are very often drained at the time of the inspection. Inspectors should attempt to find and test the ground fault devices that provide electrical safety. I have also seen spas that were caving in the house floors they were located on. Note: spas are mini-pools and have the same child safety concerns. They also require chemical maintenance.

Saunas are not inspected. I recommend finding out if these were permit approved; if not, have an electrician inspect the installation further.

#8 Code Compliance

This was covered in chapter 11, so I won't repeat the issues with code compliance here.

#9 Zoning. Just as important as *building code compliance* is *zoning compliance*. In part, this is a legal issue (and is discussed in Chapters 7 and 9). Zoning determines what types of usages you can utilize the property for. Do not assume anything on this. More than a few people have purchased a property with the idea of running a business from the property where the town's zoning simply does not allow this.

One zoning pitfall is <u>setbacks</u>. Each town typically has a zoning map that delineates, for each zone, how close one can build to the property line and the street frontage. The setbacks, frontage requirements, height limitations, lot size requirements, and allowed usages will vary between municipalities and within each zone in the municipality. As noted earlier, a deck or addition may have been built too close to a neighboring property (in other words, it did not meet the required setbacks). <u>In this situation, you could conceivably be required to remove the structure</u>. Also, don't assume you can put up a garage or permanent building unless you know you have enough room to do this without violating the setback requirements.

Zoning matters if you are planning to make any change of use in the property. This could be adding an in-law unit (not allowed in many municipalities), adding a rental unit, or running some type of business out of the home (home offices generally are not a problem – but any business with people going and coming, or multiple employees may be). See the previous chapters on this also.

Where relevant, you could also possibly talk to neighbors to see if they would support you in getting a variance for a new deck, garage, etc. They may be supportive when the change does not affect them or when you are replacing a decrepit structure with something better.

Lastly, I would advise that you not buy any property where neighbors are con-testing the construction of the home based on zoning compliance – even if a building permit has been issued. This includes concerns such as height issues. Land courts can sometimes reverse the issuance of a building permit. A home-owner in a well-to-do town in the North Shore had to tear his new home down due to lawsuits by neighbors over the height of the home. He had been issued a building permit by the town, but a Land Court judge overturned this – after the home was built. See the legal issue in chapter 7 also – and talk to your attorney.

#10 Egress issues

Egress issues are important for fire safety but they are not formally addressed by the home inspection. Why? Egress standards are a code issue and most older homes and apartments simply do not and very often cannot meet current egress requirements, especially in terms of the sizing of the windows. Neither do they have to. A lot of egress deficiencies are just not that easy to correct. The small casement, awning, and hopper windows found in homes from the 1950s, 1960s, and 1970s do not provide a viable means of egress. Nor are basement windows sized for egress. Many replacement windows decrease the size of the original window opening so that openings that may have provided egress no longer do.

New homes would be required to meet current egress standards; existing homes should have met the code standards in effect when the home was constructed. Your home inspector does not evaluate this. Compliance with current egress standards may be required in any home or building that will be used for daycare, schools, foster care, etc.

In general, all living units should have two unobstructed means of access to the ground. If you are planning on using a basement area for a bedroom, you will need to meet the required egress and window lighting provisions. You may need to have a special window unit installed that is designed to allow egress. A functioning bulkhead door in the room may be sufficient in some cases – but you still need a specified amount of natural lighting to call a space a 'bedroom.'

Although optional, you may want to have a larger window installed on an upper floor that will allow egress during an emergency. Other things are common sense:

Don't block hallways or stairwells and don't weather-strip bedroom windows so they cannot be opened.

#11 Concealed insulation and vapor barriers . . .

Concealed insulation is excluded from the inspection. Most often, this pertains to wall insulation. You'd think that determining the presence of wall insulation would be part of the inspection. It isn't. Very simply, any finished room will have enclosed walls, floors, and ceilings. Despite your inspectors' best intentions, they can't see into the walls and enclosed cavities, such as vaulted ceilings. Older homes with balloon framing may show evidence of insulation at the base of the walls but modern platform framing doesn't allow this. Most homes built in the last fifty years will have some level of wall insulation (although often minimal until the 1970s), but exceptions exist. How well the insulation is performing is another matter. Voids, poor installations, and missing insulation are common.

Another reason why this is excluded: many older homes have partial wall or ceiling insulation. My neighbor had insulation blown into two walls – and not the others. Very often, homeowners have gutted and insulated some walls during renovations and not others. Your inspector can't determine this. I recommend that you have an energy audit after moving in to assess the presence and the condition of suspected wall insulation.

Concealed insulation could also pertain to enclosed and vaulted ceilings: normally, anything done in the last 40 years – in northern areas, at least – will have some level of insulation. Where the home has been renovated, the current homeowner or permits on record may indicate that insulation was installed.

A brief word about vapor barriers – and the lack of . . .

Vapor barriers in the walls and ceilings are not an inspection concern – and should not be. The potential problem with vapor permeable materials was a big concern back in the 1970s when fuel prices started to rise, as everyone thought the water vapor penetrating through the better-insulated interior walls and ceiling surfaces would cause moisture problems. While moisture problems within walls have sometimes occurred, it wasn't for a lack of vapor barriers. What building research and experience showed was that vapor barriers were largely ineffective; moisture enters walls due to leakage from the exterior. Moisture enters attic spaces or cavities through 'bypasses,' where warm moist air can flow into the attic unimpeded. Very little moisture flows through materials – which was what vapor barriers were designed to prevent. Vapor barriers over crawlspace floors are desirable (to hold down the dampness), but for walls and ceilings, forget about this as a home buying issue, even though it is included in many report systems.

#12 Special case: The presence of urea formaldehyde insulation in the walls

I'll discuss this a bit more in the chapter on environmental hazards, but this type of insulation will not typically be visible to the home inspector. The presence of this insulation is no longer regarded as a concern – other than the stuff crumbles and tends to fall to the bottom of the wall cavities, so it is no longer effective. Ignore.

#13 The home inspection is a 'home' inspection – not a 'property' inspection.

Structures and 'stuff' that are 'remote' from the house are not part of the inspection. This could include the following:

- Remote garages (sometimes not even visible from the home). Inform your inspector about any accessory structures on the property.
- Sheds and outbuildings are not inspected. (Outbuildings and remote garages can be formally inspected, but they typically involve extra costs – and you must request that they be inspected). The electrical systems in these structures should be inspected, in my opinion.
- While sheds ARE NOT inspected, take note of their condition. Make sure they do not contain hazardous waste or noxious materials, abandoned equipment, or other items that you may have to pay to get rid of. I found one shed that was filled with asbestos tiles. Hazardous materials are sometimes present in sheds or at the back of the property.
- Remote retaining walls or other walls. These can be a source of major expense – but they may not be viewed or considered part of the inspection. Home inspectors are normally required to inspect retaining walls that affect the home. I recommend that you walk the lot and identify walls, retaining or otherwise, that could be a concern. Retaining walls over four feet in height that are in significant distress may warrant a further evaluation by a qualified engineer or a masonry contractor. The ubiquitous short timber and other walls/barriers, such as are found along walkways, are ignored. All wood walls that did not utilize pressure treated wood will have a limited life. Even walls with pressure treated wood will eventually decay. Barrier walls are not retaining walls and would not be inspected or noted. The future performance of newer segmental block walls over five feet in height cannot be determined, as your inspector can't see the buried geotextiles that keep the wall up. (Verify with the installer that these are present, if possible).
- Seawalls. Seawalls could be present but they require a structural engineer who knows what he is looking at – and a contractor who installs these and who can provide further input and cost estimates when repairs are needed.
- Remote landscaping and drainage. Large trees – and especially dead or dying trees – are a common problem. As noted earlier, large trees on your property could fall onto not only your own home – or car, or outbuilding,

or fence, or pool, or kid, etc. – but your neighbor's as well. It's your insurance that will pay if they fall down on an adjacent property. Remote drainage issues include ditches that may fill with water, swampy areas, child hazards, land unsuitable for agriculture or specific usages, etc.

- Abandoned vehicles, hazardous waste, hazardous conditions, and structures or materials not adjacent to the house would also be excluded from the home inspection.

All of the above are important. I advise that you <u>walk the property</u>, get disclosures on everything, ask questions, and have a good attorney to advise you if the property has the above 'issues.'

#14 Solar photovoltaic systems – existing – and determining if they are feasible.

The potential for installing solar photovoltaic panels is something that you may see as a positive feature. Photovoltaic (PV) systems, however, can have some negatives – not fatal, in my opinion, but something you need to be aware of.

But first, as a very brief explanation: the solar photovoltaic panels installed on rooftops are designed to capture the sun's energy and produce electricity when the sun is shining. (Note: The panels for solar hot water systems that were commonly installed in the 1970s and early 80s have largely disappeared. Different thing). You can utilize PV solar by either a *grid-tied* system that feeds the electricity back into the utility grid to offset your electrical usage or, a *grid-independent* system that generates power for your own use, with large, heavy-duty batteries used to store the electricity. Off-grid systems are most often found in remote areas where utility power is not available

Almost all systems are grid tied. These are easier to install, are much, much cheaper (although still expensive), require vastly less maintenance, and allow you to draw power from the utility when the sun isn't shining. Being off-grid sounds wonderful, but those who go this route need to understand the limitations of these systems and how to work around the limited power they provide. Basically, homeowners with off-grid systems need to use the minimum amount of electricity <u>for everything</u>. Typically, they would still need propane for cooking and hot water. You also have to know how to maintain an off-grid system or you will be replacing the expensive battery system prematurely.

So, we are down to grid-tied systems, where most of the panels installed on roofs that are south-facing although sometimes east or west-facing. The pluses for these systems are low or non-existent electrical bills if your system can generate enough power, higher resale value in many cases, and the societal benefit of offsetting the use of coal or other fossil fuels used to generate electricity.

These are great reasons to have these systems put in. But you need to realize there are limitations and possible negatives to having solar panels on the roof of a home you are buying. I don't feel these are 'fatal' defects, however, in most cases.

#1 Many people feel they are ugly. I'm not really of that persuasion. I think they are okay. You may feel differently. Large panels set on ground mounts, however, can look obtrusive if you have close-by neighbors. A local newspaper article described a recent dispute between neighbors after one homeowner put up a huge, ground-mounted tracking array. While legal, the neighbors were having fits about this. The properties appeared to be too close to each other for this type of installation.

#2 There are concerns with PV solar panels on roofs in terms of potential leaks or structural inadequacy. The roof structure is supposed to be evaluated prior to any installation. Leaks have reportedly been a problem when the solar companies did not have the best installation crews. You can't put these panels on a roof with older roof shingles.

#3 You cannot tap into your PV system if the power goes out. This is a popular misconception. You would still need a generator for emergency power.

#4 Legal and financing problems. Solar PV panels can be purchased or leased. When the panels are owned, this is fairly straightforward: you buy the panels with the home – which usually will increase the selling price. When the panels are leased, however, this can impact you in several ways. First, you don't own the panels; you can't remove them or touch the equipment. Second, your bank or mortgage company will not cover these in your mortgage. You will still have to make the lease payments. This may determine how much you can borrow on the mortgage, as the lease payments count as a semi-permanent expense, just like child care or alimony. This would normally impact first-time buyers more than move up buyers. Leasing panels is a less desirable option, in my opinion.

#15 Yard concerns

These could cover a range of items: debris left behind, abandoned recreational equipment, abandoned anything, problematic landscaping, what I call noxious vegetation (see below), holes and an uneven yard that needs regrading, stumps (should not be left in the ground near the house), etc.

#16 Noxious vegetation.

This includes poison ivy (learn to identify this!), bittersweet vines (these will kill all trees if left unchecked), multiflora roses (sort of a natural barbed wire, great for kids), many types of bamboo (your neighbors will love when it spreads onto their property), knotweed (a type of bamboo and almost impossible to control if you let it get started), kudzu (down south), and literally dozens more. A number of weeds formerly controlled by herbicides now pose risks to agricultural areas as they have become resistant to existing controls. While the state of the vegetation would seldom be a reason not to buy a home, I did one inspection where the entire property was filled with knotweed. It would take years of effort to eradicate this– with no control over the adjoining properties that were also filled with it. No gardens there . . .

#17 Fences and gates.

While you would think these are part of the inspection, these are not <u>required</u> inspection components in the states I work in – and, I suspect, in many other states. Deteriorated fences are common, however, and can be a major cost to replace. I've found that the condition of fences, for most buyers, just isn't their primary concern – and I agree, but they can still be a significant cost if you have to replace them. My advice is to take note of the condition of the fence and gates, especially if pools or spas are present. They may not be negotiable or walk-away factors, but you still need to be aware of potential expenses. (As an effective 'Band-Aid,' decaying wood posts can be bolted or strapped to pressure treated wood or metal posts) that run into the ground, providing an additional life for these structures).

#18 Lawn sprinkler systems

Some inspection companies may cover these; most don't. In northern areas, they will be winterized and can't be inspected for much of the year. What if one is present? If the system is running – and very often they aren't if the property is vacant or the seller is moving shortly, you could ask the owner to demonstrate the operation of the system; very often they will do this, if asked. If the lawn sprinkler system has been winterized, ask if it was used the previous summer. Any homeowner-installed system is inherently suspect. Any system not properly winterized the previous fall will typically be sufficiently damaged such that it will not be functional. These are shallow systems and if not 'blown out' before winter they are subject to freeze-ups and burst pipes (at least in northern areas).

#19 Debris and abandoned goods . . .

The presence of debris and abandoned materials is commonly seen and normally is fairly obvious. I'll mention that while your inspector may note the presence of debris, this issue is not covered in many inspection report systems. Take note of this and other unwanted materials. If the lot is large, be careful with what may lie at the back of the property. In a recent inspection, I found large containers that may have been used for hazardous materials in the woods at the end of the yard. Debris, unused construction materials, unwanted owner's goods, and abandoned materials may also be present in the basement, attic, sheds, etc. The general rule in real estate sales is that all debris and unwanted materials should be gone and the property broom clean by the time of the sale. Sellers are almost always 'required' to do this – but this often doesn't happen. The costs to remove large quantities of 'junk' or other debris can be high. A clause mandating debris removal is something your attorney (or buyer's agent) will normally include in the sales contract.

The presence of significant debris or unwanted items left behind is something you would check for the at the walk-through inspection. If extensive debris or other goods are still present, the closing attorney may require significant hold-backs of monies to cover the cost of removing the unwanted items.

#20 Barns

These can normally be inspected, but at added cost. For larger barns that are in obvious distress, however (which would include many antique barns), I recommend that you consider bringing in a barn specialist – or at least a contractor with barn experience to evaluate the structure – assuming you plan on keeping it. Structural engineers can sometimes be needed. Any intent to convert a barn or detached structure to living space would require follow up from: a general contractor, the local building inspector, a structural engineer, an energy specialist, a septic evaluator, and more. (In general, this idea doesn't work very well). Agricultural barns may require further evaluation from a specialist or farmer with specialized knowledge. Any change in use could be a zoning issue and even structural issue. (Many counties have agricultural schools with experts on farming requirements and issues so this could be a good resource).

#21 Lot boundaries, plot plans. Having a survey done . . .

See Chapter 7 for more information on this . . .

#22 Legal Issues. See Chapter 7.

I don't want to sound like an attorney, but the home inspection does not determine the suitability of the home (or other structures) for any specific use. This could pertain to, as a few examples: the intent to use a structure for kilns, workshops, auto repair, livestock, child care, pet care, and home businesses or hobbies of any sort, etc. Code, safety, and zoning issues all apply.

#23 Energy Efficiency: Costs to Heat and Cool the Building . . .

The home inspector's primary focus is not on energy efficiency or the costs to heat and cool the home. The energy profile is an important concern, but it is just not the *primary* concern of the home inspection. Heating and cooling costs, moreover, often reflect the lifestyle and age of the current occupants. I recommend that you request copies or a summary of the fuel and utility bills from the seller. You will want to have an energy audit after moving in. High end, specialized audits are available in some areas. Note: the energy profile of the home or building – and the potential for improvements – may be something you will want to think about when looking to buy. Some homes will have limited potential for making them energy efficient; others have great potential.

Infrared scans can be done, but they are not formally part of the home inspection. They may be utilized at an inspection to detect water intrusion in the walls – but not so much to identify areas of heat loss. You need a temperature differential to get valid results from an infrared scan, so they may only be useful during the colder months.

#24 *Comfort levels in the home*

As a related issue, determining the comfort levels in the home is impossible except by living in the home during the extreme winter and summer temperatures – and possibly during high wind conditions. A few culprits:

1. Many homes – and not just older ones – have windows that are drafty. Sometimes the problem isn't the windows, but the unsealed gaps around the windows (hidden under the casings) that were never sealed or were stuffed with fiberglass (which doesn't work). Problems with excessive air infiltration are difficult to evaluate at the inspection. Older single-glazed units, even with combination storms present, will have a degree of air infiltration. Even a lot of the double-glazed wood (and vinyl) units (especially those installed in the 80s) may be leaky when exposed to cold winter winds.
2. Homes with tall vaulted ceilings may sometimes have poor comfort levels during the winter. Big family rooms with high ceilings are great for 'cooling' climates, less so where heating is the larger concern.
3. Obviously, homes with minimal insulation and with poorly sealed walls, ceilings, and unheated basements or crawlspaces may have comfort level issues. Rooms that just don't heat up or have poor comfort levels may have missing insulation in the walls, ceilings, or floors – especially in 'overhangs.' You can't see any of this. A thermal camera may show some of these problems but, as noted, you may need cold temperatures to get a proper reading.

4.   Homes with minimal insulation in the attic and less than optimal ventilation will have poor comfort levels on the second floor during the summer. In general, rooms on the upper floors, unless extremely well insulated and properly air conditioned, will stay warm during the summer.

5.   Homes with excessive south-facing glass (such as with early solar homes) or with enclosed sunspaces, may suffer from higher summer temperatures and poor comfort levels unless effective shading is present.

6.   Undersized heating or cooling systems – or a flawed distribution system – can be a problem – see below.

As you can't predict comfort level problems, you can't do a lot until you move in. Upgrading insulation, weather-stripping, and sealing drafts can help.

#25 Oil tanks and oil feed lines . . .

Another important exclusion is the condition of oil tanks and oil feed lines. Again, your inspector may look at these (I think just about everyone does), but they are formally excluded from the Standards of Practice in my state and, I suspect, in many others. The problem with oil tanks is that they corrode from the inside out; exterior rusting may look bad but this may not indicate a failure of the tank. Specific evidence ('cysting' or an oil sheen under the tank that cannot be attributed to an overfill) will typically indicate a failed tank. Tanks can fail catastrophically on rare occasions – which is a good reason to replace any tank over 25 years of age. This can be an important concern, as the cost to replace a tank typically will run $1500 to $2500. A leaking tank – or a leaking fuel line under the slab – can entail clean-up costs of over $200,000. (Ouch!)

What to do: ultrasound testing can be done – if you can find a company to do this – but some oil tank specialists believe this may not be reliable for household size tanks. For added assurance (at extra cost) have the tank examined by a reputable oil service company. In many areas, you can get tank insurance; the program is called Tank Sure in Massachusetts. Ask your oil delivery company if they offer this. Also check as you may be able to get partial coverage through your homeowner's insurance (at extra cost). Consider routinely upgrading any tank over 25 years old to a modern Roth tank.

Tanks over 25 years old are fully depreciated and their replacement should be anticipated; older tanks often get replaced when the heating system is changed. A tank (or oil feed line) that leaks is an environmental disaster. While I routinely see tanks that are sixty years old and are still functional, I recommend that you err on the side of caution.

Unprotected oil feed lines (without an approved sheathing) that run under the floor are a potential environmental disaster as these lines can leak oil into the ground below the slab for a long time before they are discovered. Just as with failed oil tanks, the costs could potentially run into the tens of thousands of dollars (or higher) in worst case scenarios. The solution (assuming no leakage has occurred) is to have the feedline replaced with a new feed pipe in an approved conduit; these are often run overhead. Some states have required that all unprotected or non-compliant oil feed lines be upgraded immediately – but oil companies often fail to do this. Whether required or not, you want this done. What are called 'oil safety valves' may be allowed as an alternative, but some question their reliability. Better to upgrade the oil feed line entirely.

#26 The presence and condition of underground fuel tanks . . . This is covered in Chapter 13, on Environmental Hazards.

#27 The type of waste disposal system present and whether municipal sewer lines are present or will be installed.

This is an unusual one – and is not a common problem. That said, there have been instances where everyone involved in the transaction – the homeowner, the listing agent, and the buyer – thought that the home had been hooked up to town sewers, but where the older private septic system was still being used. Even the current homeowner could be unaware that the system was not hooked up to town sewers if they were improperly informed when they purchased the home. The piping is entirely underground, and all anyone can see is the waste pipe that goes out the wall. In areas where the septic systems was located in the backyard, the old sewer pipe still may go out the wall on the back side, but it was often cut and rerouted around the house to the street sewer. Usually . . .

What to do: Where it was represented that the home was hooked up to a town sewer but you are not sure about this, ask the listing agent to check on this. They have a legal obligation to do basic research with the town to verify that the sewer hook-up occurred. Or, talk to your attorney about 'covering' yourself on this issue.

> As an example of a related problem: many years ago, I inspected a home in New Hampshire where the septic system was very old. I recommended that my client have the system further evaluated, whereupon the listing agent stated that town sewers were on the street outside the home. (If true, this would have mitigated the risk of my client incurring significant expense having a new system installed as they simply could hook into the municipal system). The problem was: the sewer line stopped down the street and the town had no plans to bring it up.

#28 Combustion testing.

This is also beyond the scope of a home inspection. The inspector will normally look for evidence of back-drafting or lack of combustion air for the heating system, but the 'adequacy' of the make-up air in the home is impossible to determine without specialized testing. Another difficulty in evaluating this is that – without getting into too much detail – specific actions by occupants or weather conditions can cause problems where none normally occur. For instance, running a fireplace in a tight home could cause back-drafting down the chimney serving a conventionally-vented heating system or water heater. Back-drafting can also occur if a powerful exhaust fan is used in the kitchen or, multiple bathroom exhaust fans are run at once; running the dryer could also cause a problem in tight homes. An old, 'leaky' home may have no problems until the building 'envelope' is significantly tightened and the home made more energy efficient.

What can you do: newer gas fired heating and hot water systems very often bring in outside air for combustion, eliminating problems with inadequate air flow for fuel combustion. Second, exhaust type kitchen fans are highly desirable but be careful with high capacity fans in very tight homes or in homes with conventionally venting heating systems or fireplaces. They could cause a back-drafting of air down the chimney if too much air is being sucked out of the home. Third, make sure you have carbon monoxide detectors and make sure they are working. Fourth, if you suspect a problem, then get this checked out. Air quality or HVAC specialists can often identify the problem and outline a solution.

Interior components not inspected . . .

Some of these are common sense or routine – others not so much . . .

#29 Screen windows, screen doors, and screening . . .

Formally, the Standards of Practice in most states do not mandate that home inspectors examine storm windows and storm doors – certainly not the screening. As a practical matter, inspectors will often comment on a non-working storm door, but if it is just older or worn, it may only be noted briefly or not at all.

I see lots of homes where the storm windows and storm doors are beat up and/ or are missing storm or screen panels. The replacement of numerous storm or screen panels can be a significant expense – especially screen units for sliders or patio doors. Also, missing or damaged panels may not be replaceable on older units, so new storm windows or doors may be needed. In many homes, reasonably tight older windows are viable when they have combination storm units, but they may not be economically viable if the storm units are missing or non-functional. Replacing the storm units entirely can be a major expense. I advise taking note of the condition of the storm windows, as it may be more cost effective to simply replace the primary windows if the storm units are damaged, old, or missing. Storm doors may be desirable but they are optional. They do not provide significant energy savings. They do protect the door and are nice for the screening they offer.

#30 Interior finishes

While the condition of interior wall and ceiling sheathings and floors is an inspection concern the surface finishes are not. In most cases, the condition and acceptability of surface finishes will be obvious. You may pay more for a home that has been well kept and shows beautiful finishes (and less for one that needs a cosmetic overhaul). The general appearance of the home's interior is normally (and hopefully) reflected in the asking price. Buyers may have very different standards as to what is acceptable or not. Your home inspection will not make value judgments on the finishes.

That said, keep this in mind: the amount of work involved to prep and paint distressed walls and ceilings can be considerable. Many young buyers like this type of work as a way to build sweat equity, but if you are paying someone, it can be expensive. I don't really like to call anything a 'cosmetic' problem for this reason. Most buyers know what they are willing and capable of doing themselves also, and most refinishing work is regarded as an 'upgrade.'

#31 Carpeting and floor coverings

Carpets and floor coverings are not inspection items. Any permanent wood or tiled floor, however, is normally inspected – but not for cosmetic defects such as a worn finish or scratches. A couple of qualifications: first, you really can't see that much of the floors in many rooms when the house is full of furniture and owner's goods. Second, the appearance of (or how attractive) the floor covering is not an inspection issue. Third, carpeting is not an inspection concern. Few inspectors, myself included, can determine what is quality carpeting and what type is appropriate for different rooms. Also, the most common issue with carpeting is its appearance and cleanliness. You will most likely want to replace older carpeting unless it is pristine conditions and meets your standards. Worn but functional floors may be ignored as their condition is obvious.

What to do: look at the floors and floor coverings during the walk-through inspection to inspect for defects previously concealed. Many wood floors will very often warrant a sanding and refinish. Where this is the case, get estimates so you can have this done before your move in.

211

#32 Presence or absence of items

This is an 'outside the box' item – and I include it only because I know of an inspector who got sued because his report listed 'Fireplaces/Chimneys' as an inspection item when, in this home, there was a chimney but no fireplace. The inspector noted no problems with the chimney so he checked 'Acceptable.' The buyer sued as there was no fireplace present, which they decided they wanted. (These were not a seeing-impaired couple). So, here goes: you need to take note of what is present and what is not present in your tours of the property, especially if you have limited access or showings before making your offer. You also need to look at the listing form to see what the seller may have excluded from the sale (that nice chandelier you covet?). And finally, ask the listing agent about specific items that you may want or that you are not sure if they go with the property. The inspector inspects what is there: not whether something is or is not present – or will be there when you take possession.

#33 Appliances

Some kitchen appliances are inspected; others aren't. Many inspectors feel that they are extrinsic to the structural, mechanical condition of the home. When a home has serious issues, the time spent inspecting older kitchen appliances may not be warranted. Many states – and ASHI Standards – require that certain appliances be inspected. In my opinion, it is important to look at stoves, dishwashers, disposals, and exhaust fans.

A few cautions are in order:

First, ALL appliances have a limited life. For dishwashers, I think it is about eight years, disposals – about the same? They may be checked – but they aren't the most important part of the inspection. You can turn them on and see if they operate. If they are old, shut down, or not in use plan to replace them.

Also, some appliances can be inspected and others can't be. Some specifics:

Laundry appliances are never inspected. The washer and dryer hook-ups should be – but not the units themselves.

Refrigerators are never inspected and shouldn't be, in my opinion. They are normally considered personal property. A caution: never open a refrigerator door in an abandoned or vacant home – at least unless you are ready to bolt out the door due to spoiled foodstuffs inside. I'll reverse myself: do open the door to rule this out – but only when you are prepared to leave the kitchen quickly.

Disposals – these are easy to inspect and lots of them are bad. <u>When not used for a while, they freeze up and won't work</u>. Some will leak out when run; don't go near them if this occurs as they could be a shock hazard. Plan on replacing older units. Get rid of them if a septic system is present. When non-functional, this is something sellers often will have repaired prior to the sale if the home is still occupied as the sink will clog up if you can't run the disposal.

Dishwashers are also worth inspecting – although, to reiterate, assume that older or worn units may need to be replaced; at least budget for this. On occasion, I have had newly installed dishwashers leak all over the floor when run, so don't assume that because they are new, they are fine (usually it's a plumbing fitting that needs repairs). Also, I will note that you can hear them run – but you can't tell if they are actually cleaning the dishes. On one occasion, I had a homeowner come forward to admit the unit sounded fine but wouldn't clean the dishes. Portable units are personal property and are not looked at.

Stoves. Stoves may have faulty gas or electric burners. In my opinion, having one faulty burner may be tolerable (assuming it's not your brand new Viking unit) as you may be able to work around this. The typical cost of a serviceperson (two visits plus parts) to fix a balky burner adds up to a large portion of what you would pay for a new stove. Unless this is a safety concern, save your money. Obviously, if it is a safety concern, it should be repaired prior to the sale (or use of the stove).

Exhaust fans. You can have two types of kitchen exhaust fans: those that recirculate the air and those that exhaust the air to the exterior. Recirculating type fans are normally found. They may work and are not considered a defect, but they provide little benefit as the cooking odors and moisture from cooking are just sent back into the room. Exhaust fans that vent to the exterior are preferable but they still can have problems (outside flap not opening, poor performance, age, poor location, etc.) Your inspector may be able to give you information as to the type and apparent performance – but air flows that are too low are not quantified. Where you <u>want</u> to have a vented (exhaust type) fan installed in place of a recirculating unit, get cost estimates as this may not be cheap – and may not always be possible.

Compactors. Not worth inspecting, in my opinion. I hate them. Many are mal-functioning. I'll run them if I have to.

Microwaves. Few inspectors look at these; I don't either. They could be inspected by putting a ceramic cup full of water inside to see if it heats up.

Ice makers. Not inspected. They are prone to problems and sometimes just stop working. I will provide a caution, however: when you have the piping hooked up for the ice maker – or just open up the gate valve in the basement for this line, inspect around the refrigerator carefully for a period of time afterward for possible leaks. Don't leave the building after connecting the piping. Leakage under the refrigerator happens and will ruin your floors if it goes unnoticed.

#34 Central vacuum systems

While a desirable system to have, they are not an inspection concern. If you can find the hose attachment, plug it in and see if it works.

#35 Wood, coal, gas stoves

The installations are looked at and addressed in the inspection – but the actual stove units are not part of the inspection. Lots of older wood stoves are out there and are still in use. Old wood stoves and older gas space heaters may only operate at 40 to 50 percent efficiency. Newer units that meet EPA standards are much more efficient. Franklin type units are rarely found anymore. They are basically fireplace units – which means they are very inefficient and are not a viable heat source.

What to do: Safety concerns are paramount. Make sure that woodstoves (et al.) have had a permit issued by the fire or building department. If not, you will need to obtain one as most insurance companies require this. This is important. Do not assume that any woodstove (or coal stove) can be safely used and can be permit approved. Have the chimneys and flues inspected by a qualified chimney sweep, as noted previously.

#36 Drapes, blinds, window treatments

This is an obvious one, so no further explanation is necessary. Window treatments can be very expensive, so if they are something you would like to have, ask if they are staying with the property.

#37 Cleanliness

Not our issue. Very often, you'll need to either spend a couple of days cleaning before or when you move in – or have a professional cleaning company do this.

#38 Odors

This is another tough one. Some people have very fine senses of smell and others don't. Bad smells can be from fairly harmless or non-recurrent sources: mice that die in walls, food left out by a previous occupant; bad housekeeping, etc., but odors could also indicate mold problems or even plumbing issues, especially if a sewer-type smell is present. I would be cautious about any home where you smell a strong odor unless you can determine what it comes from and what it will cost to correct it.

Odors could also emanate from outside the home from nearby livestock pens or grazing areas. Fertilizers and especially manure will smell. In rural areas, an outside wood burning heating system used by a neighbor can produce a lot of smoke and soot and if this is upwind and nearby. A failing septic system will stink. Any adverse smells should be followed up by the appropriate specialist. *You or your buyer's agent should notify the owner or listing agent to call the gas company if gas is smelled.*

As a special case, odors and the discoloration on wood floors from **pet urine** may or may not be visible. Carpeting that has been subject to pet urine obviously needs to be removed. Whether a dark stain on wood floors can be removed is still subject to debate: a few say it can but the general opinion is that the stains aren't removable. The odor can be dealt with by using products designed for this purpose. Staining the floors dark will hide the dark spots.

#39 Cigarette smoke odors and staining.

This could fall under environmental conditions. The odors and residues left when there have been smokers in the home can be an important issue. This should be solvable – but you may have to throw out the carpeting, have the walls and ceilings scrubbed, and then have the surfaces thoroughly painted. Get estimates from a company that does fire restoration work and from a qualified painter (one company may do both).

#40 Noise . . .

This is another potential issue, especially if you are buying a condominium. You should ask the sellers about whether noise from the occupants of adjacent units is a problem. The seller typically won't be around, however, to answer this question. The problem with noise issues is that you may not be viewing the unit at those odd times when the neighbor decides to blast his stereo – or just walk across the floor. Older homes broken up into condominiums would be more at risk of noise issues. Other noise problems could come from various exterior sources (nearby nightclubs, airport flight paths, trains, etc.). Not all of these can be avoided in urban environments. Tight fitting windows will actually screen out most of the noise.

#41 Use of tempered glass in windows.

The determination as to whether windows and doors have tempered glass (safety glass or acceptable alternatives) is not specifically an inspection responsibility.

The codes in most areas going back into the 1970s have required tempered glass in windows, sliders, sidelights, etc. where the glass is close to floor level, on stairwells, or in windows adjacent to bathtubs. How often is this found? Almost never in 'older' (pre-1975) homes, although new construction is much better on this. Occasionally I'll find an old sliding glass door that does not have tempered glass. In many cases it is difficult to read the etching on the glass that would indicate it is tempered. The windows around whirlpool units very often do not have safety glass. An upgrading is recommended in all cases.

Note: a very small percentage of tempered glass units, as found in sliding glass and patio doors, skylights, and windows in specific locations, will spontaneously shatter. This does not happen often – but it can occur. (I have a nephew who had this happen).

#42 Garage door transmitters.

Not an inspection item. Get these from the owner. If they don't have them and you have an older overhead door unit, you may need to replace the doors if you can't get a transmitter that works.

#43 Alarm systems.

These include water alarms that go off if they sense leakage on the floor. These are a great idea and I recommend them – but they are not part of the home inspection.

#44 Security concerns or the effectiveness door locks.

The status and operation of whole-house alarm systems should be reviewed with the owner and the alarm company; a new contract would typically be needed. Security concerns vary according to the buyer and the location of the home. Deadbolts are desirable for exterior doors.

#45 Fire sprinklers and fire safety . . .

A lot goes into the issue of fire safety – more than I can cover here. I'll note that fire sprinklers, while highly desirable, are obviously not subject to inspection – at least by the home inspector. You do not want to have the heat go off in a home with fire sprinklers. You also need to make sure the pipes remain well buried under the insulation if they run through the attic.

#46 Fire escapes and elevators.

These are not inspection components. Elevators have rarely been found in single-family residential properties – but they are becoming more common. If present, they would require a specialist to inspect. Fire escapes are an issue that you should investigate. Many municipalities require periodic (five years for Boston) inspections – but this is not always done. If you are buying a unit on an upper floor of a multistory building, you could try to find out if the condo-minium association has had the fire escape structure inspected or if there are reported problems.

#47 Squeaky floors.

I know, I know: this is for most people a nuisance item and I am getting to the end of the list here, but I have heard of home buyers (fortunately not my clients) who went ballistic over floors that squeaked. This is a nuisance issue, and you'll commonly find them if you step on the right spot. They are more common in homes built in the 70s through the 90s as builders today generally *glue and screw* the subfloors down. Squeaky floors occur when the subfloor was nailed down and then warped or loosened slightly; the subfloor would then ride up and down slightly when stepped on. The cure is simple if you have unfinished space below. If carpeted, the floor can be screwed down when the carpet is replaced. Where the ceiling below is finished and you have a wood or vinyl floor, my advice is that you learn to live with the squeak.

Specialized systems, components, and concerns

I don't want to overwhelm you, just scan (with your eyes, not your scanner) the items below. Some of these are low risk or things you can't do anything about – but others are items you need to be aware of and things could follow up on.

Heating and cooling system exclusions

#1 The home inspection does not determine the 'adequacy' of the heating and cooling system.

Several points:

1. Precisely sizing the heating and cooling system for 'adequate' supply and optimal efficiency requires engineering or specialized knowledge and calculations. A Manual J is used for sizing air conditioning systems. Miscalculations have tended to be more of a problem with cooling systems as builders have routinely oversized units so that the home's occupants would not complain about the home not cooling enough or

quickly. The problem is that air conditioning systems work better when slightly undersized. By running more they remove moisture from the air and distribute the air better.

Oversized heating systems will cycle on and off more, making them less efficient.

2.   Despite the fact that a lot of the ductwork installed over the last 50 years was poorly designed and often poorly installed, most often it basically works. Your inspector simply won't apply today's higher standards to these installations. For instance, many 'older' homes have just one return duct while newer or better-designed systems will have a return duct in each room. Most older ducts were poorly sealed whereas new ductwork is generally well sealed. Flex ducts are not as desirable as metal ducts. For 'older' homes (over 10 years old in this case), less than optimal ductwork simply may not be noted by the inspector as long as it is functional. An upgrading of the ductwork is often justified when replacing the heating/cooling system or when it is filthy inside. <u>An initial duct cleaning should be anticipated</u>.

3.   Contractors can get the heating calculations wrong if they size the heating system to provide just enough heat during extreme temperatures. Any miscalculation can leave rooms with poor comfort levels – usually just during temperature extremes. Poor comfort levels can be problem when high vaulted ceilings are present as the warm air stratifies at the top of the ceiling. Unusually low temperatures in southern areas, where homes were not built for the cold, may lead to poor heating performance and poor comfort levels (not to mention, frozen pipes). Under-sizing the heating system may be more of an issue with new construction when the builder is trying to get the sizing just right – and not oversize the system, as was done in the past. In practical terms, it may require simply living in the home during extreme temperature conditions to identify comfort level problems. Compensatory measures to reduce heat losses or add a supplement heat source may be the easiest option.

#2 The condition of the internal heat exchangers in furnaces . . .

This is a tough one. Determining the condition of the internal heat exchangers inside furnaces (hot air systems) is *excluded from the inspection*. (The heat exchanger, I should note, is simply the metal surfaces inside the furnace that separate the hot combustion air from the household air circulated through the system to absorb the heat).

As your home inspector is inspecting the heating system, you would like to know the heat exchanger has no problems. If the heat exchanger is found to have cracks when the system is serviced, the technician will shut down and 'red tag' the system so that it can't be run. A new furnace would then need to be installed. Unfortunately, the heat exchanger surfaces are never fully visible, and on 'newer' systems, they are completely concealed from view. In many instances, moreover, a furnace with a cracked heat exchanger may operate normally and show no functional problem in its operation. It doesn't matter: if the heating technician sees a crack, either the heat exchanger or the entire system normally gets replaced. Replacing just the heat exchanger alone is occasionally done and may be both possible and warranted in a few cases – but it usually is not done, especially if the furnace is over fifteen years old.

What can you do? For older furnaces (anything over 15 years old), consider having the system checked by a gas or oil service technician. As they will not look at the heat exchanger during a normal servicing, you should explicitly ask that they examine the heat exchanger for cracks. I should note that very often even the service techs can't view the heat exchanger surfaces with special or invasive procedures.

#3 Solar hot water or solar air systems.

Solar hot water systems can still be found – especially in southern areas where they are most cost-effective – but, generally, you won't see too many working systems anymore. These systems (including any type of solar air collector) are beyond the scope of the inspection. They require a plumber or installer (or occasionally a very knowledgeable homeowner) to explain the working of the system and the needed maintenance. 'Newer,' professionally installed installations that are in use should be regarded as a plus.

#4 Photovoltaic installations

These are specialized and are beyond the scope of the inspection. You will want to ensure that the system was professionally installed and was inspected by the municipal electrical inspector. As noted earlier, if the system is leased, you – or your attorney – may also want to investigate any leasing issues that go with this. Any performance issues would be beyond the scope of the inspection.

#5 The potential for installing photovoltaic or other collectors

This is similarly beyond the scope of the inspection. Concerns would be: the orientation of the roof (if this is a roof mount), the shading (can't have ANY), the appearance (not always a plus), the cost, and for off-grid systems, the higher cost and critical maintenance required to operate the system properly and ensure its reliability.

#6 Evaluating heat recovery and energy recovery ventilation systems.

These are increasingly found in new energy-efficient homes and buildings that need a source of fresh air due to their tightness and resulting potential for air quality problems. Heat recovery ventilators (HRVs) or energy recovery ventilators (ERVs) are also found in homes where previous owners may have had respiratory concerns and want a continuous stream of fresh air in the home without having to pay the energy penalty of leaving windows open. I won't get into these systems too much as they are not commonly found. They work by bringing fresh outside air in while discharging the 'stale' household air, transferring the heat from the outgoing air stream to the incoming air. Just exhausting the air and letting new air in (which is constantly occurring due to air leakage in conventional homes) carries too much of an energy penalty.

What to do: having one of these systems is a plus – but they require a specialist to determine if they are installed and working properly. Commercial buildings have a 'commissioning' process for these, performed by qualified HVAC technicians. This can be done for residential systems also.

#7 Humidifiers and electronic air filters

These are not formally inspection items, although your home inspector may look at these.

Humidifiers must be properly installed and regularly maintained – which is usually not the case. Older style humidifiers with pans of water (typically stagnant) should be removed. A moderate amount of humidification may be desirable but higher levels often lead to mold or indoor air quality problems in the home. Electronic air filters require regular maintenance to work properly and are less often installed today. Older units, I find, are very often abandoned. In general, humidifiers, unless carefully used, cause more problems than they solve. Homes with grand pianos, wood guitars, and fine woodwork, however, may be damaged from overly dry air, so humidification may be necessary to maintain a specified level of relative humidity.

#8 Miscellaneous heating related components not inspected

These include many of the sophisticated controls for heating systems, such as boiler reset controls, which, while desirable, are beyond the scope of an inspection and are not subject to evaluation. Motorized dampers to allow zoning on hot air systems are not an inspection component.

#9 Gas meters

These are owned by and the responsibility of the gas company. That said, gas meters are supposed to be periodically replaced (seven years in my area). This is not always done. These meters can go bad – and leave you without heat in the middle of winter. This may be quickly detected and fixable if you are in the home – but not if you are vacationing in Florida for the winter.

<u>What to do?</u> If your meter appears to be quite old, ask the gas company if it is due for replacement. Keep the base of gas meters out of the ground. For maximum assurance, install Nest type thermostats or specialized sensors that will text you if the temperatures in the home fall below 40 degrees.

Electrical system Exclusions

While the home inspection includes a thorough inspection of the electrical system, there is lots of stuff that is beyond the scope of the inspection. A few of these issues are:

#1 The presence of elevated electromagnetic fields due to faulty wiring practices in the home or from electronic devices. See more on this in Chapter 14, on Environmental Hazards.

#2 Certain types of hidden wiring conditions within junction boxes, switch boxes, etc. may not be ascertainable by normal inspection procedures and equipment. Combining neutrals from different circuits comes to mind.

#3. The inspection cannot determine the adequacy of the service. This is determined by an electrician or electrical inspector, who does a load calculation of the existing and planned usages in new construction. As a general rule, 100 amps is more than sufficient for most homes. Homes with multiple large appliances (think hot tubs, air conditioning, electric heat, etc.) may require a larger service. 200 amps is the new norm. The size of the service, in almost cases, is not a safety issue.

#4 The home inspector typically does not test every outlet – nor are they required to under ASHI and other standards. You can't get at all of them. Exterior light fixtures on photocells or security sensors will only come on when it is dark. Consider buying a simple tester and testing each outlet while the home is vacant – or hire the inspector to do this at a lower cost inspection at the walk-through or just after moving in.

#5 The home inspection does not 'map' the electrical system to tell you what circuits provide power to which outlets and usages. You can do this after you move in by turning off every breaker and then documenting what comes on when you restore power to that circuit.

Over-extended circuits may only become apparent after you have lived in the home for a while. A common problem is when homeowners add window air conditioning units. These use a lot of power so when you have two on the same circuit you may find the breaker tripping. One solution is to have one or more of the room AC units supplied by a new circuit back to the panel.

#6 The type of wiring within the enclosed walls and ceilings. An inspector can usually see if knob and tube wiring is present – but there are times it may still be present within enclosed walls and ceilings – but you simply can't see it. Old hallway light fixtures are usually where knob and tube wiring is still present – and won't be seen.

#7 The presence and effectiveness of surge protectors is beyond the scope of the inspection. Few people install these – but they are always a good idea. Inspectors won't comment on the lack of these devices, however.

#8 The quality of the power cannot be determined by the inspection, nor voltage drops on various circuits. Substandard but allowed wiring practices such as 'back-stabbing' outlets and switches won't be found. The services in some multi-unit buildings will have a 208 and not a 240 volt service. This is not a safety defect. This list could go on.

#9 Low voltage systems are not inspection components. This includes the presence and operation of wiring for cable TV; telephone wiring; speaker wires, doorbells, outside lighting, Cat 5 wiring for computers, the strength of cell signals – ALL are not inspection concerns. All may warrant further evaluation and upgrading.

Plumbing System Exclusions

The major components of the plumbing system are part of the home inspection – but there are some important exclusions and things that fall through the cracks. I've noted these below with recommendations on how to pursue further investigations, where feasible.

#1. Underground or below slab pipes . . .

The home inspection does not include waste pipes that run underground out to the street, under the basement slab, or even up through the enclosed walls. And yet, a significant percentage of homes – and especially older homes – have cracked or failing sewer pipes. In a few cases, the back-up of sewage or waste water from a failed pipe may show up simply by running the water at the inspection. More often, it takes weeks of occupancy and water use for the problem to become apparent. This is especially true if the home was previously vacant or underutilized – or if the home's previous occupants were elderly and rarely ran the water. A backup of sewage could also indicate a failed septic system or even an overloaded municipal sewer line on the street.

Nails that penetrate waste (or supply) pipes in the wall take some type before they leak (the nail has to rust out). This sometimes happens months or years after renovations have been done in the home.

What to do:

1. If the water was shut off at the inspection, try to run the water hard at the *walk-through* inspection. (Better yet: make sure that the water is on for the inspection, as banks often have the home winterized. Hire the inspector to come back, ideally at seller's expense, if they can't get the water on for the inspection). See option 2.
2. Have a sewer scan done by a sewer cleaning company that offers this service. They will send a camera down the pipe to look for cracks, blockage, tree roots, etc. This evaluation is a fairly standard procedure in some areas of the country – but not yet in all areas.

#2. Home inspectors may look at – but they won't operate – stop valves. The unfortunate reality is that if an inspector even touches an extremely corroded valve that is not currently leaking – and it starts to drip, the homeowner will hold the inspector responsible for repairs. The inspector will examine a sampling of the valves present and should point out badly corroded gate valves, but no one sees them all. Also, some of the valves that are corroded work fine while others will immediately leak or fail to operate when used. ALL gate valves, however, are suspect and their replacement with 'ball' valves should be anticipated. Main shut off valves should be carefully checked by a plumber. You may want to test this yourself – but be careful: I've heard of instances where merely touching the main shut-off valve or incoming pipe caused an immediate failure with resultant flooding. (Fortunately, this did not occur on one of my inspections!)

As a special case, **the single-levered valves for washing machine hoses** may leak when operated. These valves use inferior metal and very often are corroded. The home inspector won't touch these for obvious reasons. If the valves are corroded, assume they will need replacement. This is also a problem as you very often can't get the older rubber washer hoses off without replacing the mixing valve. I recommend having your plumber replace any corroded laundry valve with *quarter turn* valves.

#3. Laundry hoses. These are more prone to failure than most types of supply piping. Everyone knows that the older style rubber hoses have a history of bursting

(assuming the pressure is left in the pipes) and home inspectors routinely recommend their replacement. The 'no-burst' metal braided hoses are considered fine – but there have even been isolated cases of these failing – usually those of advanced age. Neither your inspector nor your plumber has any predictive ability about this. The safest course of action is to turn off the water to the washing machine when not in use – but few people do this. You could also replace hoses every five years, as recommended by the insurance industry. Have a plumber install quarter turn valves (the most reliable type) and use them. Another option is to have a specialized flow control device installed that will sense the difference in water flows between a leak and normal filling and will shut the water off if the laundry hose has failed. These are especially valuable if the laundry is located on an upper floor – or you have another living unit below yours. Just remember: if a hose bursts, the water will not stop running until you come home – or you run the reservoir dry. I could tell you the horror stories – but I'll leave it to your imagination.

#4. Supply piping running through the slab or basement floor can't be inspected. Pipes running through the concrete slab under the living space or under the basement floor can't be seen. Lots of 'older' (older means pre-1980) homes have copper supply pipes that run through the slab. Slab-on-grade homes, moreover, may have extensive piping that still runs through the concrete from where the piping enters the home to the bathrooms, kitchen, and laundry areas. As long as the piping appears to be functional (water runs, no apparent leakage), the inspector can't declare it to be defective. But this is a potential problem as concrete will eventually corrode the copper. You can't avoid buying a home with piping in the slab, but at least be aware of this issue. In single level slab on grade homes, you may want to have new PEX (plastic) pipes re-routed through the attic (under the insulation). I find that this has already been done in many homes.

As a special case, radiant copper heat pipes in the slab are a problem. These were installed in numerous slab-on-grade homes in the 1960s and 1970s. I don't know the experience in the rest of the country, but in New England most of these systems have failed and have been replaced with perimeter baseboard or other systems. (The copper pipes simply corrode out and leak). Newer types of radiant floor heat systems, utilizing specific types of plastic piping, are not included in this caution. To date, these materials have not been prone to failure.

#5. Older types of thinner walled copper piping (type M) are often present for the potable supply plumbing. This will have a red label while the thicker walled pipe, type L, will have a blue label. While type L rated copper piping is now required for new piping, there is no routine requirement or recommendation for replacing older type M piping unless corrosion is visible. This is not an inspection issue. I recommend that you periodically examine all copper piping for corrosion. Although rare, reportedly there have been 'bad' batches of pipes manufactured.

6. The adequacy of the hot water system is difficult to assess. Your inspectors will – or should – look at this, but determining the 'adequacy' under all conditions is difficult. Example: my electric-fired water heater is fine for almost all usages – except when a relative visits who likes to take half-hour long steamy showers. My son's tankless hot water system is okay – as long as no one runs the dishwasher or other usages at the same time. My sister used to live in a multi-story building with a common water heater. The hot water flows were fine – except at 7:00 in the morning when everyone was taking a shower.

The newer 'on demand' water heaters may *potentially* have problems as they tend to 'scale up' with deposits due to the small tubing inside where the water heating occurs. These often require an annual or bi-annual descaling by a plumber. The jury is 'still out,' I believe, on the newer tankless hot water systems that come off of hydronic boilers.

7. The shower pans under tiled shower enclosures are concealed and are not part of the home inspection. An inspector will normally run the water in the shower stall, but in some cases the leakage only occurs after the water has been run for a longer time; in other cases, the water stains don't appear until some time after the shower was used. Some inspectors have tested these shower stalls by putting stoppers to fill the shower base. This is a great idea – which occasionally resulted in leakage and water damage on the ceilings below (and resulting lawsuits from homeowner who allege that they never had leakage from the shower before this was done). No assurances can be offered with shower pans as the critical details are hidden below the surface tile. There may be no small repairs on these. You – and your inspector – should look for evidence of leakage below enclosed showers. Also, be sure to recheck this at later visits and the walk-through prior to the sale, as homeowners could hide the evidence of leakage at the inspection.

8. Note: READ THIS: The overflow drains present in every bathtub sometimes will leak when the bathtub is filled (very often when bathing young kids). These drains depend on gaskets that seal the drain pipe to the back of the bathtub. These gaskets dry out (as they are never wetted), so when the bathtub is filled (or a lot of splashing around occurs), the water simply leaks through this opening onto the ceilings below (usually the nicely finished kitchen ceiling). You cannot tell whether the overflow drains are properly secured unless you overfill the bathtub and then check the ceiling below – which may mean you created the problem you intended to avoid! Your home inspector obviously won't test this. The solution is to not overfill the bathtub – ever.

9. **Water purification equipment** is not evaluated by the inspection. See Chapter 15 for more information on water purification equipment.

CHAPTER 14
Environmental Hazards

This chapter covers a number of environmental hazards relevant to your home buying effort that you need to know about. Please note that I have not put these in order of importance or in any predefined sequence. I suggest skimming through the list to see which may be applicable to a property you are looking to buy. Also, this is not an in-depth or technically exhaustive treatment of these items. It's just the basics of what you may need to be aware of. I'll cover the risk factors and how you can deal with many of these concerns. These include:

- *Lead paint hazards and how to avoid them*
- *Carbon monoxide risks*
- *Asbestos – what to recognize, risk factors*
- *Vermiculite insulation*
- *Radon gas in the air – risks and options for testing*
- *Exposure to electromagnetic fields (EMF) from high power lines, cell tower, other sources*
- *Problems living near windmills, radar stations*
- *Chinese drywall*
- *Formaldehyde in wood flooring*
- *Liquid underground Fuel Storage tanks (LUSTS)*
- *Proximity to hazardous waste sites*
- *Recognizing and avoiding drug or 'meth' houses*
- *Out-gassing from urea-formaldehyde foam insulation*
- *Problems with living near highways, busy roadways*
- *Air quality problems from wood burning*
- *Problems with excessive exposure to Herbicides and Pesticides*
- *Homes near major oil and gas pipelines*

Mold and Indoor Air quality

Any discussion of environmental concerns with real estate has to start with mold and indoor air quality. Due to the amount of concern with mold issues, however, I have covered this in a separate Chapter, which follows.

Lead paint and other sources of lead contamination

Lead paint and possible lead poisoning from other sources is an important concern, both for home buyers and homeowners. (Note: the issue of lead in the water supply will be dealt with in Chapter 16). Everyone needs to be aware of how lead poisoning can occur and steps you can take to avoid this. While lead paint could be present in any 'older' home (or home with older woodwork), by following commonsense precautions, you should be able to avoid most problems.

The EPA has a lot of good material on lead paint, including how to minimize your family's risk of lead poisoning. (See https://www.epa.gov/lead for more information. Also, if you are buying a newer home lead paint may not be concern – but lead in the soil or water could be.

As background: lead is a naturally occurring mineral that was extensively used in paints up until 1978, when it was formally banned. Lead paint was rarely used in the 1970s and, when used in the 1960s, was largely on the exterior. That said, no one can tell if lead paint is present unless one tests for its presence. In general, the older the home, the more likely it is to have lead-based paint. Lead was also widely used as a gasoline additive until banned in 1995; engines were developed to use unleaded gasoline starting in the 1970s, so lead was on its way out from that time. Also note that lead and lead compounds have been used in a wide variety of products found in and around the home, including paint, ceramics, pipes and plumbing materials, solders, gasoline, batteries, ammunition, and cosmetics.

Lead poisoning can occur in individuals of any age, but the largest risk is with children up to the age of six or those in utero (during pregnancy). At this age, children's brains and nervous systems are more sensitive to the damaging effects of lead. Even low levels of lead in the blood of children can result in:

- Behavior and learning problems
- Lower IQ and Hyperactivity
- Slowed growth
- Hearing Problems
- Anemia

- For pregnant and children in utero, lead exposure can result in reduced growth of the fetus and possible premature birth.

All young children should be tested for the presence of elevated lead. If high levels are detected, however, you may need to investigate where the exposure came from. It may be from your home – but it could also be from someone else's home or the yard your child plays in.

While lead paint may is most often found on woodwork, it was reported to have been occasionally used on walls and ceilings in bathrooms and kitchens. The largest risk, according to many experts, is lead dust. Lead dust may be generated from moveable surfaces, such as older painted windows or doors, or from careless renovations where the lead paint in the home is disturbed.

A few points insofar as what you need to know as a home buyer:

1. Under Federal Law, every home buyer must be given a pamphlet that explains the risks of lead poisoning. Much like the home inspection contingency, you are given the right to have the home tested for lead paint within a specified period. The home inspection contingency is not mandated, however; it is just customary. The right to a lead inspection is federally mandated.

2. If you have young children, or plan to, and you have a high level of concern about lead paint, then you may want to simply buy a newer home. As the only affordable homes in many areas are older homes, this can be difficult. Common sense cautions (such as never disturbing older paint and removing lead dust and chips from window wells, etc.) can greatly reduce the risk of lead poisoning. While I very often recommend that buyers keep and refurbish older homes (when the condition and quality of the window warrants this), you may want to replace old windows with loose or deteriorated paint on the sashes or in the tracks. Unless the paint is removed (and you properly clean all dust and paint residue from the floor), the normal opening and closing of the window may produce lead dust.

3. If the presence of lead paint will be a walk-away factor, have the home tested before you spend the money on a home inspection and appraisal.

4. Consider having a certified lead paint technician test the home for lead. They will normally use a sophisticated X-ray fluorescence machine to do the testing. In many states, your home inspector cannot legally do lead testing – and most inspectors simply will not do this as it is not part of a home inspection. You can purchase test kits from a hardware store, but I can't vouch for how reliable these are. They may work, but I think they are less likely to provide clear results when just small concentrations of lead may be present. As a home inspector, I do not

ever discourage buyers from testing for lead paint – but the safe assumption is that most older homes will contain lead paint.

5. Recognize that lead may be present in the soil and can enter the home as lead dust or other means. Homes near highways or busy roads are more at risk of having lead in the soil due to the residue from the years when lead was added to gasoline. Also, the soil around older homes may contain lead due to the flaking of the lead paint off the siding over the years. (Most of the paint used on antique homes was lead-based). I recommend that you do not plant edibles or herbs next to the foundations of older homes. You can even have your soils tested, often by state laboratories. This may need to be done by a specialist.

6. Any contractor – or homeowner – who will be working around or disturbing lead paint needs to follow lead-safe practices. The information on this is con-tained in the EPA guide to lead-safe work practices (PDF). See their website for this information. Personally, I recommend refraining from any aggressive removal of lead paint or, alteration of the older painted woodwork (that may contain lead paint) while you have young children in the home.

7. If you plan on renting your home in the future – or if you are buying a multi-family home where you plan on renting the other units –*then you will want to have the rental units de-leaded* – meaning made compliant with the standards for lead paint. If you are in an owner-occupied building, you may have the right to not rent to someone with young kids (check with your attorney on this) – but if you are not living at the property then you don't have the right to discriminate and *not* rent to families with young children. If your tenant's children are found to have elevated levels of lead, you could be paying to house them in a motel while you have the home de-leaded (which really means ripping out all of the older doors, woodwork, and windows). I won't even go into the worst-case scenarios that can happen.

Carbon Monoxide Poisoning

Carbon monoxide is an odorless, colorless, and tasteless gas that is poisonous and can be fatal when inhaled. The statistics on this are somewhat grueling, with over 500 deaths from CO poisoning in the U.S. last year. I covered carbon monoxide issues in the last chapter when discussing smoke detectors, so please read this section. Important stuff . . .

Asbestos-containing Materials (ACMs)

The home inspection does not make any determination as to whether asbestos is present or, whether materials that appear to be asbestos are, in fact, asbestos-con-taining. That said, I think just about every inspector will comment on the presence of certain types of 'suspected' asbestos-containing materials (ACMs). The most visible type of asbestos is the whitish insulation found on older heating pipes, boilers, and ductwork. You should assume these to be asbestos-containing – although there is similar looking pipe insulations that do not contain asbestos (which is why home inspectors use the term 'suspected' when discussing asbestos containing materials).

I won't go into the reputed health effects of asbestos, but exposure has been linked to asbestosis and higher rates of lung cancer and mesothelioma. (See the following section on the asbestos found in vermiculite insulation, below).

A few things you should know:

1. Home inspectors, as noted, may point out potential asbestos-containing materials that would be considered a high risk of generating airborne particles, but they can't test for asbestos or take samples unless they are licensed to do this.

2. Asbestos was used in hundreds of building products since the early part of the 20th century. These include asbestos-cement siding, composition floorings (the ubiquitous 7- and 9-inch composition tiles), asbestos-cement roofing (rarely found today), mastics on floors to secure composition type floorings, post-1910 plaster, spray-on 'popcorn' ceilings from the 1950s and 60s, and literally dozens of other building materials. Asbestos was even used in drywall joint compounds up into the 1970s. The difficulty is that no determination can be made without testing, and second, the asbestos that may be present in most of these materials is 'bound up' and does not become readily 'friable' (crushable) or generate airborne particles. These ACMs are not considered to be hazardous. That said, they should not be disturbed. Removing older floor coverings may be possible, but it is not recommended; you will have to research this if you are going to do this. It is a lot of work too, so it is usually better to just cover them. Flooring professionals normally will not remove composition floorings but will just cover them with another material. Older popcorn ceilings from the 50s and 60s should be left alone unless testing is done. The white acoustical tiles used on ceilings in the 50s into the 1970s look like they could contain asbestos, but I have never found any sources that indicate any brand is asbestos-containing.

3. The risk from asbestos is not from its being present but from airborne particles. The insulation on heating pipes and older boilers is considered 'friable,' or crushable, and this type will produce airborne particles, <u>if disturbed</u>. On the other hand, if not disturbed, it's not a health problem – it is more of a resale issue.

'So, how is asbestos regarded in real estate transactions?' you may ask. Is it a negotiable issue? First, there is nothing that says a homeowner has to remove asbestos-containing materials – so usually, depending on a bunch of factors, it stays. Many authorities recommend leaving asbestos-containing insulation on heating pipes alone – <u>assuming</u> the material is intact and/or is well encapsulated – and is not in an area that will be extensively used. (These can be big assumptions!) If it is not deteriorated, is reasonably well encapsulated – and is not located in habitable space, the risk factors of generating airborne particles would be low. Also, if the asbestos insulation was plainly visible when making your offer, it would generally be tough to make this a negotiable issue.

Conversely, when the friable type asbestos found on older (usually steam) heating pipes is loose and deteriorated, this is a concern and the material warrants removal. Your inspector may indicate this – but this may not be an issue in post-inspection negotiations if its condition was obvious to anyone walking through the home.

As noted in the chapter 11 on post-inspection negotiations, how the asbestos-containing materials are dealt with depends on:

#1 the condition of the material (is it largely intact or are numerous sections of deteriorated or loose insulation?

#2 the nature of the property (in most older homes with unfinished basements or in rental properties, the ACMs are less of a critical issue).

#3 whether the ACMs are located in an area that you plan to finish,

#4 the price of the home is the nature of the local real estate market. Environmentally concerned buyers in higher-end markets, I find, will have more concerns about asbestos than those buying an older home with an unusable basement.

#5 your own level of concern. Some people simply have few concerns about asbestos-containing materials; others regard it as something comparable to nuclear waste.

#6 whether the material was clearly visible when you make your offer. (Example: I once encountered a pile of ACM deep in a crawlspace. The buyer negotiated to have this removed, as it was an unknown up to that point and the buyer did not believe they should have to bear the cost of having this removed).

#7 was there evidence that asbestos-containing materials were formerly present but were removed by a non-professional (in other words, a prior homeowner)? This can be a problem if remnants were left on the heating pipes. The basement may need a professional cleanup by an asbestos-removal contractor, as asbestos particles were most likely left on the floor.

Vermiculite insulation

Vermiculite is a gray, pebble-like insulation, often sold under the name Zonolite that was found to contain asbestos. I, along with many homeowners, installed this in my own home in the early 1980s as it was cheap and easy for homeowners to use. Much later, it was revealed that the Zonolite brand of vermiculite from the Libby, Montana mine contains asbestos. This insulation is no longer sold, but it is commonly found in attics. Many types of vermiculite do not contain asbestos, but roughly 73 percent of all vermiculite insulation reportedly is Zonolite from the Libby mine.

A few things about this insulation . . .

The actual incidence, or percentage, of asbestos in this insulation is small – roughly 2 percent, according to sources in the remediation field. I know asbestos testers who have not found asbestos in the samples they have taken. It doesn't matter, however, as there is no rational risk assessment of this material. The standard now is to have the material removed by companies that specialize in this. This is not a do-it-yourself job. Fortunately, an asbestos removal trust (Zonolite Attic Insulation (ZAI) Trust), was set up by the W.R. Grace company that will reimburse homeowners for up to 55 percent of the removal cost, up to a maximum cost of $7500 (or a maximum reimbursement of $4125). To participate in this, however, the homeowner must go through the procedures outlined in the settlement. This is clearly laid out on the website http://www.zonoliteatticinsulation.com/faqs/ or https://www.zonoliteatticinsulation.com/. Programs like this end, so check this out.

Each state has its own regulations regarding testing and disposal, so you need to research this before beginning any removal of suspected vermiculite insulation. Although they don't recommend it, some states may allow homeowners to remove vermiculite from their own homes. Waste disposal regulations may vary from state to state, so you should check with your regulatory authorities before attempting to remove or dispose of vermiculite. The state by state regulations can be found at www2.epa.gov/asbestos/state-asbestos-contacts.

In Massachusetts at least, the vermiculite issue is normally handled by the numerous companies that offer energy audits. In most cases, it will be necessary to have the material tested by a licensed tester and lab to determine if it was Zonolite insulation and not another type. I recommend contacting your energy office in your state for more information.

As noted, the home inspection is not formally an asbestos inspection. That said, most inspectors will note the presence of suspected vermiculite, IF viewed. There are a couple of difficulties, however. First, this insulation is very often covered over with another insulation; your inspector won't go searching for this material under existing insulation. (As my opinion only: if completely covered in a largely unused attic, how much of a risk would the presence of vermiculite be – assuming the insulation will not be disturbed?). Also, sometimes it is only present in a very small quantity, sometimes in a remote section of the attic. It was also used to insulate walls where you simply cannot see it. The experts I've heard talk on this recommend leaving the vermiculite in the walls alone, as it will not readily generate airborne fibers and, realistically, may not be removable.

In any case, note any type of grayish- tan pebbly insulation in the attic and ask your inspector about this.

Radon in air . . . (note: radon in well water is covered in chapter 15)

I won't provide a detailed explanation of radon issues here as the EPA website provides a lot of good information on radon. The link: https://www.epa.gov/radon/home-buyers-and-sellers-guide-radon

As a brief overview: Radon is an odorless, colorless radioactive gas that comes from the breakdown of the naturally occurring uranium in the soil. Unfortunately, radon tends to accumulate in homes and buildings, raising the levels to sometimes unacceptable levels. Statistically, elevated levels of radon are found in 25 percent of homes nationwide. In some regions, radon is rarely present while in other areas, elevated levels are routinely found. Radon also will vary from house to house and neighborhood to neighborhood. The street where I live has numerous homes with very high levels of radon – but a small percentage of homes do not have elevated levels. You can have high radon levels in your (soon to own) house, while all the neighboring houses test low. The only way to tell is to have the home tested. The effect of exposure to radon gas is analogous to getting a chest x-ray. Living in a home with high radon levels could be the same as getting multiple chest x-rays every day. The health risk from this is an increased risk of lung cancer. (To date, I've not seen studies that link radon to other type of cancer).

Most inspection companies will offer to test for radon. Either canisters, vials, or electronic monitors can be used. Each has their advantages. Electronic monitors provide the best option as they are more tamper-proof, provide hourly results, and provide a much quicker turn-around. They are also a more expensive option and many inspectors do not have these – or offer them for all areas. Charcoal canister or vial (liquid scintillation) test kits are also available and provide a lower cost option. Despite the knock they get, they are accurate as long as the proper test conditions are observed. They are not tamper-proof (nothing is, really) and require mailing the testing devices to a lab for processing.

Radon testing involves leaving a test device at the property for a minimum of 48 hours. Canisters can be left longer than vials, and electronic monitors could conceivably be left for a much longer period. Long-term tests can be done but these are not used in real estate transactions as everything has to happen quickly.

A few notes regarding radon and radon testing:

When it was first discovered that homes may have elevated levels of radon the EPA established an 'action level' of 4.0 picoCuries per liter (pCi/L, a unit of radiation). This is not a danger level but an *action level*. In terms of real estate transactions, when the testing shows levels at or greater than 4.0 pCi/L, very often the current homeowner will have a radon mitigation installed or will make an allowance for the buyer to have this done. While not a legal requirement, this is the common protocol, as the listing agent and seller must disclose 'higher than desirable' radon levels to any future buyer of the property. Very often, a mitigation system will be installed prior to the sale; in other cases, an allowance will be made.

Exceptions to this scenario, however, can exist. In sales where the buyer is getting the property 'as is', this, in most cases, would exclude renegotiating for a radon mitigation system to address the high radon levels. For bank-owned properties and short sales, forget it. You can test for radon, but any remediation will be up to you. For the vast majority of homes, the mitigation systems for radon in air run about $1200 to $1500. Occasionally, a home may require a more elaborate or expensive radon mitigation system.

Where and when to test . . .

#1 You want to have the home tested for radon during your inspection contingency period. If there is no way this will be a negotiable issue, then wait until you are in the home, as you will have better control of the testing premises. You could then test with inexpensive canisters. Very often, you can't get the radon results back within the contingency period. In this case, the buyer's agent normally will insert a clause in the Purchase and Sale document that notes that the agreement is 'pending an acceptable radon test result' (consult your broker or attorney for the language). This gives you more time to get the result. This is routinely done.

#2 If testing, have your inspector do this; it's short money. Don't use the inexpensive testing devices you may get in a hardware store. You may wait weeks to get the results; this doesn't help you when you need the results quickly.

#3 Test the lowest *potential* habitable or usable level of the home. The original EPA guidelines recommended testing the currently used habitable space – not the unfinished basement. These guidelines were intended for *homeowners* – not *home buyers*. This created a lot of confusion as some real estate agents have argued that we should not do the testing in unfinished spaces we should not test in an unfinished basement based on these guidelines. This was not the intent of the EPA, as clarified in their recommendations in the pamphlet they provide for guidance as to where to test:

'Make sure that the test is done in the lowest level of the home that could be used regularly. This means the lowest level that you are going to use as living space, whether it is finished or unfinished.'

https://www.epa.gov/sites/production/files/2015-05/documents/hmbuygud.pdf

The highest levels of radon will always be found in the lowest area of the home (typically the basement). In older homes with unusable basements or homes with half height basements or crawlspaces, you should have the testing device placed in the lowest habitable space (typically the first floor).

#4 *If you are buying a newly constructed home, make sure you test for radon!* A lot of buyers have the misconception that radon will only be found in older homes or when there is a dirt basement or loose foundation. This is not the case. High radon levels are even more likely to be found in new construction, especially if there has been blasting to remove a ledge. I just inspected a very nice new home recently where it was apparent the builder had to blast out the ledge to allow a full basement. The radon levels came in at 166 pCi – which is what you could find in a uranium mine.

#5 Radon is a correctable problem. If you like the home, I think it seldom warrants walking away due to high radon levels. In some towns, you can't find a home that does not have 'high' (over EPA action level) radon. On the other hand, if the results are outrageously high (which is extremely rare), then maybe this is something you may not want to deal with.

Exposure to electromagnetic fields (EMF) from high power lines, cell towers, other sources

This topic really requires its own chapter – if not a book. I've provided links to websites that cover EMF exposure – many created by Michael Neuert of EMFinfo.org and EMFcenter.com. If you are electromagnetically sensitive – or just have a lot of concern about your exposure to electromagnetic fields – you will need to do additional research. I will note at the start that there are many misconceptions about exposures to electromagnetic fields and lots of studies that indicate possible problems – and an equal number of studies that downplay the risks. I'll concentrate on how you may want to approach this topic in your home-buying search. It may not be a relevant or critical concern to you - but it is a topic you should know something about.

As a brief explanation: electromagnetic fields (or EMFs) encompass the entire spectrum of the fields of energy. Visible light is part of this spectrum. EMFs include the low-frequency waves such as those from power sources, radios, cell signals, TV signals, etc. These are referred to as non-ionizing waves, as they do not heat up and thereby directly damage human tissues. By contrast, the frequencies that are higher than visible light, running from ultraviolet light and Xrays up to gamma rays, are referred to as ionizing radiation. Essentially, our bodies are part of and are affected by the whole electromagnetic spectrum.

For our purposes, there are **three types of EMFs** that we should be concerned about:

> First, to quote Michael Neuert, '*magnetic fields* are the EMF component most often linked to serious health effects in the scientific research literature (e.g., the link between power lines and leukemia). These common magnetic fields are emitted from power lines, building wiring, electrical panels, lights, appliances, and virtually every device that runs on regular electricity.

> *Electric fields* make up the other half of the common *electro*magnetic fields emitted from power lines, wiring, lights, and appliances. They are also linked to many important biological effects but have been studied less. Anecdotally, electric fields are often involved when people knowingly feel 'symptoms' and discomfort from different electrical sources. Electric fields induce significant voltages onto the skin, which are easily sensed and measured.

> Finally, *Radiofrequency or 'RF'* includes the higher frequency fields and microwaves emitted by cell towers and cell phones, TV and radio broadcast towers, cordless phones, Wi-Fi and other wireless computer components, microwave ovens, baby monitors, Smart Meters and various other electronic devices.'

While the section below goes over the largest sources of EMF exposure, it is beyond the scope of this book to delve too deeply into the possible risks from electromagnetic field exposure. I'm also not covering the concern with transient voltages, or what is called 'dirty electricity' for now. I will provide commonsense advice on how you can limit your exposure and risk when in the home buying process – as well as after you are in the home.

As noted, EMFs come in two types: ionizing and non-ionizing. 'Ionizing' basically refers to the ability of the energy to break chemical bonds into ions. Electromagnetic radiation of the ionizing radiation type (X-rays and gamma rays) is a problem as it causes DNA damage, but what about radiation from the non-ionizing electromagnetic fields?

This is where things get controversial. Because the radio frequency waves produced by cell towers are the non-ionizing low-frequency types, the telecom industry has argued that cell signals are not a problem. The studies they have done seem to support this. (A lot of the independent studies do not, as noted below). Similarly, studies on the effect of high-voltage transmission lines done by the utility companies have indicated that the level of exposure to radiation from EMFs from major power lines may not be excessive – at some reasonable distance away. They may or may not be correct – I'm not qualified to give a definitive answer. In homes with elevated EMFs, the problem may just as often be close-by power lines and wiring problems in the home and not the major power lines. A specific type of wiring defect present in up to twenty-five percent of existing homes will produce elevated electromagnetic fields. I'll explain this below

What are the reputed health concerns with exposure to electronic magnetic fields (EMF)?

Studies on the low-frequency electromagnetic fields produced by power lines and the higher frequency fields produced by cell phones, cell towers, and other RF sources (such as smart meters) do not show these to be a significant health risk. The problem is: most of the studies funded by the telecom industry do not show a link between EMF exposure and health issues, while numerous independent studies come to very different conclusions. Scientists initially assumed that, because EMFs from these sources are not an ionizing type of radiation (such as X-rays or gamma rays that do ionize, or damage, the molecules they hit), they would not be a risk to human health. Unfortunately, scientists then discovered that EMFs can cause harmful biological effects not only by heating up sensitive tissues but by influencing or interfering with sensitive 'bio-electromagnetic' processes within our cells, brains, and bodies. The human body is a living 'bio-electronic' machine, utilizing many sensitive electromagnetic processes for the proper functioning of our brains, nervous systems, immune systems, and other organs. To quote Michael Neuert again:

> ' . . . researchers have shown that our pineal gland can sense daily changes in the earth's natural magnetic field, and use this information to help regulate our brainwave patterns and wake/sleep cycle. An example of electromagnetic interference (EMI) affecting human biology is found in the fact that artificial magnetic fields (like those from power lines) can suppress the secretion of melatonin from the pineal gland at night. This is important because melatonin is the main hormone which initiates our sleep cycle. It is also a strong antioxidant which fights cancer naturally within our bodies.'

Another problem is that, as cell phone usage has only really taken off over the last ten or fifteen years, no long-term studies have been conducted on the risks from cell phone usage or exposure to cell signals.

While this remains a matter of much controversy, studies suggest that EMFs may be linked to a variety of health problems, including leukemia, lymphoma, brain and nervous system cancers, melanoma, breast cancer, miscarriage, birth defects, Alzheimer's disease, Lou Gehrig's disease, depression, and suicide. Anecdotally, EMFs have been associated with symptoms such as nausea, headache, fatigue, anxiety, dizziness, mental confusion, memory loss, sleep disturbance, seizures, tinnitus, changes to blood pressure and heart rate, itchy or burning skin sensations, and skin rashes. Anecdotally, increasing numbers of people now report 'hypersensitivity' to electromagnetic fields, similar to the way that some individuals have become 'hypersensitive' to chemicals due to over-exposure in the past.

Exposure to high magnetic and electrical fields from high transmission lines AND other power sources . . .

Transmission lines . . . There have been claims that the low-frequency EMFs from high voltage lines could increase the risk of cancer, particularly childhood leukemia. Importantly, other studies have not shown this correlation. I cannot weigh in on this, as the science or proof of health effects may not be entirely settled. In terms of what to think about when looking at homes near high power transmission lines, I think the critical factor is just how close you are to the transmission lines. EMFs decrease with distance from the source. At anywhere from 700 to 1000 feet, the level of EMFs produced by power lines should reach 'background levels' – in other words, there is simply is no elevated exposure. You may be able to see the transmission lines from your home or backyard, but if you are a sufficient distance (see below) away, this may not be a problem. In many states, including California, and in many areas in New England, the utility companies will come out to a property where homeowners have concerns about power lines and will do a survey with 'Gauss meters' to indicate the levels of electromagnetic fields that may be reaching the house. In terms of household appliances, most will produce EMFs, but if the appliances are correctly wired, you should not have any elevated exposures at one to three feet away.

The issue with exposure to high magnetic fields, however, goes beyond proximity to high voltage transmission lines. Regarding this, I'll again quote Michael R. Neuert of The EMF Center (www.emfcenter.com).

> 'It is difficult to predict a safe distance from power lines because the EMFs can vary greatly depending upon the situation. The best advice is to measure with a gaussmeter to determine the actual levels of magnetic fields

and the distance required in your particular case. (Special note: magnetic fields are EMF component most often linked to health effects in the studies. They are measured with special instruments called <u>gaussmeters</u>.)

The strongest magnetic fields are usually emitted from high voltage transmission lines — the power lines on the big, tall metal towers. To be sure that you are reducing the exposure levels to 0.5 milligauss (mG) or less, a safety distance of 700 feet may be needed. It could be much less, but sometimes more. You must test with a gaussmeter to be sure.

It's even more difficult to predict a safe distance from neighborhood power distribution lines — the type typically found on wooden poles. For example, homes with a nearby transformer will sometimes have higher EMFs because the transformer is a hub and the power lines carry more electricity for a group of homes. The issue is complicated by the fact that there can be stray electricity flowing in the metal water service pipes of the neighborhood, increasing the magnetic fields from both the power lines and from the buried pipes!

Thus, there is no reliable safety distance for neighborhood power lines. In general, a magnetic field level of 0.5 mG will be reached somewhere between 10 and 200 feet from the wires. But you cannot tell by simply looking up at the power lines. You have to test on-site with a gaussmeter to be sure.

If the electrical power lines are installed underground, the magnetic fields may be just as strong, or even stronger. This is because the power lines could actually be closer to you when only buried a few feet down, rather than up 20 or 30 feet overhead. For neighborhoods with buried power lines, you must always test with a gaussmeter.

Power lines also emit electric fields. The electric fields from high voltage transmission lines (metal towers) can be very strong outside near the wires and extend for over a thousand feet. However once inside the home, the building structure usually provides some shielding, and the electric fields from electrical wiring and cords will usually be much stronger than that from the power lines.'

On this, I'll note that I've had the voltage stick I keep in my shirt pocket start ringing when inspecting homes near power lines – but usually just when I am on the out-side of the home. It's disconcerting, but the electrical EMFs may not pose as much of a concern as the magnetic portion of the EMFs as they are easily shielded by trees and the home's walls and ceilings. The magnetic fields penetrate through the walls and are not easy to shield against.

Exposure to EMFs from power sources within the home . . .

One of the authorities on problems with EMFs, Karl Riley, found that, when conducting studies to identify the sources of high EMF levels in homes and schools, most of the time the problem was not from the transmission lines or the power lines outside the home. Instead, bad wiring practices (specifically an improper grounding of the 'neutral' wires) were the source of the problem. Some of these practices can be spotted by the home inspector – but others are concealed from view. I'll note at the end of this section about having a further evaluation by a specialist in this area.

Exposure to RF waves from cell towers, other sources . . .

Exposure to electromagnetic fields from cell towers are another area of concern. Cell phones communicate with nearby cell towers mainly through radiofrequency (RF) waves, a form of energy in the electromagnetic spectrum between FM radio waves and microwaves. Like FM radio waves, microwaves, visible light, and heat, they are forms of **non-ionizing radiation** that do not directly damage the DNA inside cells. Again, the stronger (**ionizing**) types of radiation such as X-rays, gamma rays, and ultraviolet (UV) light are thought to be able to cause cancer.

Cell towers that are a good distance away may not pose a significant risk of exposure to harmful EMFs. The problem is, you may find cell tower installations in buildings where you did not even know they were present. There are over 300,000 cell tower installations in the United States. Many now are disguised as chimneys, trees, or just boxes on commercial buildings.

> I once inspected an old church and was ascending the interior ladders in the tall steeple when I found I was surrounded by the large cables from the cell tower installation inside. I can only wonder what my exposure was for that day! In any case, I didn't know the cell tower was even there before ascending the steeple. What about the neighbors to this church? With a base station installed on top of a building where people live or work, how many people who work or live next to this are aware that there is a cell site close by – and the high levels of EMF radiation that they are subjected to every day?

To quote Michael Neuert again:

> It is also difficult to predict a safe distance from cell towers. For example, cell towers are designed to transmit most of their radio frequency (RF) energy horizontally. Some areas below the tower may have lower levels than locations farther away that are more in line with the vertical height of the antennas.

The exposure from a cell tower will depend on the type of antennas, the number of antennas, how much the antennas are actually being used, the time of day, etc. The distance needed to reduce exposures down to the General Public Precautionary Level of 0.010 microwatts per centimeter squared ($\mu W/cm^2$) is often around a quarter of a mile (1320 feet) or more. Due to the uncertainty, on-site testing with a broadband RF test meter is strongly recommended.

A German study reported that people living within 400 meters (1312 feet) of cell towers had over 3 times the normal rate for new cancers (City of Naila 2004). In an Israeli study, the relative risk for cancer was about 4 times greater within 350 meters (1148 feet) of the cell tower (Wolf et al. 1997). Based on findings like these, a minimum safety distance of 1/4 mile (1320 feet) might be considered prudent.

RF exposure from other devices . . .

Low frequency (which doesn't necessarily mean without biological effects) RF signals will also be generated by numerous sources, including radio and TV stations. Again, its proximity that is a concern: you may get more exposure when sitting right in front of a TV than you would be from exposure to the signals reaching the home from a tower some distance away. Michael Neuert also expresses concern about living next to police and fire stations, as these use a higher frequency cell signal that may be more difficult to shield within the home.

Electromagnetic and RF radiation inside the home . . .

The levels and quality of the electromagnetic fields in the home is also a concern to be aware of. Cell towers get all the attention regarding possible effects from RF exposure. These may not be the thing you should be the most concerned about, in my opinion – again assuming you are not in close proximity to the tower. I've read that you get more radiation from cell phones when a weak signal is present – so one could argue that having more towers and stronger signals may be a plus? Your exposure to low-frequency RF waves is much higher when you are actually using a cell phone than what you will get from a cell tower located some distance from your home.

Importantly, a wireless router in your home will also vastly increase your exposure to electromagnetic RFs. A wireless router basically is a low powered home-based cell tower. RF fields are also emitted from other wireless and electronic devices, including cell phones, cordless phones (may be even higher levels than cell phones), TV/radio broadcast towers, Wi-Fi, wireless computers and components, baby monitors, microwave ovens, radar, etc. There have recently been concerns raised about the electromagnetic fields generated by smart meters. I've talked to people in this field who dismiss this concern, but cautions are still in order if your living space is directly adjacent to these meters (see the list of ways to decrease your risks at the end of this section). These may be behind the walls of your condo unit, so you need to look for them.

As a general comment, I believe the overall levels of exposure to RFs and EMFs should be a concern. This is one of those topics where there is limited but damning evidence that EMFs are a significant concern versus the research from the government and 'official' sources that says, basically, that 'we don't know.' I won't wade into this here; I've provided links to websites on electromagnetic fields. I will say that the issue of exposure to EMFs from cell phones and from electrical fields within the home is not something typically subject to evaluation during the home-buying process. I don't know any inspectors who would offer this and, to be honest, one would need to test for EMFs after you have moved in, as the electronic equipment you may bring with you would also count. Your wireless router could be the source of EMFs. In many homes, the electric and magnetic fields will also carry added RFs due to the use of dimmers, fluorescent lights, computers, Wi-Fi, Smart Meters, etc. (This is referred to as 'dirty electricity').

What can you do when buying a home?

So what can you do to find a home without high levels of electromagnetic radiation due to power lines, or radiofrequency radiation due to cell towers or other sources?

1. As it isn't always possible to find where the closest cell tower is, visit antennasearch.com to find out where the towers and antennas are in your area and how close they are to your home or place of work to locate the closest tower. Cell towers located at least 700 feet from your home may not pose a high risk of elevated electromagnetic fields. You may, however, find a concealed tower nearby that you did not know existed, especially in urban areas.

2. If you want to know your exposure from the magnetic fields from a power line, you may be able to have your utility company visit the property and test for EMFs from power lines. They would not, however, test for or look for problems within the home. An option would be to simply avoid living close to high voltage power lines.

3. Consider having an electrician or other specialist who is knowledgeable about EMFs and associated wiring defects examine the home's electrical system and measure for elevated EMFs with a gaussmeter. This may be a more likely source of EMF problems. Improper wiring practices, bad connections, or other faults may produce high EMFs.

A wiring defect, whereby the neutrals are grounded or improperly routed, is one of the more common sources of electromagnetic exposure within the home. Home inspectors may be able to spot when a neutral wire in a subpanel has been improperly grounded, but not when this has been done within junction boxes.

4. Strong sources of magnetic fields from electrical panels, transformers, refrigerators, pump motors, and other common sources can often be shielded with MuMetal® type alloys.

5. If you are concerned about a nearby cell tower, you need an RF test meter. If you are knowingly sensitive to electric fields, you need a body voltage meter. If you are concerned about the potential health effects from a variety of EMF sources, you may need several test meters to detect all three types of EMFs — a gaussmeter for the magnetic fields, a body voltage meter for the electric fields, and an RF meter for the radio frequency fields.

6. If you are electromagnetically sensitive, you will need to be especially cautious about where to live and what you can do to shield yourself from EMF exposure. I should note that Electromagnetic Sensitivity (ES) is a health condition where people report heightened sensitivity and troubling symptoms related to EMF exposure. This condition is often verified when, by simply removing or turning off the EMF source or moving the person away from the EMF source, the symptoms disappear, but reappear later when the exposure is reintroduced. Anecdotally, the incidence of electromagnetic sensitivity is steadily increasing, especially with the proliferation of wireless technologies such as Wi-Fi computers, DECT cordless phones, and Smart Meters.

    People with electromagnetic sensitivity are often very affected by the normal EMF levels found in a typical home or work environment today. Thus, special measures are often needed to reduce the exposure levels even further. See ElectroMagnetichealth.org for information on the distances recommended for specific EMF generators.

7. Get rid of fluorescent lights. Use low wattage incandescent bulbs in your bedroom. Obviously, don't leave your cell phone on and nearby when sleeping. Same for your computer. Same for your cordless phone. Same for your wireless router, if present in or near the bedroom. Turn things off at night.

8. Research your options for shielding yourself (and your home) from high EMF levels. A great book for home buyers who need to avoid homes with elevated EMF's is How to Find a Heathy Home, by Jeromy Johnson. Also, Michael Neuert provides consulting services for homeowners in northern California. Contact at 707/578-1645.

Problems living near windmills, radar stations . . .

I – like most people – think windmills and alternative power sources are a good thing (not necessarily the answer to our problems – but what is?). Also, a lot of arguments made against windmills simply don't hold (kill birds [yes but not as many as claimed], too expensive, don't work all the time, etc.). Overall, however, wind turbines have proven to be economically viable and are generally accepted by most of the public.

But – there's always a 'but.' There have been complaints from homeowners living near large wind turbines who reputedly suffer migraines, insomnia, dizziness, and a general discomfort from the constant low-frequency noise, termed 'infrasound', produced by the blades. Numerous residents of Falmouth, Mass., as detailed in an NBC report in 2012, found it almost impossible to live in their homes due to the effect of the nearby wind turbines. The difficulty is that some people living near large wind turbines experience the effects and others don't. Studies have also been mixed on whether the effects are real or significant – but it certainly has been real for those who have been experiencing the effects.

I cannot comment on the science. It appears that some people are more prone to problems than others AND that the nature of the topography and site makes some properties more prone to wind turbine effects than others. In any case, you don't want to buy a home that you will be miserable in.

As far as what you can do, I recommend that you not live in close proximity to large wind turbines. (How 'close' is 'close'?) Most are sited some distance from homes – as they should be. <u>You will also need to do your own investigations</u>. There is no easily available test for infrasound, and the wind may also not be blowing when you are looking at the property. Talk to the town health officials, neighbors, and other local sources regarding complaints about windmills made by homeowners in those towns. Look at the overall evidence carefully. Some complaints have proved to be groundless.

Chinese drywall

Chinese drywall' refers to an environmental health issue involving defective drywall manufactured in China, imported to the United States, and used in residential construction between 2001 and 2009 – affecting 'an estimated 100,000 homes in more than 20 states.' Most of this was the Knauf brand (although most Knauf drywall was domestically produced and did not experience the problems of the Chinese manufacturer). Almost all the defective drywall (and reports of problems) was associated with the southeastern states, particularly Florida. A lot of this drywall was shipped in due to the hurricane damage in these years and the need for extensive reconstruction. I have not seen or heard of this in New

England or states in the west or northern regions, although I'm sure it could have been used elsewhere.

The problem arises because the drywall contains excessive levels of hydrogen sulfide that outgases due to humidity and high temperatures. Not only did this stuff smell bad, it also corroded copper pipes and other metals, including the copper coils located inside air conditioning units. The sulfide could also damage electrical wiring, gas piping, and fire alarm systems.

What to do: be aware of this issue if you are buying a home in the southeastern states. Ask whether there is any history of this material being used. This drywall would mostly be found in new construction or homes renovated due to storm damage during the noted period. If the drywall is found to be present – or was used and replaced already – research whether the piping, air conditioning, or other systems were repaired or replaced.

To research this further, the following place is a good start.
https://en.wikipedia.org/wiki/Chinese_drywall#Affected_locales

Formaldehyde in wood flooring

Formaldehyde is found in numerous building materials due to its 'binding' properties and low cost. It is also found in household products, like glues and paints, dishwashing liquids and fabric softeners, and even cosmetics and some medicines. It is hard to escape exposure to formaldehyde. That said, short-term exposure can lead to irritation of the skin, eyes, nose, and throat. Exposure to concentrated or chronically high levels can reportedly lead to respiratory issues and nasopharyngeal cancer and leukemia, according to the National Cancer Institute.

A couple of years back, batches of laminate flooring coming from China and sold by Lumber Liquidators were reported to have levels of formaldehyde six to seven times the allowable limit. There was much outcry about this (and rightly so). A class action lawsuit was brought against that company and there was money set aside for claimants. (Unfortunately, the time frame for collecting on the settlement has ended).

In terms of your buying decision, you could ask if any laminate flooring present (and the better stuff looks like an engineered wood floor) was the type that was part of the lawsuit (and implicitly, may have had the elevated levels of formaldehyde). Your inspector has no way to determine this. Testing is possible but it would have to be done by a specialist and reputedly it takes 30 days to get the results back.

Many building products, including laminate flooring, will come with some level of formaldehyde – but all currently imported flooring is supposed to meet standards for formaldehyde content.   Fortunately, formaldehyde outgases. Newer homes, very tight homes, and newly renovated homes may show higher levels of formaldehyde – but this should diminish, especially if you can 'air the building out.' The rate at which it diminishes and the residual amounts present would not be determined by the home inspection. In terms of renovations you may do, choose products with low or no formaldehyde and ventilate aggressively post-renovation. This should not, in my opinion, be a walkaway or significant long-term issue for most people – but having this flooring may be considered a 'negative'.   For those who are chemically sensitized, even residual levels could be an issue.

Liquid underground fuel storage tanks (LUSTS)

This refers to underground fuel oil tanks and does not refer to underground propane tanks. (If propane tanks leak, the gases would simply enter the air and not contaminate the site). The tanks we are concerned about are the underground tanks used to store fuel oil. Underground tanks were occasionally used to store gasoline on older estate and farm properties. Most often, underground tanks were used to store fuel oil for heating the home.

Unfortunately, these tanks sometimes leak, spilling fuel oil into the ground and sometimes into the basement. Putting metal tanks underground and filling them with oil was not, in retrospect, a very good idea. The cost to remediate the site from a tank that has been leaking can run into the tens of thousands –- or hundreds of thousands of dollars.

> As an example of what can happen: back in the late 80s, I inspected a home in an upscale suburb. The home was gorgeous and fairly priced. The only glitch was that there was a reported underground tank in the yard. My buyers were going to buy the property as is, but I urged them to make the owner have the tank removed first. When I heard from them a few months later (as they were looking to buy a different home), I found out that the seller did agree to remove the tank – and unfortunately found that it had been leaking for some time. The formerly lovely yard was reportedly now a pit ten feet deep and around 75 feet in diameter due to the removal of the contaminated soil.

I should note that most underground tanks have been removed by now and the majority did not leak. I used to see evidence of underground tanks commonly back in the 80s – but less so now. While most have been removed, a few tanks are still out there in rural areas; I encountered one in the winter of 2018. The recognition of the potential for huge remediation costs and the liability for real estate professionals created a situation – at least in my area – where agents will not even take a listing if a home has an underground tank – and many mortgage and insurance companies will not cover these properties if a known tank is present.

That said, who can tell what may be buried out in the yard? Many homeowners have purchased homes without knowing that an underground tank was present. I inspected a home a couple of years ago where there was evidence of an underground tank in the recent past – and no history of this having been removed. The owner also tried to conceal the evidence of the tank. For their own financial well-being, my clients 'walked' and found another home.

Another problem found more often is that the copper fuel lines from *above-ground* tanks in basements will sometimes corrode out and leak oil below the slab. It has been mandated in Massachusetts for several years that homeowners must have these lines upgraded to an approved type not subject to corrosion – but I still see them. Unfortunately, your inspector can't determine if these lines have been leaking. Not all states may require that these fuel lines be upgraded – but you should plan on doing this as soon as you take possession.

What to do: don't buy a home with an underground fuel oil tank, as you will still find them in many areas. Older farm and estate properties may carry the largest risk of hidden tanks. These properties were more likely to have these tanks originally – and very often the tanks were left in place, without the current owner even being aware of their existence. Also check with the town and the fire department as they may have a record of tanks being present – or having been removed.

Your home inspector is not responsible for finding underground fuel oil tanks – although one may see clues in the basement. A number of possible clues that may indicate an underground fuel tank would include: dual oil feed lines that come out of the foundation or floor slab, old oil gauges on the wall, pipes coming out of the ground in the yard (although a number of pipes are found that have nothing to do with underground tanks). I recommend that you walk the grounds. Look for pipes, look for coffee or other cans that may cover the fill pipes; look for dead vegetation. Lastly, you may want to engage a company that uses a ground scanning radar to identify fuel oil tanks. A good web site on finding these tanks is http://inspectapedia.com/oiltanks/Find_Buried_Oil_Tank.php

---

Hazardous waste sites

There are numerous hazardous waste sites throughout the country and more than 10,000 hazardous waste sites dot New England's landscape. In Massachusetts alone, more than a third of the towns have lost all or parts of their drinking water to toxic contamination. Note: a lot of these sites have been capped and may pose a minimal risk at this time.

This concern is not dealt with by the home inspection. Some inspection companies offer an assessment by Environmental Data Resources. They have databases of known contamination sites and will issue a report on sites within a set distance of the home. Another website to check is the EPA site: **https://www.epa.gov/ superfund/search-superfund-sites-where-you-live**

You may have a high risk of finding unknown or unreported contamination sites in rural or sparsely populated areas where there may have been little or no oversight over what was dumped into the ground. It is likely moreover, that there are more known and unknown contamination sites in areas where fossil fuel operations have been present.

What you can do: when walking the property, check for old barrels, dead vegetation concentrated in one spot, discolored puddles on the ground, etc. Have an environmental assessment done by Environmental Data Resources.

Drug (or meth) houses

Houses where methamphetamine (referred to meth or crystal meth) was used or made are found in many areas of the country – especially in rural areas. Properties where meth was made are likely to be contaminated.

There are a number of things to look out for so you   ELIM COMMA don't inadvertently buy a meth house. Homes that have housed meth but   ELIM "or other drug users" AND COMMA were not used to produce meth, may also contain chemical residues but at much lower levels than homes where the meth was actually made. I would advise avoiding these – or have them tested by a qualified lab. Do your research on potential contamination.

A few things that would indicate a high risk of the property being used to produce meth include:

-   Small, often isolated rural homes that are in serious disrepair – or appear to have recently been fixed up. (Meth houses may have been spiffed up by a flipper or the owner's relatives; these may appear to be a super bargain – so be careful).
-   Strong smells of ammonia and other chemicals. It will often smell like urine.
-   Packages of drugs, vials, or containers in the house or yard. Pseudoephedrine, found in cold medicines, is the key ingredient for homemade meth.

- Broken down doors, windows covered, damaged interiors (or all of these recently replaced) could indicate a former drug lab.

While testing for meth residues is reportedly possible, I advise avoiding any house where you even suspect methamphetamine was produced. Check with the local police department also, as they would normally know of properties where meth was produced.

Out-gassing from urea formaldehyde foam insulation

This is one I can dispense with fairly quickly. Urea formaldehyde foam insulation (UFFI) was commonly installed in the late 1970s into the early 80s. While most installations had no problems, a small percentage of installations were faulty and outgassed high levels of formaldehyde. Occupants of these homes sometimes became chemically sensitized, such that they could not tolerate exposures to any level of chemicals in the future. Due to this problem, UFFI was banned as an installation material.

Fortunately, it was found that the formaldehyde quickly out-gassed, such that even the problem installations had no detectable levels after a passage of time. This became a non-issue eventually. The problem we now have with UFFI installations is that the insulation turned to dust and settled in the walls, making this less than optimal from an energy standpoint. As an environmental hazard, this should not be a problem.

Note: some of the items below fall under the topic of Indoor Air Quality (covered in chapter 13). I will include them in this chapter if the exposure comes from sources outside the home.

Problems with living near highways, busy roadways

A number of recent studies indicate that living near highways and high-traffic roads carries a greater risk of developing cardiovascular disease than does living twice as far away, largely due to the effect of ultra-fine particles.

As noted by author Cory Herro in the Think Progress website, 'the worst air quality in the United States can be found within about 5 football fields of any highway — where 1 in 10 Americans live. Millions of Americans breathe this air every day. And as a result, they suffer from an increased risk of cardiac disease, according to a new study from researchers at Tufts University and Boston University.

The study, slated for publication in the journal *Environment International*, looked at 'ultrafine' pollutants from car exhaust rather than the larger pollutants that are traditionally the focus of air quality research. Researchers found that high concentrations of ultrafine particles – 500 times smaller in diameter than the width of a human hair – are just as toxic as larger particles. While larger particles settle in the lungs, smaller particles enter the bloodstream, causing inflammation and elevated cholesterol levels. Chronic exposure can cause dangerous plaque buildup in the arteries and eventually lead to heart attack or stroke. Researchers controlled for age, gender, body fat, and health indicators such as whether someone smoked – meaning that they were able to isolate the increased cardiac risk as being connected to people's proximity to highways.

Doug Brugge, one of the researchers and a professor of public health at Tufts University School of Medicine, has emphasized the unique danger of super-tiny airborne toxins for years. 'Most of the mortality, most of the economic impact [of these particulates] are coming from cardiovascular disease,' he told Tufts Medicine in 2012. 'It's not primarily asthma or lung cancer.'

The above puts it clearly: try to avoid living near highways, when possible. I will also note that, in some areas of the country with predominant winds from one direction, your exposure may be far less if your home is on the upwind side.

Air quality problems from wood burning . . .

In terms of buying a home, I won't note the general cautions on the potential for indoor air quality problems from using a woodstove or fireplace. You can <u>choose</u> to use a wood stove or fireplace. But in terms of poor air quality from exterior sources, there are two potential problems I can think of – one of which most of us would ignore and the other, as something to avoid.

In the first case, a number of regions and localities where wood is widely used for heating can suffer from high levels of particulates from the residue from wood-stoves during certain types of wintertime conditions. A few of the nasty things in wood smoke are benzene, formaldehyde, acetaldehyde, acrolein, and polycyclic aromatic hydrocarbons (PAHs). In enclosed valleys, where homeowners heat extensively with wood, the air quality may at times be very poor – especially during temperature inversions.

People love their fireplaces or woodstoves. Most adults in good health can tolerate a certain amount of low level pollution. You can also take steps to minimize the production of particulates by using good stoves, proper burn techniques, dry wood, etc. You can also improve the indoor air by proper filtration, tightening the house, and the use of effective indoor air purification devices. If a temperature inversion occurs in your area, people with compromised immune or lung systems should stay indoors or take steps to limit their time outside

What you can't control is having an upwind neighbor who has an outside wood burning furnace or boiler, where the stove is constantly bathing your house in smoke. This is unusual, but I once dealt with a homeowner who was having problems due to a neighbor running an outside wood-fired boiler all winter. Every room in the home smelled like wood smoke. Conceivably, you could have the same problem if a close by (and upwind) neighbor burns wood extensively. As none of this may be apparent during the non-heating months, you may want to ask questions of the seller about any air quality problems they may have had at that site. There may some recourse by having the town require the neighbor to shut this down or take steps to reduce the smoke. But in rural areas, there may not be a lot you can do other than encouraging your neighbor to take measures to deal with the problem. Also, this may only be an issue if the offending home is close to your property and no landscape shielding is present.

Problems with excessive exposure to herbicides and pesticides

While anyone can be exposed to herbicides and pesticides — a lot of the potentially bad stuff is sold to homeowners — you will want to reduce the risk of excessive exposure to chemicals due to factors you can't control. I will note that if any property you are looking at has a reported history of contamination from any source, you will need to be very careful. What you can't always control is the high amounts of herbicides and pesticides you may be exposed to by living in an area with industrial agriculture.

As noted in Chapter 3, our industrial agricultural system utilizes large amounts of fertilizers, pesticides, and herbicides. Those who live in localities with industrial agricultural are often exposed to high levels of chemicals with reputed health risks. These include glyphosate (sold as Roundup® by Monsanto) and atrazine. In my opinion, these are a disaster for the environment, both for the long-term viability of the soil and for the public's health. As it relates to buying a home, I recommend being aware of these issues and how you can limit your exposure. Unfortunately, homeowners (especially the poor) can't just get up and leave their homes and jobs in agricultural areas.

Pollution from fracking sites, pipelines

As noted in chapter 3, *fracking* (or hydraulic fracturing) uses high-pressure slugs of chemicals, water, and sand to crack shale formations deep underground, unlocking methane gas trapped therein. By utilizing this technology, natural gas (methane) can be produced where conventional drilling would be uneconomical. While the oil-bearing shales of the Bakken formation in North Dakota have gotten the most press, numerous areas of the country, including the Marcellus shale formations in Pennsylvania have been extensively drilled.

251

In the ideal scenario, the fracking procedure would not allow gas to enter the wells of nearby properties, and the severely contaminated liquids used to crack the rocks to allow the gas to flow out would stay deep underground when injected back into the earth.

Unfortunately, this has not been the case. A reported 20 to 40 percent of the liquids used in the fracking procedure don't stay underground. Drillers typically inject the liquids into old, dried out wells, or other deep sites. But even when the wastewater isn't bubbling up to the surface, there is evidence that shows show that injection isn't always permanent. The film 'Gas Land' shows burning water coming out of faucets in Pennsylvania homes where deep fracking wells are located. The highly toxic wastewater reportedly is commonly discharged onto surface waters, contaminating the land and streams.

CHAPTER 15
Avoiding Mold and Indoor Air Quality Problems

What you will learn in this chapter . . .

This chapter will cover a few of the indoor air quality problems you need to know about when buying a home – and specifically what to do when the home you are looking at has a 'mold problem.' This subject alone is covered in numerous books. We can't do that here, but I will try to answer the following questions about mold that may be relevant to home you may be looking to purchase. These include:

- *Why is mold found in so many homes?*
- *What are the health issues with mold?*
- *How is mold dealt with in real estate transactions?*
- *Should you test for mold when buying a home?*
- *What are the options for getting rid of mold?*
- *What are the problems with finished basements and mold?*
- *What are the problems with central air conditioning and indoor air quality?*
- *How do you deal with contaminated ductwork?*
- *What other contaminants affect indoor air quality?*
- *How can you prevent carbon monoxide testing?*
- *How do you choose a healthy home?*
- *How do you avoid problems after you move in?*

The New Four Letter Word: Mold . . .

Mold has been the hot button issue in real estate transactions for the last fifteen years or so. The issue exploded on the scene due to a well-publicized case in Texas, when an upscale home got flooded and the resulting 'black mold' made the house uninhabitable. The occupants suffered severe health issues, including possible brain damage. It was not as if indoor air quality issues were not recognized before this, but the concern with mold really came to the forefront after this case was publicized. Certainly, the experiences of homeowners in New Orleans after hurricane Katrina and the flooding that occurred in Houston have increased the awareness of the mold problems caused by flooding.

Concerns about indoor air quality have been around for a while. Over the years, there have been numerous cases of people moving into homes or entering new workplaces and suffering chronic and sometimes serious health problems. Many who are afflicted come to realize it is the air quality in their home (or workplace) that is the problem as very often their symptoms disappear when they are not at those locations. Some people have become so chemically sensitized from exposure to contaminants that they can't be exposed to <u>any</u> level of toxins without suffering health issues. Also, asthma rates have soared in recent years – due, at least in part it is believed, to poor indoor air quality and exposure to mold residues and other contaminants.

What you want to do is reduce your risk of buying a home with serious mold or other indoor air quality (IAQ) problems that can affect you and your family's health and safety. Exposure to carbon monoxide and volatile organic compounds fall into this list. You also want to know how mold issues are typically handled during the home buying process and what you can do to protect your interests. And lastly, as many types of IAQ problems are caused by the actions of unknowing homeowners, it is important to know what you can do in the future to keep your home from ruining your family's health. This is just a brief overview of this subject, obviously. I'm just trying to give you enough information to stay out of trouble. For more information, I recommend reading the book *Your Home Is Making You Sick* by Jeff May, an indoor air quality specialist located in Massachusetts. A second recommended book on mold is *Our Toxic World: A Wake-Up Call*, by Dr. Doris Rapp.

But first: what is mold, where does it occur, and why is it a problem?

Very simply, mold is fungi that break down organic or carbon-based materials – which means everything that comes from plants or living organisms. Unless made of steel or concrete with no wood or paper present, every building contains lots of digestible organic materials. For mold to grow, three things are needed: mold spores, moisture, and a food source (and a fourth, oxygen, which we assume is always present).

Some types of molds produce poisonous chemicals called mycotoxins. They can cause numerous health problems, especially for the very young, the very old, and those with compromised immune systems. Health problems that can be caused by mycotoxins include:

- Pneumonia

- Pulmonary hemorrhage
- Vascular – blood vessel fragility, hemorrhage from tissue or lungs
- Kidney damage
- Liver cancer
- Poor immune system functioning
- Gastro-intestinal disorders, including diarrhea, vomiting, hemorrhage, liver damage, fibrosis
- Neurological – tremors, loss of coordination, headaches, depression
- Reproductive disorders and infertility
- Joint pain and inflammation
- Migraine headaches
- Depression
- Severe fatigue

Other types of molds produce spores that are allergens that increase the risk of asthma and compromised immune systems.

Anyone in your household who is experiencing any of the above symptoms will need to talk to their physician for treatment. But you may also need to engage a qualified mold specialist to determine if there is 'hidden' mold or other allergen sources. (See more on this below). Unfortunately, you may not experience the health effects from mold problems in the short times you will be in the home before moving in. However, there are a number of things you can do when looking at properties to limit your risk of getting a home with indoor air quality problems.

But first, why is mold so much more an issue now than in the past?

Two reasons: first, the materials and methods used in modern construction are conducive for mold. One of the best food sources for mold is paper-backed drywall – which, of course, has been used in almost every home and building constructed in the last 50+ years. Drywall that stays chronically damp will become moldy. Wood may decay – but it has to remain damp for a prolonged time for the fungus to do its work. Most of the time, wood that gets wet will dry before significant mold develops. The plastered walls and ceilings found in older homes are much less prone to mold than are newer homes – which not only have drywall for the interior sheathings but particle board for the exterior sheathing (under the siding). Plaster is not an organic material and the wood lath found in pre-1900 homes literally needs to stay constantly wet before it decays. The particle board and oriented strand board sheathings used on the exterior walls can work fine if kept *perfectly* dry; if not, they can become what Joseph Lstiburek, a building science consultant, has termed 'vertical mulch.'

The second problem is that homes are built much tighter and are not tolerant of moisture and water intrusion conditions.

Where do you usually see mold when looking at homes?

The area where you most commonly see mold is on the roof sheathing in the attic. The reason for this lies in the 'stack effect.' Warm, moist, dust-laden air from the living space will tend to rise and will find its way into the unheated attic through numerous openings (called 'bypasses'). Warm air can hold more moisture than cold air, and as it flows up into the attic, it condenses on the cold roof sheathing (which is wood or plywood) and the roof framing. The organic dust and wood members provide a nice home for (ever present) mold spores to grow.

> Note: due to cases where what appeared to be mold and was reported as 'mold' but did not turn out to be mold – which resulted in lawsuits, of course – your inspector may report 'suspected microbial growth' or 'discoloration consistent with mold.' I usually just say 'mold' – but there are times you have to use the above phrases. Also, although it is a bit of an anomaly, the board sheathings found in the attics of older homes will often blacken due to extractive staining from condensation on the sheathing. Some of these roofs could also have mold – but when it is just darkening, it may not be mold you are dealing with. What gets tough is when you have both conditions present, as it can be difficult to distinguish between watermarking and mold. An inspector in these situations may throw up his hands and simply recommend a mold evaluation.

What do you do if the home you are looking at has a mold 'problem' in an attic?

Your home inspection will commonly find evidence of mold in the attic. Typically, this is evidenced by dark stains and black mold spots or a fuzzy white growth. When this is found during real estate transactions, a mold remediation will typically be done prior to the sale. Less commonly, allowances will be made for the buyer to have this done. There are alternatives to a conventional mold remediation to deal with mold issues in an attic, so you will want to take note of these below.

Most listing agents, I find, do not balk at asking the current homeowner/seller to have the mold conditions remediated. They know that if a buyer 'walks away' due to mold issues, the agent will have to disclose the known mold problems to the next prospective buyer. On foreclosures and short sales – or when the homeowner refuses to do anything – dealing with mold issues may fall on you. In this case, you will need to bring in one or more reputable mold remediation companies to get estimates for a mold remediation so you know what you are dealing with. If the mold problems appear to be extreme – or if you or your mold-sensitive friends or relatives can't stay in the home for much time without getting a headache or losing your voice (among other symptoms) – you may want to rethink whether you want to pursue this property.

A home inspector may recommend further evaluation by a mold specialist after evidence of mold is found. In my opinion, additional evaluation is warranted if the inspector really doesn't know if this is mold or he suspects other problems in the home – or just wants to be cautious. Typically, when the roof sheathing (or other areas) shows clearly visible or suspected microbial growth, you will just want a mold remediation to be done.

What about testing the home for mold?

Mold testing using simple kits to detect mold spore spores in the air is some-times offered by inspection companies. This is generally regarded, however, as a waste of time and money. (See the EPA's comment on this).

While certain types of mold testing can occasionally be of value (see below), just sampling the air will not give you an accurate picture of possible mold problems in the home. In the first place, mold kits have problems with both 'false positives' and 'false negatives.' A false positive could occur when someone leaves a window open; mold spores will simply blow in as the outside air is full of mold spores for much of the year. A false negative, conversely, could occur when the carpet is full of mold but no one walks across the room to stir up the mold. The random sam-pling of the air does not provide a valid or useful tool to determine if a building has a mold problem.

Mold behind finished walls simply may not reg-ister on mold tests. Testing the types of mold found may be warranted in a few situations, but it should be done by industrial hygienists or those with specialized training on what to look for. As noted, the EPA does not recommend mold testing. Their position is that if clearly visible mold is present, it needs to be removed. You don't need to test it.

You don't need to spend extra money to test mold to see what type it is: ALL mold is bad and should be dealt with . . .

A proper mold inspection should follow the ASTM D7338 Assessment of Fungal Growth in Buildings protocol. This includes an assessment of the site conditions that caused the mold, including the HVAC system.

As noted by the American Society for Testing Materials, "There are too many variables impacting the results and the sample size is too small for air testing for mold to be reliable. The type of mold will not change the necessary mold remediation. The genus of mold is just not relevant or necessary unless you are trying to frighten a client into believing that they have "Toxic" mold. Mold spore trap air samples do not have the ability to establish the presence of any mycotoxins." (ASTM International).

It may sometimes be useful or necessary to document that mold is present on interior surfaces, such as behind walls or in the ductwork. Swab type tests, when processed by a mold specialist or accredited lab, can be done to _prove_ that mold is indeed present in these areas.

What types of mold are bad? Is only black mold bad?

These are other questions that arise. The black mold that gets the most attention is *Stachybotrys* – which is quite toxic. Other black molds exist, however, that are not nearly as bad, and some of the 'white' molds, such as *Aspergillus*, are quite nasty. In fact, scientists have identified over 1000 types of mold growing in homes across America. As noted earlier, you don't always have to identify what type of mold is present, just if any type of mold is present.

In terms of the home inspection, it is important to realize that:

the home inspection is NOT a mold or indoor air quality inspection.

This deserves an explanation – and I don't want this to sound like a disclaimer, as any good home inspector should (in my opinion) look for and report on *clearly visible* signs of mold. The limitation of the home inspection is that inspectors may be able to see 'suspected' mold on the exposed roof sheathing in the attic and occasionally in the basement. Unfortunately, in some homes, the mold is concealed from view and sometimes the areas that have mold will not be readily visible or accessible. Many types of indoor air quality problems may not show visible evidence or be detectable by a visual inspection. Moldy materials could be present within enclosed walls, ceilings, or floors, and won't be visible during your brief visits to the home, including the home inspection. Sometimes the symptom is simply odors – which may be more noticeable to some people than others, and which may be evident only under specific weather or seasonal conditions.

A second problem is that people vary widely in terms of their sensitivity to mold and other environmental contaminants. I personally do not easily react to mold. Only in severe situations have I felt my lungs tighten up. Many people, however, report that they can instantly tell if the home has a mold problem and a small percentage of people are extremely sensitive. I had one client who reported that her mother would not be able to speak for a couple of days after being in a home with a suspected mold problem. As recommended earlier, it could be useful (to you – not them) to bring these people along at the second showing when you have a suspect situation. It's sort of a 'canary in a coal mine' test. Also, you may find you are having problems the previous owner did not experience. In one home I inspected, the walls were literally covered with black mold – but someone was still living there (perhaps they did not live long after this?). I couldn't stay in the home for more than ten minutes without going outside every ten minutes to breathe and take notes (and this was on a ten-degree day!).

Importantly,

> *if you are 'chemically sensitized' or if you sense unusual odors when looking at the house, or if you or others in your entourage experience asthma-like symptoms after being in the home, you will need to take your indoor air quality investigation to another level.*

Third, a lot of mold and indoor air quality problems come from how people live. Many of the afflicted cause their own problems by keeping the home too moist or allowing other conditions to flourish. (I'll cover, later in this chapter, how to minimize your risk of creating mold-conducive conditions).

How to do you determine if mold is present in a home you're buying?

As I noted, assuming your inspector has full access to the attic, then mold present there should be visible. Sometimes, however, we find semi-permanent shelving or extensive owner's goods stored in a closet; or the hatches have been sealed shut; or the attic space simply has no access at all. Similar restrictions apply to crawlspaces: some have sealed accesses; some have no means of access, and others have unsanitary conditions or are unsafe to enter. Whatever. My advice is that you *notify the seller (or listing agent) ahead of time that your inspector will need clear access to all attics and crawlspaces.* If these spaces are still blocked or sealed at the time of the inspection, request that access be provided. Most inspectors, for an extra fee, will come back to inspect attics or other areas that could not be viewed at the inspection. Without doing this, you won't know what is present in these spaces.

Cautions on mold remediations in an attic . . .

The cost of attic mold remediations varies widely, as the levels and extent of the mold will be different in each property. The price will also depend on the type, quality, and level of remediation performed by the mold remediation company. Mold remediation companies show a wide range of expertise as to what they can and will do. Market conditions could obviously make a difference in the price. I've seen low-cost remediations in the range of $2500 to $3000 that *appeared* adequate (these were attics with limited mold) and others that were incomplete or seriously flawed. Some of these homes needed a more extensive (and most likely, more expensive) mold remediation. I've also seen remediations that cost $15,000. Maybe it was necessary to spend this, but sometimes the remediation costs appear exorbitant. Different companies utilize different techniques and the amount of mold and size of the attic obviously matters. Specific coatings can be applied <u>after</u> the mold is removed that will prevent mold from developing in the future. This is usually done.

The conditions that caused the mold problem must also be dealt with. This is often done – but not always. A standard recommendation to prevent future mold is to add ventilation in the attic, typically soffit and ridge vents if not already present. This can help – but <u>only</u> if the vents actually work and the openings (bypasses) that allow warm, moist household air to enter the attic are adequately sealed. Increasing the ventilation in the attic may actually make the mold problem worse, in some cases, if not combined with air sealing efforts.

> As an example of why simply adding more ventilation is not enough, I did a consult on mold problems in a relatively newer home. The owner had recently had the roof shingles replaced along with the plywood roof sheathing. He had soffit and ridge vents added– and the underside of the new roof was already covered with mold. It was easy to determine the problem. Pulling up the insulation on the attic floor revealed numerous wide-open cavities and other openings that allowed the household air (humidified, no less) into the attic. The added ventilation was simply drawing more of the warm, moist air up into the attic and was doing more harm than good.

-Bypass openings that allow moist household air to enter the attic occur at the chaises or gaps between chimneys and floor framing in the attic, wiring and duct boot openings, pull down stairwells, doors to attic stairs, loose hatch covers, wall cavities that open up into the attic and, perhaps the biggest culprit for attic mold problems: bathroom exhaust fans that improperly discharge into the attic or to the eaves. Bathroom fans, importantly, must be vented to a dedicated wall or (ideally) roof hood so the moist shower air is discharged to the exterior.

A problem is that, in an insulated attic, it can be difficult to find – much less seal – all the bypasses that may be present. It can also be impossible to view exhaust ducts that run under the insulation.

Third, rectifying mold problems in an attic (or basement) will often necessitate removing the existing insulation and installing new insulation. This is usually done by the better (and more expensive) mold remediation companies. It may not be warranted in less severe cases or where the insulation in an attic was tightly covered with flooring.

The most important cure for attic mold problems, however, is something that may fall on the homeowner (which means YOU): *control the moisture levels in the home and keep the moist air from the living space out of the attic*. I've noted the critical need to have the bypass openings sealed between the living space and attic. While most mold remediation companies will attempt to do this, it is difficult to do this perfectly. You also need to keep moisture levels at reasonable amounts within the living space. A problem is that some 'experts' have recommended keeping the indoor air at 50 percent relative humidity during the winter. This may be okay for mid-Atlantic or southern regions, but in northern areas, which experience much colder temperatures, these levels will produce excessive condensation (and mold) in the attic. The excessive use of furnace-based humidifiers is a major culprit, as these either aren't needed or are set too high. As an example, I did a mold consult to investigate why an eight-year-old upscale home had an attic full of mold. The problem came down to the fact that he central humidifier was constantly running. I should note that family members in this home were reportedly suffering serious health issues.

In terms of keeping mold from occurring in the attic in the future, you need to

#1 Have bathroom (and kitchen) exhaust fans vented to the exterior and run them for a sufficient time after showering. Having the fans exhaust into the vented soffits – or even to soffit hoods – does not always work as the moist air simply re-enters the attic.

#2 Have fans on a timer so that you have the option of letting them run after you leave the bathroom is a good idea. This is often required in new construction. New construction built for superior energy performance may be so tight that continuous ventilation is necessary.

#3 As recommended, have a qualified energy retrofit company identify and seal the bypasses.

#4 Turn down – or better yet, TURN OFF – your humidifier.

#5 And lastly, it is critical that you control sources of moisture and water in the basement and crawlspace. Moisture present in these areas will end up in the attic.

Other ways to deal with mold problems in an attic when buying a home . . .

One alternative to having a standard remediation done when mold is found in the attic is to simply *have the entire roof sheathing (plywood or boards) removed along with the roof shingles*. This may be a better option when the roof shingles are aged and close to needing replacement. In homes with attic mold where the plywood sheathing is delaminating due to condensation, the roof sheathing would need replacement in any case when the roof is re-shingled. Doing a total strip off of the roof sheathing (down to the exposed roof rafters) along with the shingles sounds drastic. It pushes up the cost of replacing the roof (whereas normally just the roof shingles would be replaced) – but it may be cheaper than having an expensive mold remediation done inside the attic. Although not warranted in limited remediations or when the roof shingles are fairly new, this can be a better solution than trying to remove the mold from the roof sheathing. The rafters may still need to be cleaned and treated, however.

If this appears to be the better option, get estimates from a roofer on the added cost of replacing the roof sheathings when the roof shingles are replaced. You could then possibly negotiate for an allowance on this extra cost as opposed to having a complete mold remediation that leaves the existing roof sheathing in place. Talk to your buyer's broker and attorney, as this recommendation sometimes goes over everyone's head and they just want to mold (or mold residues) gone as quickly as possible.

The spray foam option . . .

When mold is found on the roof sheathing, it can be more effective and less expensive to have spray foam insulation blown into the rafter cavities and exposed end walls rather than have a mold remediation done. The foam encapsulates the existing roof sheathing, mold covered or not, such that it is no longer an issue. Installing spray foam in the rafter cavities is also desirable from an energy standpoint and eliminates the need to add ventilation, as the attic now becomes 'conditioned' space. As a few cautions: this may not be appropriate or even the best solution for all attics; second, it can be expensive – but very often less than a mold remediation, which also can be costly; and third, if the plywood roof sheathing has delaminated, you may need to deal with that first. Also, spray foam installations, if done improperly, carry their own risk of outgassing noxious chemicals (see below). Lastly, either 'closed cell' or 'open cell' foams can be used, although there is a general preference for the closed cell type. Open cell foams will work, but you have to be diligent about controlling moisture levels in the home, as this type of foam will allow moisture to pass through the insulation.

When could you possibly forego a full mold remediation?

I've inspected homes where extremely small amounts of suspected mold were present on the roof sheathing and the attic was fully accessible. I – along with most inspectors – would point out the visible mold and normally recommend a mold remediation. How you proceed is entirely up to you, but in a few of these cases, twenty minutes with an appropriate mold removal product (not bleach!) will deal with the problem. Many mold remediation companies can't do a job for less than $2500. So, you could override your inspector's recommendation if you are comfortable with this.

Lastly, I won't diminish the concern when mold is found in an attic. It needs to be dealt with, but the more serious concerns are what is happening in the basement and, at some properties, within the walls.

Homes that have been vacant – and especially those that have not been kept heated – are at more risk of problems. Stagnant air is conducive for mold to develop. Homes with a reported history of burst pipes would present a high risk of concealed mold.

Mold that is not indicative of a mold 'problem' . . .

Certain types of mold we commonly encounter may not indicate a home with a 'mold problem.' You may see dark stains on unfinished concrete walls in a basement. This is typically mold on dust particles that have settled on the concrete. If left in place, this could aggravate allergies – but this type of mold typically just needs a simple cleaning. The mold one sees on bathroom ceilings is unsightly and needs to be cleaned, but it does not indicate (by itself) that the home has a mold problem; more likely, it's a problem of long hot showers by family members – or a lack of an effective ventilation system (meaning, no exhaust fan). Mold does not grow on concrete, and it does not easily grow on wood framing unless the wood stays chronically damp – and if it does grow there, then you are faced with decay and damage, which is a whole other problem. Personal goods are also subject to mold. Just leave paper goods or leather in your basement or garage and see what happens.

Other mold problems in homes . . .

Although mold in the attic is what home inspectors see and report on, from an indoor air quality standpoint, this may not be the most serious issue. Mold on roof sheathings in the attic may not always increase the health risks for the home's occupants as this air doesn't normally find its way back down into the living space. It doesn't matter. Mold on the roof sheathings is not acceptable when buying or selling a home and is something you don't want to have. The larger risk for your family's health, however, is mold that could be present in enclosed walls, ceilings, and floors – and, most importantly, in the insulation and finished walls of the basement.

Mold and IAQ problems in finished basements . . .

Of special concern with mold and IAQ is the finishing of basements – and specifically the installation of fiberglass insulation in the ceilings and walls. Basements in most of the country (the colder regions anyhow) are below ground and are generally cold. If finished, the foundation walls will still be cold.

Unfortunately, unless a finished basement has been kept heated, dry, and dehumidified over its life, it has the potential for mold problems. Mold in the walls or ceilings of a finished basement poses more of a risk to your health than does the mold found in the attic. Jeff May, an indoor air quality specialist from Massachusetts, has seen so many problems arising from the finished basements that he doesn't advise people to even consider finishing off below-grade basements. I would not go this far, as there are ways to get a finished space that is dry and mold free, but you have to use the right materials, have continuous heat or dehumidification in the space, and ensure that the basement doesn't take on water. You also need to control mouse infestations.

Why are finished basements a problem? One problem is that the paper-backed drywall present in almost every finished basement is prone to mold. It's paper – and paper becomes moldy if you look at it. The paneled walls found in basements finished in the 50s and 60s are actually less prone to mold than drywall; they do, however, have their aesthetic issues. The second cause of mold problems in the basement is the very fact that, by insulating the walls, the foundation stays cold and damp. This is conducive for mold.

A third culprit in finished and unfinished basements is the use of fiberglass batts on the walls and in the ceilings. Fiberglass acts like a sponge when water intrusions occur. The insulation is adjacent to the paper-backed drywall which, as noted, is prone to mold. Fiberglass batts also perform as a filter for mold spores and other contaminants in the air as well as those deposited by rodents or insects. Mice love to nest in fiberglass insulation.

If you are looking at homes with nice finished basements, I should note that not all basements have a problem – or a problem you can't deal with. Continuously heated and dehumidified basements with no water problems do better than basements where the heat has been intermittently on. Walk-out basements are less at risk. Some of the basement finishing systems also do a good job of preventing mold from being an issue.

If you will be finishing the basement, the new approach of using spray foam insulation along the top of the basement walls and rigid foam insulation on the walls is a good way to avoid mold problems. (In may not, however, be so good in terms of termite issues). Obviously, any finished basement needs to be kept dry – which usually means you will need to install a dehumidifier. You will also want to avoid the temptation to open windows during the summer doldrums (when hot and humid), as this allows moist air to enter the basement and condense on the cooler surfaces.

The use of one or more sump pumps will very often be needed as you will want to ensure the space stays dry. The only guarantee of a dry basement in many homes, however, will be to have a sub-slab 'French' drain system in place. These have drainage pipes installed under the slab along the perimeter plus ways to capture water that may flow down the basement walls. The pipes run to a large sump pit with pumps that will discharge the water away from the home. If a sub-slab drainage system is present in the home you are looking at, consider this is a plus. If not present and the basement gets water, you may need one. Warning: they are expensive. I should note that some basements just don't get water – a minority, perhaps – but they are out there.

Another problem with finished basements is that the insulation and suspended panels installed in the basement ceilings provide the ideal nesting spots for mice. Unless the mouse infestations have been controlled over the life of the home (or since finishing off the basement), the insulation is often full of mouse urine, droppings, and dead bodies. Gross – but that is what is often present. You may not see this during the home inspection and your own visits – but you need to be aware of this as an air quality issue. You may, in some cases, need to have the insulation and finished materials in the basement entirely removed after you move in. An indoor air quality assessment, if done by a qualified specialist, will often identify these problems.

Dirt floors and crawlspaces . . .

Uncovered dirt floors are commonly found in crawlspaces and occasionally in basements. For a basement that you will use, plan to have a concrete slab poured. For a crawlspace, a tight-fitting vapor barrier may be present – and if not, you should have one installed.

Having a crawlspace is not always a problem – but it often is. Having a crawlspace under the first-floor living space is typical for much of the country. But there are 'good' crawlspace practices and 'bad' – and 'bad' have generally been the rule. The traditional, code-mandated design for crawlspaces was to have an uncovered dirt floor, fiberglass in the ceiling, and vents in the walls (ostensibly to remove moisture from the space). This design has proven to be a disaster with mold and decayed framing rampant.

Building science has found that sealing that crawlspace floors and walls, dehumidifying the crawlspace, and insulating the perimeter walls – not the ceilings – is the most effective way to keep crawlspaces dry. No air interchange should be present between the crawlspace (or basement, for that matter) and the living space above.

Crawlspace retrofits are now common in many of the mid-Atlantic states, due to the mold concerns that were commonly found. Problem-free crawlspaces often have concrete slab floors or a layer of plastic over the floor as a vapor barrier. With an effective vapor barrier, many crawlspaces will stay reasonably dry – assuming any vents or openings in the walls are kept sealed. Crawlspaces that are sealed on the perimeter but are left open to a heated basement (or just containing the heating system) usually are dry and not a problem.

In terms of what you should be looking at, all moldy or mold-prone materials in a crawlspace – and in an unheated basement – should be removed or encapsulated. You need to realize that you may be able to get a seller to remove debris or abandoned goods from the basement – but you will not get a seller to do anything about air quality issues or problems in a crawlspace. An ideal solution is to have a company that specializes in crawlspace problems do a complete retrofit (eliminating the insulation in the ceilings, uncovered dirt floors, and vents in the walls). In New England, a company called Neutocrete (http://neutocrete.com/) offers a nice repair option that you could look into.

The air quality problems from central air conditioning . . .

Read this if the home you are buying has central air conditioning – or you plan to install it.

You may – like most people – believe that if you have central air conditioning, this will help you to have a healthier home. Central air conditioning provides the promise for controlling moisture in the home during the summer months and filtering the air of contaminants. That is the 'promise' – and if everything worked perfectly, life would be wonderful.

Unfortunately, that is not what happens in actual practice. One finding reported by Jeff May (the IAQ specialist I mentioned) is that, when doing a statistical analysis of the homes, a far greater percentage of the sick homes he investigates have central air conditioning than not. But why, if central air systems dehumidify the household air when running and have filter systems that could screen out dust and other contaminants, do they often present more of a problem than a benefit?

A few reasons come to mind.

First, central air conditioning systems have what is called an evaporator coil (that looks like an upside down 'V' inside the ductwork plenum above the heating system). When the air conditioner is running, the warm household air is blown over the cold coil to remove the heat and moisture from the air. The moisture in this 'return' air essentially condenses out and drips into an internal 'pan,' which drains to a condensate pump (ideally). This is how central air conditioning works. Meanwhile, the filter on the air handler is supposed to screen out the dust (which are largely organic particles) before the return air reaches the evaporator coil. So far so good. But things don't always work as intended.

The problem is that the filtration systems on most furnaces are either very poor at removing dust from the return air or are very poorly installed, with big gaps along the sides that allow the filter compartments to be open to the basement. In many cases, we find that the filter is missing entirely. And while the system may have a good filter now, past owners may have ignored this. The result is that you have organic dust ending up on the moist evaporator coil and pan below. This obviously leads to a moldy mess in the pan. The furnace fan then blows air over the pan and sends the mold spores all over the house. Mold spores in the pan or ductwork will be distributed to the living space during the heating season as well.

Do all central heating and cooling systems have this problem? Not always – just most of the time. The air conditioning system should not have internal mold issues IF the system has a very effective filter (such as a pleated or media filter that is tightly installed); AND the evaporator pan and coils have been kept clean, AND the ductwork does not contain organic residues. The problem is that – although this is changing – most of the evaporator coils and pans (underneath the coils) are never looked at by the HVAC technicians. This is not something that your home inspector can view either. For many older air conditioning systems, there is no easy way for an air conditioning technician to even access the coils.

So, how does this affect you as a buyer? If you – or other household members – have severe asthma or other serious health issues, or if you are chemically sensitized or extremely allergic to dust, you may want to consider buying a home that is heated by a forced hot water system. For homes with old, dust filled ductwork, it will be desirable to have the ductwork professionally cleaned – or better yet, replaced. If you have central air conditioning, the plenum above the furnace should be opened up and the evaporator coils and pan cleaned yearly when serviced by your HVAC technician. As I noted, *this is almost never done*. When a new furnace is installed insist on having the evaporator coil and pan made readily accessible. Adding an effective, tight-fitting filter is a necessity.

By the way: a note on filters and ductwork. The fiberglass or mesh filters (usually blue) are not effective at removing contaminants and dust from the air; HVAC technicians refer to them as 'boulder catchers.' Depending on the system, you want either media filter (best) or an insertable filter rated at MERV 8 or, when allowed by the heating system installer, MERV11 (the ratings are normally on the filters when you buy them). MERRV 5 filters may be okay. (The higher the number, the finer the particles the filter will remove). The higher rated MERV filters may be usable in some furnaces but not others. Filters, by the way, are sometimes accessible at the home inspection but the ductwork is not. When the return registers and ductwork can be viewed, one often sees layers of dust and debris from the years of use by a prior owner. In this case, the ductwork needs to be thoroughly (which usually means professionally) cleaned – or, as noted, replaced. Lastly, there are systems that use ultraviolet light devices next to the evaporator coil to supposedly kill any mold spores. I used to think this was a good idea – but studies now indicate this is not an effective option.

The problem with carpeting and indoor air quality . . .

Carpeting tends to attract dust and dirt. The surface area in carpeting is thousands of times larger than on a solid surface floor. Old wall-to-wall carpeting, or <u>any carpeting that has not been kept rigorously clean, will lead to indoor air quality problems.</u> In most cases, I find buyers intend to have older carpeting replaced. I recommend assessing the age and visible appearance of the carpeting. Home inspectors do not typically inspect carpeting, as it's difficult to tell what the quality of existing carpeting, what may be in it or under it, and what off-gassing it may experience. Assume plywood or rough board subfloor is present under carpeting – unless proven otherwise.

Homes subject to past flooding – or other sources of water intrusion, such as burst pipes, sewerage back-ups, or other water sources . . .

Besides the issue of whether you want to live in a location where flooding has occurred and has a high probability of occurring again (covered in previous chapters), you want to be especially careful when there is a reported history of past flooding. Be aware that water intrusion due to a burst or clogged pipe could also be a problem. You would want to verify that the walls and enclosed areas that were inundated were thoroughly and properly cleaned. This means a professional cleaning by a company that is following the established protocols for this type of work. In general, anything that got water soaked needs to be removed. This means a complete gutting to the studs for homes that flooded, plus a removal of all residues. Water from a leaking pipe may require just a partial gutting of the affected areas. In some cases of water leakage, companies that specialize in restoring fire and water damaged homes can dry out the affected spaces before mold develops. The inspection really can't tell if the proper procedures were followed so you will need to ask a lot of questions and do research on the reported remediation. You don't want to buy a home with intractable mold problems.

Other indoor air quality issues . . .

Before I get into how to avoid – or deal with – homes with indoor air quality problems, it's important to note that mold is just one type of indoor air quality issue. A few others that you want to avoid are below.

Odors

Odors can occur from any type of off-gassing, whether from mold or from building materials. Odors could be due to the contamination of the current owner's goods, but they could also indicate something worse. Bad odors are a symptom of something that will need further investigation. Note: Externally generated odors from wood combustion, general air pollution, highways, nearby commercial establishments or factories have been covered in previous chapters. Smelling oil fumes is not normal and is something you would want to have checked out. Oil fumes could be from a range of problems. It may be that the heating system needs to be serviced. More seriously, it could indicate venting problems or some type of oil tank or line leakage.

Allergic reactions, sources of allergens . . .

Allergens are the small particles in the air (or food) that our bodies react to. What we are concerned about here are the types of microscopic particles and chemicals found in homes that people have 'allergic' reactions to – in other words, the things that would make you sick or get asthma. Many allergens are mold spores produced by allergenic molds. If you can make a reasonable determination that indoor air quality problems are remediable, this may not dissuade you from pursuing a particular home. But you need to know where the problems may lie – and how to avoid homes that will make you sick.

Dust mites, the microscopic creatures that actually live on our skin, our beds, clothing, etc., are a source of allergenic reactions. Dust mites digest the organic matter we constantly slough off. You can't escape them by taking enough showers. Breathing in the fecal particles from dust mites increases the risk of asthma and allergies. Changing pillowcases regularly and vacuuming with a high efficiency or HEPA vacuum can help to control dust mites. This is more of a home cleanliness issue than an issue for home buyers – except that you may need to thoroughly clean the home before moving in.

Mice and rodents, including squirrels, bats, and raccoons. I've covered these in Chapter 13, so I'll just note them here. Obviously, you don't want any of these in the home, but mice are ubiquitous in many areas. They come in during the fall to take advantage of the warmth and sometimes available food. Mice are incredibly destructive and their urine will stain and ruin whatever they are nesting in. They need to be controlled (as with the other pests, noted above). I recommend snap or bucket traps, as they are the quickest and most humane way to control mouse infestations. I commend those who trap the mice and let them off in a wooded area. This may generate good karma – but it's too much work for most people.

As noted, mouse residues are especially prevalent in attic insulation and the insulation installed in basement ceilings. In crawlspaces, forgot it: the insulation put in the ceiling very often ends up being an apartment building for mice. Mouse-infested insulation should be removed – but you may need a mold removal person to do this. A good respirator and post removal cleaning would be the minimum. Having the crawlspace ceilings (and/or) walls covered with spray foam insulation is ideal not only from an energy standpoint – but to prevent mice from nesting in the insulation.

Pets. Everyone loves their pets, so I won't say don't have one. But many people react to pet dander – and if the former occupant had a dog or cat that you would be allergic to, you will need to thoroughly clean the home and throw out the wall-to-wall or other carpeting. Pet urine in flooring may require a removal of the flooring and subfloor if it cannot be effectively sealed or removed. Older stains are usually more of an aesthetic issue. Most of the time, these can be sealed and even hidden if you have the floor stained a dark color. You may need a professional duct cleaning also. Pets kept in bedrooms, such as in fish tanks or in enclosed cages (e.g., rabbits, hamsters, etc.) could be a problem. If the former owner had these, you may need to do extra cleaning. Fish tanks don't do much for the indoor air quality.

Cigarette smoke residues left from prior owners (or your own smoking habits) are a common problem. Many people can instantly tell if there has been a smoker in the house. In severe situations, the walls and ceilings are stained a nicotine yellow. Homes with tobacco smoke residues can normally be made right with a good cleaning followed by a complete painting of the exposed surfaces on the walls and ceilings. Some authorities on cleaning recommend cleaning with a vinegar solution. Most painted walls can be sufficiently cleaned to eliminate the smells, but severe problems may call for painting with a sealer (such as Kilz) before repainting. Getting rid of existing carpeting is a given. Do further research if you have this problem.

A problem to be aware of, however, is when you are buying a condominium or have common walls with a neighbor who smokes. In some cases, you can have an air interchange between the units. Also, do people smoke in the hallways of the building you are looking at? Look for cigarette butts in the hallways; some people can determine this by the smells. This is a real nuisance.

Smoke from woodstoves or back drafting. The particles may be present if a woodstove or fireplace was extensively used and experienced poor drafting. A past usage of a woodstove or fireplace in the home is unlikely to lead to a chronic condition, in my opinion, but a more extensive initial cleaning could be needed. Your use of a woodstove may or may not lead to significant deterioration of the indoor air quality, depending on the quality of the unit and how much and how properly it is used. Fireplaces, despite their charms, don't do a lot for the indoor air quality, especially if extensively used (which few people do anymore). The aesthetic pleasures of a fireplace can outweigh these concerns.

Soot from a back-drafting oil-fired heating system. On occasion, I find soot-covered insulation in the basement that was caused by an oil-fired heating system. Usually, repairs have been made to the heating system to correct this problem. The 'sooting,' if extremely minimal, may be tolerable and not have an effect, but if the insulation is black with soot, in my opinion, the insulation should be removed. Even light 'sooting' presents poorly to a future buyer, if nothing else.

Chemicals or pesticides used by the former owner(s) or cleaning professionals.

The improper use of chemicals or pesticides by past owners could, in some cases, be a problem for a new owner. There is a famous case in Massachusetts where the company hired to clean up a basement with a soot back-drafting problem contaminated the house through the use of improper chemical cleaners. Pesticides and herbicides are also inherently nasty chemicals. Try to avoid them. Where you must have them, store them outside the home (in a shed or garage). You probably won't be able to find out what products were used inside the home in the past. Chemicals used to treat termite infestations may be present but they are apparently not as problematic as the chlordane used in the past. Those who are chemically sensitized may not be able to tolerate any residues of these materials.

Off-gassing from newly installed building materials. See the comments in chapter 14. High formaldehyde levels may be found in newer household materials (such as cabinets, wood flooring, and especially laminate flooring). Avoid any excessive exposure, but for most people (those who are not or do not become chemically sensitized), this may not be a long-term problem as the formaldehyde will outgas and become less serious in time.

The newer the construction and the greater the use of synthetic or composite materials, the greater the risk of experiencing reactions to the indoor air. A few of the culprits for the chemically sensitive could include polymer-based leveling compounds, flooring adhesives, laminate flooring, fiberglass screens, and new carpeting. Older homes, while perhaps dustier, would be at lower risk of chemical outgassing than new construction.

If you are chemically sensitive or just concerned about this issue, you may want to look at older homes. They may have wood cabinets instead of particleboard and hardwood or tile floors instead of carpeting, etc. If building new or renovating, it is possible to have homes built without toxic or potentially problematic materials. There is a lot to research here.

Non-organic contaminants: lead dust, asbestos, fuel combustion byproducts, etc.

Obviously, lead dust, dust from asbestos residues, and fuel combustion byproducts, such as from poorly vented systems, can also impact the indoor air quality. For lead paint and asbestos dust, the trick is to not generate airborne particles. See chapter 14 on these. Removing asbestos-containing materials may be desirable – but it is not always warranted, strictly speaking, for health reasons, assuming the material is not exposed or deteriorated. Removing asbestos in embedded materials, while desirable during a major renovation or gutting of the home – from a practical standpoint is simply not feasible. Vermiculite insulation in attics, if found, is recommended for removal. Vermiculite in walls is ignored as you simply can't get at it.

Off-gassing from newer spray foam installations. Spray foam insulation provides a super-efficient way to insulate a home – and the vast majority of the spray foam installations have not had problems. Unfortunately, there have been spray foam installations that were not done properly and the foam outgassed, producing a really nasty odor – smelling something like dying fish or ammonia. In the worst cases, this made the homes unlivable – or the insulation has had to be completely removed and the surfaces it was on sealed. As a buyer, I would be careful if the home was <u>recently</u> subject to spray foaming. You could also ask the current homeowner (or occupant) for any problems they may have experienced with the spray foam installation. Try to sense if there is any lingering smell present. <u>Close the open windows at the inspection.</u> If a recent installation was done and it smells like dead fish, just 'run' from the property. Fortunately, this has not been a problem in the vast majority of installations. If you are going to have spray foam used to retrofit your home, only hire a company that has been doing this for a number of years. Spray foam cannot be installed on overly cold or overly hot days, and it has to be mixed and installed exactly according to manufacturer's instructions.

Candles. Most of these are petroleum based. <u>Don't use them</u> – or use them as little as possible. As a buyer, you may need to clean the soot off the walls or ceilings if the former owner had a candle fetish.

Hot tubs, pools, greenhouses inside or open to the home . . .

Occasionally we find hot tubs, pools, or greenhouses that are not isolated from the interior of the house. Usually, these are outside (where pools and hot tubs belong) or are isolated from the interior space and have exhaust fans to vent the moist air. Where these are open to the interiors, be careful. Hot tubs and pools produce a lot of moisture. They also require chemicals so they don't become pools of algae. Whatever chemicals or nasty organic stuff that is present in the water will be discharged into the air. Pesticides could have been used in the greenhouse. These installations may be desirable features, but you need to be aware of the moisture and chemical issues that these present. For hot tubs especially, you would like to keep these isolated from the living space so the area can be properly vented when they are in use.

Other Indoor Air Concerns

Carbon monoxide

I've covered carbon monoxide in Chapter 12, but as this an important concern, I will briefly note this below.

Carbon monoxide kills hundreds of people every year – and sickens many more. Carbon monoxide is produced by incomplete or faulty combustion of any carbon-based fuel. Carbon monoxide is particularly insidious, as you can't see or smell it. At lower levels, the symptoms of carbon monoxide poisoning are similar to getting the flu – but with carbon monoxide poisoning, no one gets over this until they leave the home (if they make it out). If you are getting chronic headaches or just feel lousy (and it isn't because you have teenagers or toddlers) when you are in the home, be aware of this as a potential cause. Many fire departments or even gas companies will test the home if elevated levels of carbon monoxide are suspected.

Insofar as the inspection goes, most inspectors will not test for carbon monoxide due to the fact that elevated CO levels may only occur during certain weather or environmental conditions that one can't reproduce on demand. Doing the testing at the time of the inspection may reveal no problem – and you still get poisoned after moving in. The way to avoid getting poisoned is to install new carbon monoxide detectors in the home prior to moving in, test them regularly, and change them every five years. That – and have all combustion equipment in the home serviced annually, along with an initial and periodic check of the chimneys and venting systems.

Drug houses.

Need I say more? See chapter 14. Avoid. I will say that a home where drugs were used may be subject to an effective remediation and clean up whereas a property where drugs were *produced* is probably not. This will warrant further investigation on your part. Also, a home where pot was grown would represent less of a problem than a property where meth was made.

Gas combustion byproducts . . .

Gas stoves that burn cleanly don't produce carbon monoxide – at least once they have warmed up. Not all, however, burn completely cleanly. All will put combustion byproducts back into the air. Using a gas stove does not seem to be a problem for most people. If you are asthmatic and/or react when the gas stove has been running for a time, you may need to have the unit checked. As a worst case, switch to an electric-fired stove (the best stoves have gas burners and electric-fired ovens). Flames that are constricted will produce CO and noxious aldehydes. If the home is moderately tight, consider cracking a window in the kitchen when the gas oven will be on for a long period. In very tight homes, such as newer energy efficient homes, you really can't have a gas stove for cooking. Use a portable gas or propane-fired stove outside when you need to barbeque.

Another potential problem is **ventless gas stoves.** These stoves do not vent to the exterior but instead vent the combustion byproducts back into the household air. Lots of indoor air quality experts condemn these – but they are allowed. I've seen them work without *apparent* problems when located in wide open spaces in upscale condos. If you want to use one of these you must follow the manufacturer's recommendations (which briefly include: don't use it for a long length of time or as a primary heat source; don't use in a restricted space; don't alter the gas logs as this could cause flame impingement, and make sure you have good carbon monoxide detectors present). Better yet, don't use it or use it minimally.

Fuel oil leakage or spillage.

Have any strong oil smells resolved – or don't pursue the property, as you don't want to own a home where fuel oil has been leaking into the ground or below the slab. Tanks corrode from the inside out so a rusting tank, while not a good sign, may not indicate a failing tank. Have older or suspect tanks evaluated further. Tanks over 25 years of age are considered 'fully depreciated.' Consider replacing.

What you can do when looking at homes . . .

When looking at a home you are considering making an offer on, be cautious – but not paranoid. The list below could be 'red flags' of indoor air quality problems.

1. Be careful if all the windows in the home are open when you look at the home. Open windows may not mean anything, but if the weather conditions really don't warrant having multiple windows open, then perhaps this could indicate an odor is present that the owner doesn't want you to smell. Very often, however, windows are opened to hide cigarette smells. Close the windows and see if things change. Any type of fuel oil smell would be a serious 'red flag.'

2. Be aware if the current owner has a large number of air 'fresheners' installed in the outlets that could be hiding smells. You see these all of the time – so they may not always indicate that the owner is hiding something (IF TO IS) – but there is a limit to everything; a couple

of these things may be okay – but not a house filled with them. Get rid of them after you move in too; they may smell like flowers – but they may be filled with toxic chemicals. Some types are reputed to be a fire hazard.

3. As noted, bring along friends or relatives who are sensitive to mold on a second visit to the property. If you are really concerned about mold or other indoor air quality issues – or you just want to rule out air quality issues in the home you are looking at – consider having a qualified indoor air quality specialist look at the home. Don't just get someone who sticks out a few mold testing kits. Industrial hygienists or qualified IAQ specialists would be candidates for this evaluation.

4. Be careful with finished basements. If the insulation appears to be full of mouse droppings, this is an issue that will need to be dealt with. If the finished basement shows evidence of water penetration, there is a higher risk of concealed mold behind the walls. Be aware if the sump pump is running constantly. This may not be a concern for an unfinished basement – but a finished basement is another matter.

5. Be careful with unmaintained or older central air conditioning systems. Ask if the system has been serviced in the last year. It's not an intractable issue, but servicing and a possible duct cleaning will be needed.

CHAPTER 16
Evaluating Water Quality and Private Wells...

What you will learn in this chapter

- *The types of private wells you could have...*
- *Issues with private wells you need to be aware of...*
- *Water quality testing... what you need to test for...*
- *Issues with municipal water... cautions...*

Most of this chapter will deal with the issues that come with having a private well supply your water. You should know what type of well is present, the problems you can encounter, how to evaluate private wells during the home buying process, and lastly, what *water quality tests* you can and should do. As most homes are served by municipal or community (but private) water supplies, the subject of water quality from these also needs a discussion. For those who are interested, I've provided more information on what may be in your municipal water supply and what you can do to increase the likelihood that the water is 'safe to drink.'

PART 1 Private well systems...

Private well systems serve roughly 15 million homes or 15 percent of the population, mostly in rural areas. They are very common in the northeast, outside urban and suburban areas. Having a private well system isn't necessarily a negative: many homeowners get superior water from their wells and they don't have to pay the sometimes exorbitant municipal water bills. But private wells do have risks and there are things you need to know when buying a home that gets its drinking water from a well system. Unless a comprehensive test was recently done and the results are available, you should plan to have the water tested during your home inspection contingency period. I'll go over the options for water testing and will include links to various EPA and other sites with information on wells and water quality.

What type of well could you have?

The first thing you need to find out is the type of well the property has. Almost always this will be a deep (drilled) well – but shallow (dug) wells and point wells are also found. While rare, you could have a spring or surface water source. If not obvious, the seller and/or the listing agent should be able to tell you what type of well is supplying the water. If they have no idea (and surprisingly, I see this a lot), then plan on getting a well specialist out the property to examine the system – either when the inspection is done – or before. On some properties, the well head is below ground and the sellers will have no idea where it is. The location of the well needs to be determined either before or during your contingency period.

Dug and shallow wells . . .

Dug wells were the original source of water for most antique homes. Many were stone-lined; newer dug wells may have large round tile casings set into the ground. 'Point' wells, made by driving a pointed steel pipe into the ground, are usually (but not always) moderately shallow. I'll lump these in with dug wells, although they are not quite the same.

What are the most common problems with shallow well systems?

#1 *Bacterial contamination* is number one. Dug wells utilize surface water in addition to water that comes from the water table. In my opinion, some dug wells (those tied into springs) can produce a generous supply of good quality water. These are the exception. Dug wells are more prone to bacterial contamination due to surface water intrusion. Testing for bacteria should pick this up, but some wells may be fine in the winter and not so good during the warmer months. Test initially and retest periodically.

Any type of surface water supply, such as water pulled out of lakes or streams, is inherently at risk of contamination and would not be recommended for use as drinking water. For other usages, this water could perhaps be utilized.

#2 *Limited capacity during drought periods* . . .

The second problem with dug and shallow wells is that many will provide an adequate supply of water in normal rainfall years but will run dry or have limited water during droughts – or just routinely during the summer months. The dug well I had at my first house would be great most of the year – but it could get very scratchy during late summer conditions. (By contrast, a neighbor's dug well had unlimited water and was once used to supply a barn full of livestock).

277

Insofar as buying a home with a dug well, I would be careful. Ask the owner whether they have ever run out of water. Ask the local plumbing inspector if that area of town has widespread problems with water issues during the summer. Your home inspector is not doing a capacity evaluation. A problem is that no one cannot predict whether a well that appears to provide unlimited water in the spring or winter may run out during a drought or during summer conditions. In my area, many wells with no previous capacity issues ran dry during the 2016 drought. Also, what may be adequate for the current homeowner may not be adequate for your family if your water usage is higher. You may have a larger household or want to use the well to water your garden or lawn. Well capacity can change over time and nearby development can also reduce the amount of water supplied by the well (and this is true for both shallow and deep drilled wells).

If you determine the well has capacity issues – or intractable quality issues – you should plan on having a drilled well installed. Costs on this can vary greatly, so I recommend getting an estimate from a well-drilling company.

#3 Safety. This is not a common problem, but occasionally I encounter old dug wells with no covers or easily removable covers. I've even lifted planks in a basement floor and found a dug well going down 25 feet. A dug well with a poorly secured cover is obviously a child safety hazard. The presence of a poorly capped dug well would be an urgent safety concern.

#4 Well equipment. Shallow wells will have either suction or jet pumps that are located above ground, usually in the basement. Jet pumps can be used on wells down to 160 or so feet and are commonly found on 'point' wells. A good pump normally will last anywhere from 10 to 20 years, occasionally more – but just realize: they are a mechanical system. Putting a whole surge protector on the incoming electrical service is a good idea, as nearby lightning strikes or other surges will sometime knock out well pumps (as well as electronic equipment). Find a well company that can service the system after you move in.

Evaluating drilled wells . . .

Most of the private wells in my region and, I suspect, most of the country, are drilled wells. These wells utilize metal casings that run into the bedrock and tap into the water present in the aquifer, the water in the bedrock deep underground. Sometimes the pumps may be drawing from groundwater, which is less desirable. Drilled wells have submersible pumps set deep inside the well casing. The pump controls and a pressure tank are typically located in the basement.

As far as the inspection of these wells, your home inspector will typically run the water to ensure there is adequate flow over a limited time span. As noted, you can also have a well specialist look at the system. This may reveal problems or issues you will need to follow up on. Unfortunately, even with drilled wells, it is difficult to predict what the water flows may be during drought periods. The majority of deep wells, from my experience, do not have significant capacity issues, but specific geographic areas will tend to have capacity limitations even with deep wells. Ask questions and do the investigations I've detailed below.

Problems you commonly find with deep well systems include:

 # 1 The capacity of the well to supply an interrupted supply over the course of the year.

As noted, the majority of the drilled wells do not have serious capacity issues. Much like with shallow wells, however, drilled wells could run dry or experience limited water flows during droughts. Limited flows can also occur when the well driller never hit a good source of water. If you find out that the well is 800 feet deep, that tells you the well driller had problems finding adequate water at normal depths. This is a red flag in my opinion; expect a lot of mineralization from these wells, even if you get an adequate supply of water.

Another problem you can have is that new development can affect the capacity of nearby wells. In a neighboring town, the municipal wells stopped producing adequate water when a golf course drilled their own wells near the town's. In my neighborhood, the owner of a 'newer' home impacted water flows at a neighbor's well by using a large volume of well water to irrigate his yard.

#2 *Age.* Wells may undergo a decreased flow of water over time as the pores in the aquafer rock clog up. In some cases, older wells with limited flows can be 'fracked' with high-pressure water streams to open up the pores in the bedrock (just like energy companies do to open up the pores to produce natural gas). This can work, but it often produces excessive mineralization in the water. All submersible pumps, as mechanical systems, will eventually fail – and sometimes prematurely. (I recommend getting a whole house surge protector as nearby lightning strikes will often 'fry' the well equipment).

#3 *Bad wells. READ THIS!* Occasionally, you can have a well that either doesn't provide enough water – or the water has so many contaminants you may need to have another well drilled. It can be hard to determine if the well has insurmountable quantity or quality issues during the short home buying period – but where you can, try to resolve this. To provide an example of how this can be a problem: I inspected a very nice, upscale two-year-old home for young buyers a couple of years ago. The home was well built and had few issues – except for the fact that the water came out of the taps an orange color, indicating extreme mineralization. (When I inquired about the well at the start of the inspection, it was reported to be 800 feet deep, so I wasn't surprised. But orange water: really?) Besides taking a water sample, I referred them to a company that does well evaluations. Their suggestion was to drill another well. I think this issue blindsided my clients, and they weren't prepared to renegotiate or walk away due to this issue. This home was going to need an expensive water treatment system (possibly $10,000+) to get reasonably drinkable and usable water.

Other problems with wells are cracked casings, casings that don't run far enough into the bedrock, bad fittings, poorly fitting caps – all of which may allow unwanted surface water to enter the well. Unless you can engage a water testing company that offers a camera scan for the interior of the well, you will not be able to determine if these conditions are present during your inspection contingency period. A well that continues to show bacteria in tests done after it has been 'shocked' could indicate one of the problems noted above.

Where the well is old, where the water tests revealed bacteria problems – or just for maximum assurance – consider having a well inspection done within your inspection contingency period.

#4 *Close to roadways – or ponds, marshes, waterways . . .*

Wells that are close to heavily salted roads will be prone to high chloride levels. This is not the end of the world, but the quality of the water may be affected. Wells close to ponds, marshes, lakes, other waterways reportedly are more prone to surface water contamination, as the subsurface water will very often find its way into the well. Wells near the ocean are prone to salt contamination due to the intrusion of the salt water into the freshwater aquifer. This can also be a problem for municipal wells in towns close to the ocean.

#5 *REGIONAL CONCERN Wells in areas where fracking is occurring for natural gas generation*

I've covered this in prior chapters, so I'll be brief here. Well contamination due to hydraulic fracturing (fracking) is becoming a significant problem in many areas of the country – especially in Pennsylvania and those western states where drilling for oil and gas is occurring.

The wells drilled for natural gas typically go deep into the bedrock (up to two miles) and were not intended to impact the water found in the shallower aquifers tapped for drinking water. The chemical-laden waste water that comes back to the surface, meanwhile, is supposed to be injected back deeply into the ground so that it also will not contaminate the water used for drinking or irrigation. Unfortunately, a high percentage of the contaminated wastewater and chemicals reputedly ends up on the ground.

And, for whatever reason, cracked or misaligned casings, poor design or installation – or perhaps just an unintended consequence of trying to drill for natural gas at one depth and thinking that this will not impact the aquifer water at a lesser depth – wells that used to supply water for drinking and agriculture have become contaminated. Where natural gas drilling is occurring, methane (natural gas) is sometimes now found in the well water. A documentary a few years back, *Gas Land*, showed people setting fire to the water coming out of their taps. This is apparently not an isolated phenomenon. As an understatement, this would not be pleasant.

My advice is to think twice about buying a rural property in areas where drilling for natural gas using fracking techniques is occurring. Portions of rural Pennsylvania seem to be particularly at risk, which is a shame, as these areas are particularly beautiful and fertile (or, least, 'were'). It can be hard, by the way, to determine how much natural gas drilling is affecting the water in a particular area, as the energy companies have been quick to settle lawsuits alleging contamination of the wells or surface water; those settling have to sign non-disclosure agreements so they cannot do anything to publicize problems they may have had.

Getting back to more typical well problems . . .

What do you do when the home you are looking at has a well system?

#1 Ask the owner about the well location, type, and history. When they don't know the location of the well, this should raise a lot of red flags. Occasionally, the well cap is buried and no one can find it. Well caps buried underground are prone to surface water intrusion and will need repairs in all cases. I also recommend asking for the age of the submersible pump. The homeowner may or may not know this. Roughly 80 percent of the submersible pumps, from my experience, will fail sometime between 15 and 25 years old; a good average is 20 years. With inferior pumps or poor installations – or the luck of the draw – you may get fewer years.

#2 Ask the owner if they have ever run out of water or if they have limited water during the summer months. While not all homeowners will give you honest answers, most will. Don't bother asking the listing agent about this, as this is not something they would know. From my experience, wells that are over 600 feet deep indicate possible lower flow-rates and a higher likelihood of excessive mineralization. Ask the owner if the well has been 'fracked.' This opens up the pores in the rock – but, as noted, may also cause excessive mineralization.

#3 Run the water and take a glass to taste. Much like with municipal water, sometimes the water tastes lousy but may not have serious health contaminants. The opposite, of course, could be true, as some types of contamination (for instance, arsenic) can't be tasted. Your inspector should run the water at the inspection to at least determine normal flows and pressure. Warning: you will not get the volume or pressure from a well system that you get from a municipal system. This is not a problem – unless the system can't supply at least 4–5 gallons per minute of water on a continuous basis.

#4 Have the water tested during your contingency period. Many – if not most – inspectors who work in rural areas will do water quality testing. Plan on having this done. FHA and VA mortgage lenders require specific water tests. If you are getting an FHA or VA mortgage, notify your inspector – or whoever will be doing the water testing – ahead of the inspection so they can plan on doing the required tests. There are tests you may want to have beyond what the FHA and VA require – see below.

I recommend a 'Comprehensive' test that covers most of the naturally occurring minerals (including arsenic), bacteria, radon in water, and a number of organic chemicals. It is possible to do even more expensive tests for pesticide and environmental contaminants. I do not explicitly recommend doing these tests as they are quite expensive – but neither would I discourage you from doing them if you are so inclined. Ask your inspector if you want these. Special test kits may need to be ordered ahead.

#5 If you have serious concerns with the well, you can have a company that specializes in well inspections do a scan of the well interior to look for cracked casings and sources of water intrusion above the bedrock. This can get expensive and most buyers just go with having the water tested. This type of evaluation may be needed, however, if the well has serious water quality issues and/or the well is 'suspect' due to age or other evidence. Some well companies test the amp draw on the motor as part of their well evaluation. This may indicate an older or 'tired' pump, but in most cases if the pump is still working it is considered 'functional.' If it no longer delivers water, that is another matter.

Contaminants in well water . . .

Contaminants are classified as either primary, which means they are a health concern, or secondary, which means they affect taste and quality. A few of the health concerns you may find with wells include:

1. Bacteria. Fecal coliform bacteria are the most worrisome, as their presence typically indicates intrusion of surface water containing animal or human wastes. This is known to cause cramps, diarrhea, intestinal illness, and serious kidney disorders in humans. A finding of bacteria in the well water – and especially fecal bacteria – is usually considered 'not acceptable' in real estate transactions. In most cases, the well will need to be 'shocked,' a procedure where a specified amount of bleach is put into and run through the system. After being shocked, the water can then be retested. Note: viruses and parasites could also potentially be found in well water – but they are difficult to test for.

2. Lead. This is included in a lot of standard water tests but, in my opinion, it can be difficult to test for due to the difficulty of getting an accurate sample. A point-of-use filter for the drinking water may be needed – as well as replacing old lead feed pipes if high levels are found in the water sample.

3. Arsenic in the water. Chronic exposure to arsenic is also associated with an increased risk of skin, bladder, and lung cancer. There is also evidence that long-term exposure to arsenic can increase the risk of kidney and prostate cancer. High levels of arsenic in the water are obviously not desirable, and steps should be taken to limit your exposure (and this does not include drinking bottled water).

    Plan to have the water tested for arsenic. I should note that moderately elevated arsenic levels are very often something the buyer deals with after taking possession. This is not written in stone, as each situation is different, and homes with extreme levels of arsenic in the water – or where a buyer has an extreme level of concern – could be exceptions. Either point of use (for drinking water at the kitchen sink) or whole house systems could be installed. Depending on what the water will be used for, either could be appropriate.

4. Heavy metals, including cadmium, chromium, selenium in the water. Fluoride, although not a 'heavy' metal, could be lumped in with these. Cadmium and chromium would most likely occur from industrial byproducts.

5. High levels of nitrates in the water. High nitrate/nitrite levels are most commonly found in agricultural areas or areas with fertilizer runoff. This mainly affects infants, who can develop a condition called

methemoglobinemia. Most basic water tests will include nitrates. Treatment options would need to be determined by a water treatment professional. (Some authorities recommend finding another source of water – especially for infants, when this is present). High levels of nitrates are rarely seen in most of New England, from my experience.

6. High levels of radon or uranium in the water. Radon can be present in the well water as well as the household air. Radon in water is measured in the thousands of picocuries (pCi/L). Much of your exposure to radon gas from the well water would occur when you are in the shower or running high volumes of water. (Having an exhaust fan in the bathroom limits your exposure). Unfortunately, there is no EPA standard 'action level' for radon in water as there is for radon in air. Each state sets its own 'non-binding' action level. In Massachusetts, for instance, the action level is 10,000 picocuries (pCi/L); in New Hampshire it has been 2000 pCi/L, now reportedly being raised to 5,000 pCi/L. Other states will have their own action levels – and some may have no standard at all. If testing reveals high levels of radon in the water you – and most buyers – may not find this acceptable. I've tested wells that showed levels of 100,000 pCi/L of radon in the water. Homes with levels this high need a radon-in-water mitigation system. These are expensive to install (typically $4000+). You may find even lower levels of radon in water to be 'unacceptable.'

7. Volatile organic chemicals from oil or gasoline spills, chemical dumping residues, pesticides. Methyl *tert*-butyl ether (MTBE), a chemical added to gasoline in the past, is occasionally found in drinking water. Perchloroethylene (PCE) and chloroform are the most commonly found volatile organic compounds after MTBE. Volatile organic chemicals can be tested for – and I advise doing a test for the most common organic chemicals – but this is more expensive than just testing for naturally occurring minerals and bacteria. You would have a higher risk of pesticide contamination in agricultural areas and areas downstream from them.

8. Other organic chemicals that may be ffound in well water, whether private wells or municipal, are chloroform and perchloroethene (PCE). The list of possible chemical and volatile organic compounds is nearly endless. Please see the links to the EPA's web site on well water https://www.epa.gov/privatewells.

9. Environmental contaminants found due to pesticide and herbicide applications. You are more likely to find high levels of atrazine, glyphosate, and other potentially harmful chemicals in agricultural areas. Municipal systems may occasionally test for these contaminants, but I'm not sure how often. For private wells, specialized tests are needed to determine if herbicides and pesticides are present.

Note: One plus with getting your water from a private well system is that you would not typically have chlorinated water. The chlorination byproducts commonly found in municipal water would not be present.

Commonly found contaminants that affect taste and quality . . .

This is just a short list of what is termed secondary contaminants, those that may affect taste and quality.

1. Hardness. Hard water contains magnesium and calcium carbonates, formed when water percolates through limestone and chalk naturally present in soil and rock formations. Hardness is commonly found in well water and is especially common in the Midwest states. Hard water is not unhealthy; in fact, a small degree of hardness in the water may be good for you. Hard water can encrust plumbing fixtures and makes it more difficult for soap or detergents to work. Hard water can be dealt with by adding a water softening system. I recommend ignoring results that show mildly hard water as overly soft water is not ideal either.

2. Iron and manganese. These are commonly found in well water and can affect both taste and quality. They may also tend to cause laundry to stain – especially light-colored clothing when using bleach. High levels of these minerals will also tend to clog pipes over time. If you see a lot of red or black staining in the bath-tubs or toilets, this may indicate elevated levels of iron or manganese in the well water. Excessive levels of iron and manganese are something you will want to correct. Water softeners, if correctly designed and using specific salts, can often be effective at lowering high levels of these minerals. Other methods could be specified by the company that designs the water purification system.

3. pH, indicating the alkalinity or acidity of the water, is generally tested for. Waters with low pH (more acidic) may need to have acid neutralizing systems installed.

4. Chlorides. Chlorides are salts from chloride combining with other metals. These can be naturally occurring – but most typically high chloride levels are found in wells near heavily trafficked roadways subject to heavy salting during the winter. Saltwater intrusion at wells drilled near the ocean or inland waterways also causes elevated chloride levels. Low levels of chlorides are not regarded as a health concern, but they definitely can affect the taste of the water. They are not easily removable except with reverse osmosis systems, a type of point-of-use system.

5. Copper. Where high, this most typically would indicate 'aggressive' water affecting copper pipes. A small amount of copper, like many things, is okay. Too much, not good.

6. Sulfur, generally experienced as hydrogen sulfide gas, may be present. My clients can usually smell this immediately. I have a poor sense of smell, I confess, so I rarely pick this up. High sulfur content may show up more when running the hot water.

Sulfur is noxious, especially at higher levels, and warrants correction with an appropriate water treatment system. Sulfur easily volatizes, I should note, and is therefore not always picked up by water tests. If you can smell it, it's there. The presence of sulfur, according to water specialists I've consulted, normally indicates the presence of some type of bacteria. Small amounts of sulfur may be tolerable if it is just intermittent or decreases with the higher volume of water flows that comes with living in the home.

Testing the water . . .

I advise that homes with well water be tested during your contingency period. Most home inspectors – at least those that work in rural areas – will offer this. I recommend a comprehensive test that includes bacteria, naturally occurring minerals, heavy metals, arsenic, and radon in the water. As noted, the VA and FHA require specific tests for their mortgages; you will need to let your inspector know that if you are going for a VA or FHA mortgage and that the home has well water. In terms of where the test is taken, the labs that I use advise taking the water from the tap after it leaves any whole house water treatment system that may be present. This gives you a good idea of what you will be drinking or bathing in. You could test the water before, as it comes into the house, to get an idea of what is in the water prior to treatment, but the downside is that it gets expensive when you are doing a second set of tests. Testing the source water may be the better choice when a water treatment specialist is designing a new treatment system or determining why an existing system isn't working as intended. Lastly, many homes will have a point-of-use filter at the kitchen sink for the drinking water. I think these are a great idea, but again, your home inspector normally doesn't test the water from these devices. Assuming these systems are maintained and working properly, they should be regarded as a plus. Filters must get changed, however, or they can negatively affect the water quality.

Exceptions . . .

People occasionally drill wells to supply their lawn sprinkler systems. Your home inspector won't test this water. One thing you may see is orange staining on the house and bushes. This means this well water has too much iron and manganese. It won't hurt the plants, but the staining turns everything an ugly orange.

If the home has a point-of-use system to get rid of the arsenic in the water, you could have the water tested after the treatment to see if the system is working as intended.

Caution with vacant homes . . . When the home has been vacant, typically the water has not been run for some time. Unfortunately, this allows the minerals in the water to become concentrated. A water sample may then show levels of primary or secondary contaminants that are higher than what you would have than if the home was lived in and the water was used normally. To work around this, try to have the water run for several hours or so (and discharged outside so nothing overflows inside!) when buying a vacant home with a private well. You may then get a better idea of what is in the water.

New construction and new wells . . .

With new construction – or any new well – many towns will require specific water tests and require that the builder ensure the well water meets the standards for potable water. This is to your benefit. What may be required, however, can vary from town to town and state to state. Some towns require expensive 'radon in water' mitigation or other water purification systems that other towns have no requirements for. Few municipalities, however, get involved with or mandate correction of secondary contaminants. In other words, the water can still taste bad or contain stuff you don't want to drink. In much of the country, I suspect there is little or no oversight on the wells drilled in new construction. Also, I've seen towns that require testing for some exotic item – but have no requirements to test for radon in water or organic chemicals, etc. Lastly, municipalities in the same state may require specific tests that may only be offered by certain labs. If you are buying new construction where a well is present, I recommend finding out from the town which tests they require and – just as important – which tests they do not require. You may need to test for things beyond what the local jurisdiction requires and use a specified lab for the testing.

Post inspection negotiations due to water quality – and well capacity – issues.

With the exception a couple of items, it is generally hard to renegotiate for a water treatment system to correct deficiencies in the quality of the well water. This doesn't mean you have to accept everything, it is just that, from my experience, most of the time it is up to the new owner to install whatever treatment system may be needed or desired. As noted above, for new construction, the rules are different, as some municipalities require that the private well water meet specific standards for occupancy approval. In perhaps the majority of homes with private wells, I should note, water treatment systems are needed due to taste and quality issues. When the municipal water is supplied by drilled wells, high mineralization will sometimes mean that some type of water treatment could be desirable here also.

Health and functionality issues are more likely to be subject to negotiation, such as when testing reveals bacteria in the water or high arsenic levels. I would like to see buyers be a little more cautious when the water is extremely poor quality, as this can entail a significant expense to correct.

In terms of concerns about the <u>quantity of water supplied by the well</u>, extreme capacity issues should be (in my opinion) a negotiable issue (drilling a new well is expensive!), but it is difficult to determine if this is a problem until you move in and run the water at normal levels through drought (or just dry) summer conditions.

Water treatment systems . . .

A number of water purification systems exist to remove contaminants that may be present in water supplies. Determining which may be needed for any given home will depend on the testing results – and the input from a qualified water treatment professional. Your home inspector may have a basic familiarity with these systems – but that is all. Water softening systems, filters, and reverse osmosis systems are often recognizable, but unmarked canisters are often present where you would need to look at the installation paperwork to determine what they are doing. Get information from the homeowner (if knowledgeable) or a water treatment specialist. Further research is often warranted when exotic systems are present. If the equipment is older, you may want to have a water treatment professional look at the system after you move in (and after doing a water test to see what is present in the water). If a treatment system is present but not used, look at the results from the testing. I sometimes find a system no longer in use and the water test results do not warrant its reactivation.

Aeration systems to reduce the levels of radon in well water could be present. Numerous point-of-use systems that utilize carbon filtration, reverse osmosis, or arsenic reduction media are also commonly installed. Sediment filters are commonly present. You need to regularly change the filters in these or they will lead to poorer water quality than if one was not present. Although unusual, sediment filters can even 'explode' and leak water into the basement if they become clogged.

Cautions:

First, boiling water may kill pathogens, but it will also concentrate undesirable compounds in the water.

Second, any water treatment system has to be maintained. As noted, filters that are not periodically changed can result in worse water quality than what you started out with.

Third, using bottled water, perhaps except in emergencies, is not a good idea, in my opinion. A lot of the bottled water is drawn from municipal water supplies (although it goes through additional purification), and just putting water in plastic is not a good idea. What is leaching from the plastic? Plus, bottled water leads to an enormous increase in trash generation and wasted energy used to make and transport the bottles. Just my opinion.

Note: this chapter just gives you the basics on possible problems with your well or water supply and water purification issues. More sophisticated testing and investigation of esoteric problems are possible – but they are beyond the scope of this book.

Municipal supplies and community well systems . . .

The section below has information on the water supplied by municipalities. This may be less of a concern to you as a home buyer. If so, feel free to skip this section. If you have concerns about what could be in the water, read on . . .

Most homes in the US have water supplied by municipal well systems. These may get their water from surface supplies (reservoirs or rivers) or from drilled wells. The good news is that municipal water supplies and private well companies are required by the EPA to test for the contaminants that are health issues. By adding chlorine or by utilizing other disinfectant methods, most municipal water supplies provide a reasonable degree of assurance that the harmful bacteria present in the past (and that caused epidemics such as cholera) are not present – at least when the water leaves the water treatment plant. For most of the municipal water supplies, what comes out of the tap should be fairly safe to drink.

That's the good news. The bad news is that not a lot of testing gets done on what comes out of the tap – and the effectiveness of this testing has been called into question. According to a recent New York Times article, nearly 77 million Americans live in places where the water systems were in some violation of the 1974 Safe Drinking Water Act. Many water supplies have been found to have high levels of lead, arsenic, or other chemicals. Where violations have been found, they are very often not reported. Where reported, there have been almost no fines, as it is up to the states to enforce the provisions of the Act. Again, as this chapter is not designed to be an exposé of these problems, I'll just touch on the issue. A lot of water systems do a good job of monitoring the water supplies and providing quality water. That said, U.S. Health Officials estimate 900,000 people each year become ill and possibly 900 die from waterborne diseases present in municipal water supplies. If you are buying (or live) in an area where an unregulated utility supplies the water (common in rural areas in the southwest), what is in the water supply may be a complete unknown as they simply don't test the water.

Every regulated utility is required to provide a Consumer Confidence Report to their customers, also known as an annual drinking water quality report. A lot of the bad stuff (for example, lead), however, may enter the water through the water mains, the feed pipes to the home, or the house plumbing and fixtures. A third issue is that the water leaving the water treatment plant can meet all of the health standards – but can still be *substandard* in drinking quality. This is especially true where a lot of chlorine has been added to ensure the water is bacteria free.

Commonly found contaminants with municipal water (and how would you deal with these)

#1 Lead in the water . . .

Unlike many types of environmental contaminants, exposure to lead has immediate and provable effects on health and brain development in young children and those in utero (not yet born). (It is not good for adults either). In older areas of the country, especially the northeast, north-central, and older cities everywhere, lead water mains are still in use. Although not as commonly found today (as many of these have been replaced), lead feed pipes are still around, either in water mains or the pipes that bring the water to the house. This was the problem in Flint, Michigan, where a new, more corrosive water source leached lead from the old pipes. (Note: the lead problems in Flint's water are not an isolated occurrence. A study by Reuters in 2016 revealed that, in over 3000 cities with municipal water supplies, testing revealed lead levels equal to or higher than those in Flint. Numerous schools and daycare centers also showed high levels of lead).

Many cities – at least those that are fiscally healthy – are replacing the older lead, wood (yes, these are reportedly still in use), and steel pipes. This is a noble effort, but it is a slow and expensive process. Your family's exposure to lead in the water, however, may come from lead solder used to connect the copper piping or from lead present in older brass plumbing fixtures. Prior to 1986, lead solder was used for copper piping and was commonly present in plumbing fixtures, including faucets and gate valves. You should assume that lead could be present in almost every home built before the 1990s. For homes built after 1986, it was required that copper pipes have a lead-free solder. Restrictions on lead in fixtures, however, came much later. How much lead may leach from the pipes depends on a bunch of factors, including:

1. How long did the water sit in the pipe?

2. How aggressive is the water supply? Acidic water and water devoid of minerals will tend to leach out more lead.

3. Is there a coating inside the lead pipe that may inhibit the leaching? It may be present but this cannot be verified.

Issues when testing for lead in the water . . .

Testing for lead in the water is possible. Some home inspectors will do this – although, given the problems with this testing, I do not routinely recommend it. When testing the water for elevated lead levels, you have the choice of doing a 'first draw' test or a test after the water has been run for a time. The problem with a 'first draw' test, however, is that when the home is occupied, you have no way to ensure that no one has run the water that day. A second problem is that, if the home has not been occupied and you do a first draw test, you may get levels of lead that don't reflect what your normal exposure would be. You get a better sample when you can control the testing. A third problem is that, to be absolutely sure you are determining what the lead exposure may be, you'd need to test the water at each fixture, as individual fixtures could be causing elevated levels at that location. A gate valve below a sink could be the culprit.

I recommend assessing the risks when deciding whether to test for lead in the water. If you are buying a property in suburban areas developed since the 1940s, you are not likely to have lead water mains. If the home you are looking at has a lead feed pipe, you should take common-sense measures to limit your exposure or simply use bottled water – until you have the feed pipe from the street main replaced.

Measures to limit your exposure to lead in the water include:

First, routinely run the water for a short time from the taps before drawing water for drinking or cooking. Water that sits in the pipes will have a higher lead content. You could even fill a pitcher full of water after flushing and put it where it will be used. Note: don't worry about bathing in water that may contain lead; lead will not be absorbed by your body.

Second, don't use hot water from a tap for drinking or cooking, as this water will typically have higher levels of lead. Use only cold water.

Third, consider installing a point of use treatment system for the drinking water. Sometimes you need these systems just to improve the water quality.

Fourth, have the water tested by a qualified testing lab after you move in, when you can get a proper sample.

Fifth, research your treatment options. Even Brita type water filters, with a specified filter, are reportedly able to lower the lead content in the water.

#2 High levels of volatile organic byproducts from chlorination of the water . . .

Chlorine is added to public water supplies to kill disease-causing pathogens, such as bacteria, viruses, and protozoans. Whatever the 'negatives' to chlorination, these are far outweighed by the elimination of diseases such as cholera, dysentery, and typhoid fever.

Nothing good, however, comes without a dark side. The problem with chlorination is that the chlorine reacts with organic compounds to form disinfection byproducts such as trihalomethanes (THMs) and haloacetic acids (HAAs). These are believed to be carcinogenic. Various studies have indicated that drinking chlorinated water is linked to significant increases in bladder, rectal, and colon cancer. In his book, Coronaries/Cholesterol/Chlorine, Joseph M. Price, MD presents evidence that trihalomethanes are the 'prime causative agents of arteriosclerosis and its inevitable result, the heart attack or stroke.'

Various alternative methods have been utilized to eliminate or reduce the addition of chlorine into the water supply, including using chloromines, UV radiation, and ozonation. Not all of these work in every situation and they often entail much higher costs.

What can you do to limit your exposure to chlorination byproducts?

Where the water appears to be heavily chlorinated, it is desirable to have some type of water treatment system – or strategy – to limit your exposure to chlorine byproducts. One is getting a point-of-use water treatment system. Consult a reputable water treatment company regarding this. Note: a plus with having a well system is that you would not typically have chlorinated water. This is both good (no chlorination byproducts) and bad (more risk of harmful pathogens that would have been killed by the chlorine).

As an ad hoc (and unproven!) measure, some people reportedly swear that by filling a pitcher of water and letting it set for a day (presumably in the refrigerator). Some of the chlorine will dissipate, as it is a volatile gas when in solution so this has some logic to it.

#3 Fluoride.

This can be naturally occurring, but more often it is an issue when added to the municipal water supplies as a dental hygiene measure. I'm going to avoid getting into the pluses or minuses of this here, as one can't discuss this issue in a paragraph or two. This is one of those issues where each side can provide persuasive evidence to buttress their case! Where you want to remove the fluoride in water, it is possible to get water treatment systems that will screen this out.

#4 Contamination from pesticides and herbicides . . .

This is both a regional problem with the drinking water and a national problem in terms of the residues of pesticides and herbicides left on the food arising from our industrial agriculture system. There is a lot of bad stuff out there, but two stand out as something prevalent in the water supplies in agricultural regions.

The first is atrazine.

Atrazine is a potent herbicide. Studies have indicated that atrazine is a potent endocrine disrupter. Exposure to even trace levels will affect numerous species, causing what is equivalent to a 'chemical castration.' Studies have also shown links of atrazine to cancer.

Atrazine is found in 94% of U.S drinking water tested by the USDA – more often than any other pesticide. An estimated 7 million people were exposed to atrazine in their drinking water between 1998 and 2003. (Note: Italy and Germany banned atrazine in 1991. Of course, it is still widely used here). The highest levels of contamination are in the Midwest, where it is widely used on corn fields. USGS monitoring shows drinking water concentrations typically spike during the spring and early summer, as rains flush the freshly applied herbicide into streams – and into local water supplies.

Data from the EPA's Atrazine Monitoring Program show that atrazine levels in drinking water can spike above the legal limit of 3 parts per billion in many water supplies. Although the EPA bases its limit on an annual average (not seasonal peaks), the monitoring results reveal alarming levels of human exposure.

According to **NRDC's 2010 analysis** of the most recent EPA data, drinking water in 67 public systems had peak atrazine levels above 3 parts per billion (ppb), with one as high as 60 ppb in Ohio. Six water systems had average annual atrazine concentrations that exceeded the EPA limit entirely. And these figures are for *treated* drinking water – raw water samples contained even higher levels.

The second herbicide that is found in the water supplies in states where industrial agriculture is dominant – and is found in the food supply nationally as well – is glyphosate, also known as Round-up™, produced by the justly maligned Monsanto corporation (referred to by many as the most 'evil' corporation on earth). I'll let that go here. (Roundup also has inert ingredients besides glyphosate that independent studies have indicated may also be problematic).

In addition to being a potent endocrine disrupter, in 2015, a WHO International Agency for Research report indicated that glyphosate is 'probably carcinogenic to humans.' Another study, done by Paul Winchester, medical director of the neonatal intensive care unit at the Franciscan St. Francis Health System and professor of clinical pediatrics at Riley Hospital for Children in Indianapolis, Ind., found glyphosate residues in 90 percent of the women patients. The high levels of those residues appeared to correlate with shortened pregnancies and below-average birth weights adjusted for age. The findings, regarded as preliminary, however, alarmed the researchers because such babies are at increased risk of diabetes, heart disease, high blood pressure, and lower cognitive abilities. Roundup™ usage has roughly doubled, from 85–90 million pounds in 2001 to 180–185 million pounds in 2007. (Where it is now, one can only guess!)

#5 Bacterial contamination after the water leaves the water plant . . .

Even when the water leaving the treatment plant may be free of bacterial contamination, it is possible that not all the water that leaves the treatment plant arrives at your home in the state it was originally in. Reportedly, the water in the mains occasionally may leak out and then get sucked back in; who knows what is in the water at that point. Other potential issues (such as parasites, fungal contaminants) may only be detected by expensive environmental scans. As most municipal water does not have these problems and the tests are expensive, I do not routinely recommend that you test for these when buying a home – but you could do this if you have a reason to be concerned. These are more likely to be done on water from private wells. Nevertheless, you do these after moving in if you are experiencing health issues and suspect the water could be the cause.

#6 Water quality.

Municipal water systems are required to test for contaminants that affect health and not the contaminants that may affect the water's taste and quality. In my region, some towns have great water quality; others not so good. In some regions – and particularly the southern states year-round and during the warmer months in much of the country – you will find high levels of chlorine in the water. Municipal water may be deemed 'safe to drink,' but it still tastes awful. Again, you may want to install some type of point-of-use system in the home to improve the quality.

CHAPTER 17

How to Evaluate Private Waste Disposal (Septic) Systems

What you will learn in this chapter . . .

- Understanding the type of waste disposal system that is present on the home you are purchasing
- The plusses and minuses of various exotic systems
- The problem with 'mounded' leaching fields
- How systems fail . . . How to identify a failed system
- Evaluating septic systems when buying a home
- 'Red flags' for a failed system
- Knowing how to maintain a system so that it will last

One in five homes in the United States, serving some sixty million people, have a private waste disposal system (as opposed to municipal sewers) for getting rid of household wastewater. If the property you are looking at is served by municipal sewers, then feel free to skip this chapter and go on to the other stuff. There are lots of other things you need to be familiar with. Also, I'm just going to cover the basics of how these systems work and how to have them inspected.

My primary caution, however, is this: if you are not proactive about understanding these systems, what can go wrong, and how to evaluate them properly, you could be facing tens of thousands of dollars in costs to replace a failed or inadequate septic system. You don't want this to occur just after you move in – or even a couple of years 'down the road.' The cost to replace a failed system can run in the tens of thousands of

'if you are not proactive about understanding these systems, what can go wrong, and how to evaluate them properly, you could be facing tens of thousands of dollars in costs to replace a failed or inadequate septic system.'

dollars. In the state I reside in, there is a requirement that each home with a private waste disposal system have a specific type of septic inspection done at the time of a real estate transaction. This is referred to as a **Title 5** inspection. It provides a degree of protection for home buyers – but even this inspection is not foolproof. Most states, however, have no requirements that private waste disposal systems be inspected at the time of a real estate sale and most don't have a recognized standard of what should be done. It's a case of caveat emptor (buyer beware!).

So, if the property you are looking at has a private waste disposal system, you will need to know something about how these systems work, the type of system that could be present, how they fail, and how to have them evaluated. You should also understand the limitations and inadequacies of most septic evaluations. And lastly, you should know how to maintain these systems so you can avoid a premature failure. There are lots of pitfalls to avoid!!

You might ask: are there any benefits to having a private waste disposal (PWD) system? Well, one is that you won't have to pay municipal sewerage bills or the possible large assessments that sometimes go with tying in to a municipal sewer system. While I feel that having the home's effluent go to a municipal sewer is preferable (out of sight, out of mind), in many towns and areas, especially in rural areas, septic systems are the norm. There is no other option. My own home is served by a septic system. If the system is 'newer' and was properly installed – or just has plenty of life left, there is no reason to avoid a home with a PWD system.

But how does a private waste disposal system work? Knowing this will help you understand how they fail – and how to keep them from failing. Basically, the function of a private waste disposal system (and in most cases this means a 'septic system,' so I may use these terms interchangeably) is to allow for an on-site disposal of household water and sewage wastes.

Conventional systems . . .

If the home you are looking at has a private waste disposal system, most of the time this means a conventional septic system. How do these work? To quote Inspectapedia

' . . . A 'septic system . . . receives wastewater and solids from a Building's plumbing facilities (bathrooms, kitchens, shower, laundry), treats, and then disposes of the effluent from this waste, by permitting it to absorb into soils at the property.'

'Treatment' is partially accomplished by bacterial action in the 'septic' or 'treatment' tank but most treatment is done by the bacteria in the soil around and below the soil absorption system (SAS), commonly referred to as the 'drain/ leaching field.'

This bacterial action is needed to reduce the level of pathogens in the effluent before it discharges into the soil.

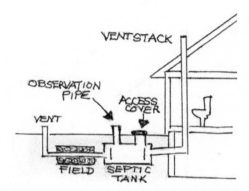

The principal components of a private on-site waste disposal system usually include the following:

- the piping connecting the building to the treatment tank
- a septic or treatment tank which retains solid waste
- piping connecting and conducting clarified effluent from the treatment tank to a distribution box.
- a distribution box connecting the effluent line from the tank to the absorption system or 'septic field.'
- an absorption system which permits effluent to drain to soils below. This is typically a gravel bed installed below the perforated plastic pipe that carries the 'gray water' from the tank. It can also be one or more pits that does the same thing as a leaching field.
- a bio-mat or bio-mass of pathogen-digesting bacteria, which forms in soil below the absorption system.'

Basically, the sewage and wastewater enter the septic tank, where bacteria digest the organic matter, with the undigested solids falling to the bottom of the tank. A top layer of bacterial scum floats on the top of the tank. The 'gray water,' which is still full of organic effluent, flows out from the middle of the tank. (If the scum layer floated out to the leaching field, this would cause a premature failure of the soil absorption system). The gray water effluent then flows out to either a leaching field of some type or to leaching pits, to allow the water to disperse into the soil. The bio-mat of bacteria that surrounds the piping (or pits) digests the bacteria in the effluent. If everything is working correctly, by the time the septic effluent reaches about 12 feet underground, it is (supposedly) clean enough to drink (although I certainly wouldn't).

Mound and pump chamber systems (If you have a mound system, read this)

Mound systems are conventional systems with a septic tank and a leaching field – but with a twist. To elevate the soil absorption system (leaching field) a set distance above the highest seasonal ground water level, the system will have an elevated 'mound' that rises above the surrounding terrain. Mound systems will typically have a second tank after the main septic tank, often referred to as a 'pump chamber.' This tank has an ejector pump that pumps the watery effluent out (and 'up') to the leaching field in the elevated mound. These systems are commonly found where the water tables are relatively high or in sites where the terrain is steep. In many states, new systems must have four feet of separation between the annual high groundwater level and the bottom of the leaching field bed, which requires a pump chamber and mound system.

The problem with mound systems . . .

#1 Mound systems cost extra. They require an extra tank (the pump chamber) and an elevated mound. In some cases, retaining walls are necessary to enclose the mounds or to allow an installation on a steep slope. The added cost of a pump chamber and possible retaining walls to enclose the field) can vary widely. When I had my system replaced, the quote for just a pump chamber (no mounds) was less than $5000. But typically, the complete cost for a mounded or retaining wall system will run anywhere from $15,000 to $40,000. I know of systems on hilly sites that cost $75,000 to install. You need to understand what you could be facing. If the home you are looking at has what appears to be a problem site (high groundwater, adjacent wetlands, steep site, lots of ledge), try to find out what it would cost to replace the system IF it fails. As noted earlier, I had a client years ago who walked away from the property due to the likely costs of replacing the septic system – even though the system was still working at the time of the inspection.

2. Mound systems have an ejector pump, so they require electricity (pumps do not cost much to run, fortunately) and will need periodic pump replacement (which is not a minimal cost). Most pumps last 10 to 16 years, on average. If you lose power, by the way, you will have to stop running water as the system will back up if the pump is not running. Having a generator will be desirable if your area experiences power outages and you have a pump chamber in your septic system.

3. Mound systems can be ugly. In many installations, the septic installer can elevate the area over the septic field by contouring the land so that there is no mound. You will just have a change in the topography. I've even seen people use the re-contouring to get the flatter lawn they wanted. On the other hand, you can have some really ugly

mound systems. One house I inspected had a concrete retaining wall around the leaching field that took up most of the yard. In another instance, one of my clients disclosed that he was moving from his old home as he could not look at the ugly mound in the middle of the yard after a new septic system was installed. I saw it – and it was ugly.

Tip: this may apply to Massachusetts only. In Massachusetts, a property cannot be sold unless there is a passing 'Title 5' inspection; if it doesn't pass, a new or repaired system would need to be installed. Sometimes even what appear to be working systems will not pass due to high groundwater issues. The problem is that you may not know what will be installed before you commit to the purchase. The new system could include an 'ugly mound' that ruins your yard. To avoid this, you could ask to get a look at the plans for the new septic system. I had clients who did this. As they were buying a home with lovely landscaping in the backyard, they requested a look at the plans for the new system before they would commit to the sale. If it was going to ruin the nicely landscaped backyard, they would not proceed with the purchase. (In this case, the septic plan integrated the elevated mound into the landscape, so they did go ahead with the purchase).

Note: a limitation of the Title 5 inspection is that it does not involve running a high volume of water as part of the inspection. A system that works fine for a small household could pass the Title 5 inspection with flying colors – and fail prematurely when your household of five moves in! You may want to 'read between the lines': If the system is 'older' or you will be using the system more intensively, you may need to anticipate replacing the system. Although rare, I've also encountered what I would regard as fraudulent Title 5 inspections.

A commonly found system is **Enviro Systems**, named after the New Hampshire company, Presby Environmental systems, that invented these. These use a series of large corrugated plastic tubes surrounded by coarse sand or gravel with geo-textiles to keep the sand out of the pipes and promote dispersion of the septic effluent into the ground. These are increasingly installed in New England and elsewhere. These systems will have a vent pipe at the end of the septic field to allow air to enter the pipes; this encourages an aerobic (oxygen supported) digestion of the septic wastes in the system. The advantage or the Enviro systems is that they may require a smaller leaching field and, at least in some states, may not need to be four feet above the high groundwater elevation. I have had one of these systems installed for my own home. These systems are commonly found in some states, while in others they are not approved.

In terms of performance, the record is mixed. Many of these systems seem to have performed well, but in many neighborhoods the systems are getting replaced after ten or so years. This may be an installer issue, as this design requires a higher grade of coarse sand around the piping to keep the leaching system from filling up – which will happen when finer grades of sand are used.

Other types of waste disposal systems . . .

I'll just go over these systems briefly, as they are not the commonly found – and if the home you are looking at has one you'll need to know a lot more than I can provide here.

Aerobic and other high tech systems

Aerobic systems are appropriate where a conventional system may not work, such as sites adjacent to a wetland, or in rocky or steep sites. This is a recognized technology and these systems can reportedly work. Basically, they utilize a special tank that continually aerates the sewerage effluent while they keep it in motion. The waste (gray) water that comes out of the system is much cleaner than the effluent from a conventional septic system. The size of the leaching field may also be much smaller than with a conventional system.

The disadvantage of an aerobic system is the higher upfront installation cost. (How much this would be I have no idea so you would need to research this). Also, these systems must have professional maintenance on a yearly basis to ensure they are working correctly. This gets costly – and some towns *require* an annual inspection and professional maintenance at added cost. Lastly, these systems may allow building on a site that never really should have been built on due to the soil conditions (for instance, ledge or with high-water tables).

I would not rule out a property that has an aerobic system, but you will want to verify that it was professionally designed and has been maintained. If I thought I may need to have one of these systems installed, I'd research the costs first.

Various **Material Media Filtration** systems are also in use. One type utilizes recirculating sand filtration. Again, these systems are more likely to be found in 'difficult' sites where a conventional system would not work. They also reportedly produce a much cleaner gray water effluent. The downside would be a much higher cost and higher maintenance. A more detailed description of the various media filter types is best explained on the website https://inspectapedia.com/septic/Septic_Media_Filters.php

Cesspools are a more primitive type of system. Basically, with a cesspool, the solid and liquid effluent from the toilets, bathtub, and sink drains, etc. is dumped into a large porous tank; sometimes an overflow tank is connected. The effluent flows out into the soil around the tank. Due to the amount of solid particles that will eventually clog the soil, a cesspool is more prone to failure. The advantage of septic systems over cesspools is that the solids are separated out in the tank, so only the 'gray water has to be discharged into the soil. The solids are pumped out periodically, as needed.

We find cesspools less and less. A town close to where I live, however, still has a lot of cesspools in use. On sites where the soil is mostly gravel, cesspools could perhaps be 'functional.' My advice, however, if you are buying a home with a cesspool, is to anticipate replacing this with a properly designed septic system. Get cost estimates accordingly.

Tight tanks

Tight tanks are systems where the sewage effluent – and ALL of the water that runs from the sinks and other usages – empties into a large holding tank. Nothing flows out of this. When filled, you hire a septic pumper to come and pump out the tank. These systems are most often found on lakeside properties or properties that adjoin marshes or wetlands. In some cases, it would be difficult, very expensive, or downright impossible to have a conventional septic system at these sites as the effluent from the gray water would contaminate the groundwater, nearby lake, or wetland.

Tight tanks are obviously less desirable, due to the need for a more frequent pumping. This can get expensive. Unless it is a seasonal property, having a tight tank will greatly reduce the value of the home. I have a friend with a tight tank at a summer house. They are extremely careful with the amount of water they use, so the system works fine for them. Avoid them, however, for year-round properties (unless you are prepared to drastically limit your water usage).

Lagoon systems, which utilize wetlands plants to 'digest' the gray water effluent.

I don't think these would be commonly found (although plenty of rural areas have had unofficial 'lagoon' systems, where the septic effluent is dumped into a pond or stream or over the side of a hill). Any designed lagoon systems would need a careful evaluation by a septic engineer. Properties with unofficial 'lagoon' systems will need a septic system. Get cost estimates from a septic installation company.

Waterless and low water separation systems . . .

This could include outhouses, composting toilets, etc. These may allowed in some areas – but not in others. I won't cover them here. If you have one make sure that #1, it is allowed; #2 is working properly; #3 is not contaminating the groundwater or nearby wetlands.

Identifying a failed – or failing – septic/cesspool system . . .

First, a couple of important cautions.

One of those frightful things you could have nightmares about is falling into a septic pit – or having a child or guest fall in and drown. This has happened and would not be a pleasant way to go. While in most cases the property owner will know the location of the septic tanks, cesspools, or leaching pits (if present), there still could be older, steel lined tanks or weakly covered cesspools. You would be more likely to find these in rural areas. This writer's first home, bought long before septic inspections were the norm, was an old metal tank covered with steel pipes to keep the cover from falling in (this was changed after I moved in!).

Not only can one drown if one falls in, but the tanks are full of methane gas – which will asphyxiate anyone who enters or falls into the tank. You don't want to enter any tank to do repairs and be careful even when leaning in to look inside the tank. Also, if you are walking the yard where there has been no disclosure about where the private waste disposal is located, you need to be aware of possible hidden tanks. One inspector related how he narrowly avoided falling into a poorly covered tank only by jumping out of the way and grasping nearby branches.

How and why they fail . . .

Remember, a private waste disposal system (cesspool or conventional septic system) works by having the gray water containing the sewage effluent percolate into the ground through a bio-mat of bacteria (this is the stinky, nasty black stuff you smell when a septic system fails). It is important to understand that <u>every system will eventually fail </u>as the pores in the soil eventually get clogged. New systems that are properly sized and constructed, however, can last a long time. I've seen some that are still working after 40 years. A lot depends on how well the system was designed and installed, whether the site had good soil conditions (sand or gravel: good; clay or silt, bad), and whether the degree of usage was limited and the system was properly maintained (see Addendum). While many older systems are still functional, in general, the older the system the more suspect it is. Don't assume newer systems are okay, however, as I've seen systems less than ten years old that have failed (usually due to an improper installation).

The symptom of a failed or failing system would be back-ups of the waste plumbing (although this can have other causes – such as blocked baffles or pipes), bad odors emanating from the lawn, sewage effluent on the lawn, or extremely verdant lawns where the leaching field is located. These are dead giveaways. Any system where the bottom of the septic field (soil absorption system) is below the high groundwater level is technically in failure, even if it appears to be working properly (at least by Massachusetts standards).

Lastly, with problem sites, waterfront, or small lots, I would find out what it would cost to install a new septic system should the existing system fail.

Evaluating septic systems – IMPORTANT . . .

#1 Many states do not have any requirements for evaluating private waste disposal systems. As noted, Massachusetts, where I reside and do most of my work, does have a requirement that a specific evaluation (called a Title 5 inspection) be done at the time of a real estate transaction. This is normally done by the seller prior to the sale – but this is not written in stone; in a few cases it has fallen upon the buyer to do this. Very often, however, the seller won't do the Title 5 inspection until after the home is under contract and the inspection period is over. This poses some potential problems, as noted below. In New Hampshire, it is standard practice to have the septic system evaluated by a septic professional – but this is not mandatory. Other states may or may not have requirements; your real estate agent should have information on this.

What is critical is that you don't let this issue slide. To reiterate: you could be facing tens of thousands of dollars in repair costs or reduced value to your home should you have a failed or inadequate system – and you don't find out about this before you are committed to purchasing the home. Also, having the septic evaluation done after your inspection contingency period ends means that you won't know if a new system will be needed and what it will look like (see previous comments on mound systems). In my opinion, the septic system evaluations should be done before putting the home on the market – but I don't write the laws.

#2 Not all septic inspections are equally useful. In many states home inspection companies may offer to inspect septic systems. The problem is that, unless they are digging up the components you really can't tell that much. Dye tests are almost always worthless. A system has to be grossly failed and 'breaking out' for this to reveal anything – and if the sewage effluent is 'breaking out' (coming to the ground surface), you can see and smell it. Digging up the outlet baffle will often tell you if the system is failing. Digging up the distribution box and/or a portion of the septic field (or pits) will tell you even more.

I recommend that you find a company that does septic evaluations in your area and have this done *within your inspection contingency period*. Talk to several companies to see what they do and what they charge. Having the tank pumped may not be necessary. If the owner states the system was 'just pumped,' by the way, this tells you nothing – and may make it more difficult to determine if the system has problems.

#3 Be aware of red flags . . . These would include:

1. Older systems (over 20 years) where there is little information on the system and no documented history of servicing, pumping, or repairs. Abandoned or currently unlived in houses may fall into this category. The more rural or isolated the spot, the higher the risk of problems as no one may live close enough to detect the aftermath of a failed system (the really nasty odors). States or municipalities with no oversight of existing or new systems would be at higher risk.

2. Wintertime can make it difficult to inspect systems – although the companies that do inspections in New Hampshire often use jackhammers to get through the frozen ground. This may not always work, depending on the winter. You may want to have your attorney get some type of escrow agreement, where you will have the right and ability to evaluate the system once weather and soil conditions allow, with monies set aside for a new system, should the existing one be failed. This is ideal – but escrows can be challenging to get done.

3. The performance of a septic system depends a lot on the level and type of usage. A system that works fine for a home with one or two occupants – or just old people (as they don't take as many showers) – may fail when you move in with kids and start doing multiple laundry loads every week. Similarly, vacant homes may have systems that appear to be okay – but won't be when normal household usage occurs. (Septic evaluations that dig up the leaching field, however, very often can still detect failed systems in vacant houses). ALL septic evaluations have a degree of uncertainty: the systems lie underground and <u>even septic evaluators are not testing their functional capacity</u>. I have yet to hear of any company that does septic system inspections provide a warranty or guarantee on the systems. Also, poor practices and a lack of maintenance can doom a system that is currently working fine.

4. Relating to the above, even a properly working system, one that adequately serves a household with several members, may fail catastrophically if subject to extremely high water usage (such as from a party or function at your home, with lots of people attending). This happened to a homeowner in California. Their system worked fine – until they had a political event at their home with a large number of people attending. Their septic system failed due to the heavy use of the bathroom, and the stinky septic effluent was running out of the tank down the driveway. This must have been embarrassing, to say the least. Septic evaluations, no matter what type, do not involve running a large volume of water to see how well the system will work in high usage conditions. Remember this caution before you host an event!

Tip: You could run the water hard prior to a septic evaluation, but you would have to watch to make sure that nothing overflows or backs up into the living space or basement.

5. Owners who say they have the system pumped yearly – or just pumped the day before – could be a red flag.

You should not need to pump out a septic tank annually. While this may not be a sign of a problem system (some owners think they need to pump yearly), it is still a caution as most systems do not need to be pumped that often (unless an old, small tank is present).

Read between the lines . . . When a homeowner indicates that the system was 'just pumped,' this does not tell you anything. The pumping of the system just prior to your inspection period may indicate an effort on the seller's part to have everything up to date – or could indicate an attempt to hide a failing system. You may need to let the system fill up before evidence of failure will become apparent. Don't let an owner dissuade you from having the system evaluating by trying to convince you how great the system works and how they've never had problems.

5. Replacing the septic tank or doing repairs to the D-box or tank components may not represent a large expense. Replacing the actual septic field or installing an alternative system, however, can mean HUGE costs. This cost will vary greatly depending on the site, the soils, and the local regulations. Research this. If the system is old or has already failed, get estimates on the likely replacement cost. Costs in some areas will be half or less than in others. I've heard of systems being installed in Maine for one-third of what they would cost in Massachusetts.

6. Be careful with problem sites. Examples of these would include areas adjacent to wetlands or waterways where the groundwater levels appear to be high (next to a marsh or lake?); steep or rocky properties with a lot of ledge where you may not be able to put a conventional system. New systems near lakes must often be relocated so they are 100 feet or more away from the water. Expensive alternative systems may be needed for these locations.

7. As noted, if the system has failed and it is represented that a new system will be installed before the sale, find out what the new system will do to the yard. Installing a new system that is compliant with current regulations may require a 'mounded system.' The problem, as discussed earlier, is that you may be looking at an ugly mound out in the nicely landscaped yard.

8. Lastly – and this may pertain more to when you are living in the home – don't get taken to the cleaners by a septic installation company. I once had a backup

of sewage into the basement (small amounts, fortunately). The septic company I hired to pump the tank and find the problem indicated a total failure and the need for a new system. I requested that they first clear the baffles (which turned out to be blocked). When this was done the system performed normally.

9. Be careful if you are planning to enlarge the home or add bathrooms . . .

The existing septic system may be performing admirably and the septic evaluation reveals no problems but if you will be expanding the home you may need to have a new or expanded system to account for the added bedrooms or bathrooms. Ka-ching. Think this through ahead and find out if you would face exorbitant costs to replace or expand the existing system.

Maintenance

Maintaining your septic system is important as this could be difference between a system that provides years of use and never fails – and a premature replacement of the system. A few tips are provided below.

#1. Have the system pumped out periodically. The standard recommendation is every two years. For many households, it really isn't necessary to pump that often. We (my wife and I) have a relatively newer system with a 1500 gallon septic tank. I had it pumped after four years and the pumper said there was almost nothing in the tank. A lot depends on the family size and degree of usage. When in doubt, however, have the system pumped every 2-3 years.

#2 This one is obvious: do not drive anything heavy over the tank or leaching field.

#3 Don't bother with the 'additives' that are widely promoted as necessary for your system to function or that will save a failing system. Bacterial septic additives are actually banned in some states. They aren't needed and, interestingly, by digesting the solids in the tank, they may send more organic matter out to the leaching field, aging the system quicker. Dumping the additives into the distribution box, however, could be beneficial – but you won't have easy access to the D-box.

#4 Be careful what you put into the system. Anything that kills the bacteria that digest the septic effluent is not good. This means: don't use anti-bacterial soaps (they don't work, anyhow). Use septic safe toilet paper and liquid laundry detergents. Limit the amount of bleach you use in the laundry. Don't put anything into the system that can't be digested (no plastics).

#5 No disposals. Septic systems are generally not designed for disposals and you may void any warranty on a newer septic system by putting one in. Disposals labeled as 'septic safe' are available, but I've not been able to verify whether these really are 'safe.' If you are one of those who just can't do without their disposal, then use it sparingly and don't put most of the organic matter you generate down the unit). Maintain it properly. Compost your organic waste.

#6 Never, ever flush paint into the system or even clean your paint brushes in a slop sink. Paint creates a film that will fill the pores in the septic field, causing a premature failure of the system.

#7 Try to stagger your laundry usage. I know, this is almost impossible as people will do most of their laundry on weekends. But if you can stagger your washing machine usage you won't overload the system as easily. Front-loading washers will use a lot less water than most top loaders, saving on your water bill as well as easing the burden on your septic system. Low flow toilets will also help.

Separate 'dry well' systems for laundry usage are no longer allowed in many states, but if you have one (and it is working) these can greatly prolong the life of your septic system.

CHAPTER 18
A Brief Review of New Construction Concerns

What you will learn in this chapter. . .

- *The advantages and disadvantages (and risks) with new construction. . .*
- *The negatives that go with buying a new home. . .*
- *Concerns specific to new construction. . .*
- *What the code oversight does. . .*
- *Problems home inspectors often find with new construction. . .*
- *The pluses and minuses of having a home built. . .*
- *The good and the bad of modular and panelized homes. . .*
- *Energy efficient options. . .*

Any detailed treatment of new construction problems would take an entire book (or multiple books). What you should do when having a new home built – or doing any portion of it yourself – would be several more books. I think I'd lose you if I get too deeply into this. Instead, I'm going to outline a few of the things you need to think about if you are buying a newly built home. The issues that come with new construction can be different than those that come with an 'existing' (already built) home. <u>New construction carries both the least risk and – in some cases – the highest risk of unanticipated problems.</u> But before we get into those, let's list the pluses and minuses of buying new construction. A lot of these are obvious – but some won't be.

Advantages to buying New Construction . . .

What are the advantages to buying new construction? There are several and they are substantial:

First, when things are done right, everything is new and finished! (or so you hope . . .). You will not be buying a fixer upper. Any home over ten years old that was not maintained – or that was not well built – will require a varying degree of work (which means either money or time – or both). How much depends on the age of the home, whether it has been maintained and

New construction carries both the least risk and – in some cases – the highest risk of unanticipated problems.

improved – and the quality of the original construction. A lot of the materials used on new homes are fairly maintenance free: vinyl or composite sidings that don't need painting, vinyl composition trim and metal claddings that won't decay, pressure treated wood or composite decking that are not prone to deterioration. With a new home, you shouldn't have to spend your weekends painting the home or doing endless projects. The fact that you are buying a home that is largely finished has enormous appeal for people who are involved with work, their family, or other pursuits. If you get involved early in the process you may also be able to customize a lot of the finishes.

Second, new construction very often will have floor plans that meet modern lifestyles. However much I may like the look of 'older' homes (and 'older' can mean anything over 40 years of age going back much further), newer homes very offer the open space design, contemporary features, and larger kitchens that people want today. A lot of the single-family homes being built today – at least by the better builders – really look great also. (This isn't always the case, unfortunately)

Third, new homes are often subdivisions with cul-de-sacs that are more child friendly than other types of residential neighborhoods. Many new subdivisions may also be safer and have more security measures than existing homes. Gated communities come to mind.

Fourth, most of the new systems for heating and cooling are far more efficient than older systems. They are also NEW and will typically carry a minimum five-year warranty. The kitchen appliances are also new. Many states have a one-year builder's warranty which give you a degree of assurance that certain types of problems must be addressed by the builder in the first year. This would normally include water intrusion into the basement.

Fifth – and this can be important: due to the revised energy codes homes are built for much greater energy efficiency than 'older' (meaning anything built prior to the 2009 code changes). New construction in the states that adopted the IRC Energy Codes require minimal air changes (meaning less outside air entering the home and heated air escaping), increased levels of insulation, and high efficiency heating and cooling systems. New homes that conform to these standards should cost far less to heat and cool when compared to homes built prior to 2009 – and especially those built prior to 2000. You can now even get net zero homes that, through the installation of photovoltaic panels, generate more energy than they use. Even for homes that are not net zero, many builders are building tighter homes that are far more efficient than the homes built in the 1980s or 90s.

Sixth, new homes should not have lead paint (although no home built after 1978 should – and most built in the 1970s back into the 60s did not either).

And the potential negatives to new construction? I'll list several.

First, you'll pay more for what you get. New homes are like new cars: drive them off the lot and they are worth 20 percent (or whatever that figure is) less. The tradeoff is that, with any luck, you won't have to replace major components or systems for many years – but you do pay a premium with new construction.

Second, potentially shoddy construction. This may not be true everywhere, but there is a lot of subpar construction out there. A well-constructed, problem-free home depends on choosing the right site, an experienced builder and subcontractors, and proper code oversight of that project. While you would like to determine this before you 'sign on the dotted line,' this is not always easy to do. (I'll go over this further in this chapter).

In my own state, the code oversight on most new construction seems to be good. However, I know of towns where the oversight is, to put it charitably, somewhat lacking. In more rural areas, the code oversight and enforcement may be getting better, but really, this can vary from town to town and builder to builder. It certainly wasn't so great in the past. As an example, in the spring of 2018, I inspected a fourteen year-old upscale home where the deck stairs were in danger of falling off, the flashing at the deck was faulty (causing leakage and decay), and the foundation was bolted back together.

Third, adherence to the code doesn't guarantee quality construction. Codes are minimum standards in many ways. The workmanship can still be lousy, while the home meets code standards. Also, *it is important to understand that municipalities and the municipal code officials cannot be sued for negligence if they overlook something or don't bother to enforce the 'required' standards. They are 'off the hook.'* Home inspectors routinely find numerous defects and lack of adherence to the codes that the local building inspector didn't see – or simply didn't require the builder to fix. Much of time, it is 'small' stuff; occasionally, it is significant defects.

Fourth, if you are buying in a subdivision, over-55 development, or a condominium, you will need to abide by the covenants of the Homeowners' Association. This should be regarded as potential plus, as well as a negative.

Fifth, cookie cutter design. While this is true, builders put up what people want to buy. I've talked to developers who wanted to build smaller homes while putting more attention into the design and features – but this was not what their younger buying clientele wanted. Their buyers basically just looked at the square footage and the price when deciding on what to buy. Another caution is that the attractiveness of the design may not be reflected in the quality of the construction. One local builder in my area builds gorgeous, architecturally designed homes. Unfortunately, they are also poorly constructed and very often need major reconstruction within the first 15 years due to the poor flashing and decay. Obviously, the opposite is also true. I see new homes that are somewhat generic and boring – but that are well constructed and come through the inspection with flying colors.

The plain truth is, however, that older homes, unless butchered, simply look better in terms of their exterior design and curb appeal than newer homes. The fact is, however, that it doesn't necessarily cost a lot more to build a well-designed home than what you very often find.

Sixth, the hassles of ongoing construction in the neighborhood. I've heard it said that you don't want to be the first home in the neighborhood that is built – or the last. While it may be a temporary problem, if the neighborhood is being built out you will have to put up with a certain amount of noise, dust, and construction vehicles for the first year or so. This may be a temporary condition, but it is still a pain.

The problem with being the last house in the development is that this is sometimes the poorest location of the bunch. In some cases, the last house will be located next to the retention pit for the storm drains or at a low point in the development subject to a seasonal pooling of water; some lots simply never dry out.

Perhaps the worst case is buying into a development that is half-finished and the developer goes 'belly up' and can't finish building out the project. You may end up with unfinished houses and unfinished roads.

Seventh, you think you are done with major projects or expenses on the home – but you aren't. Maybe the home you are buying (or having built) will have a yard and landscaping finished, but just as often you will need to do a lot of work to get them where you want. After stripping the top soil off the property, what the developer puts back very often isn't much. It is common to see sunken areas next to the foundation due to subsidence of the soil plus erosion and gullies if the lawn is not established. This does not always indicate the builder did something wrong, but you should anticipate the need to fill in low spots, add topsoil, add more grass seed and vegetation, and even create drainage swales where water flows across the lot.

Eighth. Many of the materials used today will work fine — but only if they are installed precisely to manufacturer's instructions. Most builders are okay with this; others, not so much.

Ninth: Risk. This is the big one. The home has no history. The flashing defects and substandard construction that may prove to be a problem are now concealed from view, buried below ground or covered by the drywall on the inside and the siding on the exterior. The attractive finishes, granite countertops, and new bathrooms may go along with well-built construction — but they don't have to. A lot of spiffy looking homes have serious flaws that won't show up until someone has lived in the home for a while.

You never know what will show up later — whether one year or five or ten. 'Older' — or just existing — homes have had time to reveal the latent defects that may be present. Granted, in areas with code oversight and quality builders, these risks may be minimal. As an example of what can go wrong, I know an experienced inspector in the Boston area who inspected a newly constructed home (for a friend, no less). The home appeared to be well built and everything checked out fine at the inspection. Six months later, all the windows started to leak. They were improperly flashed and needed major repairs to correct. The siding had to be removed to view the flashing details. No one could have foreseen this problem after the siding was on. This is not an isolated occurrence!

Concerns with New Construction . . .

So, what are some of the concerns you need to be careful of when buying new construction? In no particular order:

#1 *The reputation and financial health of the developer and builder.* In most cases, the developer who is subdividing the property will also be building the homes — but not always. In many cases, they will be selling the lots and either a chosen builder or a builder of your choice will be constructing the home. In either case, you will want to assess the reputation of the developer AND the builder. Try to get a feel for the financial health of their company. A large successful developer with largely satisfied clients is a lot better risk than a developer just starting to build out a new subdivision.

In terms of on-line searches, this can be incredibly useful, but I have a couple of caveats. Large national home builders may have quality projects in some areas and problem developments in other areas of the country. You can't always judge one from another. A lot of the variation could depend on the code oversight, the prices for the homes, and very simply, the competence, commitment, and oversight of the local managers. Also, satisfied customers don't leave remarks: only those who were unhappy will vent their feelings online.

You could possibly talk to other homeowners who have already purchased a home in that development. Checking your state's attorney general's or consumer complaints office would be prudent, especially if you have a lack of confidence or lack of information about your builder. You could even talk to the local building inspector. You may have to 'read between the lines,' however, on what they tell you.

It is also desirable to have your own attorney when buying new construction. Many large builders will have mortgage companies that can provide the financing, as well as attorneys who can do the title search and handle the closing. This makes sense from the builder's standpoint, as they want everything to go smoothly. There is nothing wrong with this – except that the Purchase and Sales documents may be written to favor them – not you. The financing they offer, however, may be more attractive than what you can find elsewhere.

#2 Will the home be finished when promised? Try to ensure that the home will be finished when promised. This is a common problem. When times are good and the developer has a number of homes in construction, things don't always get done as fast as promised. They will get one house to a certain point, but they may have others in a different stage of construction that they want to sell. Delays, however, don't always indicate that the builder is at fault. Things always take longer than expected, the wrong windows get delivered or are damaged in transit, subcontractors may not get their work done on time, doors don't fit or were damaged and have to be replaced; weather issues can play a role; the wrong cabinets got delivered due to a mis-communication between you and the builder. Lots of stuff can go wrong, even when the builder will produce a good finished product. You need to a bit forgiving on time lines and expect that things may not be finished when initially promised. When possible, don't schedule your move at the earliest expected finish date.

Conversely, you should – as much as is feasible and warranted – try hold the builder to your scheduled close date when the home you are purchasing is still under construction. This is especially important when you need to move by a certain time or your belongings will have to put into storage. It's one thing if the delay is not critical and is beyond the builder's control. It's another when the home simply isn't getting done because finishing it is far down on the builder's priority list.

One reported problem is that the builder gets bored – or distracted – as the home nears completion. A common complaint of new construction buyers is that they can't get the builder to finish things and make the small repairs and alterations they have promised to make. Your recourse here is to withhold final payment until the critical items have been completed. Talk to your attorney about this.

#3 *Getting locked in early in the building process . . .*

When buying new construction while the home is still being constructed, you very often have to make a commitment early in the process that you will be purchasing the home. Short of the builder simply not finishing the home, you may have a legal commitment to go through with the purchase. In most cases, you will certainly have a financial commitment. This is, to a large extent, unavoidable – so you had better do your homework on the builder and the development ahead of time. You will also need to look at the options for materials and the potential for desired changes – and what these will cost you. You will normally have the opportunity to do the home inspection – it's just that the 'walk away' option with no financial 'penalty' may not exist, as would be the case with buying a home that is not new construction.

#4 *You may not always be getting accurate or truthful information.* I don't mean to disparage all builders. Many and perhaps most are honest, but you can't talk to homeowners who have purchased new homes without finding out that they weren't always given accurate information about the property. Just a few areas of concern would be:

- The boundaries of the lot. Make sure that you look carefully at the plot plan for the property. Is the driveway or yard really on your property? Are the nice trees along the perimeter of the property going to be removed?
- Are there any 'paper roads' adjacent to the property?
- Where is the retention pond for the development going to be located?
- What are the plans for the further development around your home? (You need to question the listing agent about this. They have no obligation to tell you about future development – unless you ask!)
- Are the high-end appliances present going to be the same units that are present when you go to move in. (It is hard to imagine, but I've been told that, on occasion, builders have swapped out the expensive appliances you saw when viewing the home for lower quality units).

#5 *Was there proper code oversight during construction?* The building code governs new construction and new work. It is intended to ensure that the building meets minimum standards for construction. Normally these inspections occur in stages, with an inspection after the foundation is completed, a framing inspection once the home has been framed, and rough and final inspections of the electrical, plumbing, and heating systems. I'll go through what is normally looked at in the stage inspections below, but just realize that the codes are designed to enforce only the minimum standards. They do not ensure good workmanship; they are occasionally followed minimally or not at all. At least some code officials are overworked and simply do not have enough time to do a proper inspection.

Code Inspections with New Construction . . .

When buying a new home, you have a couple of options for doing the physical inspection of the property. One option is to find a home inspector who will do 'stage' inspections that your municipal inspector is doing (or supposed to be doing) throughout the building progress. The second option, which is what normally occurs, is to do the inspection when the home is substantially completed: the heat is on, the electrical and plumbing systems are finished, and the decks and entryways are finished.

In terms of the stage inspection, these would normally include:

- A building permit should have been issued for the home. This would normally have addressed some of the site and soil issues.
- If a septic system will be installed, the site would normally have had a perc (percolation) test to make sure that a septic system will work at that site and what type of system may be needed, given the level of the ground water and other factors.
- A pre-foundation inspection. This would occur after the footings have been poured. In some cases, this inspection occurs after the foundation has been poured but before the back-filling has been done. This includes excavation, footings, foundation walls (or slab), waterproofing, backfill and compaction, and underground plumbing.
- Framing Stage – This includes wood or steel framing, exterior wall and roof sheathing, exterior trim and siding (and/or stucco/brick), windows and exterior doors, and roofing. Municipal inspections are typically performed on the rough framing. Some municipalities inspect the roofing.
- Rough Plumbing, Mechanical, Electrical – This includes water and waste/vent piping, plus setting of the water heater; ductwork, venting and furnace installation, and wiring and electrical panel installation.
- Insulation and Drywall Stage – This includes wall insulation (but not attic insulation at this time), and drywall installation, taping, and texturing. This stage cannot begin till the rough stage inspections are passed. Many municipalities do not inspect the insulation but rely on the contractor's 'certification' of installation. Some municipalities have a drywall nail/screw inspection prior to taping and texturing.
- Paint, Trim, Finish Stage – This includes finished flooring, cabinets, countertops, wall tile, mirrors, shower doors, final electrical (including fixtures), final plumbing (including fixtures), and final mechanical.

A few points about stage inspections. First, they may not include an evaluation of the site, the soils, and the lot drainage and grading. Problems with the soils should have been addressed prior to the start of construction. One of the big problems I see with new construction is the water management concerns. While a lot of these issues can be evaluated at the final inspection (when most inspectors look at the home), the grading and site issues should have been addressed before construction ever started.

In terms of stage inspections, I won't do them. Nor will most inspectors I know. This is for a few reasons.

First, in the areas I inspect, the code oversight is fairly good. I hate to charge a lot of money for an overview of work that may have already been checked by the municipal building inspector – who usually is more knowledgeable about the building code than I am. In regions with inherent problems with the soils that require precisely engineered foundations, however, I would encourage you to hire an inspector who specializes in stage inspections. (Areas of Texas and the upper plains come to mind).

A second reason why most home inspectors will not do stage inspections is that home inspection is not a code inspection, and most inspectors are not experts on the building code. The expertise and knowledge a home inspector and a code official must have overlap – but they are not the same. Nor can your home inspector cite the code unless they are a code official. The home inspector can note, as an example, non-conforming or missing hand/guard rails – but they will cite this as a safety concern and not a code issue.

Lastly, your home inspector lacks the power to enforce corrective actions. All they can do is note deficiencies and potential problems and recommend correction or further evaluation.

Another issue: builders can and sometimes deny home inspectors access to the property during the construction process.

Lastly, the codes are constantly changing, and the code officials I know are having a hard time keeping up with the changes in the energy codes.

Now, despite the above concerns, I won't discourage you from having your own inspector do the stage inspections. However, you really need to find an inspector who is knowledgeable about the building code followed in your state. Expect to pay for these inspections as they require multiple site visits.

New construction home inspections . . .

There is a common misperception that you don't need to do an inspection on new construction. Many buyers end up skipping the inspection when they are purchasing a new home. The listing agents who work with the builder certainly aren't going to recommend an inspection. And I must confess: I've done new construction inspections where I could not find anything wrong with the property – <u>but these were the exceptions</u>. Usually, these were very high-end (expensive) construction or garden style condominiums.

What types of problems and conditions have I commonly found when inspecting brand new homes? A partial list follows:

- Grading and drainage problems. This is perhaps the most common problem I find with new construction. Very often, we find voids or low areas next to the foundation; a lack of a positive pitch away from the home, or reversed grading that directs water toward the home.
- Siding not installed according the manufacturer's instructions.
- Unfinished landscaping; no lawn established. (This is typically something the builder will agree to take care of. Just make sure they rake out the rocks and put down topsoil before reseeding, as I've seen yards where the topsoil was so thin or rocky it will never provide a suitable lawn).
- Dead or dying trees (common when the site has been bulldozed)
- No gutters – even when it is apparent they are needed to reduce the risk of water intrusion into the basement or damage due to splash-back, they very often will not be installed by the builder. Very often, it is left to the buyer to install these after moving in.
- No handrails on stairs (extremely common; inspectors will recommend hand and guard rails – but the fact is, if the code inspector did not require this, then usually they won't get installed)
- Defective windows, cracked panes.
- Warped wood flooring. (I inspected one home that required a complete replacement of the wood floors due to uncontrolled moisture in the home during humid summertime conditions).
- Interior doors that bind up; no stoppers (not required by the building codes, however).
- Leaking dishwashers.
- Improper or non-conforming deck framing practices.
- Plumbing defects, including drip leaks from the plumbing (surprisingly common); vent stacks terminated in the attic (not run through the roof); leaking whirlpool units; inoperable shower valves.
- Improperly wired electrical outlets; non-working arc fault breakers.

Lastly, you will always find unfinished work. Uncompleted items are something the builder may be planning to finish, but it is still a good idea to document these so that nothing is overlooked. Unfinished or marred paint surfaces are common. Many real estate advisors recommend using small colored labels and applying these to the spots that show blemishes or paint discrepancies. (Just make sure they are a type that will come off easily when removed).

Important: the home inspection may reveal items that need correction or finishing – but it does not provide you with the punch list to give to the builder. I always tell my clients that I will point out the visible blemishes or surface defects I see– but I am not doing the 'punch list' of items that will be presented for correction or completion. You need to compose your own list for these types of items. I find that many of my clients (especially women clients) have a finer eye for picking up the small blemishes that may be present on the wall surfaces in new construction. Everyone   ELIM 'ALSO' has their own standard for what is 'acceptable.' Also, you may have agreements on the finishes and the installed components that your home inspector is not aware of. These don't always match up with what was installed. Beyond what the inspection comes up with, you will need to make your own list of items that the builder needs to correct or finish.

Another reason to have a home inspection with new construction is to test the home for high levels of radon gas. I often inspect homes that are a few years old and find that no one ever mentioned to the original buyer about testing the home for radon. If you don't test, however, and high radon levels are found when you go to sell, it will fall on you to install a radon mitigation system. Builders in my area will very often rough in the piping for a radon system during construction, with the provision that they will not install the completed system if high radon levels are found. When the rough-in is done, the cost to install the radon fan should be minimal. Also, *the highest radon levels I've found have been in new (or newer) construction* – not older homes. Testing the well water can done if this has not been done by the builder. Most towns in the states I work in require that specific water tests be done on new wells. Where this is not required or where you want additional items tested (such as arsenic, radon in water) then have your inspector do these additional tests.

And lastly, another reason to do an inspection on new construction is that – when done properly – it should give you an education on what you need to do to maintain the home. It should also inform you of some of the common conditions that you should expect to see during the first year – many of which are routine and just require maintenance. A few of the conditions you will routinely have with new construction include: hairline cracks in the foundation and floor slab, small cracks over doorways, caulking that is failing due an improper installation, soil subsidence, and water seepage or dampness in the basement. Depending on the degree of the problem, these may or may not be a significant concern.

Having a Home Built . . .

What about having a home built? Again, there are literally hundreds of books on this subject so. I'll just VERY BRIEFLY note the pluses and potential minuses of going this route.

The pluses:

1. It should be possible to have the home designed to specifically meet your needs and wants. Engaging an architect can help you realize this. In my opinion, it's crazy not to have an architect either do the design – or just tweak something you've decided on.
2. You can choose a design that is more interesting, functional, and beautiful than most of the new construction you find. Look at some of the options listed at the end of this chapter. Many are high end – but others may not cost more than the standard new home.
3. You can get a very energy-efficient home. It is possible to build a home that uses very little fuel or electricity to heat and cool the home. Energy efficient new homes can, when photovoltaic panels are installed on the roof, generate more energy than they use. Although not true for most developments, you can find builders (at least in New England) with whole subdivisions of energy efficient ('high performance') homes. While these homes may cost more than conventionally-built homes, the energy savings you realize may greatly outweigh the higher cost of the monthly mortgage payment.

    That's the good news. The bad news is that the vast majority of homes being constructed today are not high-performance homes. Builders build what they know and what their buyers demand – which is nice-looking homes in a desirable location. Unfortunately, these homes will cost far more to heat and cool than a home built to a higher standard of insulation and air sealing.

    You will also find a lot of regional variation in terms of the adoption of model Energy Codes that mandate builders build a more energy-efficient home. At the time of this writing, only nine states have adopted 2015 International Energy Code and the majority of states have not even adopted the 2012 model energy code.

    My advice is to do some research and find builders who building high performance homes that will use very little energy. Better yet, look into 'net zero' homes that will generate more energy than they use due to the output from photoelectric panels.

For information on zero energy homes, see the below links:

https://zeroenergyproject.org/2016/09/20/
prefab-zero-energy-homes-lower-cost-efficient-wider-availability/
https://zeroenergyproject.org/get-started/

You can find a lot of good information on line. Google 'zeroenergyproject.
org' for good information on this subject. I've included the above links in
the website that goes along with the book: TheHomeBuyerHbook.com

4. A third reason to build new is that you control the process from start to
    finish, and you get input on the features, components, and finishes that
    will be installed. If you are an experienced homeowner and know what
    you want, designing and building a new home can be the way to go. I've
    known people who acted as their own general contractor and made out
    great – but they had already built a couple of homes and knew how to
    handle the process. They also found a builder who was happy to work
    with them.
5. Cost savings. (Note: the cost factor will go into the plus side and nega-
    tive list, provided below). In terms of the pluses, some (usually) younger
    homeowners get to own a home by building it themselves. This is more
    likely the case in rural areas, where reasonably priced building lots can
    sometimes be found. Not everyone has the skills or resources to do this,
    but this could be a route to homeownership for those in the trades or
    with the right skills. My advice to them would be to spend a little more
    money and thought, so they will get home that looks right and offers
    superior energy performance.
6. Another plus is that you when you own the lot, you can then site home
    properly, taking advantage of the natural features of the land. You'll
    never find builders doing this, by the way: it's bulldoze the lot flat, put
    the house facing the street and go from there.

The negatives of having your own home built?

1. First, it's a lot of work. Obviously, unless you have a lot of resources
    – which includes a great builder who you can work with – this is no
    easy project. You need to be involved in the process to make sure things
    go smoothly. (Note: this doesn't mean you belong on the building site
    while the work is going on).

Although not required, you would want to educate yourself on design
and energy options. It's crazy not to build a home that you can heat (and
cool) using a minimal amount of fossil fuels. It's also not a lot more work
(or expense) to build a superior-designed home than something that

looks like a box with a roof. You can find newer homes that show a lot of 'curb appeal' in their design. Better yet: hire an architect to design the home or modify a plan you like.

2. You must be able to deal with issues that come up civilly, as there will always be disagreements, miscommunications, and things that go wrong. You want a builder (and architect) with whom you enjoy working and who gets back to you when you have questions or concerns. The ability to communicate and work through the issues civilly also includes you. Some people are wonderful at this; others aren't. I once did a new construction inspection on a high-end home where the buyers and builder spent four straight hours hashing out various details about the project without ever once getting angry or defensive. Each had their points, and each conceded where they needed to concede. If you feel you can't communicate with your builder – or if you expect perfection or can't handle disagreements civilly – don't have a house built.

3. You will need to research potential problems with the site, the neighborhood, and town ahead of time. Are there restrictions on what you can build? Are there neighbor problems you should be aware of? Don't proceed if there is a hint of threatened litigation over your right to build the home at this site. As noted in Chapter 7 (on legal issues), there have been instances where a land court ruled that a building lot was not legal – and the newly home built on the lot had to be torn down.

4. Risks you didn't think of. You should try to eliminate as many of these as possible. A few possible concerns:

    -   Is there a ledge on the property? (This will make installing the foundation and the septic system much more expensive and could require relocating the home and/or septic system).
    -   Is there a high likelihood of problem soils? (This can be more of a problem in some regions than others).
    -   How costly will it be to have the utility lines run to the site?
    -   Are they any legal impediments that will impact on your ability to access the lot, run utility lines, and build what you want?
    -   Are there streams, lakes, marshes, or other waterways on the property? These will affect where you can site the home, plus locate the septic system, the driveway, and the well.
    -   What are the risks of rising sea levels? This includes water backing up in river basins.
    -   Be careful when building in areas that have problem soils. The clay soils of the southwest come to mind. Expansive soils are commonly found in Colorado, Texas, the Dakotas – and the southwest region in general. They could be present in other regions, but this is where this seems to be a recurrent issue. The problem very often relates to

the clay content in the soil – especially bentonite, which will greatly expand when moist and shrink when dry. Homes built over expansive soils require engineered solutions, with deep piers, special foundations and/or drainage measures to keep the foundation slab from heaving. Some may have foundation watering systems that need to stay on so that the soil maintains a uniform moisture content.

Expansive soils are something you will need to do further research on – especially if you are looking at newer construction in the above regions. While poor soils can be a problem in the northeast, it tends to be less of a problem. (That doesn't mean it can't occur).

In new construction, where there is any concern about the soils, a qualified engineer should provide an analysis prior to construction. Whether this has been done in the past will need to be researched.

- Be careful with new homes built on steep slopes. Obviously, many homes have been built on slopes and the majority are fine. Numerous homes in New England and the western areas have been built on hillsides and mountains and show no problems. With proper engineering and construction one can build almost anywhere. Almost. But building into a hillside poses potential risks, if the builder did not have the foundation and site properly engineered, if the slope is extreme, or if problem soils are present. The foundation could crack and, even worse, push in from the pressure of the uphill soils. The driveway may be prone to wash-outs. Buildings set into a steep slope that rest on un-compacted fill are always a disaster. Homes at the top of a hill may be okay but will entail longer driveways. Homes set at the very bottom of a steep slope would be more prone to water problems. Most of these factors can be compensated for – with proper engineering and design – and knowledgeable and diligent contractors. In general, be careful with newer construction as the problems may simply not have shown up yet.
- Areas of the country with poor code oversight would post more of a risk, obviously. (See the section on utilizing soil and civil engineers in Chapter 11). When in doubt, don't buy newer construction built on a steep slope where code oversight is poor.

5. Cost. Things will always cost more than you think – especially when building a home. Nothing will come in on budget. You need to anticipate this. However, not only will the cost of building the home be higher than expected, you may not know what it will cost to put in the well, the septic system, the roadway, etc. until after the work has started on

these. Sometimes, it isn't the house that will cost you more than what you will think, it's the lot and the site work.

6. Cost and availability of land. This is a major problem in many areas. Along with the high cost of new construction, the prices for lots in areas that are already 'built out' tend to be outrageous. In many areas, after factoring in the cost of the site work, you could buy a finished home for what you'll pay for the lot. Even in the rural areas of New England I frequent, I don't see a lot of bargains – at least for attractive lots. This is why I discourage most people from building a new home.

What about Modular and Panelized Homes?

Before we get into the pluses and minuses of modular homes, it is important to understand the difference between mobile/manufactured homes and modular homes. Modular construction refers to homes that are built largely offsite in panels that are trucked to the site and are reassembled on a permanent foundation. Modular homes ARE NOT mobile homes (which are also called manufactured homes – just to confuse the issue!). Mobile homes are entirely built in a factory and are then towed to a site where they are dropped on piers that support the metal frame. (See Chapter 19 for more on mobile homes). Modular homes have to meet the same building standards and code compliance as conventional stick-built homes, whereas mobile/manufactured homes are required to meet HUD standards.

The difficult part of discussing modular homes is the sheer variation in what you can find. A couple of doors up from my house sits a very attractive, interesting home – that was brought in as a series of boxes. Believe me, you would never know this was a modular home. You can also go on-line and see pictures of modular homes that are gorgeous. Some are very interesting architecturally, and modular homes designed for superior energy efficiency are now being built. Conversely, modular homes were originally designed simply to provide an inexpensive home that could be put up quickly. The result was designs that were boxy and generic. Many of today's modular homes still fall into this category.

A second area of confusion with modular homes is that you can now find homes built that offer the ultimate in energy efficient design and performance that utilize *panelized* construction. The most energy efficient of these are called *passive houses,* as they require only little or no fuel input to keep them heated during the winter. The panels that form the home are built in a factory and are reassembled on site. The homes are not restricted in terms of their design. These manufacturers stress that these are not 'modular' homes, they are 'panelized' homes. In my opinion, these form one of the more attractive options you new construction. (For instance, see ecocor.us with the link below or the links in the website homebuyersHBook.com)

If you are looking to buy a new modular home you should understand how widely these may vary. You should also understand the pluses and minuses of modular homes (see below).

Advantages of Buying a new Modular Home . . .

1. The construction should be as good – if not better – than most stick-built homes (homes built entirely on-site). The quality control in a factory is probably a lot better than what you will find on a lot of job sites. Also, materials don't get left out in the rain, the windows would be installed correctly, etc.

2. It's faster. Once the building has started, it may only take a few weeks to have the home delivered and erected on site. This can be an important reason to choose a modular home.

3. They can be less expensive than a stick-built home. (That's 'can be' – see the cautions below).

The disadvantages – or just cautions – on buying a modular home are several:

1. There may be a bit of a negative associated with modular homes, again due a confusion with mobile/manufactured homes. A lot of the modular homes put up in the past have boring, cookie-cutter designs and offered cheap finishes on the interior. Many were built as entry level homes. This may be true for many – but not all – of today's modular homes. A lot of the panelized options offer attractive and flexible designs.

2. They are more difficult to customize than most stick-built homes – at least, once they get started.

3. As with all new construction, the costs for the home don't include your costs for the land, foundation, site work, a septic system, well, etc. You need to own a plot of land before you can do anything. You would need to research your costs on the site-related items. Septic systems, in particular, can be a large expense. The same for driveways, retaining walls, and the site prep.

4. The loan process can be a bit more complicated.

5. Due to the past confusion of mobile homes with modular homes, you can find restrictive covenants in some areas that may not allow them. This restriction may not be warranted anymore – but you still will need to research this.

6. The sections of the modular housing could get damaged in transit to the home, but they should be less at risk than with mobile homes (which are transported in

one large piece). Also, the foundation must be precisely sized and leveled prior to dropping the home on it or nothing will work right.

CAUTION: this has probably (we hope?) not happened a lot, but there have been instances where a buyer purchased what he thought was a modular home and it turned out to be a double-wide mobile home set on a foundation. Does a mobile home constructed entirely in a factory become a modular home when it has a permanent foundation? I don't think so. Even if everything was done right, these homes would carry a negative for resale (see above). I recommend you research any company you would be buying from to make sure you don't have this done to you. It is not a bad idea to set a mobile home on a permanent foundation, by the way; it's just that this will still be considered a mobile home.

See the website below for a more detailed list of the pluses and minuses of modular homes. If you are not reading this on-line you can also follow the links on line at ThehomebuyersHBresource.com

https://www.maxrealestateexposure.com/pros-and-cons-of-modular-homes/

Interesting new construction options for design and energy efficiency . . .

(This is just a random sample, among many). Or just visit an architect whose work you admire, or where you've seen homes they've designed that appeal to you. Check out their websites).

https://www.ecocor.us/rethink-building
https://mainecohomes.com/
https://www.connormill-built.com/
http://www.earlynewenglandhomes.com/
http://www.gologic.us/
http://timbercrafttinyhomes.com/
https://www.davisframe.com/our-homes/panelized/
http://bensonwood.com/
https://shelter-kit.com/
http://transformations-inc.com/

CHAPTER 19
Condominiums, Condexes, Over-55 Developments...

What this chapter covers. . .

- *Choosing the right condominium for your needs. . .what to research. . .*
- *About legal due diligence. . .*
- *Pluses and minuses of condexes. . .*
- *What needs to be inspected with condominiums . . .*
- *When to inspect the entire condo development and when just the individual unit. . .*
- *A few important cautions. . .*

At the start, I should note that the term 'condominium' just refers to the type of legal ownership of the property – not the type of construction. While you may think of attached townhouses when you think of condos, in fact, condominiums can be small to enormous, cheap to fabulously expensive apartment-style units in high-rise buildings; multi-families that have been broken up into condos, or simply single-family condos in newer developments. Over-55 developments typically function more or less as condominiums. Condexes, also referred to as duplexes, are usually two-unit buildings that legally are more like single family homes – but they share some of the concerns we would find with condominiums, so I'll cover those here.

Before getting into what you need to research when looking to buy a condo, I don't think we need to spend a lot of time going over the attractions of condo living. Condominiums provide a great option for people who don't want the hassles of taking care of a typical single-family home: yard work, snow plowing, exterior maintenance, many types of needed repairs, etc. They can be great for those just starting out, as many are less expensive than single-family 'starter' homes. They are a nice option for people at certain stages of their life: pre-kids, no kids, post kids, living alone or, as noted, when you don't want the hassles of maintaining a single-family home. Condos are often the only option for in-town or urban living. They can be cheaper to heat and cool, as they are usually smaller and are often more energy efficient than the average single-family home. Depending on the type of complex, they may have amenities such as pools, work out rooms, and social activities, as just a few options. Condominiums may provide a higher degree of security than living in a single-family home. And lastly, many of the newer condominium complexes are better designed and more attractive than nearby single-family developments.

Lots of positives . . . I think most of you recognize these. But there are decisions that you need to consider when buying a condo. They aren't negatives as much as things you need to research so you'll make the right choice and won't get stuck with expenses and restrictions you didn't expect.

In terms of what you need to think about:

First, obviously buy the type of condo that meets your needs and budget. Many higher-end condominiums, as noted, will come with amenities such as workout rooms, tennis courts, swimming pools, golf course membership, and on and on. Great stuff, if you will use it. On the negative side, you will pay for these features. For many, these amenities will be a reason for buying into a particular condo development. If you are looking at keeping your costs down or are unlikely to use the facilities, it will make more sense to buy a condominium that doesn't come with these added features.

Second, you will want to research the following concerns to make sure the condo is a good 'fit.' You'll want to get an idea of how restrictive the condominium's bylaws are. Specifically:

1. Can you have pets? Some complexes won't allow pets – or dogs over a certain size. Goodbye Fido. If you are allergic to dogs, however, you cannot exclude them from elevators or common areas where you may be exposed to them.
2. Can you have a garden in the backyard; is there a designated area where you can have this? Can you keep plants on your deck?
3. How many parking spaces can you have? Are they underground with access to the unit (a real plus if you live in the snowbelt). Do you have deeded parking (a plus) or is the parking lot first come/first served?
4. Can you rent the unit out? Does the condominium association have restrictions on the percentage of units that can be rented; will this affect you?
5. If you are buying in an over-55 development, can you have kids or grandkids move in? How long are they allowed to stay?

6. If you have young children, are there playgrounds or areas where they can play or hang out?

7. Can you walk to anything from the condo?

8. How much storage space is present in the unit and the storage area? You will probably need to do serious purging if you are moving from a single-family home. (This can be a good thing).

9. How much living space is there if you are downsizing?

10. Are there any pending special assessments that will be levied on the unit owners due to a shortfall in the reserve funds (see below)?

11. Do you have or can you put a washer and dryer in the unit? Lots of garden style apartments that were converted to condominiums do not have laundry hook-ups in the unit. This may matter little or a lot to you. Where it matters a lot, ask if other unit owners have done this. It may require a plumber, however, to provide a final opinion on whether this is 'doable' or not.

12. What are the condo fees? These can range from minimal in limited unit condos with no amenities, to quite high, depending on what you are the nature of the unit and the complex. Take into account, however, that the condo fees may include heating costs and many of the expenses you would have in a single-family home.

13. Can you live with the restrictions and rules that are a necessity with condo living? Condominiums are subject to rules and regulations called Covenants. These outline how the condo association operates and the rules and regulations that all unit owners must adhere to. You will want to read and understand these so there are no surprises.

Third, while condominiums come with less maintenance and repairs, as the homeowners' association (HOA) monthly fee normally will cover the exterior maintenance, landscaping, and trash removal (and sometimes the heating costs), you still have things you will be responsible for. A few of these would be:

- Maintenance, repair, and replacement of heating and cooling systems. In larger buildings, the heating and cooling is sometimes provided by the association. In some multi-story buildings, the association will provide the heat – but you may be responsible for the cooling system. In multi-story buildings, the association may provide the heat or cooling source – but the unit owner will 'own' the heat pump or extraction system.
- Plumbing leaks and other plumbing problems stemming from problems within the unit will be your responsibility
- Repairs or replacement of doors and windows. In some cases, mostly in multi-story buildings, the condominium association will be responsible for these. In most complexes, the windows are the responsibility of the unit owners.
- The kitchen (and other) appliances are yours.

- Garage door openers, where you have your own garage space, will be yours.
- Decks are usually the responsibility of the association – but not always.

You may want to talk to other unit owners about how quickly the condo associa-tion responds to complaints or the need for maintenance. In some cases, you may be able to get work done faster on your own – but you do need to get approval from the association for any repairs or maintenance done on the exterior. Condo owners sometimes will get permission to re-stain their deck (with the approved color stain!), rather than wait for the association to do the work.

Legal Diligence . . .

It goes without saying that legal diligence is critical when buying a condominium. This oversight is both routine and essential. Your attorney will typically examine the bylaws and articles of incorporation. When buying a condominium you will need 'clear title' for the unit and, for lack of a better phrase, a lack of legal entan-glements for the complex as a whole.

One of the things that fall under the legal umbrella – but is typically investigated or disclosed early in the sale process – or should be – is whether there are pending assessments for major repairs or renovations to the complex that will not be funded by the existing reserve accounts. Examples could be: the need for a total reroofing of the buildings, repairs to the buildings exteriors or structure that are far more expensive than anticipated; total heating or cooling system replacement; a replacement of the windows; repaving the parking areas and roadways, etc. Again, many condominium complexes will have adequate capital resources that will cover expenses in these areas without having to levy assessments. You may find, how-ever, with inexpensive or limited unit condos (such as 3 or 4 family buildings broken up into condos), that no such reserve exists. Also, large unanticipated expenses sometimes arise that will exceed the capital budget of the association.

Another possible source of a pending assessment could come from lawsuits brought against the association. This could be from alleged negligence; for instance, someone falling due to ice left on a sidewalk, ice falling off a roof and causing injury, unsafe roadways or walkways, or a multitude of other conditions that could be deemed unsafe, unwarranted, or improper. In some cases, the likely adverse judgment may not be substantial. Where it could be, have your attorney assess the likelihood of the lawsuit being successful and whether this will have a financial impact on the association. Lots of lawsuits without merit are reportedly filed. I would avoid buying into a condo embroiled in lawsuits between the unit owners and the Board (of Directors). These are probably not all that common, but they make for great reading on the web. Lawsuits against the building developer or the management company would also be a red flag.

Also, look at what may be deeded structures on the property that you may or may not have the rights to. In limited unit developments, a stand-alone garage may be deeded to a single unit owner. The same can be true for decks, porches, portions of the yard, etc. This type of stuff normally gets disclosed up front, but if you aren't getting this information, then do your research and ask questions. Don't assume you have the right to use a rooftop deck unless your attorney has verified this is included in the deed for your unit.

Another issue that falls under the legal umbrella is determining what is covered under the Master Policy for the association. While the exteriors may be covered under the master policy, anything within or belonging to the unit will need to be covered under your policy. If you are planning on renting out the unit, you may need to get additional property and liability coverage to make sure you are covered should your tenant get hurt anywhere on the premises.

What about condexes?

Condexes usually refers to a type of construction consisting of side-by-side attached units. As noted, these are also be referred to as duplexes (but duplexes could legally be a condex or a condominium). They are very popular with builders, as they can sell two properties for little more than the price of one. I don't think they are always great for a town or neighborhood, but they could allow you to get into something close to a single-family home for a lot less money.

The nature of condexes presents two types of problems. First, you are living right next to your neighbor, so you had better share the same values concerning late night noise, maintaining the yard, etc.

Unlike a condominium, moreover, each unit is legally separate; there is no 'Association,' and there may be no bylaws governing what can and can't be done. Again, you had better hope that you and your close neighbor share the same lifestyle (at least as it affects the property). One problem I see is that the newer condex units look great for some years — until one of the owners has no money or no interest in keeping up their half of the property. This would not be so great if you are living on the other side of the duplex. With this type of ownership, your inspector will only be looking at the side you are looking at — not the entire building.

Inspecting condominiums – what can be different . . .

Many – but not all – condo buyers do an inspection prior to the purchase. On average, the extent and range of problems in large complexes are less than you would find with single family homes – but you still see lots of deficient conditions.

I could present a long list – but just a few of these from the last few months prior to writing this include:

- A dangerous electrical panel located in a closet, in a high-end urban condo.
- Non-operable windows or windows with damaged hardware.
- Windows fogging due to 'breached seals.'
- Ground fault devices missing or not-working.
- A central air conditioning unit that was over 28 years old and was just worn out.
- Faulty kitchen appliances.
- Leaks at the waste drains.
- Air conditioning coils full of debris and mold.
- And on and on . . .

What the inspector won't find . . .

A few of the problems that even a qualified inspector won't find include: improper sizing of the heating and cooling systems; air infiltration problems that may only show up during windy, cold conditions, workmanship defects in the framing that will cause cracks (but that haven't shown up yet); heat loss and comfort level problems, anything to do with environmental contamination (although it may be possible to test for radon). Units in multi-story buildings may require an inspection by a company that can bring a higher level of technical expertise to the job, given some of the problems with defective construction and defective materials that can occur.

What needs to be inspected with condominiums . . .

This is important, as you'd think this would be obvious: but it isn't. Condominium units can be inspected in one of two ways. First, for large complexes or buildings, the home inspector will typically just check the components and systems that are part of the individual unit. This makes sense, as your inspector can't look at all of the roofs, decks, common areas, etc. (at least, without you paying a lot for this). These inspections will typically have a lower cost than inspecting single-family homes.

As a second option, when you have a limited number of units in the condominium, as is commonly found where a 2-, 3-, or 4-family building has been converted to condos, I recommend that you have your inspector look at the exteriors and accessible common areas and not just the unit itself. After all, if there are only three units in the association and the roof is close to failing with an expected repair a cost of $15,000, you may be faced with a $5000 assessment if this money is not available in the capital reserves. As an example, I once inspected a five-unit condominium where the exterior stairs, porches, and trim needed an estimated

$25,000 in repairs; none of this was known or disclosed before the inspection. My client would have been hit with a large bill that she was not anticipating. This inspection will typically run close to what a single-family inspection will cost (or at least more than the inspection that confined itself to the individual unit), but it is necessary if you really want to know the overall condition of the building. Unlike larger condo developments, these 'small,' limited unit condos very often have had limited maintenance and repairs – so there are more 'unknowns' regarding the condition of the building.

You may also want to have your unit tested for radon as part of the inspection. Only do this, however, if you have a ground level unit or living space on the lowest level. In some condominiums, however, it may be difficult to have a mitigation system installed; you may need to determine this prior to testing.

Another issue: at least some (or perhaps many?) large buildings that were built as or converted to condominiums may have serious issues with the major systems and structures (especially the exterior claddings or HVAC equipment) that will end up costing the unit owners a lot to fix. These problems (or future problems) may not have been recognized yet or, if they were known, they have not been disclosed to prospective buyers. There is a value, then, in having a very knowledgeable inspector examine the overall systems with these types of buildings. These may be engineering firms, building science experts, or construction professionals with experience relevant to large building construction (and failures) who have the training and equipment to assess these types of structures. Many inspectors who are otherwise well qualified may not have this expertise.

As a few basic warnings when looking to buy a condominium . . .

First, do a bit of research on the HOA. While the vast majority of HOAs are probably well run and represent the unit owner's interests, this is not universal. Stories abound of over-zealous boards or board members who make life miserable and rule the complex like it is their own fiefdom. You don't want to buy into a building where the residents are warring with the board members. Nor, as noted, do you want to buy where the lawsuits are occurring, either due to disruptive owners or unresponsive board members (both can be a problem). These situations are not common, but they do occur. And, obviously, make sure that you can live with the necessary restrictions that will be present in every condo development.

Second, I think it is appropriate to caution you about buying into a new condo development – and especially one that has not yet been completed. Yes, I understand that you may be able to get a better price if you get in early, but this carries a risk. Specifically, what if the development (or building) is not finished? Who gets the builder (or developer) to finish what they promised? What if the builder goes bankrupt? At least, don't be the first to buy.

Also, whatever future problems that may arise due to deficient or substandard construction may not show up until the owners have lived there for some time. Everything looks shiny and perfect, with granite countertops, new appliances, and perfect walls and ceilings, so it is easy to think everything will be fine. It may be . . .

Time reveals all: a condo complex in a city near to where I live was built over a toxic waste dump. No one (allegedly) knew about this when the complex was approved. Unfortunately, the health (and resale) issues did not arise until the complex was fully occupied with new buyers. As with new single-family construction, any shortcuts or mistakes the builder made may not show up for a while. A lot of the problems may be buried in the walls. You would like to think that the municipal code oversight during the building would catch these problems, but, unfortunately, that is not always the case. Many code inspectors are overworked, some are not competent, and some could be compromised. As noted previously, municipal code inspectors and the municipalities that employ them *cannot be sued for damages* if they failed to provide proper oversight. They may do their best, but with 'no skin in the game,' the repercussions from failed oversight are limited.

Third – and **important**: avoid buying a condominium where the developer or one investor owns most of the units in the complex. In this situation, they *ARE* the board of directors, and they decide whether and where to put money into repairs and capital improvements. Unlike the case for a unit in a condo that is controlled by the unit owners through their association, any needed repairs or improvements may not be done in a timely manner (or done at all) AND, the developer can choose who does the work and at what cost. On occasion, they will have their own management company that will do the work (very often at an exorbitant cost). Could there be some conflicts of interest in this situation?

CHAPTER 20

Special Types: Vacation Properties, Investment Properties, Mobile Homes . . .

What this chapter covers. . .

- *What you need to consider when buying a vacation property. . .*
- *A few things to consider when deciding on investment property . . .*
- *Links to useful articles on buying multi-families and other investment property. . .*
- *Buying a mobile home? Pluses and minuses. . . What to be careful of. . .*
- *Assessing the quality of the unit. . .*
- *Inspecting a mobile home. . . Special considerations. . .*

This chapter will provide advice for those who are looking at specific types of property. This is not a comprehensive treatment of these areas. Investment properties, for instance, have guidelines and ratios that determine for how much a rental property may be worth, given the rental income you may realize. I will provide links to sources of information on some of these areas.

Vacation properties

Buying a vacation home can be a nice way to get away and have a place where the family can spend time together – but, with the exceptions below – don't consider these properties 'investments.' In reality, if you plan on using the vacation house just for your own family's use, they are the opposite of an investment. The number one rule is to make sure that you can afford to own it so it won't take all of the money you may need for retirement and your kid's education.

Vacation properties have the same costs you would have for a primary residence:

   a.   Mortgage and financing costs (or just purchase costs if you won't have a mortgage)
   b.   Real estate taxes
   c.   Maintenance and repairs (painting, carpentry repairs, driveway, etc.)
   d.   Plowing costs (for northern areas) if you want the property to be accessible in the winter.
   e.   Utility costs including cable TV and internet
   f.   Insurance (This is often higher for vacation homes).
   g.   Gas costs or airline tickets to reach the vacation house
   h.   Appliance repairs and replacement
   i.   Desired and necessary improvements

Although the above expenses probably will exceed any potential income from renting the property I've met people who own vacation homes on New England lakes who tell me they have made out extremely well from renting their properties. The catch is: they brought these properties when they were a lot cheaper than today; and second, they don't use these properties themselves (although some may rent them for the summer and use them in the fall and winter). Also, they have to strip the properties of their personal goods and anything of value if they are going to rent them.

I'll repeat myself: if you can afford it, a vacation house can be great – just don't regard it as an investment. I strongly recommend checking out what you will pay in real estate taxes. Homes on the big lakes and in many areas often have exorbitant property taxes. I can't for the life of me understand what these small towns are spending the money on – but it is going somewhere.

I should note that, for vacation properties that you rent, you can take numerous write-offs against the income you receive, just as with other investment properties (see below). You can also rent the property for up to 14 days without claiming the rental income. I would sit down with your accountant, however, regarding what you can claim and what you can't. Also, if getting rental income is needed for you to afford the property then maybe you should re-think its purchase.

A few things you need to be aware of when buying a vacation property:

#1 How long does it take to get to the home? If you can spend extended time at the property, this may not matter. If you plan on going up weekends, then you may want to set a limit on how far you will go.

#2 Don't rely on pictures that may show a lake you can see from the property. These may have been taken from someone else's land. They may also show the lake looking across a lakefront property in front of yours – property that you can't cross to access the water (I know of situations where this has occurred).

#3 Some vacation homes can be used in the winter. You may like this if you are into snowmobiling or skiing. There are a lot of added costs, however, as you need to keep the heat on and the property plowed. These expenses may or may not be worth it to you. If you plan on eventually relocating and living 'up north' or near that beachfront property, you want a winterized property or one you can convert to year-round use. Unless you like to snowmobile or ski, however, having a vacation property for seasonal use can make more sense. (It's colder 'up north' and a lot of seaside communities can be pretty desolate in the winter).

#4 Caution: if you are buying a vacation home with a masonry foundation where the winters are severe, you may need to think about keeping the basement heated during the winter. Unless a lot of attention was paid to the drainage on the exterior and you have a reasonable expectation that surface and subsurface water will drain away from the foundation, having an unheated basement can be a problem. Water accumulating next to the foundation will expand as it freezes and can sometimes push in a foundation. There are cases where this has required pouring a new foundation. Ouch!

Investment properties

I won't even begin to go over the things you need to think about if you are looking to buying an investment property. Buying an investment property can be a source of future wealth – or, on another scale, a way to not have to rely on social security when you retire. But you must do your homework. You ideally want to buy at the right time – preferably when the economy is suffering and the real estate market has reached a low point. (I don't dare say 'buy low, sell high' at this point!) There are rules for investing in real estate, such as only buying when the costs of owning the property are 'X' times what you will realize in monthly rental income. When you get the right property at the right price with the right tenants, having a rental property can work out. If you are a younger buyer, buying a two-family and keeping it after you move into a single family can be one of the smartest investments you can make. Conversely, when you get a lousy tenant, it can make your life miserable. Do your research – but sometimes, with tenants, it's just the 'luck of the draw.'

As some of you may not be reading this online, I've copied a WikiLeaks article below that has some useful information. You can view this article in its entirety at (http://www.investopedia.com/articles/investing/090815/buying-your-first-investment-property-top-10-tips.asp?lgl=myfinance-layout-no-ads

'A few things to consider when deciding on investment property . . .

#1 Make Sure it's for You

Do you know your way around a toolbox? How are you at repairing drywall? Or unclogging a toilet? Sure, you could call somebody to do it for you, but that will eat into your profits. Property owners who have one or two homes often do their own repairs to save money. If you're not the handy type and you don't have lots of spare cash, being a landlord may not be right for you. (See also: *Becoming a Landlord: More Trouble Than It's Worth?*)

Your first property will consume a lot of your time as you learn the ins and outs of being a landlord. Think of it as another part-time job. Do you have the time?

2. Pay Down Debt First

Savvy investors might carry debt as part of their investment portfolio, but the average person should avoid debt. If you have student loans, unpaid medical bills, or have children who will soon attend college, purchasing a rental property may not be the right move at this time. As contrary advice: some parents with kids going to college have purchased a condominium for their kid to live in while going to school. Depending on where the school is located and the local real estate prices, this could be an option.

3. Get the Down Payment

Investment properties generally require a larger down payment than owner-occupied properties, so they have more stringent approval requirements. The 3 percent you put down on the home you currently live in isn't going to work for an investment property. You will need at least 20 percent, given that mortgage insurance isn't available on rental properties.

4. Beware of Higher Interest Rates

The cost of borrowing money might be cheap right now, but the interest rate on an investment property will be higher than traditional mortgage interest rates. Remember, you need a mortgage payment that's low enough so that it won't eat into your monthly profits.

5. Calculate Your Margins

Wall Street firms that buy distressed properties aim for 5 percent to 7 percent returns because they have to pay a staff. Individuals should set a goal of 10 percent. Even when the building is in reasonably good condition and the systems have been updated, estimate maintenance costs at one percent of the property value annually. Other expenses include insurance, possible HOA fees, property taxes, and monthly outlays, such as pest control and landscaping.

6. Don't Buy a Fixer-Upper

It's tempting to look for the house that you can get at a bargain and flip it into a rental property. But if this is your first property, that's probably a bad idea. Unless you have a contractor who does quality work on the cheap or you are skilled at large-scale home improvements, you're likely to pay too much to renovate. Instead, look to buy a home that is priced below the market and that needs mostly minor repairs.

7. Calculate Operating Expenses

Overall, operating expenses on your new property will be between 35 percent and 50 percent of your gross operating income . If you charge $1,500 for rent and your expenses come in at $600 per month, you're at 40 percent. For an even easier calculation, use the 50 percent rule. If the rent you charge is $2,000 per month, expect to pay $1,000 in total expenses. (Note: I assume, by 'operating expenses,' they don't include the mortgage, tax, and insurance payments. If this is the case, then these operating expense estimates may be too high. In any case, your total expenses should be covered by the rental income – excluding those times when you are between tenants.)

8. Determine Your Return

For every dollar you invest, what is your return on that dollar? Stocks may offer a 7.5 percent cash-on-cash return (if you are lucky and good), while bonds may pay 4.5 percent. A 6 percent return in your first year as a landlord is considered healthy, especially given that number should rise over time.

9. Get a Low-Cost Home

The more expensive the home, the higher your ongoing expenses will be. Some experts recommend starting with a $150,000 home. (Good luck with that in today's market!)

10. Find the Right Location

Look for low property taxes, a decent school district, a neighborhood with low crime rates, an area with a growing job market and plenty of amenities like parks, malls, restaurants and movie theaters.

> The Bottom Line
>
> Keep your expectations realistic. Like any investment, a rental property isn't going to produce a sizeable monthly paycheck for a while and picking the wrong property could be a catastrophic mistake. Consider working with an experienced partner on your first property or rent out your own home to test your landlord abilities.

Just a few of the useful links you can follow are provided below:

https://www.investopedia.com/articles/investing/090815/buying-your-first-investment-property-top-10-tips.asp?lgl=myfinance-layout
(http://www.investopedia.com/articles/investing/090815/buying-your-first-investment-property-top-10-tips.asp?lgl=myfinance-layout-no-ads
http://www.investopedia.com/articles/06/rentalrealestate.asp
https://www.irs.gov/businesses/small-businesses-self-employed/tips-on-rental-real-estate-income-deductions-and-recordkeeping
https://www.irs.gov/publications/p527
https://www.thebalance.com/rental-income-and-expenses-3193476

Every Landlord's Guide to Finding Great Tenants
Every Landlord's Guide to Managing Property
Every Landlord's Legal Guide
Every Landlord's Tax Deduction Guide

Mobile Homes

Some 20 million Americans, or roughly six percent of the population, reside in mobile homes. Many are located in 'trailer parks,' but at least in New England, mobile homes are found throughout rural areas. Reportedly, two-thirds of the mobile homes sold today are installed on individual lots owned by the buyer. Mobile homes are more affordable than most single-family homes and, especially for those on a fixed or limited income, they provide an attractive way to avoid paying the rental costs of an apartment.

The negatives for mobile homes are several.

First, there is a stigma some would apply to living in a trailer park. To be honest, most of the people who live in the parks could care less. It's affordable living and better than renting. Many of the parks form a community that can provide positive social relationships plus access to 'common' amenities available to the unit owners.

Second, 'mobile' homes really are not an accurate term as most of these units are not moveable once placed on the lot. They are more accurately described as a manufactured home of a certain size and type that can be towed and dropped onto a small lot. Over time most mobile homes will depreciate in value – although upgrades and improvements will help them to maintain their value. 'Manufactured homes,' unfortunately, do not have antique value as they get older. The land under the units, however, will tend to appreciate over time.

Third, you own the structure, but you may still pay rent on the lot. Traditionally, with most 'mom and pop' trailer parks, the rental fees were reasonable. Unfortunately, as typical for everything that can be monetized in our country, investors have found that owning trailer parks is a goldmine. Large investors have brought up thousands of the trailer parks in the U.S. For example, Equity LifeStyle Properties (ELS), the largest mobile home park owner in America, now has a controlling interest in nearly 140,000 park lots. When the mobile home parks get bought from the original owners, moreover, it is typical to see large rent increases on the land. While these parks may still be an attractive alternative to renting or single-family homes, you may not have a lot of control over what you will be paying to rent the land under your unit. Let's face it: in the American tradition, the new owners will gouge you for as much as they can get away with. Where possible, I would try to buy where the residents have managed to buy the park and turn it into a coop development. You may also just want to put the unit on your own lot – which is where most mobile homes sold in many states reportedly end up.

Regarding what to look for, I would advise the following:

First, I would avoid mobile homes built before 1976. Units manufactured after 1976 had to meet the standards set by the U.S. Department of Housing and Urban Development ('HUD'), so the quality of construction will be higher. You can find very 'substandard' conditions on units built before that. Mobile homes do not age well like a well-built single-family home (that, of course, is maintained and invested in over time).

Second, when looking at the mobile home, obviously assess whether the property has had improvements and upgrades. You may pay more for a unit that has had money put into it – but you won't have to spend the money yourself on the 'necessary' improvements, and it will make life more enjoyable living there. Desirable enhancements include:

- Having a gable roof installed over the entire structure. These allow the structure to handle snow loads better and should prevent ice dams and other sources of leakage. They will also afford greater insulation levels (and thereby lower heating costs). The original low-pitched roofs that come with the units are prone to leakage and flashing problems.

- The hot air systems typically found have an average life of 20–25 years. If the furnace in the unit you are looking at is approaching this age, then anticipate replacing it. For air conditioning, the same expected longevity applies as with single-family homes: ten to fifteen years in southern areas and 15 to 27 years in northern areas. The mid-Atlantic and other middle-tier states probably fall in the middle.
- The original stairs for these units are usually substandard and are often unsafe. The primary entrance stairs will usually have been upgraded (and if not, they should be) – but the metal stairs built for the back side egress are very often still in place.
- Adding screened porches or enclosed rooms to these units, where space allows, can make for a much more comfortable living space. Some will add wood or pellet stoves to these rooms. If you drive around the mobile home developments you'll see improvements that really make the places look attractive.

Assessing the quality of the unit. . .

Better quality units differ from economy models in a number of ways. Note: I've provided information from home inspectors in Florida who have extensive experience inspecting mobile homes. They have literally dozens of articles you can learn from. Check out their site at http://www.mcgarryandmadsen.com

How can you tell if a mobile home is well constructed?

The quality and longevity of a mobile home depend a lot on its price when it was built. A budget model will only meet minimum HUD standards while a more expensive model will have better quality materials and construction details. A premium line of mobile homes will likely be sturdier and last longer. Budget models can begin to show signs of deterioration within 10 years, if not maintained.

How can you tell a budget model from a premium one? The basic mobile homes look bare-bones and are never confused with a site-built home. The mid-range units are still clearly mobile homes but have a more house-like proportion and detailing, while the premium models can sometimes be mistaken for a site-built home.

Many of the details of superior construction are hidden within the floors, walls, and ceilings of the home. This includes the R-value of the insulation and size and spacing of the floor joists. I've listed below some key visible areas where you can determine if you are looking at a budget, mid-range, or premium mobile home:

1. Roof Pitch – Budget models have a low roof pitch of 2/12 (2 inches of rise for every 12 inches of length). This is best gauged when looking directly at the side of the home. As the quality increases, the

roof pitch does also. Note: many of the budget and mid-range models will have had a pitched roof that was added over the structure. This should be regarded as a plus.

2. Roof Overhang – The most basic homes have a zero or minimal roof overhang at the front and back. This means that water runs down those walls every time it rains – which can often result in water intrusion and decay in the walls. Better quality units will come with a roof overhang – but again, lower grade models will sometimes have had a gable roof structure added that will provide an overhang.

3. Ceiling height at the exterior walls – Budget homes may only have a 7-foot ceiling height, measured where the ceiling meets the front and back walls. Because door height remains constant at 6-foot 8-inches, you can get a good idea of the ceiling height from the outside, by checking the distance from the bottom of the fascia (the board that wraps around the edge of the roof) to the top of the door. Just a few inches means a 7-foot ceiling inside. Above 2-feet means a 9-foot ceiling and a premium home.

4. Siding – Older mobile homes have metal siding, regardless of price range. Today, budget homes have economy-grade vinyl siding. Better quality homes may have heavier vinyl siding or a fiber-cement siding. The less expensive homes from the 1980s into the 90s may have a wood or hardboard siding. A 'hardboard' or 'Masonite' sided home, combined with no roof overhang will be prone to moisture intrusion problems and wood rot. (Usually, these homes have been sided over with vinyl).

5. Front Doors – Lesser quality mobile homes often have a thin, light-weight aluminum front door, something like you might see a travel trailer. Better quality homes have a steel front door that closely resembles what you would find on a site-built home. Again, be aware that the owner of a budget model may have had a metal insulated door installed. This is good – but the unit is still a budget model. Very often the front door has been upgraded – but the rear door is still the thin metal type.

6. Roofing – Lower-priced homes will tend to have lightweight three-tab grade shingles. Better quality units will have 'architectural' shingles that are thicker and provide a more attractive profile. They should also last longer. Economy grade shingles have a shorter lifespan and are more prone to wind damage – although any shingle that is older, was improperly nailed, or was nailed into a substandard sheathing will be prone to blow-offs. I also see asphalt roll roofing used over the original surface when the roof is almost flat. This material has a poor longevity record.

7. Interior walls – Budget homes may have vinyl-covered wallboard that is butted at the sides. Better quality homes have battens covering the seams, and the best quality homes should have finished drywall.

8. Windows – mobile home windows in the past utilized a single thickness of glass. More recently, better quality homes have double-pane

insulated glass windows. Very often, the windows have been upgraded. This is a desirable improvement.

	Component	Budget	Mid-Range	Premimum
①	Roof Pitch ★	2/12	3/12	4/12 and higher
②	Roof Overhang	Front/back, none to 3"	Front/back, 6" to 8"	All sides, 8" to 12"
③	Ceiling at Exterior Walls	7'-0"	7'-6"	8'-0" or more
④	Siding ★★	Economy vinyl siding or wood/particleboard	Foam-backed vinyl	Fiber-cement siding (such as Hardi-Plank)
⑤	Front Door	Aluminum less than 3'-0" x 6'-8"	Steel 3'-0" x 6'-8"	Steel 3'-0" x 6'-8"
⑥	Roofing	Economy 3-tab shingles	Standard 3-tab shingles	Dimensional shingles
⑦	Interior Walls	Vinyl-covered wallboard	Vinyl-covered wallboard with battens, or finished drywall	Finished drywall
⑧	Windows	Single pane	Dual-glazed (insulated)	Dual-glazed and Low-e

★ Roof pitch is epressed in inches of vertical rise per inches of horizontal run. So a "2/12" pitch roof rises 2 inches for each foot of horizontal run.

★★ Older mobile homes have metal siding regardless of price range.

This is not intended to be a rigid guideline. We recommend that you check these eight construction details, then use them as a jumping-off point for your own assessment of the quality of the home. Some homes will straddle two categories based on their combination of features. '

Having the Mobile Home Inspected . . .

Mobile home should be inspected. Normally these will cost less to inspect than single-family homes. A few typical problems your inspector should look out for include:

- Substandard or damaged windows that need upgrading. Substandard may be okay – but upgraded windows are a worthwhile investment in all but the newest mobile homes (where the windows are also newer).
- Aluminum branch wiring and defective electrical panels; Improperly wired outlets; lack of ground fault protection.
- Termite activity and damage on accessory structures built onto the unit.
- The 'belly wrap' under the unit that encloses the insulation in the floor cavity will often be damaged, with the fiberglass insulation falling out. This can be a problem as the space between the insulation and floor above will be a prime nesting spot for mice and other vermin. Also, this allows increased heat losses and the potential for frozen pipes.
- Missing or damaged skirting on the exterior. These metal skirting panels are needed to keep vermin from entering the space under the unit. When missing or damaged they make the place look run down. (The condo association may require that missing or damaged panels be replaced).

- Polybutylene plumbing. Common from the 1980s into the 90s. This is a gray plastic plumbing. It is a 'delisted' material due to the problems with leaking pipes and fittings. Not all of this piping has failed. It is still present in mobile homes and lots of condo complexes – but it's best to anticipate its replacement.
- No vapor barrier on the ground under the unit.
- Non-conforming or absent 'hold downs' or anchor straps. These may be required in many states but perhaps not all. They were not required by HUD prior to the revised 2008 Standards, so your inspector may find pre-2008 units with no hold downs or anchors.
- Note: this is not an inclusive list.

More on hold downs . . .

These are especially important in areas prone to hurricanes and tornadoes. Florida, reportedly has very stringent requirements for anchors and tie-downs. Where I inspect in New England, I don't routinely see evidence of anchoring systems. These are largely buried in the ground or slab under the home. The difficulty with this issue is that each state may have specific requirements, there are default requirements under HUD standards, and towns or mobile home communities may have their own requirements. You should anticipate that older units, unless proven otherwise, may lack adequate hold down or anchoring systems. It's doubtful that the anchoring standards required for newer units will be present in an older unit. Given the complexity of this issue, many inspectors will disclaim an evaluation of the anchoring system. I recommend that, where possible, you get a home inspector who is knowledgeable about mobile homes. Also, talk to the local building inspector about the hold down requirements and any listed compliance for the unit you are buying. This is especially important in areas that are prone to tornadoes, as even a mild tornado may severely damage an insufficiently secured unit. With the most severe tornadoes, by the way, there may not be a lot you can do other than know how to shelter where you can survive.

Difficulties in inspecting . . .

1. In northern areas, it is difficult if not impossible to look under the unit during heavy snow or ice conditions.

2. Your inspector needs to look under the unit – but no one crawls through this space. Very often the ground is moist, filthy – or contains numerous obstructions and insulation lying over the ground. Typically, your inspector will just examine the space from a couple of access points.

3. As noted, some inspectors see a lot of mobile homes and are knowledgeable about the hold down and anchoring requirements required or found in that area. Where you can get them, they would be the inspectors to use.

4. In southern areas, I would imagine that you would need to be aware of the possibility that snakes are present under the unit. Tread carefully . . .

Modular Homes . . .

Modular homes are not mobile homes (which are also called 'manufactured homes'). I've discussed modular homes in Chapter 17, so please check there for information on these. Regarding the inspection, modular homes would get the same inspection as a single-family home. They do have their idiosyncrasies, however, and you may ask ahead of time if there were any reported problems (such as if the unit was dropped onto the foundation or the foundation was improperly sized). You'll want to assess the overall quality of the unit and the reputation of the company that built and installed the home.

Please see the website HomeBuyersHBook.com for more information and https://evergreenhomeinspection.com for more information on my services. Feel free to contact me directly at esimpson@evergreenhomeinspection.com.

9 781545 656624